Dealing with Economic Failure

Albrecht Cordes / Margrit Schulte Beerbühl (eds.)

Dealing with Economic Failure

Between Norm and Practice (15th to 21st Century)

PETER LANG
EDITION

Bibliographic Information published by the Deutsche Nationalbibliothek
The Deutsche Nationalbibliothek lists this publication in the Deutsche Nationalbibliografie; detailed bibliographic data is available in the internet at http://dnb.d-nb.de.

Cover image:
R. Cambers ed., The Book of Days, A Miscellany of Popular Antiquities in Connection with the Calendar Including Anecdote, Biography, & History. Curiosities of Literature and Oddities of Human Life and Characters, vol.1., London & Edinburgh 1869, S. 488. , scanned by the editors of this book.

ISBN 978-3-631-65825-3 (Print)
E-ISBN 978-3-653-05026-4 (E-Book)
DOI 10.3726/ 978-3-653-05026-4

Peter Lang Edition is an Imprint of Peter Lang GmbH.

Peter Lang – Frankfurt am Main · Bern · Bruxelles · New York · Oxford · Warszawa · Wien

This publication has been peer reviewed.

www.peterlang.com

Contents

Preface

On 20/21 February 2014 the editors hosted an international and interdisciplinary conference on "Dealing with economic failures: extra-judicial and judicial conflict regulations". Nine of the thirteen papers presented on that occasion are published in this volume; subsequently Jasper Kunstreich submitted his article. All papers were thoroughly revised before publication.

The editors met under the roof of the LOEWE Research Focus 'Extrajudicial and Judicial Conflict Resolution' (2012–2015), a project organized mainly by the Goethe-University Frankfurt a.M. and the Max Planck Institute for European Legal History. LOEWE is an ongoing programme of research funding by the state of Hesse, mainly focused on natural sciences, medicine and engineering; our research focus was among the few social science projects. Margrit Schulte Beerbühl was one of our research fellows, and Albrecht Cordes a member of the steering committee. While Albrecht Cordes is interested in the history of commercial law during the middle ages and early modern times in general, Margrit Schulte Beerbühl has done research on spectacular series of bankruptcies, namely the chain of collapses which originated in Hamburg in 1799 and subsequently shook the economy in Western Europe and even across the Atlantic Ocean. The crossroads of our interests and of the LOEWE subject were quickly identified: The ways medieval and modern societies dealt and deal with economic failure, concentrating on but not limited to the reaction on bankruptcies. Is the failure of an enterprise the ultimate defeat, a punishable crime and the terrible disaster? Or is it more like an incident, a bump in a mercantile career which can be overcome and possibly even leads to a welcomed opportunity to get rid of a suffocating amount of debts? The answers differ in space and time. The authors reflect on this subject from their respective economic or legal standpoints, some more with their individual case studies in mind, others from a more general angle.

The editors would like to thank the LOEWE research focus which funded the conference and the publication, to the whole LOEWE team under its managing director Andreas Karg, to the publishing house Peter Lang, to the Max Planck-Institute of European Legal History which hosted the conference, to the translator Sophie Costella, to the makers of the index Sonja Breustedt and Christina Voellinger, to Clemens Butzert who published the conference proceedings in

H-soz-Kult to the chairs, discussants and other participants of the conference, and to all contributors of this joint enterprise between jurists and historians. We hope that our readers will not have to deal with too many failures within this book.

Albrecht Cordes

Introduction

Writing in 1697 on bankrupts Daniel Defoe, the author of Robinson Crusoe, thought the English law on bankruptcy "has something in it of Barbarity". He continues:

> It gives a loose to the Malice and Revenge of the Creditor, as well as a Power to right himself, while it leaves the Debtor no way to show himself honest: It contrives all the ways possible to drive the Debtor to despair, and encourages no new Industry, for it makes him perfectly uncapable of any thing but *starving.*[1]

With these few words Defoe describes the hardships unfortunate traders faced in early modern England. Defoe suffered from the fate of a bankruptcy himself. After various unsuccessful ventures, among others in the wine trade with Portugal, and underwriting in insurance, he was declared bankrupt for more than £17,000 in 1692. Harassed by recalcitrant creditors he was committed to prison for several months, after a composition had failed, because four of his 140 creditors had refused to consent to an agreement. As the contemporary bankruptcy law contained no provisions for discharge Defoe remained liable with his future earnings. The harshness and cruelty of the law towards the debtor, he argues, "cast [him] out of Human Society, and expos'd [him] to Extremities worse than Death" Moreover, he thought that the bankruptcy laws were not only inhumane to the debtor but also of no advantage to the creditor.[2]

The bankruptcy laws of the early modern period treated the insolvent debtor as a criminal who had to be sanctioned severely. The perception of bankruptcy as a sort of theft or robbery of the creditor's property was not only a central element in the European bankruptcy laws but also in nineteenth-century America.[3] In Britain the insolvent debtor even had to face capital punishment until 1820.[4]

The shift from creditor-friendly towards more debtor-friendly legislation was a slow and uneven process lasting far into the twentieth century. The idea that

1 Daniel Defoe: *An Essay upon Projects.* London 1697, p. 192.

2 Ibid. pp. 192–194, see also his articles on the fate of bankrupts in his Review: "*A Review of the State of the British Nation*" April 17, 1707, p. 115 "Miscellanea"; April 19. 1707, p. 119.

3 For the U.S.A. see among others Scott A. Sandage: *Born Losers. A History of Failure in America.* Cambridge Mass., 2005; Bruce H. Mann: *Republic of Debtors. Bankruptcy in the Age of American Independence.* Cambridge Mass. 2002.

4 1 Geo IV c. 115; see Emily Kadens: The Last Bankrupt Hanged: Balancing Incentives in the Development of Bankruptcy Law. *Duke Law Journal* 59 (2010), pp. 1229–1319.

prevails today, that bankruptcy law should be debtor-friendly, is a far cry from the creditor-friendly laws that dominated for centuries. Historically, according to Mike W. Peng, "entrepreneur-friendliness and bankruptcy laws are like an 'oxymoron', because bankruptcy laws used to be harsh and cruel".[5] Entrepreneur-friendly bankruptcy regimes are now advocated to make it easier to start afresh after a bankruptcy. Recent business literature highlights the role of entrepreneurs as agents of growth. As institutions decisively influence the level of entrepreneurial activity, business scholars pledge for entrepreneur-friendly institutional contexts that provide stimuli for innovation and risk-taking.[6] Although the New Institutional Economics have long emphasized that institutions matter, the relationship between entrepreneurship and bankruptcy regimes has hardly been looked into. Only within the last few years, induced by the growing concern of governments around the world to facilitate the re-entry of bankrupts, have scholars begun to inquire into indices for entrepreneur-friendly bankruptcy laws.[7] A strong interest in the question how bankruptcy laws impact on business activity resulted from various factors, the big financial crash in 2008, intensified global competition among business and states, the overall high number of failures even before 2008, and also from awareness that the percentage of firms that fail within the first five years is much higher than those that survive.[8]

The following papers are the outcome of an international conference that focused on the norms and practice of dealing with economic failure within and outside the courts from a long-term, international and interdisciplinary perspective. The papers cover the period from the early sixteenth century until today. Without

---

5 Mike W. Peng et al.: Bankruptcy Laws and Entrepreneur-Friendliness. *Entrepreneurship. Theory and Practice* 34 (2010), pp. 517–730, here: p. 518.

6 Ibid; see also F. Wei and M.I. White: Personal bankruptcies and the level of entrepreneurial activity. *Journal of Law & Economics* 46 (2003), pp. 543–69; Paolo Di Martino: Legal institutions, social norms, and entrepreneurship in Britain (c. 1890–c. 1939). *The Economic History Review* 65 (2012), pp. 120–143, here: p. 122f.

7 For that discussion see Peng, Bankruptcy Laws, pp. 517–730; Seung-Hyun Lee et al.: How do bankruptcy laws affect entrepreneurship development around the world. *Journal of Business Venturing* 26 (2011), pp. 505–520 or John Armour and Douglas Cumming: Bankruptcy Law and Entrepreneurship. *American Law and Economics Review* 10 (2008), pp. 330–350; see also contributions in: Stijn Claessens et al. (eds): *Resolutions of Financial Distress. An International Perspective on the Design of Bankruptcy Laws.* Washington 2001 to name only a few.

8 Peng, Bankruptcy Laws, p. 518 FN. 2: Germany experienced a considerable rise of insolvencies already before the 2008 crisis. They rose from a total of 15.302 in 1992 to 154.04 in 2006: failure among businesses rose from 10.900 to 30.357 (www.destatis.de).

claiming to give a comprehensive overview, the papers presented here – by addressing some central issues – should give an impression of the protracted process of modernization and adaptation. They focus on Europe's leading commercial centres, for it was here that the impact of economic change was first experienced. Here we find information on the earliest examples of alternative conflict regulations and efforts by the town councils to search for more viable ways of dealing with bankruptcies. The volume concludes with a paper on today's bankruptcy law in Germany to show where we are now.

The contributors to this volume are from various disciplines, social and economic as well as legal history and contemporary law. In Germany – perhaps more so than in Anglo-American countries – social and economic historians on the one side and legal historians on the other have for a long time approached the history of bankruptcies from diverging angles. Social and economic historians have used legal records like bankruptcy files predominantly for analyzing social and economic developments, or more recently turned their attention to cultural factors such as reputation, trust and the impact of social relations such as family, kin, or co-religionists on firms and companies.[9] Vice versa, legal historians have focussed on the law, paying only secondary attention to economic and social aspects.[10] Only within the last few years are some tendencies towards a broader approach visible in both disciplines. One of the aims of the conference was to intensify the dialogue between the disciplines.

A word needs to be said about the terms used: failure is a broader term that includes, but is not limited to, bankruptcy. A business may fail for lack of assets without undergoing a formal procedure before the courts. The term bankruptcy goes back to the Italian "banca rotta" meaning the break-up of a trader's business, when he was not able to pay his debts. "Bankrupt" or "banqueroute" or "Bankrotteur" frequently used to have a negative connotation applying to a fraudulent failure,[11] the term failure or the outdated continental version of "falliment", "fallissement"

---

9 Given the vast literature on the cultural and social impact on economic relations the reader is only referred to the Douglass, C. North: *Institutionen, institutioneller Wandel und Wirtschaftsleistung.* Tübingen 1992; Oliver E. Williamson: *The economic institutions of capitalism: firms, markets, and relational contracting.* New York 1985; on trust, Niklas Luhmann: *Vertrauen.* Stuttgart 2000; Francis Fukuyama: *Trust. The Social Virtues and the Creation of Prosperity.* New York 1995.

10 Anke Meier: *Die Geschichte des deutschen Konkursrechts, insbesondere die Entstehung der Reichsordnung von 1877.* Frankfurt a. M. 2003.

11 Oxford English Dictionary online; Peter Hertner: Article: Bankrott. *Handwörterbuch zur deutschen Rechtsgeschichte*, vol. 1, 2. ed. 2008, column p. 428f.

for bankruptcy or "fallit" for the debtor did not carry the negative implication of bankruptcy. In the past "insolvency" was applied to small traders and non-trading groups in Britain, who had to undergo a different court procedure than a bankrupt.[12] Some of the papers in the volume are written by lawyers or legal historians. The character of the German legal language tradition may have connotations that are not to be found in the same English term. To open the German quotations in the articles to a non-German reading public, terms were adapted to the language used in the contemporary U.S. Bankruptcy Code.

Since the discovery of the Americas the world has changed fundamentally. The expansion of trade to distant non-European shores produced the financial revolution of the late seventeenth century followed by the industrial revolution.[13] The rise of the European commercial empires was not, however, a history of continuous growth but was also accompanied by birth pangs and setbacks. Trade with the non-European world offered surprising economic opportunities and profit prospects, but traders had also to cope with new and unpredictable risks. Although we do not have comprehensive and reliable figures on failures, those we do have suggest that the number began to rise with long-distance trade and first became an accompaniment to commercial life in the early modern commercial centres such as Antwerp, Augsburg or Nürnberg. For Augsburg, for example, Mark Häberlein counted 62 bankruptcies between 1529 and 1580 and a further 57 between 1580 and 1620. Even large firms such as Höchstetter in 1529 failed along with middling and small merchants.[14] A similar rise in bankruptcies can also be noticed in England during the sixteenth century.[15] Compared to the eighteenth

12 Debtors were divided in three classes, merchants and traders owing at least £100, only this group came under the bankruptcy law, small tradesmen or mechanics owing less than £100 were dealt with at the Court of Common Pleas and later at insolvency courts. The third class consisted of persons with small debts of £20 and less. (Ian P.H. Duffy: *Bankruptcy and Insolvency in London during the Industrial Revolution.* New York / London 1985, see the first three chapters).

13 On the commercial revolutions see the still valuable publication of Peter G.M. Dickson: *The Financial Revolution in England. A Study in the Development of Public Credit 1688–1756.* London, New York 1967.

14 Mark Häberlein: Merchants's bankrupts, economic development and social relations in German cities during the long 16th century. In: Thomas Max Safley (ed.): *The History of Bankruptcy. Economic, Social and Cultural Implications in Early Modern Europe.* London, New York 2013, pp. 19–33, here: p. 21f.

15 W.J. Jones: The Foundations of English Bankruptcy: Statutes and Commissions in the Early Modern Period. *Transactions of the American Philosophical Society* 69 (1979), pp. 1–63, here: p. 5.

century the numbers were low. Two centuries later the numbers were several times higher in the leading commercial centres and jumped with the advent of industrialisation. In England they rose from an average of between 172 and 278 per year in the first half of the century to an average of 762 yearly in its last decade. A similar trend, although much lower in absolute numbers, can be perceived in Amsterdam and even in Stockholm.[16]

Given the economic change on the one side and the harshness of bankruptcy laws on the other, the question arises to what extent the laws were enforced and to what extent alternative solutions were sought. Researchers should not only study the provisions of the bankruptcy laws, but look at the practice of handling failures by the parties concerned.[17]

The penalizing treatment of the unfortunate trader had a more than thousand year old tradition dating back to the Roman times. As well as imprisonment, the bankrupt had to endure bondage and corporal punishment. The Romans already distinguished between the honest and the fraudulent debtor. While the fraudulent debtor faced bondage, incarceration and death, the honest debtor, whose misfortune was caused by external accidents, was granted a cessio bonorum and did not suffer the disgrace of losing his citizen's rights, if he surrendered his property voluntarily.[18] This distinction and the institution of cessio bonorum was lost with the decline of the Roman Empire and only slowly re-discovered in the early modern period. In some countries it took even longer before it was written down.[19]

Given the increase of risk and failure from the sixteenth century onwards, the question arises how debtors and creditors as well as the lawmakers and courts responded to the changing economic environment. Imprisonment for debt robbed the bankrupts of the opportunity to pay back their debts. For the creditor, imprisonment, death or flight of the debtor to some unknown place could mean that

---

16 For London see Margrit Schulte Beerbühl: *The Forgotten Majority. German Merchants in London, Naturalization, and Global Trade 1660–1815.* New York / Oxford 2015, pp. 198f.; Julian Hoppit: *Risk and Failure in English Business 1700–1800.* Cambridge 1985, Appendix 1; for Amsterdam W.F.H. Oldeweit: Twee eeuwen Amsterdamse fallissementen en het verloop van de conjuncture (1636 tot 1838). *Tijdschrift voor Geschiedenis* 75 (1962) p. 421–435, here: pp. 432f.; for Stockholm see Klas Nyberg and Håkan Jakobsson's contribution in this volume.

17 Karl Gratzer, Introduction, in: Karl Gratzer, and Dieter Stiefel (eds): *History of Insolvency and Bankruptcy from an International Perspective.* Södertörn 2008, p. 18.

18 Gratzer, Introduction, p. 20f.

19 First examples of the re-introduction of the cessio bonorum are found at the end of the fifteenth and early sixteenth century (Gratzer, Introduction, p. 23).

he would have to write off losses and in the worst case be drawn into the failure, possibly facing bankruptcy himself. Given the laws, the questions will be: What opportunities did debtors, creditors and the court have for alternative instruments of conflict regulation and conflict reduction? What changes can be perceived in the level of imprisonment?

Law sources provide us with interpretations of what was considered right or wrong at a given time. These provisions vary in time and space as they are embedded in cultural values and responsive to social change. As Lawrence Friedman and, more recently, Jérôme Sgard have pointed out economic and social developments do not only have an impact on legal and judicial structures, but vice versa as well; the two spheres shape each other.[20] Reciprocal influences do not imply that changes correlate immediately. Legal norms may react much more slowly to changes, because lasting cultural perceptions, such as the criminal perception of economic failure for example, retarded change in the law. Furthermore, the early bankruptcy laws were often attempts to solve immediate problems and thus were vague and had defects.[21] By looking at judicial and non-judicial practices in dealing with bankrupts the impact of social relations on the outcome of a procedure should be taken into account.

The inability to repay debts opens up a Pandora's box of conflicts not only between debtor and creditor, but also between the creditors. It was conflict-prone on many issues, economic, social, cultural and legal, which had to be solved quickly and individually. Given the penalizing character of the pre-modern laws, bankruptcy was something to be avoided at nearly any price. Thus conflict reduction and prevention for the benefit of good governance have been the guiding principles throughout the centuries.

Powerful trading enterprises with trade links extending to the New World already existed in the first half of the sixteenth century. Well-known examples are the Fuggers and Höchstetters of Augsburg or the Imhoffs of Nuremberg. These firms had invested not only in long-distance trade but in mines and other early modern industrial enterprises. They were, moreover, money-lenders to the crowns and nobility of Europe. Although they were family firms, capital did not exclusively come from family members or dowries but also from non-related shareholders.

---

20 Lawrence M. Friedman: Legal Culture and Social Development. *Law & Society Review* 4 (1969), pp. 29–44; Jérôme Sgard: Do legal origins matter? The case of bankruptcy laws in Europe 1808–1914. *European Review of Economic History* 10 (2006), pp. 389–419, here: p. 389.

21 Jones, Foundations of English Bankruptcy, p. 7.

To prevent internal litigation and conflict among the active and silent partners that could end in bankruptcy, the Höchstetters, Imhoffs and other large family enterprises had concluded company agreements detailing the rights and duties of the governing members and providing instruments to deal with existing or threatened conflicts. Three measures proved particularly effective to prevent litigation, as Mechthild Isenmann explains in detail in her contribution; firstly they institutionalized regular and obligatory shareholder meetings that provided a platform for regulating internal conflicts. In case of unforeseen and imminent disputes the contract provided for extraordinary shareholder meetings. Secondly, if these could not be settled at the meetings the articles prescribed mediation either internally by a family member and kin, or if the matter could not be settled internally, they were to call in external mediators. Litigation was the last resort and only started when all other forms of conflict regulations had failed. Isenmann comes to the conclusion that mediation practices were generally preferred for several reasons. One was that information on internal business habits should not be laid open to the public, and a mutual agreement or mediation could be more advantageous to the parties concerned.

Another preventive measure to evade the threat of social death that accompanied bankruptcy in the early modern period is described by Wolfgang Forster. The commercial developments after the discovery of the New World began to shake the social and economic foundations of the traditional social elite in Spain by the new wealth of the mercantile middle classes. Traditionally, social status was based on landownership that needed to be displayed by a conspicuous and elaborate dress code and consumption rituals. The obligation to demonstrate noble status through a luxurious lifestyle and extravagant dowries for daughters was a financial strain. Unlike the mercantile classes they faced falling revenues from a declining population. Various instruments existed to prevent or delay bankruptcy of a noble family: creditors could grant a respite, a partial remission of debt was another option or the crown could intervene and hustle creditors and debtor into an agreement. When all of these possibilities failed only a "cession bonorum", i.e. relinquishing all assets to the creditors, remained in order to avoid imprisonment and disgrace. Surrendering all assets, however, implied losing noble status which was inalienably bound to the memoria of entailed estates in Spain. Faced with this problem the Spanish lawyer Salgado de Somoza developed a legal solution by separating administration from possession which allowed the over-indebted nobility to retain its social status.

Some factors allow the sixteenth century to be seen as a first turning point in the history of bankruptcy: around the turn to the sixteenth century a more systematic bankruptcy system began to emerge in Europe resulting from the expansion of trade and credit relations, the frequent wars and rising number of bankruptcies. Suitable solutions for handling bankruptcy had to be found. In medieval cities creditors could take debtors to prison without the intervention of a court, and the old instruments for dealing with insolvent debtors led to tensions and discontent. The inadequacy of the old bankruptcy regulations was first felt in the commercial centre of Antwerp, whose mercantile community had grown considerably and become more international.

In response to rising litigation the Antwerp City council, as Dave De ruysscher elaborates, issued an ordinance in 1516 that for the first time introduced collective bankruptcy proceedings. Up to that time creditors who first made a claim to the assets of a bankrupt were prioritized over those who claimed compensation before the courts at a later stage. The new law imposed restraint on the individual creditor who sought full repayment at the expense of others. Besides the introduction of collective bankruptcy proceedings a second important measure was introduced in the 1520s and 1530s. During these decades de Ruyscher notices a certain shift from creditor-oriented to more debtor-oriented legislation that to some extent alleviated the debtor's fate, although its aim was primarily to encourage him to come forward and forfeit all his property. This development resulted from the economic and financial crises between the Frisian war of 1517 and the Italian wars of 1521 and went along with further changes, such as a distinction between unfortunate and fraudulent debtors, and the introduction of voluntary bankruptcy.

Furthermore, the council of Brabant and the urban government took an active role in hustling the parties into compromise, allowing the debtor to apply to the council of Brabant to commission the Antwerp aldermen to mediate a compromise, encouraging the creditors to consent to postponement of payments, and allowing a debtor to continue business at least during the negotiations. Although, as De ruysscher points out, the number of arrangements increased considerably in the 1530s. The new regulations were clearly adapted to the needs of a commercial hub, but the city authorities lacked effective instruments to force all creditors into a lasting compromise.

The eighteenth century marks a step up in the history of bankruptcy. It saw the evolution of a commercial bankruptcy regime adapted to the needs of a commercial society. The bankruptcy system of Antwerp was a local regulation, but during the eighteenth century commercial opportunities and risk extended beyond the few city centres. After the fall of Antwerp in 1585 trade shifted to the north, to Amsterdam, later on to London. Besides the two leading financial hubs many larger and smaller trading and commercial centres had emerged by the eighteenth century. Non-European regions had become interconnected forming an early modern global trade by European trade companies, adventurers and individual merchants, who had established far-reaching trade networks.[22] New financial institutions had been created during the course of the seventeenth century such as the Wisselbank in Amsterdam as early as 1609, the Hamburg Bank in 1619 or the Bank of England in 1694 along with insurance companies and other financial instruments to meet the rapidly growing credit demand of private businessmen and governments.

Although bankruptcy laws had been amended to some extent during the early seventeenth century they had become inadequate to meet the requirements of the commercialized economies at the end of the century. That did not only hold true for Britain. The laws had been suited, as Daniel Defoe remarked, for "the Circumstances and Time of the Evil they were made against", but were "now a Public Grievance to the Nation"[23] and their "severity served neither the creditor nor the debtor".[24] Suffering himself from the dreadful fate of a bankrupt, Defoe began to advocate a reform of the bankruptcy law that would allow a 'full and free discharge' of debts. His struggle for a reform resulted in the new bankruptcy law of 1706 (4 & 5 Anne c. 17). It can be seen as a turning point in the history of bankruptcy legislation as it introduced for the first time the possibility of a discharge from debt and a debt-free fresh start for the honest traders.[25] The law of 1706 alleviated the fate of at least some honest traders, but it neither abolished the traditional penalizing provisions (on the contrary, it even exacerbated punishment for fraudulent debtors by introducing the death penalty), nor did it introduce voluntary bankruptcy.[26]

Given the long period of wars between 1689 and 1714 (the Nine Years' War and the War of Succession) and a marked increase in failures, the perception that reforms were necessary induced many lawmakers across Europe to consider them. Besides Britain, Denmark passed a new bankruptcy law in 1706, Bremen followed a few years later in 1711. Further towns and countries followed during the next

22 Meanwhile a vast literature on the early modern globalisation has been published, among others see a short valuable summary of the literature in: Bernd Hausberg: *Die Verknüpfung der Welt. Geschichte der frühen Globalisierung vom 16. bis zum 18. Jahrhunderts.* Wien 2015.

23 Defoe, *Of Bankrupts*, pp. 196f.

24 Ibid., p. 192.

25 The law became a model for the American legislation after the independence. See Charles Jordan Tabb: The Historical Evolution of the Bankruptcy Discharge. *American Bankruptcy Journal* 65 (1991), pp. 325–371.

26 A discharge depended on the consent of four-fifths of the major creditors. It was certified by granting a certificate of conformity.

few decades. The new laws, however, only reflect a minor part of the reform efforts and changes in dealing with bankrupts. In the case of the free City of Hamburg, for example, discussions on a reform of the bankruptcy law already started before the end of the seventeenth century. Several attempts at new legislation followed, and discussions continued throughout the next fifty years, before the new law was finally passed in 1753. Even the new law did not stop further discussions.[27] Similarly in Britain discussions continued throughout the century, only a few amendments were passed, but all in all legislation became more lenient during the course of the century.[28]

The introduction of the distinction between unfortunate and fraudulent bankrupts was a first step by the lawmakers of the sixteenth century to take into consideration that failure did not automatically result from fraud. The novel dimension of speculation and financial crises causing huge bankruptcy waves changed perceptions as to the causes of failure. Especially from mid-eighteenth century onwards crises and bankruptcies grew in number and geographical reach. The financial crisis of 1763, which for example started in Amsterdam, sent out shock waves that were felt in places as far apart as Stockholm or Venice.[29]

In many countries, laws already granted security from imprisonment at least for a limited period during the bankruptcy procedure to encourage debtors to come forward and also to allow the unfortunate some subsistence. The growing risk of domino effects, that the failure of debtors could draw creditors themselves into bankruptcy, increased the willingness to come to an arrangement. By a composition, the creditor could at least get some of his money back, and it allowed a quicker return than a formal court procedure which could last decades. Furthermore, allowing a debtor to start again could raise the prospects of getting fully paid at some future time or being compensated by future business.[30] Willingness to come to a compromise, however, depended on the circumstances of the failure and the social embeddedness of the debtor. Creditors were more inclined to an

---

27 Staatsarchiv Hamburg: Senat 111-1-CI VIII; The political and commercial elite of Hamburg were more or less the same. In dealing with economic failures they had often responded flexibly to the changing commercial situation and felt little need to change the law.

28 E.g. amendments of 1718 or 1732, Jay Cohen: History of imprisonment for debt. *Journal of legal history* 3 (1982), pp. 153–171, here: 156f.; Duffy, pp. 10–14.

29 See below the contributions of Klas Nyberg / Håkan Jacobsson and Magnus Ressel.

30 In the eighteenth century out-of-court arrangements could induce creditors to a moratorium or creditors would consent to a dividend in the hope of future business with the debtor that would compensate to some extent for his losses.

arrangement if the debtor was a reputable and trustworthy man embedded in an influential family and kinship network and whose misfortune was caused by external circumstances.

We have no means to evaluate the volume of private compositions, as only comparatively few cases left traces. What can be perceived is that the bankruptcy laws increasingly reacted to the spread of composition and entered clauses that provided for composition, since private and voluntary compositions suffered from a lack of any obligation. Taking the example of the bankruptcy law of Hamburg passed in 1753, it encouraged the courts to push the conflicting parties into composition. Similar to the Venetian law on bankruptcy the Hamburg Senate envisaged three categories of bankrupts. Besides the fraudulent and the unfortunate bankrupt it introduced a third type, the careless debtor, reflecting that speculation as well as careless bookkeeping could result in bankruptcy. For both cases, the unfortunate as well as the careless merchant, the courts were to advocate composition.

The perception that speculation, risk and failure were integral parts of any trade was no longer confined to the leading commercial centres, but had also spread to peripheral countries such as Sweden. Rising numbers of bankruptcies caused by crises abroad initiated, as Klas Nyberg and Håkan Jacobsson shows in their paper, a fundamental reform of the Swedish bankruptcy law. First vague provisions to regulate the bankruptcy procedure had already been introduced in 1734. Only in the aftermath of the bankruptcy wave in Stockholm, originating from Amsterdam, did the government include detailed provisions regulating the bankruptcy procedure in the bankruptcy laws of 1767 and 1773. They encouraged the debtor to come forward and deliver his assets by granting them free passage, protecting him from imprisonment, forbidding the creditors to seize the property individually, and fixing a strict time limit on the procedure in order to avoid unnecessary costs that wasted the bankrupt's assets. According to the findings of Nyberg and Jakobsson court officials induced parties, whenever suitable, to come to a composition. Before the opening of a formal and costly process a preparatory meeting of creditors, debtors and a justice was frequently used for an arrangement. Both authors also assume that the new business-friendly regulation contributed to the increase in bankruptcy declarations in the last quarter of the century. A similar well-regulated procedure as in Sweden was practiced in Venice in the second half of the century as Magnus Ressel illustrates in a case study on the German merchant and textile entrepreneur in Venice who failed in 1773. The Venetian bankruptcy law, although dating back to the early seventeenth century, was well adjusted to the needs of a commercial elite and diverged fundamentally from the laws in Italy as it did not distinguish between inhabitants and foreigners, and encouraged negotiations among creditors and debtors that were to be sanctioned by the Venetian court.

In all, settlements between creditors and debtors, either private or under the surveillance of a justice, in the period between the first official proclamation of insolvency and the formal opening of court proceedings became a widespread feature in eighteenth century Europe.[31] Formal time and asset consuming court procedures were used as a last resort when efforts for arrangements had failed.

Despite the growing leniency of law and the encouragement of private or court-surveyed compositions the Damocles Sword of imprisonment was still hanging over the debtor. Imprisonment for debt was not abolished until the 1860s and 1870s in European countries.

Until right into the nineteenth century bankruptcy laws applied only to the commercial classes. They excluded petty debtors such as labourers, craftsmen, tradesmen and non-commercial classes. A prevailing reason for excluding non-trading classes from the benefits of the bankruptcy laws was voiced by the famous lawyer W. Blackstone:

> "They [the laws] allow the benefit of the laws of bankruptcy to none but actual traders; since that set of men are ... the only persons liable to accidental losses and to an inability of paying their debts, without any fault of their own. If persons in other situations of life run in debt without the power of payment, they must take the consequences of their own indiscretion"[32]

England was not the only country that excluded non-traders from the bankruptcy laws. Similar regulations are to be found in German towns such as Hamburg or in France.[33] As mentioned above petty debtors in England came under the insolvency laws which provided for imprisonment and unlike the big merchants they remained liable for their debts. The distinction between bankruptcy and insolvency was repealed in England only in 1861 and imprisonment for debt even later in 1869.

Like the commercial elite the middling and lower classes were embedded in a network of credit and reciprocal obligations. Financial crises and bankruptcy waves similarly plunged them into economic failures.[34] By the last quarter of the eighteenth century rising dissatisfaction and public critique against traditional

---

31 For Britain see especially Sheila Marriner: English Bankruptcy Records and Statistics before 1850. *Economic History Review* 33 (1980), pp. 351–366.

32 Quoted after Cohen, History of Imprisonment, p. 160.

33 See the papers of Jasper Kunstreich, Erika Vause and Viera Rebolledo-Dhuin in this volume.

34 For the credit networks of the middling and lower classes see Margot C. Finn: *The Character of Credit. Personal Debt in English Culture, 1740–1914.* Cambridge 2003; Craig Muldrew: *The Economy of Obligation: the Culture of Credit and Social Relations in Early Modern England.* Basingstoke 1998; Gabriele, B. Clemens (ed.): *Schuldenlast*

imprisonment practices had already given rise to a more liberal interpretation of the term trader and other groups.[35]

The use of imprisonment seems to have deviated considerably from the provisions of the law. Napoleon's Code de Commerce constituted the first detailed description of the bankruptcy procedure. It stipulated strict surveillance and control of the bankruptcy proceedings and imprisonment at least until proceedings could be initiated.[36] In her paper on the credit problems and the development of bankruptcies among Parisian book traders in the 1820s and 1830s Viera Rebolledo-Dhuin raises the question to what extent the provisions of the code for imprisonment of the insolvent debtor and the loss of commercial rights was enforced. Based on a sample of 141 bankruptcy files of nineteenth-century Parisian book traders and publishers Rebolledo-Dhuin reveals that only four of the sample were imprisoned. Further reforms in the 1820s and 1830s limited imprisonment further and eased the fate of the debtor and his family by allowing the unfortunate trader to keep his tools, furniture and money. Thus bankruptcy among the book traders did not necessarily end their career but was frequently used as an opportunity for a restart.

Based on the internment records of the debtor's prison in Lyon between 1835 and 1840 Erika Vause researches the social composition of the imprisoned debtors and the reasons that induced creditors to jail them. Starting with the French law of 1832 that limited the time in prison for debts below 500 francs, and exempted certain persons such as women and minors from imprisonment unless they had incurred commercial debts, she analyzes the social composition of the imprisoned debtors and how that institution functioned for both debtor as well as creditor. Lyon used to be a centre of the silk industry for centuries, but none of the 318 imprisoned debtors belonged to that industry. A conspicuous number came from the hospitality industry such as tavern keepers and artisans. The sums they were indebted for were generally under 500 francs. The creditors who came from the

---

und Schuldenwert: Kreditnetzwerke in der europäischen Geschichte 1300–1900. Trier 2008.

35 In 1772 a philanthropic society was founded for the release of imprisoned persons for small debts and after the turn of the century further reliefs were granted for petty debtors. Acts in 1785 and 1786 restricted the time of imprisonment for small debtors and in 1808 an act was passed to release petty debtors for sums below £20 from prison. A Court for Relief of Insolvent Debtors was established a few years later to decide on prisoners' petition for release (Cohen, Imprisonment for Debt, pp. 163f.; Duffy, *Bankruptcy*, pp. 56–106).

36 Sgard, Legal Origins, pp. 400, 403.

moneyed classes used imprisonment for three main reasons: to compel the debtor to mobilize alternative credit resources from family or friends, as a means of initiating legal proceedings for bankruptcy, or to initiate a composition.

Practices for dealing with insolvent debtors did not only vary considerably depending on time, respective laws and judicial institutions, social status of debtors and creditors and their relationship, but the gap between norms and practice also broadened. By the mid-nineteenth century the old bankruptcy laws and institutions had become obsolete. Neither imprisonment nor the distinction between merchants/traders and non-traders were any longer suited for industrialized and commercialized societies which were structured according to negotiable instruments and large-scale investments in industrial enterprises. Substantial reforms in Europe were not implemented until the 1860s.[37]

The next three papers present some information about the changes in law and practice in Germany from the mid-nineteenth century onwards. Until unification in 1871 the German states and free cities had their own bankruptcy laws. Jasper Kunstreich throws light on the practice of coping with financial crisis in the last decades of Hamburg's independence before unification. The local bankruptcy law of 1753, already mentioned, was well suited for a highly commercialized local society that was socially and economically closely interwoven. The mid-eighteenth-century bankruptcy law of Hamburg was to Kunstreich a particularly business-friendly piece of legislation designed to overcome liquidity problems and provide for a structured renegotiation procedure and a fresh start. The old law and long-established practice of dealing with bankrupts was still flexible enough to manage the global crisis of 1857 which was also felt in Hamburg. Faced with a wave of bankruptcies the Senate installed a crisis management. It resorted to temporary instruments already utilized in the eighteenth century to overcome transnational financial crises.[38] Among others it established an institution called "administration" that allowed businesses to continue under the control of officially nominated administrators. In all 118 firms applied for it. Besides this measure

37 For these reforms see Duffy, *Bankruptcy*, pp. 122 ff.; Paolo die Martino: The Historical Evolution of Bankruptcy Law in England, the US and Italy up to 1939: Determinants of Institutional Change and Structural Differences. In: Gratzer / Stiefel, *Insolvency*, pp. 263–279; Sgard, Legal Origins, op. cit.

38 For the institution of "administration" see also Margrit Schulte Beerbühl: Die Hamburger Krise von 1799 und ihre weltweite Dimension. *Hamburger Wirtschafts-Chronik, Neue Folge* 10 (2012), pp. 85–110, here: p. 104f.

some clauses of the bankruptcy laws were suspended and loan institutions were created to overcome the liquidity squeeze.

The rise of big industrial enterprises employing a large workforce had already challenged the old bankruptcy system from the early nineteenth century onwards. Given the special situation of Hamburg, management of the 1857 crisis in that city may be seen as a late survival of the commercial bankruptcy regime. Due to the rise of big industrial enterprises with a large workforce and new corporate and managerial structures in the latter part of the century the old bankruptcy regime was replaced by industrial bankruptcy regimes in the European countries.

After the unification of Germany the local and regional bankruptcy laws were abolished and replaced by a new national law in 1879. It provided for two types of proceedings: the distribution procedure and compulsory composition. While the distribution procedure allowed the creditors to assert their claims even after the closing of a bankruptcy procedure, compulsory composition, described in detail by Ulrich Falk and Christoph Kling, provided several advantages for the debtor. Compulsory composition shortened the procedure considerably, and the creditors were compelled to accept the court's decision. From 1886 to World War I and the 1920s between 21% and 29% of bankruptcy cases ended with a compulsory composition. Only privileged creditors were exempted from compulsory composition, and an amendment of the law in 1898 refused to allow composition in those cases when the expected quota was below one fifth of the claims. The authors maintain that compulsory composition had been a rather effective and simple institution until the first half of the 20th century. They attribute the decline that followed to the growth of credit securing instruments which increased the number of assetless bankruptcies.

The final paper concludes the volume with an insight into today's German bankruptcy law. Peter von Wilmowsky analyses the role and principles that govern contemporary German insolvency law regarding stock companies and the various interests of both creditors and public in either keeping the firms going or closing them down. Among the aims of contemporary insolvency law are a ban on individual collection by creditors and a distribution of the assets according to hierarchy and order of claims. The law should also guarantee a neutral decision concerning the future of the firm.

Some issues addressed here are taken up again in the current debate on the impact of bankruptcy laws on entrepreneurship and the demands for entrepreneur-friendly bankruptcy regimes. Incentives to facilitate a fresh start for bankrupts are currently seen as imperatives for good governance. European societies were slow to accept failure as the Janus face of success and likewise that financial crises and bankruptcies are integral features of the capitalist economy. According to the Schumpeterian view, bankruptcies are a sign of creative destruction. The level of speculation, risk-taking and failures are seen as indicators of growth which require a business-friendly legal framework.[39]

The path of change and relationships between creditors, debtors, laws and practice certainly diverged in the European countries over the past centuries depending on economic development and established cultural diversities. Despite variations some problems in dealing with bankruptcies reveals common features which all states had to cope with. In this volume the aim was to highlight some features of interaction between private and judicial conflict regulation.

Basic institutional and legal instruments to cope with the rise of risk and failure were missing at the beginning of the early modern age, and cultural perceptions of bankruptcy as a criminal act had to be overcome as well. Given the lack of a structured procedure, merchants and traders generally preferred to resort to private or extra-judicial conflict resolution, as this promised more advantageous and practical solutions. However, they needed laws as conflict-reducing devices against recalcitrant creditors and fraudulent debtors. In the early centuries lawmakers and judges generally possessed little expertise in commercial affairs.[40] The institution of commercial courts and commercial court judges was first introduced in France during the French Revolutionary and Napoleonic Period and spread after the turn of century to other European towns and countries.[41]

Compared to the pace of economic change norms and institutions responded only slowly, but they were receptive to the realities. The result of legislation reforms was often pragmatic measures to solve immediate problems, trying to

---

39 Werner Plumpe: *Wirtschaftskrisen. Geschichte und Gegenwart*. München 2012, p. 14; similarly Kim Christian Priemel: Was ist Spekulation, wer ist Spekulant? In: *Jahrbuch für Wirtschaftsgeschichte* 52, 2 (2013), pp. 99–26, here: p. 10, also Toni Pierenkemper: Von der Tulpenkrise zum Finanzkollaps. Das Allgemeine im Besonderen, in: ibid, pp. 139–159.

40 Concerning the influence of judges and their expertise on the bankruptcy procedure see Kenneth Ayotte: Matching Bankruptcy Laws to Legal Environments. *Journal of Law, Economic & Organization* 25 (2007), pp. 2–30.

41 On the French commercial courts and the predecessors see Rebolledo-Dhuin's contribution in this volume. In Hamburg the first commercial court was instituted in 1816 and Bremen 1845. (see August Schiebe, *Über einige Institutionen Frankreichs in Bezug auf Handel und Industrie*, [Leipzig] 1846; Willy Silberschmidt, *Die Entstehung des deutschen Handelsgerichts*, Berlin 1894.

generalize and legalize established practices, but the normative implementation could certainly also open up space for new practices and procedures. In all, the relationship between bankruptcy law, practice and economic change does not reveal straightforward interdependence but a complex and multifaceted configuration.

Margrit Schulte Beerbühl

Mechthild Isenmann

Before Bankruptcy: Conflict Solution Strategies of Upper German Trading Companies in the Fifteenth and 'Long' Sixteenth Centuries

Introduction

As an organisational form,[1] family companies formed a central basic constant in the economic centres of Nuremberg and Augsburg in the Early Modern Era.[2] The term 'family' is defined in a very broad, variable and dynamic way here, as a family recruited members from among its close or distant relatives, people related by marriage and, in some cases, those linked only by friendship, thus constantly changing, expanding and shrinking. In addition, the Upper German companies of such "relationship families"[3] formed a "contract-based association of multiple persons for gainful economic employment",[4] whose identity was designed above all for longevity, continuity and trust[5] and that were active in trading goods and credit with the help of flexible networks and clientele structures.[6]

---

1 The author thanks Sophie Costella for the translation of the German text.

2 For background: Denzel, Markus A.: "The Merchant Family in the "Oberdeutsche Hochfinanz" from the Middle-Ages up to the Eighteenth Century". In: Cavaciocchi, Simonetta (a cura di): *La famiglia nell'ecconomia europea secc. XII–XVIII* (Fondazione istituto internazionale di storia ecconomica "F. Datini". Serie II – Atti delle "Settimane di studi" e altri convegni, 40). Firenze 2009, pp. 365–388.

3 Fouquet, Gerhard: "'Freundschaft' und 'Feindschaft': Stadtadlige Verwandtschaftsfamilien in deutschen Städten des Spätmittelalters". In: Spieß, Karl-Heinz (ed.): *Die Familie in der Gesellschaft des Mittelalters.* Ostfildern 2009, pp. 107–135, here p. 111.

4 Kobelt, Hans: *Die Entwicklung der Handelsgesellschaften und ihres Rechts in der Schweiz insbesondere in St. Gallen bis Ende 18. Jahrhunderts.* Diss. jur., Bern 1916, p. 31.

5 Hildebrandt, Reinhard: *Quellen und Regesten zu den Augsburger Handelshäusern der Paler und Rehlinger 1539–1642. Wirtschaft und Politik im 16./17. Jh.* (Deutsche Handelsakten des Mittelalters und der Neuzeit, 19,1). Stuttgart 1996, p. 21.

6 For basic and detailed information on trade networks cf. the edited volume by Fouquet Gerhard/Gilomen, Hans-Jörg (eds.): *Netzwerke im europäischen Handel des Mittelalters.* (Konstanzer Arbeitskreis für Mittelalterliche Geschichte). Sigmaringen 2010, here especially Fouquet: "Netzwerke im internationalen Handel des Mittelalters – eine

Increasingly operating throughout Europe, these companies were led by 'governors' ("regierer") or 'principals', i.e. managing directors, as personally and unlimited liable partners.[7] The liable cooperating partners and potential successors might have a minor interest-paying capital investment in addition to their capital contribution in the company. However, they did not immediately make decisions regarding the economic, staff-related or financial orientation, but they had rights of approval granted by company statutes. Furthermore, additional members, especially women with their dowries, were permitted to contribute capital to the company as committed, non-active members.[8] Paid factors and merchants' assistants also worked for the company at its headquarters and in its branches.[9]

Einleitung". Ibid., pp. 9–17; Selzer, Stephan/Ewert, Ulf Christian: "Netzwerke im europäischen Handel des Mittelalters. Konzepte-Anwendungen-Fragestellungen". Ibid. pp. 21–47 and Gilomen, Hans-Jörg: "Netzwerke im europäischen Handel des Mittelalters – Versuch einer Bilanz". Ibid., pp. 341–364. Häberlein, Mark: *Brüder, Freunde und Betrüger. Soziale Beziehungen, Normen und Konflikte in der Augsburger Kaufmannschaft um die Mitte des 16. Jahrhunderts.* (Colloquia Augustana, 9). Berlin 1998 and id.: "Netzwerkanalyse und historische Elitenforschung Probleme, Erfahrungen und Ergebnisse am Beispiel der Reichsstadt Augsburg". In: Dauser, Regina (ed.): *Wissen im Netz. Botanik und Pflanzentransfer in europäischen Korrespondenznetzen des 18. Jahrhunderts.* (Colloquia Augustana, 24). Berlin 2008.

7 Schulte, Aloys: *Geschichte des mittelalterlichen Handels und Verkehrs zwischen Westdeutschland und Italien mit Aussschluß von Venedig.* 2 volumes (Vol. 1: Darstellung, Vol. 2: Urkunden). Leipzig 1900, Vol. 2, p. 270; Strieder, Jakob: *Zwei Handelsgesellschaftsverträge aus dem 15. und 16. Jahrhundert, ihre Geschichte und ihr Recht.* Diss. jur., Leipzig 1908, p. 47; Hildebrandt, Reinhard: "Unternehmensstrukturen im Wandel. Familien- und Kapitalgesellschaften vom 15.–17. Jh". In: Gerhart, Hans Jürgen (ed.): *Struktur und Dimension. Mittelalter und Frühe Neuzeit.* FS. für Karl Heinrich Kaufhold (Vierteljahrschrift für Sozial- und Wirtschaftsgeschichte (*VSWG*) Beiheft, 132/133). Stuttgart 1997, pp. 93–110, here: p. 95–98; The term 'principal' was also common, cf. Bauer, Clemens: *Unternehmung und Unternehmensformen im Spätmittelalter und in der beginnenden Neuzeit.* (Münchener volkswirtschaftliche Studien, N.F., H. 23). Neudr. d. Ausg. Jena 1936, Aalen 1981, p. 66. Examples in Lutz, Elmar: *Die rechtliche Struktur süddeutscher Handelsgesellschaften in der Zeit der Fugger.* (Studien zur Fuggergeschichte, 25,1 and 2). Tübingen 1976, Vol. 1, p. 282.

8 Denzel, "The Merchant Family" 2009, p. 374.

9 Bauer, "Unternehmung" 1981, p. 34 and o. 140; Hildebrandt, "Unternehmensstrukturen" 1997, p. 95; finally Denzel, Markus A./Westermann, Ekkehard: *Das Kaufmannsnotizbuch des Matthäus Schwarz aus Augsburg von 1548.* (*VSWG* Beihefte, 215). Stuttgart 2011, pp. 42 sq.

The conflicts

The business success of these companies could be threatened by conflicts within or between families, resulting in bankruptcy.[10] This was in part due to the specific character of the companies – bound by economic interests on the one hand and family structures on the other – and meant that conflicts and the overcoming thereof always swung between purposive-rational and affective-emotional actions.

Conflicts[11] arose due to inadequate accounting, unaccepted statements of accounts, dissatisfaction with the ascertainment and distribution of profit, and expense and fee accounts. In addition, they could erupt because of misappropriation, impermissible special transactions, violation of the duty of care under corporate law, controversial decisions in the economic corporate strategy, unresolved controversial issues in personnel or succession planning, and finally unreliable, incompetent, wasteful or insubordinate successors or partners who were already active. Further disputes arose as contract extensions approached or company agreements were controversially realigned. Liquidation problems, or even simply rumours of not being solvent or creditworthy, also caused controversy. The death of a partner was also a potential source of conflict when it came to the question of how to proceed with the heirs, as well as the way the shares in the business were distributed. In addition, there were succession problems between fathers and sons, conflicts between brothers, uncles, cousins, brothers-in-law, sons-in-law and the children of first, second and third marriages.

Taken together, the cause of these conflicts was a tense relationship and a mixture of flexibility and conservatism in questions of succession, the further selection of personnel, the mental constitution of the members, the economic orientation of the company and internal accounting.

Conflicts and crises demanded a series of "strategies" and "means and ways" to counteract them.[12] It is important to distinguish between strategic behaviour for conflict prevention and variable means and ways of managing conflicts and crises

---

10 An overview of company bankruptcies in Southern Germany in Häberlein: "Merchants' bankruptcies, economic development and social relations in German cities during the long 17th century". In: Thomas Max Safley (ed.): *The history of bankruptcy. Economic, social and cultural implications in early modern Europe.* (Routledge: Explorations in Economic History, 60). London, New York 2013, p. 19–33.

11 On the wide range of conflicts and verified using many examples: Häberlein, "Brüder" 1998, passim.

12 Moreover, in future the monograph (as part of the DFG project of the same name at the Department of Economic and Social History at the University of Leipzig, Markus A. Denzel): Isenmann, Mechthild: *Strategien, Mittel und Wege der inner- und*

that were adapted to the acute situation. However, the intention was the same, the goal being the continuity, consolidation and economic success of the company.

Strategies, means and ways for preventing and resolving conflicts

The following strategic measures for protection against conflict were available to the family companies: a careful, increasingly formalised commercial apprenticeship, the purpose of which was professional "knowledge management within commercial undertakings"[13] in the young succeeding generation; a targeted marriage policy; the creation of a binding normative and legal foundation through company and employee agreements; conducting obligatory shareholders' meetings; and disposal by will.

Where conflicts had already broken out, the following means and ways were available for resolving them: convening extraordinary shareholders' meetings; consulting brokers, who were ideally provided by "mediators" associated through family relationships, by external persons, such as representatives of the town council or members of other companies or trustworthy and experienced merchants ('boni viri'). Other options included transferring, buying out or excluding family members and, as the ultima ratio, settlement in arbitration tribunals or courts.

Three measures in particular proved especially effective. One was the company agreements, which governed the ideals, obligations, rights, demands and sanctions of every company as its normative foundation. Above all, they served to prevent conflicts from arising in the first place and set out initial specifications on how they were to be counteracted.

In addition, shareholders' meetings were an effective measure for preventing conflicts and dealing with those that had already arisen. It is important to distinguish between obligatory and extraordinary meetings here. Held at defined intervals, obligatory meetings formed key institutional components of a company in line with the company agreements, as well as being an effective instrument for determining the economic and personnel-related orientation, and provided a platform for conflicts to break out and be dealt with. Issues such as expanding the group of

---

zwischenfamiliären Konfliktlösung oberdeutscher Handelshäuser im 15. und ‚langen 16. Jahrhundert‘ (typoscript).

13 Denzel, Markus A.: "Professionalisierung und sozialer Aufstieg bei oberdeutschen Kaufleuten im 16. Jahrhundert". In: Schulz, Günther (ed): *Sozialer Aufstieg. Funktionseliten im Spätmittelalter und in der frühen Neuzeit* (Büdinger Forschungen zur Sozialgeschichte 2000/2001), Munich 2002, p. 425.

partners, questions of succession in case of death, and regular departures or exclusions of partners were discussed at the ordinary meetings. These were particularly sensitive issues that all ultimately affected the continuing existence of the company. This makes the question of how decisions were made even more interesting.

In contrast, in acute cases of conflict, extraordinary shareholders' meetings were summoned, at which disputes were discussed and ideally resolved. These have so far been all but entirely ignored by researchers. Minutes were kept of the meetings, and there were memos, letters, strategy papers and legal documents, but these are difficult to find, as well as being laborious to decipher and analyse.

The dynamics of the meetings mean that the legal, social and formal structures of a company can be revealed. Who was the governor or principal? Who had what authority? How was the relationship between family members? How did the partners deal with extreme situations, such as a conflict that threatened the company? Which measures came into play during the meeting to resolve these conflicts? Did family structures play an important a role here as economic ones?

Another effective measure in case of conflict was mediation. Here, too, rational, reconciliatory statements and advice often culminated in and collided with emotional, affective, often even extreme reactions, which were to be averted through intensive communication by trustworthy mediators.

The company agreements for preventing conflict

The legal act of founding a company was agreed in the form of a contract by the governors[14] and entered in the company's books.[15] This joint action was agreed 'out of loyalty, love and friendship, well-advised, considered and with unanimous good will',[16] with the aim of managing the company for the best possible benefit

14 Lutz, "Handelsgesellschaften" 1976, Vol. 1, p. 160; Söhnchen, Marcus: *Die historische Entwicklung der rechtlichen Gründungsvoraussetzungen von Handels- und Aktiengesellschaften vom Beginn der Neuzeit (etwa 1500) bis zum Anfang des 19. Jahrhunderts.* (Schriften zur Rechtsgeschichte, 118). Diss. jur., Berlin 2005, p. 33.

15 Lutz, "Handelsgesellschaften" 1976, Vol. 1, p. 200.

16 Company agreement of the Augsburg-based Meuting company of 4th October 1436, Staatsarchiv (StaatsA) Augsburg, Reichstadt Augsburg, Akten 213: "von mer trew, lieb und fruntschaft wegen [...] mit wolbedachtem mute, guter vorbetrachtung und ainmüttigem gutem willen". Printed in Strieder, Jakob: *Zur Genesis des modernen Kapitalismus.* Leipzig. 2nd ed., 1935, pp. 220–223, Lutz, "Handelsgesellschaften" 1976, Vol. 2, pp. 1'–4', Möncke, Gisela: *Quellen zur Wirtschafts- und Sozialgeschichte mittel- und oberdeutscher Städte im Spätmittelalter.* (Ausgewählte Quellen zur deutschen Geschichte des Mittelalters, 37). Darmstadt 1982, pp. 292–295. Cf. in detail: Isenmann,

and with reliable order ("bessers nutzen und richtikait willen").[17] This ideal, or at least a slightly modified version, and perhaps also the topos, was listed as a declaration of intention in the preamble of almost every company agreement that has survived, for example in the agreement of the Upper German Meuting company of 4th October 1436, quoted here. In the context of oaths and sworn contract law, it formed the self-conception of all economic actions linked by family relationships.

Furthermore, the community bound together by oath[18] undertook to conduct trade, purchases and sales honourably and peacefully, in the best interests and to the advantage of the company, and to avert disadvantage, as stated in the agreements of Nürnberger Imhoff or 1481 or 1527[19] and in the agreement of Augsburger Höchstetter of 1514 (1515),[20] for example. The agreements also governed the company's staffing, legal and financial structure and features. The targets, purposes and needs of the company were planned,[21] obligations and rights listed, the voting procedure defined, provisions made regarding succession and inheritance, and clauses formulated to prevent capital being withdrawn and unauthorized guarantees taken out.[22] In addition, a code of conduct was formed that affected changes in the personal lives of the partners and included specific provisions such as bans on gambling, debauchery and wasting money.[23] Every agreement also contained further exceptional, varying provisions adapted to the needs of the company in question.

Mechthild und Eberhard "Das Innenverhältnis einer spätmittelalterlichen Handelsgesellschaft und die Ausweitung interner Konflikte – Hans Arzt und Gesellschaft, Anton Paumgartner und die Reichsstadt Nürnberg (1447–1471)". *VSWG* 101, 2014, p. 438.

17 StaatsA Augsburg, Reichsstadt Augsburg, Akten 213.

18 Lutz, "Handelsgesellschaften" 1976, Vol. 1, p. 171–177 assessed the oath or promise of fidelity in the company agreements as a "strengthening of the contractual obligation" (171) and emphasis of the particular trust relationship within a company (176), less as legally binding.

19 Lutz, "Handelsgesellschaften" 1976, Vol. 2, pp. 5'–6', here p. 5' and 60'–69', here: 60'.

20 Niedermayr, Hans: "Ein Gesellschaftsvertrag der Höchstetter von 1515". *Zeitschrift des Historischen Vereins für Schwaben (ZHVS)* 76, 1982, pp. 76–91, here p. 86. The agreement was concluded on 1st April 1514, but this copy originates from 15th December 1515. The preamble was composed by Ambrosius Höchstetter senior himself, the other 23 articles by Stefan Gabler, the company's representative in Nuremberg.

21 Stromer, Wolfgang von: "Binationale deutsch-italienische Handelsgesellschaften im Mittelalter". In: Rachewiltz, Siegfried de/Riedmann, Josef (eds.): *Kommunikation und Mobilität im Mittelalter. Begegnungen zwischen dem Süden und der Mitte Europas (11.–14. Jahrhundert)*, Sigmaringen 1995, pp. 135–158, here p. 137.

22 Lutz, "Handelsgesellschaften" 1976, Vol. 1, pp. 202 sqq., 242 sqq., 276 sqq., 388 sqq., 396 sqq.

23 Ibid., pp. 339–340.

Because the question of profit ascertainment and distribution, which was only determined by the governors and impossible to check, held particular potential for conflict, the governors attempted to counteract such controversy from the start through contractual provisions. For example, in their agreement of 26th July 1527, the Imhoff partners stipulated that the company book, in which the share capital, the contributions of the main partners in question and the company agreement itself were entered, could only be opened through a resolution passed by a majority: 'our company book shall be sealed by the three present here during the main calculations or who hold [the book] at their premises and shall not be opened unless by the will and with the knowledge of the majority of the partners'.[24] After all, even if the exact procedure for profit ascertainment could not be seen in detail, it can be considered a certain prerequisite that the foundation for profit ascertainment was provided by the amount of capital brought in by the partner in question (pro rata profit ascertainment[25]). The fear here was of the danger that figures for the capital could be manipulated in the company book if this were too easily accessible. In the case of the Imhoff company, the book was therefore sealed with the three seals of the main partners and stored at the home of the oldest of the three brothers, Hans Imhoff.[26] The company thus tried at least to prevent conflicts regarding the calculation basis for the profit ascertainment, although the specific method of profit ascertainment was not shown in the agreements. However, the Meuting company of 1436, for example, at least explained that the accounting and profit ascertainment had to be conducted either unanimously or through a majority decision: 'All that is won and lost, through general or majority company accounting, once it has been calculated and estimated, given to or deducted from each one of us, and this verified by accounting'.[27] Each individual partner was 'to accept the result without

24 Ibid., Vol. 2, p. 60'–61': "unser geschelschafft puch solen albegen drey die pey den haubtrechnungen hie sein, oder in irem haus haben, versigelt werden, und nit geofnet, es geschech dan mit willen und wissen der merreren teil der geschelschaffter".

25 Mayer, Valentin: *Die 'Fürlegung' in den Handelsgesellschaften des Mittelalters und des Frühkapitalismus.* Munich 1925, p. 73; Bauer, "Unternehmung" 1981, p. 63. Strieder, *Zwei Handelsgesellschaftsverträge* 1908, p. 53 referred to the agreement of the Haug company of 1557 as evidence of pro rata profit ascertainment. Lutz, "Handelsgesellschaften" 1976, Vol. 1, pp. 396–397 also referred to the 30th title of the Nuremberg municipal law reformation of 1479, in which this mode was defined. However, this is only a proposed subsidiary formula; the specific calculation remained a secret.

26 Lutz, "Handelsgesellschaften" 1976, Vol. 1, p. 250 and Vol. 2, S. 61'.

27 StaatsA Augsburg, Reichsstadt Augsburg, Akten 213: "und was [...] gewunnen oder verloren würdet nach gemainer gesellschaft oder der merer tail rechnung, als daz gerait und uberslagen wirdet und unsser yeglicher mit rechnung zugefugt oder abgezogen wirdet".

dissent'.[28] A resolution, given particular weight by the agreement of the majority of governors, was also intended to prevent any potential conflict regarding profit.

In addition, the partners used contractual provisions in an attempt to prevent conflicts that resulted from transgressions in their personal lives and that could threaten the company, even as far as bankruptcy. This initially included non-specific, generally dishonourable behaviour, followed more specifically by unauthorized exchange transactions and guarantees, and finally uncontrolled gambling, especially among young successors and other partners.

The Augsburg-based Höchstetter company was a particularly significant example here, having attempted to counteract these dangers on the backround of their structural economic changes and risky strategies of capital accumulation across multiple contractual periods. In the early decades of the sixteenth century, the Höchstetter company enjoyed an unparalleled economic rise over a period of around 20 years, which was followed by a purportedly sudden fall. During this time, it moved the focus of its business commitments increasingly from the textile trade to mining and mercury, including attempts to gain monopolies, for which it received strong criticism from contemporaries.[29] The Höchstetters covered the high level of capital needed for this by giving almost anyone – even the smallest of investors – the chance to invest capital in the company at a fixed interest rate.[30] The result was that the company ultimately had to deal with the promised interest claims of a disproportionately large group of capital investors. After the company suffered increasing economic imbalance from around the mid-1520s and the creditors demanded repayment of their investments and interests all at once, bankruptcy became unavoidable in 1529.[31]

28 "an dem sol er ain gantzes benigen han". StaatsA Augsburg, Reichsstadt Augsburg, Akten 213.

29 On the involvement of the Höchstetters in mining up until their attempt to form a monopoly in mercury extraction, cf. e.g. Safley, Thomas Max: "Staatsmacht und geschäftliches Scheitern. Der Bankrott der Handelsgesellschaft Ambrosius und Hans, Gebrüder Höchstetter, und Mitvervandte im Jahr 1529". *Österreichische Zeitschrift für Geschichtswissenschaften*, 19/3, 2008, pp. 36–53, here pp. 44 sqq. On this and the subsequent case studies in future Isenmann: *Strategien, Mittel und Wege.*

30 Häberlein, Mark: "Hatt das glückh wunderbarlich mit uns spilt". Joachim Hoechstetter d. J. (1523–1597) in der Geschäftswelt des 16. Jahrhunderts". *ZVHS* 95, 2001, pp. 53–72; Safley, "Staatsmacht" 2008, p. 41 even counted the Höchstetters "among the pioneers of this kind of capital widening."

31 Höchstetters and the bankruptcy that attracted widespread attention were chiefly examined by Thomas Max Safley in various publications, e.g. Safley, "Staatsmacht" 2008, pp. 49 sq.

This highly-risky corporate strategy was also taking place at the same time as certain conflicts within the company, which initially appeared unspectacular but were no less of a threat. The Höchstetters initially tried to offset both the dispute with their former co-partner Bartholomäus Rem, which went on for many years, and the increasingly problematic mental attitude of some towards those family members and co-partners who tended towards waste and gambling, with the help of contractual obligation. The agreements particularly dealt with issues of conflict settlement, including the causes of conflicts. Two surviving company agreements, which saw modifications due to changed company circumstances in the form of additions, omissions and clarifications, shed more light on this.

In the first surviving contract from 1514,[32] for example, the Höchstetters dealt generally with conflicts and measures to counteract them in four articles: In Article 10, they demanded amicable and, above all, internal agreement in the case of general disputes between the partners following clarification of the situation. In the case of conflicts arising from dishonourable behaviour of a partner, Article 14 does not prescribe amicable collaborative agreement, but instead grants the principal, Ambrosius Höchstetter senior, the right to dismiss the respective partner immediately. In Article 13, the partners undertake to avoid all conflict during a contractually-demanded period of restriction preceding liquidation at the regular end of the company. Finally, Article 23 governs cases of conflict potentially arising from controversial company decisions regarding purchase, sale or exchange transactions. In this case, following clarification of the case, the gathered meeting of partners was to come to a majority decision that was to be complied with immediately.[33]

The very specific list of different conflict triggers of 1524 was evidently not sufficient to cover every facet of possible disputes. As a result, in their later agreement of 1524,[34] the Höchstetters no longer dealt specifically with the various conflicts and solution strategies, but used a single article (13) to demand, in a concise and general way for all conflicts, that they be resolved amicably and, above all, internally, in a gathering of all partners.[35] However, the two agreements concur that conflicts were always to be resolved within the company.

In their agreements, the Höchstetters also reacted to acute, genuine conflicts and dangers with modified elements of the agreement, adapted to the situation. In 1514, the dispute with the former co-partner Bartholomäus Rem was still very much on

32 Niedermayr, "Gesellschaftsvertrag" 1982, pp. 80–91.
33 Niedermayr, "Gesellschaftsvertrag" 1982, pp. 85–86, 90.
34 Mayer, "Fürlegung" 1925, pp. 113–119; Lutz, "Handelsgesellschaften" 1976, Vol. 2, pp. 39'–48'.
35 Niedermayr, "Gesellschaftsvertrag" 1982, p. 85'

the minds of all the partners.[36] The context was a disputed profit statement from the company's mandatory general financial statements of 1514, from which Rem claimed 33,000 fl. for his six years of service, while the Höchstetters only granted him 26,000 fl. plus 2,000 fl. for expense allowances. The conflict came to an end, albeit only a preliminary one, before Augsburg City Court on 7th October 1517, which decided that the Höchstetter company was to pay 28,000 fl. plus 2.000 fl.[37] The Höchstetters accepted this decision, but Rem did not, and the conflict continued. This conflict situation was the target of the detailed preamble of the 1514 agreement, compiled by the Principal himself, in which the complete liquidation of the old company and the full payment of all financial claims of former partners – predominantly meaning Rem – were emphasised.[38] By 1524, the conflict was still not settled, forcing a reaction in the form of the tangible and often-used practice of capturing a partner while he was travelling, in this specific case at the instigation of Rem. In contrast to the limitation of ransom payments demanded in 1514 (Art. 8),[39] an unlimited level of ransom money was therefore defined.[40] The Höchstetters were worried that the ongoing conflict with Bartholomäus Rem could escalate further and therefore wanted to assure their travelling partners that they would be released.

Another acute risk situation arose in 1524 from the group of partners, which was new and younger compared to in 1514 and some of whom displayed a precarious mental constitution. The wasteful gambling habits of the two young co-partners Hans-Franz Paumgartner and Joachim Höchstetter in particular resulted in a demand for a stricter absolute ban on gambling in the new agreement of 1524, in contrast to the 1514 agreement, which permitted limited gambling as long as it served the purpose of social and commercial communication. It is only on the surface that this aspect of the agreement, which also reflects the reality of life, appears incidental. After all, aside from the sheer level of gambling debt,[41] the

36 Sender, Clemens: "Die Chronik Chronik der Stadt Augsburg". In: *Die Chroniken der deutschen Städte* 23, Vol. 4 *Augsburg*, Leipzig 1894, p. 147. Sender addressed the case in detail, pp. 146–149.

37 Sender, "Chronik", p. 147. The calculation is based on Ehrenberg, Richard, "Das Zeitalter der Fugger", Vol. 1, "Die Geldmächte des 16. Jahrhunderts", Jena 1896, 2nd reprint Hildesheim 1990, p. 213.

38 Niedermayr, "Gesellschaftsvertrag" 1982, pp. 81.

39 Lutz, "Handelsgesellschaften" 1976, Vol. 2, pp. 44'.

40 Lutz, "Handelsgesellschaften" 1976, Vol. 2, pp. 45'-46'.

41 According to the Augsburg chronicler Clemens Sender, „Chronik", p. 221 the two players managed to lose the enormous total of 30,000 fl. in one night through gambling: "dann sein sun Joachim und sein tochtermann [seit 1519, Hans] Franz Paumgartner haben auff ain nacht in ainem panget thüren laussen auffgan und verthon 5.000 oder 10.000 fl.

respectability and thus the creditworthiness of a company was affected. Where further economic threats were also in evidence, as was the case for the Höchstetters, gambling debt could pose a danger to the company – a situation that needed to be prevented by contractual regulation.

A table summarising the relevant articles of the two agreements from 1514 and 1524 clearly shows the modifications adapted to the needs of the time. The specific occasion is listed, followed by the directive defined as a result:

Table: Company agreements of the Höchstetter company

1514	Directive	1524	Directive
Conflicts between partners	Clarification of the situation, amical and internal agreement	All conflicts compactly and in general	Amicable and internal agreement through gathered full meeting of partners
Conflict arising from dishonourable actions of a partner	The governor had to dismiss the partner immediately		
Waiting period to prepare the liquidation at the regular end of a company	Period of restriction with ban on conflict		
Conflict case resulting from controversial company decisions	Clarification of the case by the gathered council of partners and majority decision; this had to be complied with immediately		
Ransom money for hostage-taking	For each, 1,000 Rh. fl. capital and a capital credit[42] of 100 Rh. fl. each	Capture of a partner by B. Rem	Unlimited ransom
Gambling	Limited gambling accounted for by social communication	Gambling	Tightened, complete ban on gambling
Confidentiality clause	Main partners	Confidentiality clause	Main partners and silent investors

und auff ain mall 10.000 oder 20.000 oder 30.000 fl. verspillen." Cf. Wilhelm Krag, *Die Paumgartner von Nürnberg und Augsburg. Ein Beitrag zur Handelsgeschichte des 15. und 16. Jahrhunderts*, München/Leipzig 1919, p. 56; Häberlein, "Brüder" 1998, p. 278.

42 A capital credit ('Fürlegung') is an amount credited and allocated to the shareholder or merchant's assistant in the books, i.e. a fictional calculation amount that increased the capital and therefore all the percentage profit calculated at the end of the contract period on a pro rata basis, Bauer, "Unternehmung" 1981, p. 71.

According to Lutz, it is impossible to take stock of the number of partners tempted by gambling, as the problem appeared to have been so common.[43] The Nuremberg-based Imhoff company, for example, trod a similar path to the Höchstetters in their agreements of 1481 and 1527. While the agreement of 1481 did not contain specific articles dedicated to a ban on gambling, a ban on securities and unauthorised financial transactions, these issues were dealt with in detail in the later agreement of 1527. The personnel at the Imhoff company had changed that year, with an impact on the company's structural character. The three brothers Konrad, Hans and Peter Imhoff initially formed the company in 1481; significant reinforcements came in 1527 in the form of the heirs of the first generation of partners, the brothers Peter, Ludwig, Hieronymus and Simon and – and this is what seems to have necessitated the amendment and supplementation of the contract – of their sometimes still young sons, who were not of equal status to the main partners – the governors. In contrast to the agreement of 1481, the new agreement therefore included prohibition of gambling, romantic affairs, lending and granting guarantees, and 'other unseemly and improprietous actions' ("anderes unziemliches und ungebürliches Handeln").[44] The governors threatened the personal liability of the perpetrators as a sanction.

In general, a company agreement was a presentation of the targeted ideal, which obligated the signatories to adhere to the contractual postulates principally through vow and oath. Contracts were part of a network of different strategies and, at the same time, as a normative foundation, essential in guaranteeing the continuity of a company. The examples from the Imhoff and Höchstetter companies showed how various modified contracts could be used to shape the company and its business dealings successfully over a long period of time. The Imhoff company existed from the mid-fifteenth century until 1635 at least, while bankruptcy became unavoidable for the Höchstetters in 1529, after around 60 years in business, as a result of high-risk corporate strategies, problematic staff, excessive numbers or/and demands from creditors, liquidity problems.[45] Although reality often collided with the contractual ideal and individual clauses sometimes proved impossible to implement, these agreements were a necessary component of conflict prevention and thus formed a strategic sub-field of bankruptcy prevention.

43 Lutz, "Handelsgesellschaften" 1976, Vol. 1, p. 339.

44 "pulschafft [...] ander unzimlicher und ungepurlicher hendel", Lutz, "Handelsgesellschaften" 1976, Vol. 2, p. 67'.

45 Safley, "Staatsmacht" 2008, pp. 49 sqq.

The company meeting as a means of conflict resolution

Annual and extraordinary general meetings were another effective instrument for resolving conflicts. Some of the many case studies in this field are offered by the Nuremberg-based companies of the Arzt family in the mid-fifteenth century and "Endres Imhoff und Mitverwandte" in the mid-sixteenth century, as well as the Augsburg-based Herbrot company in the mid-sixteenth century.

A particularly sophisticated and well-considered strategy in this field was employed by the Nuremberg-based Imhoff company, which existed from at least 1528 as "Endres Imhoff und Mitverwandte" with Endres I., Gabriel, Ludwig, Hieronymus and Lienhard as the main partners and joined in 1531 by the Augsburg resident Simon Imhof.[46] On the initiative and under the leadership of the company's governor, the economically and politically influential Endres I. Imhoff senior († 1579) an incipient conflict with relative and co-partner Paulus Behaim was averted. The conflict revolved around the termination of cooperation with Paulus, considered necessary from the company's point of view. Thanks to a stroke of archival luck, the circumstances surrounding this separation, first planned and then conducted in autumn 1556, can be traced from the personal records, the "journal", of Paulus Behaim[47] – albeit with the distance necessitated by a subjective 'self-witness'.

---

46 The latest research on the Imhoff family: Fleischmann, Peter: *Rat und Patriziat in Nürnberg. Die Herrschaft der Ratsgeschlechter vom 13. bis zum 18. Jahrhundert.* (Nürnberger Forschungen, vols. 1–4). Nuremberg 2008, Vol. 2, pp. 601–631, here p. 614; Imhoff, Christoph Freiherr von: "Die Imhoff – Handelsherren und Kunstliebhaber". In: *Mitteilungen des Vereins für die Geschichte Nürnbergs (MVGN)* 62, 1975, pp. 1–42, here p. 32. Working closely with the sources, Helga Jahnel: *Die Imhoff, eine Nürnberger Patrizier- und Großkaufmannsfamilie. Eine Studie zur reichsstädtischen Wirtschaftspolitik und Kulturgeschichte an der Wende vom Mittelalter zur Neuzeit (1351–1679).* Phil. Diss. masch., Würzburg 1950, developed the first comprehensive history of the Imhoff family. In doing so, Jahnel pursued issues in economic history, social history and prosopography. Unfortunately, Jahnel's source-rich dissertation was never printed.

47 Stadtarchiv Nürnberg (StadtAN), E11/II FA Behaim, No. 601. These records were mentioned multiple times in the research, albeit with only brief references, e.g. in Kamann, Johann: "Aus Nürnberger Haushaltungs- und Rechnungsbüchern des 15. und 16. Jahrhunderts". Teil I. *MVGN* 6, 1886, pp. 57–122, here p. 60; id.: "Aus dem Briefwechsel eines jungen Nürnberger Kaufmanns im 16. Jahrhundert". In: *Mitteilungen aus dem Germanischen Nationalmuseum* 1894, pp. 9–22 und 45–56, here p. 12; Hildebrandt, Reinhard: "Diener und Herren. Zur Anatomie großer Unternehmen im Zeitalter der Fugger". In: Burkhardt, Johannes et al. (eds.): *Augsburger Handelshäuser im Wandel des historischen Urteils.* (Colloquia Augustana, 3), Berlin 1996, pp. 149–174,

The imminent conflict, the counter measures and finally Behaim's separation from the Imhoff company took place in a series of steps. During the ten-year period between 1546 and 1556, at the obligatory general meetings, conflicts regarding disputed profit and fee calculations arose, to be followed by extraordinary general meetings in order to prevent the conflict.

For 20 years, from 1536,[48] Paulus Behaim was responsible in line with his agreements,[49] first as a merchant's assistant, then as co-partner with a capital investment in the company's profit and loss, for the following tasks: he kept the journal and the register of debts at the Nuremberg headquarters, as well as conducting goods and financial transactions, including exchange transactions.[50] Finally, his duties also included travelling to the Frankfurt trade fair and to Antwerp, where the Imhoff company maintained one of its most important trading stations.[51] For this work he was paid a fixed salary, plus a fee of 200 fl. per year and 50 fl. in expenses for his journeys to Antwerp.[52]

Even during his period of service, in 1552, Paulus was stripped of his fee of 200 fl.[53] because he was refusing to travel to Antwerp – the trip to Frankfurt trade fair was as far as he would go. It was at this point that trust – so central to the agreements – began to ebb away on both sides, to be replaced by scepticism, doubt and mistrust.

---

p. 156; id. 1997, p. 97; Schmid, Barbara: *Schreiben für Status und Herrschaft. Deutsche Autobiographik in Spätmittelalter und früher Neuzeit*. Zürich 2006, p. 107. A transcription with analysis is currently being compiled: Mechthild Isenmann, '*Das Handbuch Herrn Paul Behaims*'. *Lehrjahre und Handelspraxis eines Nürnberger Kaufmanns und Financiers*. (in preparation).

48 StadtAN, E11/II FA Behaim, No. 601, fol. 2r.

49 His employee contracts from 1548 and 1552 have survived: Nuremberg (N), Germanisches Nationalmuseum (GNM), Historisches Archiv (HA), Behaim-Archiv Fasz. 25.

50 NGNM, HA, Behaim-Archiv Fasz. 25: "der gleichen des marcts und des verkauffen, auch mit wesseln und demselben in gehorig und also von notten ist, alles verwalten und nach seim pesten zustand ausrichten".

51 NGNM, HA, Behaim-Archiv Fasz. 25; Seibold, Gerhard: "Die Imhoffsche Handelsgesellschaft in den Jahren 1575–1635". In: *MVGN* 64, 1977, pp. 201–214, here p. 203.

52 NGNM, HA, Behaim-Archiv Fasz. 25: "sol im darzu die vier jar ein icliches derselben zweyhundert gulden fur all ding gegeben werden [...] ein oder mer jar gen Anttorff geschickt [...] so sol im darfur ein icliches derselben jar noch zu dem forigen 50 fl. gegeben werden."

53 Paulus Behaim then complained about this in his records, StadtAN, E11/II FA Behaim, No. 601, fol. 31v.

This did not abate during the subsequent four-year period of the agreement, leading to unwillingness among the Imhoff governors to employ their co-partner of many years any longer. The governors' idea was for Paulus Behaim to make the separation himself when his agreement came up for renewal on 1st August 1556, and they were entirely successful. At several shareholders' meetings, they first pushed Paulus into submitting the initial proposal for what he thought his future role at Imhoff should be. At the extraordinary general meeting held in Nuremberg on 3rd August 1556, Behaim thus agreed with the Imhoffs that he would commit to them again for the same conditions, profit and fee as before. In doing so, he made a limitation that appeared small but that would turn out to have severe consequences for him: because his health appeared to be weakening, he no longer wanted to travel to Frankfurt for trade fairs, although he did state his willingness to step in for the trips if no-one else could be found.[54]

To Behaim's exasperation, the Imhoffs' reaction to this proposal was to send him out of the meeting and make him wait outside for half an hour so that they could first discuss their course of action alone. The result of the internal meeting showed that the Imhoffs used Behaim's initial proposal as an opportunity to present him a counter-offer at conditions he would not be able to accept: they would accept the level of profit from his investment, but would withdraw the fee and compensation of outlay, and his presence in Frankfurt to represent the company would be mandatory.[55] This was followed by a postscript that was particularly insulting to Behaim and clearly showed the governors' merciless attitude towards an aging employee who had been with the company for many years: they told

---

54 StadtAN, E11/II FA Behaim, No. 601, fol. 37r/v: "Uber 3 tag hernach zaigt ich an, die weyl sy mir ein bedacht geben hetten, wen verner mein gelegenhait sein wolt, wie wol ich mich versehen gehabt, sy soltten mir us ersten ein furschlag gethan haben, aber ich wolt es gleich anzaigen und nemlich so feer sy mir das jenig thon wollen, das sy mir izt thon haben, als die summa gelt zue gewinn und verlust und die belonung, so woll ich mich alhie gprauchen lassen, doch diewyl ich alle mess zu Farnckfurtt besücht hab und mir allerlej beschwernüs und kranckheit in solcher zu gestanden werre, wer mir beschwerlich, die selben hinfur alzeitt zu besüchen, wollt mich deshalben versehen, sy würden mich denselben zum tayls erlassen, wan es aber di gelegenhait geb, das sy sonst nitt leutt hetten, soche mess zu besüchen, so woltt ich gern ein ubrigs thon, auff solche dret ich auf."

55 StadtAN, E11/II FA Behaim, No. 601, fol. 37v. "Nemlich so woltten sy mir auff gewinn und verlust in handel nehmen allein die 3.500 fl. und kein belonung nit geb[en]. Darumb soltt ich verpflicht sein, alle mess gen Franckfurtt die mess zu versehen, alhie das marcks mit verkauffen aus zu warttn, und auch so her Imhoff nitt hie sein würdt, die bücher zu haltten."

him curtly that they did not know how else they would be able to use him at the company.[56]

Behaim then described the sense of injustice that he, as a member of the company for many years, felt as a result of this unacceptable proposal that affected his honour as a merchant and partner. He stated that the proposal was an insult to him and that he considered it a mockery, as he was expected to work more yet earn less. Consequently, he informed them that he would have to reject the proposal, as he had to think to the benefits for him, his honour and his welfare.[57] He came to the conclusion that the partners' intention behind the proposal was to make it clear that they no longer needed him.[58] The consequence was that the Imhoff partners bought Paulus Behaim out and dismissed him from the company, thus achieving their envisaged aim evading an uncontrollable conflict.

Although Behaim initially felt that the way in which the separation had happened was an insult to him, it was also an opportunity for a new beginning for him, and he founded his own company in the period that followed. This company focused predominantly on credit transactions and, after a while, also became involved in successful business relations with his former Imhoff company.[59]

Surviving records of the Nuremberg-based Arzt company of the fifteenth century provide a unique example of conflict resolution through shareholders' meetings. What makes the source on the meetings so exceptional is not only its volume, but also the fact that it reveals contrary positions of the parties concerned.

---

56 StadtAN, E11/II FA Behaim, No. 601, fol. 37v.

57 StadtAN, E11/II FA Behaim, No. 601, fol. 38r: "Ich west mich aber auff irem furschlag dismal mit inen nitt einzulassen, dan ich auch bedenckhen must, was mein nuz, eer und wolfart werdt."

58 StadtAN, E11/II FA Behaim, No. 601, fol. 38r: "dan erst hinther sich zu dienen und minder zu nemen, das konth mir niemantt rhatte, diweyl sy mir dan solches mith furgeschlagen, must ich bey mir gedencken, daß sie inen sonst ferner nit mer notturfftig werden und mein nitt begertten."

59 This prosaic and pragmatic business connection after a conflict settlement, founded on economic benefit, began with a reconciliatory letter from Endres Imhof senior shortly after the separation on 5th September 1556. In it, Endres briefly addressed the events that had occurred, before expressive a hope that their friendship was not suffer as a result: NGNM, HA, Behaim-Archiv, Fasz. 29g, No. 14: "wie ich mich dem solchen anzeigen nach anderst nitt versehen, und deinem schreiben nach [...] anderst nitt, alls wille und freuntschafft zu dir verdrosten und nitt darfur achten will, mich oder die meinen erforderst, in ainige pös verdechtt solst haben und warin dir [...] moge wilfarhen, solst mich anders nitt als jederzeit ganz guetwillig fruntschafft und hiemit merers mit mein in all."

In particular, statements of claims[60] and responses ('defamation')[61] from two opposing parties in a case before the Nuremburg Council give an indication of how such meetings were organised and provide deeper insight into the turbulent internal dealings of a trading company beset by mistrust and discord. Furthermore, data-based information recorded by the parties and the auditors provide a deeper insight into the inner life and the business success of the company and into disputes between the partners and the 'overlord', conducted through threats, coercion and misappropriation of accounting documents.[62]

Following the death of the founder, Ulrich senior, in 1436, the company was continued by his sons, Hans Arzt and his younger brother Ulrich, their brothers-in-law Hans Ulstatt, husband of Justina nee Arzt and Sigmund Gossembrot, husband of Ursula nee Arzt and Thoman Oheim (Öhem).[63] Another sister, Clara Paumgartner nee Arzt, was also part of the company, and the question of the extent and manner to which her husband, Anton Paumgartner, was also involved later led to an extensive legal dispute. The two brothers and their brothers-in-law were involved in the company in terms of both capital and work; the sisters with capital.

When the main profit statement was presented at an obligatory meeting in 1447, the result shown was a surprisingly low profit for most of the co-partners of just 7% in two years[64] and an underlying low company capital. Being suspicious of these disappointing profits, the senior[65] Thoman began to look for reasons and came to the conclusion that Hans Arzt, who chaired the headquarters in Nuremberg and was responsible for all accounting,[66] had withdrawn company capital

60 Staatsarchiv (StaatsA) Nürnberg, Reichstadt Nürnberg, 7-farbiges Alphabet, Akten, No. 168, fol. 1r–2v, "Hannß Artzts zettel".

61 StaatsA Nürnberg, 7-farbiges Alphabet, Akten, No. 168, fol. 5r–17v.

62 Isenmann, Mechthild und Eberhard, "Das Innenverhältnis" 2014, p. 452.

63 Thoman Öhem, a wealthy Augsburg citizen connection to the Augsburg Welser and Rehlinger families through the marriage of his daughter. He presumably also knew (in a friendship and business capacity?) the company founder Ulrich Arzt senior there and, due to this shared past, was also linked to his sons as a kind of senior, Blendinger, Friedrich: "Ulrich Arzt (um 1460–1527)". In: Pölnitz, Götz Freiherr von (ed.): *Lebensbilder aus dem bayerischen Schwaben*. Vol. 6, Munich 1958, p. 88–130, here pp. 61, 91.

64 StaatsA Nürnberg, 7-farbiges Alphabet, Akten, No. 168, fol. 6v, 73r.

65 This is how Anton Paumgartner described him in later proceedings: Hofbibliothek Aschaffenburg, Dep. Stiftsbibliothek, Ms. Pap. 9, Aschaffenburger Codex (Aschaffenburger Codex), fol. 14v.

66 However, Hans Arzt disputed that he was the sole managing director and thus responsible for the bookkeeping. StaatsA Nürnberg, 7-farbiges Alphabet, Akten, Nr. 168, fol. 6v; cf. ibid. fol. 89r/v (Sigmund Gossembrot und Ulrich Arzt an den Städtebund 1452).

for his own purposes and not recorded these withdrawals in full in the accounting book. Therefore, Öhem called an extraordinary general meeting, at which he first referred to an oath he had given to the late father Ulrich Arzt senior and that now obligated him to represent the situation openly: 'A significant sum of money is missing from the company and you, Hans Arzt, are to blame for this'.[67] This resulted in a fierce exchange of words between Öhem and Hans, who denied the accusation and accused Öhem of lying. Öhem, in turn, vehemently denied this and repeated his accusation, adding that Hans Arzt had always gone behind his siblings' backs, as he could prove from the books ('he (Öhem) could prove to his siblings using the books that he [Hans Arzt] had given them the run-around and defrauded them'[68]).

At first, the brothers-in-law and siblings did not want to believe that a relative had defrauded their shared company. However, another examination of the books showed that Hans Arzt had not kept full accounts and that, due to the failure to record his budget management and living costs, there had been no separation between private and company assets. He had also failed to enter and offset accounts receivable paid to the company ("gemaine schulden") in the main book,[69] quite apart from other significant benefits he had received from the company assets.[70] The severe accusation of embezzlement therefore arose.

When confronted with the accusations, Hans Arzt admitted that irregularities may have occurred. During the meeting, which became noticeably more emotional as time went on, Hans Arzt asked his co-partners 'imploringly and in tears' to let the matter rest for the moment and to grant him a deferral of a year and a day, to allow him to work out the missing amount and to balance the books, i.e. to make it impossible to bring charges against him.[71] They granted the deferral on the condition that Arzt would then repay what he owed the company.

---

67 StaatsA Nürnberg, 7-farbiges Alphabet, Akten, No. 168, fol. 1v, fol. 5v–6r: "Es mangelt ein mercklich summ gelts in der geselschafft, Hanns Artz, da bist du schuldig an".

68 Ibid., fol. 7r: "das er seine geswistrigitt geneyset und gealfantzt hett, des wolt er in weisen mit den buchern".

69 Ibid., fol. 6v: "das sie fremd nam nach sollichem redlichem handel, die sie in solanger zeit gehabt hetten und wurden dem also nach synnen un genawer suchen, ob ichts vergessen oder in der rechnung us beliben, oder mit zu geschriben were worden. Da erfand sich, das Hanns Arzt imselbs nit vollkomenlich und gantz zugeschriben hett, was er dieselben gesellschafft schuldig was und darus genomen hett, in etwie vil und mancherlay stucken, die dann an die vorgemelten rechnung nit komen waren und der gesellschafft dran ussenstand."

70 Ibid., fol. 90r.

71 Ibid., fol. 7v.

Hans Arzt's description of the situation, however, was entirely different. In his version, because he did not want to accept such doubt, defamation and suspicion, he had put pressure on the co-partners to seal the books and then to take them in hand and examine whether he alone had neglected anything, owed anything or, in particular, spend anything for his own benefit; if this were the case, he would pay for it. After sufficient inspection, he said, they returned the documents to him, exonerated him and asked him to let the matter rest and not to resent them for it.[72] In addition, they asked him in 'humble solicitude and with reddened eyes' and many friendly words to keep them and their money 'with him in the company and the trade'. Hans claimed that, in an appeal to their family relationship, they asked him not to break away from them like a stranger, but to stand by them as a 'loyal brother' as he had in the past; they also thanked him for having made them 'rich and happy' in the past.[73]

His siblings refuted this version and explained their continued relationship exclusively with rational considerations and the wish to maintain the "honour" of all of them, without the rumours ('Geschrei') becoming too extensive and defamations being made.[74] The trust between relatives – the strength of any company formed within a family – had been destroyed and had to be secured by a 'note of alliance': a settlement under company law. In it, Hans Arzt was given two messengers who would assist with and keep an eye on business, in order to rebuild trust within the company.[75]

In 1450, after a little under three years of business activity, a new incident led to the final separation of Hans Arzt and the co-partners at the annual general meeting and on the presentation of the general balance sheet. According to the co-partners, Hans Arzt had not adhered to the agreements they had made few years ago and had, 'by his own will and whim', frequently taken business decisions without the

72 Ibid., fol. 1r.

73 Ibid., fol. 1r/v.

74 Ibid., fol. 9r: In a letter from Sigmund Gossembrot and Ulrich Arzt to the Städtebund (Association of Cities) on 23rd March 1452, they explained that they had considered that Hans Arzt was their brother and brother-in-law and that they did not want to disclose the great damage in order to protect their honour. Cf. ibid., fol. 90r.

75 Ibid., fol. 8v/9r: "Er sollte auch nit gewalt haben, allein von der gesellschafft wegen ichtz zu hantieren, dann es were der zwayer dyener einer oder die bede hie dabey." In the presence of Hans Arzt, Ulrich Arzt, Sigmund Gossemprot and Clara Paumgartner, Caspar Nagel had to pledge to them, but not Hans Arzt, not to overlook any "geverlicheit", any malicious or fraudulent behaviour, should he become aware of such. Ibid., fol. 9r, cf. fol. 90v.

obligatory consultation of the company's assistants, whom he had sent away.[76] Finally they wanted Hans Arzt to formally complete and seal the note of alliance, which had been in his hands for three years and which he had (apparently?) not yet taken care of.[77] They therefore no longer wanted to be "in company" with Hans, completed the balance sheet with him and 'took the business into their hands'.[78]

According to Hans Arzt, however, the co-partners and the merchant's assistant Caspar Nagel had met in the office of the company's headquarters, and after having locked the door behind them,[79] demanded him to pay the 3,200 guilders he owed them, making the most terrible and brutal threats. If he did not pay, they would – in place of documentary evidence and witnesses – "übersiebnen" and "überschwören" him through character witnesses, i.e. convict him and bring him to the gallows that way.[80]

In their subsequent response to the Nuremberg Council,[81] the co-partners claimed to have examined, with the permission of Hans Arzt and the indispensable assistance of Caspar Nagel, the accounting documents he had voluntarily given them – books, journal, registers, accounting notes –, made an abstract and, alongside smaller amounts, determined a missing amount of around 4,448 guilders.[82]

Hans Arzt accepted the sum, although he would later claim to have done so only under 'situational pressure'.[83] After this agreement on the old and new account,

76 Ibid., fol. 10r/v, 90v.: Hans Arzt accused the opposing side of having joined together conspiratorially against him and taken from him servants, menial staff and maids, while the co-partners claimed that Hans Arzt had secretly wanted to persuade his brother Ulrich to form a company with him in order to force his siblings out of the company and servants for himself, ibid., fol. 2r.

77 Ibid., fol. 8v–9r.

78 Ibid., fol. 90v.

79 The opposing side did not represent the locking of the doors as duress and coercion, but that they wanted to keep the servants and third parties out of the meeting room as usual in order not to be disturbed. Ibid., fol. 11r.

80 Ibid., fol. 73v.

81 Ibid., fol. 5r–17v.

82 Ibid., fol. 13v. Under cross-examination by the Nuremberg Council, Caspar Nagel later stated that Hans Arzt had personally entered the accounts into the 'company books' and then noted this in his contradictory book, his "Gegenbuch", das man "verraitpuch" nenne. (Ibid., fol. 78v). Nagel saw this as proof that Arzt was always the top manager of the company and not Oheim, as Arzt maintained.

83 Under cross-examination, the merchant's assistant Caspar Nagel represented this as follows: After the agreement on the 4,448 guilders, during which he was on the market, Ulrich Arzt said to him that he was amazed that Hans Arzt had not objected to the write-down of this sum, even though he had explicitly advised him to do so. He

according to the reports of the co-partners, Hans Arzt declared that he recognised that they, the co-partners, no longer trusted him and no longer wanted to remain in the company with him, and thus proposed options for buying him out.[84] All partners agreed with this and the company was liquidated.[85]

At the meetings, the allegations and accusations had led to the accumulation of counter-semantics to the postulates, moral values and maxims in the company agreement regarding the ideal internal relationships within a trading company: disloyalty, theft, dishonour, defamation, vilification, mistrust, disunity and division, hatred and hostility ('Neid') between brothers, even crimes ('Frevel'), false imprisonment, violence and coercion were raised by the family members in mutual accusations and threats.

In short, there are differing assessments of the Arzt family's shareholders' meetings as a conflict resolution strategy. On the one hand, they allowed disputes to be kept within the company for many years, from the outbreak of the first conflicts in 1447 to the separation in 1551, as well as enabling joint actions to be continued, albeit in a fragile state. It was only once the company had been separated that, on the other hand, the conflicts became public, chiefly through a case brought before the Nuremberg Council by Hans Arzt, entailing long-lasting controversies, conducted both judicially and politically. However, the looming bankruptcy of the Arzt company due to financial problems caused by years of dubious accounting, which could have resulted in possible difficulties in liquidation, had been avoided.

Mediation as a method of conflict resolution

Measures characterised by the intensive communication of mediators chiefly linked by family connections also stood at the heart of conflict management. Mediation proved itself as an effective means of finding a solution in cases of conflict, and tended to be more of a long-term process than a short-term measure. This process, demanded by the company agreements, illustrates both the rational

knew nothing of any coercion, but Ulrich had said to his brother Hans that if he were to complain to the Council and mayor about the matter, "so wolt er in woll an einen galgen bringen." (Ibid., fol. 72r/v). Later again: "Willst Du das Geld nicht geben, so wollen wir das ainem ratt clagen, und werstu ein fremder, so wolt ich dich mit recht [auf gerichtlichem Wege] an einen galgen bringen." In contrast to Ulrich Arzt, Sigmund Gossembrot had apparently argued multiple times against negotiations with Hans Arzt and in favour of legal recourse. Ibid., fol. 73v.

84 Ibid., fol. 15v.

85 Justina Ulstatt stated that they agreed confidentiality so that nobody's honour would be affected. Ibid., fol. 31v.

approach of 'mediators' who were experienced in business and familiar with the family, and the reaction to affective and emotional behaviour on the part of the partners involved in the conflict.[86] The mediator needed various skills and, as far as possible, to be a person who was respected by everyone within the family and often equipped with stable authority.[87] Initially, internal mediators were preferred, although the contractual parties also considered the family's wider environment 'internal'. Besides internal mediation, external mediation by negotiators, representatives and arbiters, which generally followed internal mediation. This kind of "arbitration court of fellow professionals"[88] was demanded in some company agreements, which also governed their composition.[89]

Between 1545 and 1555, the ongoing conflicts between the Imhoff family[90] and their relative Wolf turned into a large-scale mediation process in which a total of seven parties were involved. The dispute and the mediation activities were recorded in extensive correspondence stretching to over 300 letters.[91] According to these records, Wolf was active as a factor of the Imhoff company in Naples and later in L'Aquila, the centre of saffron cultivation and trade. The Imhoff governors accused Wolf not only of violating his contractual obligations as a factor, the execution of proper saffron trading and above all the obligatory and regular accountability in Nuremberg, but also of having gambled and used his gambling gains to pay off his own debts in the accounting of the foreign trading post ('I won 1,200 scudi through gambling in the same year and used it to settle

86 As in the aforementioned Meuting agreement of 1436: StaatsA Augsburg, Reichsstadt Augsburg, Akten Nr. 213.

87 Bauer, "Unternehmung" 1981, p. 77.

88 Lutz, "Handelsgesellschaften" 1976, Vol. 1, pp. 471 sq.; Bauer, "Unternehmung" 1981, p. 77. A notable example of this is the aforementioned conflict between Bartholomäus Rem and the Augsburg Höchstetter partners regarding disputed profit calculations. The conflict could not be contractually resolved until 1522, through the arbitration process chaired by the arbiter and entrepreneur Jakob Fugger, Sender, Clemens: "Chronik", p. 147; Ehrenberg, Richard: "*Das Zeitalter der Fugger*". p. 213.

89 E.g. in the Manlich agreement of 1548, Lutz, "Handelsgesellschaften" 1976, Vol. 2, p. 136'; particularly detailed in the Schreiber-Weißhaupt-Ditmar agreement, ibid., p. 18'.

90 Fleischmann, Peter: „Rat und Patriziat in Nürnberg" 2008, Vol. 2, p. 601; Imhoff, Christoph Freiherr von: "Die Imhoff – Handelsherren und Kunstliebhaber" 1975, p. 32.

91 NGNM, HA, Imhoff-Archiv, Fasz. 39, No. 8.

the damages'[92]). The governors feared that this behaviour could become public and that this would bring about 'little good repute and general good'.[93] The tangible basis of the fears lay in the negative impact on the company's standing and the loss of faith this would result in due to the poor reputation of a member of staff. The company reacted to this tangible danger with a multi-layered strategy that switched between monitoring, coercive action and repeated mediation.

Initially, mediation remained internal among the partners of the family in Nuremberg and Augsburg, before being joined by external mediators in the form of the Nuremberg Council, the Emperor's chancellery, the chancellery of the Vice-King of Naples, the representatives of the Vice-King, his brother and, increasingly at the end, the Hallers in Frankfurt and Nuremberg, who were related by marriage.[94] This case thus represents extensive internal and external mediation that had become necessary in an often highly emotional conflict. However, only particularly striking key points can be addressed here.

During the many years of disputes, Wolf repeatedly threatened, concealed and gave the impression that he could cause great damage to his masters. These threats appeared realistic as, according to a letter about Wolf from a partner ordered by the Imhoffs to attend a mediation meeting in Naples, Wolf would disclose secret i.e. forbidden transactions of the Imhoffs if he considered it necessary.[95] In further mediation meetings with an Imhoff nephew working on behalf of the principals, it was finally possible to move Wolf 'not to act against honour', and he assured his masters in a letter that he would ensure that their secret transactions were not revealed.[96] This critical situation for the company was thus at least defused.

Furthermore, mediation and simultaneous demands from the relative and principal Endres Imhoff succeeded in persuading Wolf to meet in Nuremberg his obligatory accountability duty based on his factory bookkeeping hold in Naples. During his stay in Nuremberg in 1545, however, Wolf did not meet any of his contractual obligations, nor had he corrected his balance sheet, which had been judged flawed and incomplete by the governors. He thus remained a 'non-exonerated merchant's

92 Ibid., No. 8g (34b): "so ich mit spillenn dasselb jar ob scudi 1.200 gewunnen und den schaden gut thonn".

93 Ibid., No. 8h (25b): "wenig glimpf oder guttem".

94 On the role of the factor, most recently Denzel/Westermann, "Kaufmannsnotizbuch" 2011, p. 42.

95 NGNM, HA, Imhoff-Archiv, Fasz. 39, No. 8g (24g-h).

96 Ibid.: "wider eer nitt handeln […] findt mich willig, habt ir willens es zu vertragen, dorfft mir frolich vertrauen, wil in der heimlichkait handeln das es nit geoffent sol werden, das es aus ewrm pevelch gescheh, das will ich mich hiemit verschreiben haben."

assistant'.[97] In addition, he increasingly protracted the negotiations until, on 2nd November 1546, to the outrage of his principals, he 'moved away without their knowledge and has so far remained outside [Nuremberg]'.[98] They therefore resorted to coercive action and, with the help of the imperial notary's office and the Vice-King of Naples, had him imprisoned in Naples' notorious prison, refusing his subsequent requests for help in paying bail. From then on, correspondence between the governors in Nuremberg (and Augsburg) and Wolf was characterised by disappointment, mistrust, a lack of respect and breach of contract, ultimately making internal mediation impossible. External mediation thus became necessary – a role finally taken over by the related Haller family in the final phase of the dispute. Through their mediation activities, which can only be verified here, the ten years of disputes were resolved in 1555 with the departure of factor Wolf from the company. This meant that, despite the long duration of the conflict and the threat to the Imhoff company's vital saffron trade, there was no reason for the company to fear longer-term damage or even the danger of bankruptcy.

The conflict between Jakob Herbrot and his son-in-law Simon Manlich in 1541–1545 also saw internal mediation conducted by the family and subsequent external mediation by members of the Augsburg Council build upon one another. Through his debauched lifestyle, Simon had brought about a marital crisis between himself and his wife Marina, resulting in Marina wishing to leave her husband.[99] The case showed that a connection by marriage was not always an advantage; marital conflicts could also present the danger of "disintegration"[100] and, due to the husband's unreliability and addiction to wasting money, became an economic threat to the company. After Simon Manlich had been taken to prison at the behest of this father-in-law, mediation within the family initially helped Simon to be released by causing him to promise his father-in-law that he would behave reliably once again and thus restore trust.

As this had not resolved the specific points of conflict, the next step was for the Manlich and Herbrot families to seek external mediation from the Augsburg Council ('to request amicable negotiation from some councillors'[101]). In 1545, the council negotiators succeeded in creating an agreement by conciliatory proceeding,

97 Ibid., No. 8a (4, 1): "ungeledigter diener".

98 Ibid., (13f): "unssernt halb ganz unwissend weck zog und er also pis itz aussen ist plieben".

99 Häberlein, "Brüder" 1998, p. 387.

100 Denzel, "The Merchant Family" 2009, p. 375.

101 StadtAA, Ratsprotokolle, 18/II (1544), fol. 2v: "auch etliche van rats wegen zu gutlicher underhanndlung zuervordern".

called a 'Richtung',[102] with the two parties. This averted the threat to the economic and social position of both parties – Manlich and Herbrot.

Summary

As well as working towards economic success, doing business together in a family company also demands constant efforts to harmonise ideals of peace, justice, friendship, love and honour with the realities, not to allow looming collisions between ideal and reality to come to the surface, or to defuse or compensate for them. The family companies presented here served to use specific examples to draw general conclusions about strategies, means and ways to prevent or resolve conflicts. Due to their effectiveness, contractual obligations made under oath and intensive communication at meetings or through mediators transpired as particularly frequently chosen measures here. Often they initially appeared doomed to failure but, as most of the cases showed, they generally served to clarify and rectify situations that threatened to produce conflict. This could certainly mean a separation of the company in its current form, thus nearly always paving the way for joint business and trading activities – between the newly-separate companies – in the future, in the sense of economic and social reasoning.

During the period, the companies usually chose the conflict resolution by litigation in the court only as a last resort; after all, it involved completely laying open all files, business processes and even correspondence. For this reason, the company agreements contained various provisions regarding the avoidance of this method before a 'religious or secular court'.[103] The parties often used judicial proceedings in order to integrate them into mediation activities running in parallel or subsequently.[104]

Besides disputes being decided before a ordinary court, the other option, generally preferred by partners, was to settle them before an arbitration court. The

102 Ibid., 19/I (1545), fol. 97v–99r.

103 Lutz, "Handelsgesellschaften" 1976 pp. 469 sqq. with numerous relevant examples of contractual articles like this.

104 The interaction between the legal recourse and the mediation in the aforementioned conflict between the Nuremberg Imhoff company and Wolf Imhoff was handled in a particularly virtuoso manner. Both the Nuremberg City Court and the Royal Court in Naples were called upon. Between these steps, internal mediation was conducted by the extended family and external mediation by Council members. This interplay between mediation and judicial coercion ultimately led to conflict settlement.

arbitration process complied more closely with the opponents' understanding of conflict, because it was more moderate with regard to the disclosure of business documents, more discreet with regard to their economic activities and finally – the decisive reason – orientated towards consensus.[105]

105 The conditions for proceedings in courts of arbitration were laid down in some company agreements; in particular detail in the Schreiber-Weißhaupt-Ditmar agreement of 1491, see Strieder, "Zwei Handelsgesellschaftsverträge", p. 38; Lutz, "Handelsgesellschaften", Vol. 2, p. 18.

Wolfgang Forster

Failed Memoria: Rights of Patronage and of Burial in Bankruptcy

I. Memoria and majorat

Nobility relies on reputation – and thus on a fluctuating and transient social commodity. If the reputation was to be retained, it had to be constantly reaffirmed. In the Early Modern Age, this was achieved through maintaining a magnificent way of life, also characterised by the term "conspicuous consumption".[1] The nobility experienced a high level of social pressure in this regard. For example, many Spanish nobles sent their apologies for a banquet held in 1643 in honour of an ambassador in Madrid, as they were unable to display more luxury than the host, and it would have made a negative impression had they gone to less expense. Of course, their absence also harmed their reputation,[2] but that appears to have been the lesser of two evils, compared to the consequences of providing an insufficient display of splendour.

Although the individual could, and indeed had to, affirm his nobility in public, he was unable to acquire it himself. A noble had to be known to be of noble descent. The quality of being noble depended on the duration and social significance of the remembrance of the (noble) ancestors. The formation of the nobility group was based on the memory of those from whom the property of being noble was inherited; without memoria there was no nobility.[3] However, both ostentatious

---

1 Cf. Atienza Hernández, Ignacio: *Aristocracía, poder y riqueza en la España moderna. La casa de Osuna, siglos XV–XIX*. Madrid 1987, pp. 332–334; Williams, Patrick: *The great favourite. The Duke of Lerma and the court and government of Philip III of Spain, 1598–1621*. Manchester 2006, p. 5: "In this court, men were measured by the extravagances of their display and by their spending on secular, religious and cultural affairs." Veblen, Thorstein: *The theory of the leisure class*. New York/London 1899, which shaped the expression, was interpreted as social criticsm.

2 Jago, Charles: "The 'crisis of the aristocracy' in seventeenth-century Castile". *Past & Present* 82–85, 1979, pp. 60–90, pp. 81–2.

3 Oexle, Otto Gerhard: "Memoria als Kultur", in: id. (ed.), *Memoria als Kultur*. (Veröffentlichungen des Max-Planck-Instituts für Geschichte 121). Göttingen 1995, pp. 9–78, p. 37f.: "Memoria, memory, is the crucial moment that constitutes 'nobility'. Naturally, in each group memoria brings about "the explanation and consciousness of oneself" (J. G. Droysen). However, it is not the 'sense' of the group formation equally in each

wealth and visible memoria had to be financed. In order to perpetuate the memory of the noble descent, which was the only way to create the property of being noble in itself, it had to be based on respective income and wealth.

In Spain, the nobility sought to perpetuate its assets through their constant commitment to family entailed estates, known as "mayorazgos" (majorats), which in principle made all the assets brought into them inalienable and non-mortgageable. The creation of a "mayorazgo" was seen as the important first step on the road to the longed-for title of nobility. Almost everyone who had generated sufficient funds to acquire continuously productive assets, such as seigneuries, annuities or government stocks, aspired to found a majorat, especially the middle class.[4]

However, if the noble status was confirmed and the memoria substantiated on an economic basis, the institutes in which this happened were not independent of economic life. The dream of permanently securing the "splendor familiae" was often dashed by the harsh economic realities of the 17th century. While large quantities of cash were required for maintaining an elaborate way of life and especially for dowries of daughters – an essential requirement for marriage within the social class[5] – the income of noble families, based on letting agricultural land, suffered under the declining population and the ensuing declining income.[6] In order to raise cash, the nobles took on debt by selling annuities by contracts of so-called "censo", that is by selling annuities for cash. Thus, they strained their income – which depended on agriculture and therefore was uncertain – with fixed annual payments to the annuity creditors. Although there was the option of buying back the annuity by paying the basic sum to the annuity purchaser, for economic reasons this was seldom possible. In addition, due to the generosity

---

group. The case of nobility is different, as the nobility of the individuals and the groups to which they belong, i.e. the noble 'houses' and 'lineages', is significantly created through the quality and above all the duration of their memories. Therefore, without memoria there can be no 'nobility' and thus no legitimation for noble rule."

4 Also, during the economic crisis of the 17th century, withdrawing their capital from production and trade in order to invest it in bonds of the Spanish crown and annuity purchases helped the middle classes to invest their earnings with a low monetary risk, cf. Kamen, Henry: *Spain 1469–1714. A society of conflict.* Abingdon [4]2014, pp. 238–40.

5 Casey, James: *Early modern Spain. A social history.* London 1999, p. 139: In the case of the Dukes of Gandía, one dowry alone amounted to roughly double their annual income; p. 147: "Undoubtedly mobilising cash for dowries was the single biggest headache in the lives of most aristocrats in the early modern period."

6 Jago 1979, p. 71: "The House of Bejar shared with other Castilian aristocrats the experience of 'income erosion'."; ibid.: The income of the Duke of Feria fell 44% (!) between 1635 and 1641.

with which royal permissions were given to mortgage the majorat components themselves as a security ("facultas ad hypothecandum"), the majorats turned from a non-tradeable fund into the most important collateral for procuring money – collateral that could then be used for economic purposes by the creditor. This "adapted the *mayorazgo* to the capitalistic environment of the sixteenth century".[7] In consequence, majorats could be broken up to liquidate the assets. In 1573, the lawyer Luis de Molina complained that many majorats no longer showed any signs of old families, because the assets had been passed on to other families.[8] He especially blamed the huge dowries for the alienation and destruction of mayorazgos.[9] Furthermore, the unavoidable short-term need for cash and the use of long-term debt instrument of the "censo", an annuity sale which in turn put a strain on future cash income, formed a downward spiral. In Spain, this spiral led to a level of indebtedness in the nobility that was seen as catastrophic even at the time, and which often led to insolvency proceedings.[10] In 1573, the Cortes de Castilla bemoaned the ruinous financial state of the Castilian nobility,[11] just as a

---

7 Jago, Charles: "The influence of debt on relations between crown and aristocracy in seventeenth-century Castile". *The Economic History Review* 26, 1973, pp. 218–236, p. 222.

8 Molina, Luis de: *De hispanorum primogeniorum origine ac natura.* Cologne 1601, IV, 3, before 1: "prima causa ex qua Maioratus extinctio seu diminutio, vel etiam alteratio contingit, ea est, quae ex Regiis facultatibus resultat. Ex ipsis namque bona, quae alias Maioratui subiecta, atque inalienabilia erant, libera & alienabilia fiunt, ita ut nulla iam in pluribus Primogeniis extent antiquarum familiarum vestigia, sed in extraneorum familias adversus institutorum voluntatem pertranserint." Apparently the new holders of the assets removed the coats of arms of the original bearers from the transferred buildings as they incorporated them in their own family entail.

9 Molina 1601, IV, 3, 3: "Vidimus namque proper semper ex amplissimarum dotium constitutione, bona Primogeniorum extingui, atqe abalienari, & in alienas familias transire, deperireque".

10 Cf. Jago 1979, 68: "It was a type of impoverishment peculiar to the rich; although no doubt derisory from the viewpoint of the masses of poor and starving peasants, it could lead to the loss of prestige or, worse, to bankruptcy." On the debt crisis of the Spanish nobility cf. Forster, Wolfgang: *Konkurs als Verfahren. Francisco Salgado de Somoza in der Geschichte des Insolvenzrechts.* (Norm und Struktur 32). Köln 2009, pp. 256–294.

11 *Actas de las Cortes de Castilla. Tomo cuarto. Contiene las celebradas en Madrid el año de 1573.* Madrid 1864, p. 497–8: „Otrosí dezimos, que una de las causas de donde procede estar los grandes señores y caualleros y la gente principal destos reynos, gastados y consumidos, es las muchas mohatras y deudas que hazen y contraen, y lo que toman á cambio". The Cortes go on to complain that the nobles use commoners as bailsmen, who then are incarcerated as the nobles default.

French traveller in the first half of the 17th century generally described the Spanish nobility as being insolvent.[12]

Modern research has confirmed these contemporary observations. In the year 1591 the Dukes of Osuna, for example, had already accumulated debt in the amount of 194 contracts of censo. By 1606 the number of contracts had risen to no less than 349,[13] notwithstanding the fact that the patrimony of the Duke of Osuna had been put under administration by the Council of Castile in 1594.[14] In 1592, Pedro Ramírez de Arellano, sixth Count of Aguilar de Inestrillas, declared bankruptcy as a result of facing a short-term debt of 100.000 ducats.[15] In the year 1610, the debts of the House Enríque amounted 20 times its annual income.[16] The Duke of Feria had to use 59 % of his annual expenditure of 1623 for debt service, the Duke of Medinaceli in 1660 no less than 84 %.[17] In 1625, the House of Osuna was indebted with annuities based on a sum of 1.321.566 ducats; in the same year, its arrears alone more than doubled its annual income.[18]

II. Labyrinthus creditorum concurrentium – the insolvency proceedings of Castilian court practice

1. Early modern insolvency proceedings

The ius commune provided several legal ways of dealing with insolvency. They ranked from the incarceration of the debtor on one end of the scale to a moratorium imposed by the sovereign on the other end. A joint meeting of the creditors ("concursus creditorum" in its literal sense) was required for the four other legal procedures:

---

12 Cf. Kamen 2014, p. 235.

13 This is the number of claims that had to be categorised in 1606, Atienza Hernández 1984, p. 57 n. 25, so the numbers of claims may have been even higher. Cf. Atienza Hernández 1987, 340.

14 Atienza Hernández, Ignacio: "La 'quiebra' de la nobleza castellana en el siglo XVII. Autoridad real y poder señoral: El secuestro de los bienes de la casa de Osuna." *Hispania* 44, 1984, pp. 49–81, p. 53.

15 Moreno Ramírez de Arellano, Miguel A.: "La quiebra de la casa de Arellano en el contexto de la crisis señorial castellana de finales del siglo XVI. Analisis de las causas determinantes del concurso de acreedores recaido sobre el señorio de Cameros y condado de Aguilar en 1592". *Berceo* 114–115, 1988, p. 155–170, p. 168.

16 Domínguez Ortiz, Antonio: *La sociedad española en el siglo XVII*. Vol. 1. Madrid 1963, p. 237. On p. 235–241 further examples of over-indebted nobility.

17 Kamen 2014, 235.

18 Atienza Hernández 1987, 286.

1. The majority of the creditors – corresponding to their claim against the debtor – could grant a respite to the debtor.
2. They could, with judicial confirmation, grant him a partial remission of the debt. That possibility was not seen as an option in medieval legal doctrine until the 15th century, as there was no clear precedence in Roman law. Yet it was accepted in the statutes of Italian towns as well as in Spanish legal learning. Finally, it became part of the continental ius commune.[19] In case of an imminent economic breakdown of a noble house, the Spanish crown could supervise an arrangement between the noble debtor and his creditors that could combine respite and remission with setting aside a portion of the debtor's income for debt service; in line with the literal sense of "concursus" this arrangement was called "concurso".[20]
3. Among themselves, the creditors would dispute the order of priority of their respective claims. The classification of a claim in relation to the claims of other creditors – the so-called "graduatio", graduation – was crucial, as any prior-ranking debt had to be completely fulfilled before inferior-ranking debts would be served. In consequence, creditors with inferior claims faced total loss, as the debtor rarely had enough property to satisfy all debts. That, in turn, caused the inferior creditors to arraign the existence of any better ranked claim. The Castilian judge Francisco Salgado de Somoza (1591–1664) experienced such disputes as his daily practice.[21]
4. If a settlement could not be reached and no respite was granted, only "cessio bonorum" remained: By relinquishing all his assets to the creditors, the debtor could end the enforcement measures undertaken against him and avoid both incarceration and infamy.[22] Further proceedings involved determining the content and status of each creditor's claim, before liquidating the debtor's assets

---

19 Riesenfeld, Stefan: "The evolution of modern bankruptcy law. A comparison of the recent bankruptcy acts of Italy and the United States". *Minnesota Law Review* 31, 1947, pp. 401–455, p. 440: "the practice of judicially approved majority compositions spread all over Europe, and ... finally became firmly established in theory and practice as the common law." Cf. Forster 2009, 212–218.

20 Kamen 2014, 235.

21 Salgado de Somoza, Francisco: *Labyrinthus creditorum concurrentium ad litem per debitorem communem inter illos causatam,[...].* Lyon 1651, I, 1, 26: "solet contendi, controverti [...] de viribus, & veritate iurium [...] maxime ii, qui inferioris gradus sunt, quotidie certant penitus excludere privilegiatos, & anteriores hypothecarios, ne consumant bonis debitoris, prout praxi quotidie experimus". On Salgado and his works cf. Forster 2009, pp. 7–85 and pp. 295–362.

22 On cessio bonorum cf., for example, Forster 2009, p. 89–108.

at a public auction and assigning the proceeds among the creditors according to their classification.

Francisco Salgado de Somoza's description of bankruptcy law in his work "Labyrinthus creditorum concurrentium", first published in 1651, served as a reference work on the topic. In it, he describes a procedure that was developed in Castilian court practice, drawing on the institution of "cessio bonorum" in Roman law and on the legislation of the Spanish monarchy in the Early Modern Age,[23] thus turning Castilian court practice into a European model. Salgado's treatise, in which the keywords on "maioratum" and "facultas ad hypothecandum" alone fill multiple index columns, gives proof of the debt crisis of the Castilian nobility and the frequency of insolvencies of family entails. Indeed, he especially referred to the higher nobility: Dukes, Marquises, Earls and other powerful noble persons were weighed down by debt and filed for bankruptcy.[24]

2. Salgado's procedure of concursus creditorum

The concursus creditorum could only be initiated by a declaration of the debtor. It was the debtor who petitioned for bankruptcy.[25] Neither the creditors nor a judge could open this type of insolvency proceeding. In the legal context of his time, this was Salgado's key argument to secure the exclusive competence of a single judge, thereby avoiding the problem of multiple and competing jurisdictional competences that riddled the early-modern Castilian legal system.[26] Together with his declaration, the debtor had to provide two complete lists: one containing his assets and one naming his creditors and the respective debt to allow a computation of his debt. Both registers had to be confirmed by oath. The judge then cited the creditors.

23 For details, cf. Forster 2009, pp. 89–120, 186–207 and 226–255.

24 Salgado 1651, I, 24, 32: "duces, Marchiones, Comites aut alias nobiles potentes personae, quae aere alieno gravatae sunt, & ad iudicium concursus provocant suos creditores".

25 Salgado 1651, I, 4, 8: "concursus causatus a debitore communi"; I, 1, 11: "illum format debitor"; I, 4, 12: "hoc concursu per debitorem formato". Cf. Forster 2009, 319–20, 339.

26 On this problem cf. Kagan, Richard L.: *Lawsuits and litigants in Castile 1500–1700.* University of North Carolina Press 1981, p. 31–32: "Together, ambiguous laws, conflicting fueros, and special juridical privileges helped to fashion a legal order which one historian has compared to the Cretan labyrinth. The image is apt. Castilian justice in the sixteenth and seventeenth centuries was a hodgepodge of confused laws and competing jurisdictions […] The labyrinthine state of Castilian law had its institutional analogue: an array of law courts and legal tribunals so bewildering that lawsuits regularly became lost in a confused jurisdictional morass."

If all these prerequisites are fulfilled, the concursus comprises the debtor's total property, be it real estate, movable goods, titles or claims, as well as all his creditors. The concursus was, in this sense, universal. No creditor could submit a claim against the debtor at another court; any execution in any property of the debtor was suspended. The concursus furthermore absorbed all pending proceedings against the debtor – the so-called attractiveness of the concursus.[27]

After having declared cessio bonorum and relinquished all his property to the court, the debtor no longer was allowed to administer it. He could no longer conclude contracts, nor collect any debts or rents. Also, he could not personally satisfy the claims of his creditors. In respect to his property, he was considered dead: "nec habet nolle, nec velle, & pro mortuo ad id habetur".[28] Interfering with the property by leasing land or by accepting payments after having declared cessio bonorum was a criminal offence of the debtor. Salgado reported that while he, Salgado, was writing on that aspect, a nobleman was incarcerated by order of court for this reason.[29] Furthermore, the creditors could demand that an administrator, elected by them, was installed by the judge. The administrator acted in the name of the judge, not in the name of the creditors or of the debtor.

The judge then examined the claims of the creditors in order to be able to classify them according to a complex system of precedence that had been developed from norms of Roman law concerning hypothecs (generally to be classified according to the time of their creation,[30] but subject to special privileges) and personal privileges (to be classified according to their cause[31]). The resulting verdict on the order of the creditors, the "sententia graduationis", was the essential juridical outcome of the proceeding.[32]

The final act of an insolvency was the liquidation of the assets by means of an auction. In all European nations, such auctions were held in the form of so-called

27 Cf. Forster 2009, 318, 336–7.

28 Salgado 1651, I, 14, 18.

29 Salgado 1651, I, 14, 100: „Atque ita Senatus severe punire solet audaciam tantam debitoris, qui se inserit in administrationem, aut alienationem bonorum concursus, prout, dum haec scribo, carceribus detentum habet quendam nobilem virum, qui de hoc crimine accusatus fuit per creditores."

30 C. 8.17.3: "sicut prior est in tempore, ita potior in iure".

31 Dig. 42.5.32: "Privilegia non ex tempore aestimantur, sed ex causa." For example, Dig. 42.5.17 pr. contains a privilege for the claim of a creditor that has advanced money for a funeral.

32 In later legal development, this judgement would be split in in two decisions: One sentence on the existence of the claims ("sententia liquidationis") and one on their classification ("sententia graduationis").

candle auctions, that is, a burning candle defined the time in which bids could be given. The expiration of the flame ended the auction, so that the highest bidder at that time won.[33] As mentioned above, if majorats had been indebted via a "facultas ad hypothecandum", the assets that constituted them could be auctioned off, thereby breaking up the majorat. The single further requirement was that no more free assets were extant, as the "facultas" rendered the majorat only a subordinate collateral. Salgado reports that such divestiture of family entails as a consequence of outstanding debts was decreed daily.[34]

After deducting the costs of the administrator, court fees and other costs of the liquidation, the proceeds of the auction were distributed among the creditors in the order of their graduation in the verdict: The antecedent creditors received full payment on their claims until the proceeds were consumed; therefore, at one point in the graduation the outcome for the creditor concerned (and all creditors that followed him in the graduation) was zero. Especially the creditors with no hypothec or privilege – called "creditores chirographarii" with reference to the handwritten deed of their claim, the only argument they could forward regarding their graduation – were in danger of receiving nothing out of the auction. On the other hand, the liquidation and distribution of the debtor's entire property as such only suspended the execution of the "sententia graduationis". It did not exempt the debtor from his remaining obligations. He remained liable to execution in his (future) property, e.g. in case of a later inheritance. Therefore, the bankruptcy proceeding, and consequently the administration of the debtor's goods, came to a judicial end only with the fulfilment of all his debts.[35]

III. Capellaniae

1. The capellania as an instrument of family perpetuation

One legal institution that had a particular connection with family memoria was the capellania (Spanish: capellanía). It was a foundation through which a family created a position for a cleric – who did not necessarily need to be a priest – by

33 Cf. Forster 2009, 206–7.

34 Salgado 1651, III, 4, 1: "quotidie distrahi mandantur quoties reditus maioratus non dufficiunt; ad eorum integram solutionem". Cf. Forster 2009, 357.

35 Salgado 1651, III, 16, 61: "omnibus consumptis bonis ..., si tamen aliquis, vel aliqui posteriores creditores non fuerunt soluti; non dissolvi concursum, nec litem creditorum finiri ... lis non finiatur, quamdiu aliquis creditor non est satisfactus."

devoting a certain income to it, gained from assets accordingly dedicated.[36] The incentive to do this resulted from two aspects: On the one hand, the capellaniae served to provide a living for younger male members of the family. In doing so, it was still possible to take the interests of the family succession into account by avoiding a life-long religious position. This was possible because only lower levels of ordination were required, and these were not indissoluble.[37] If the older brother died without a male heir, the younger could leave his religious position, take the place of the deceased and thus continue the family in the male line. The capellaniae therefore fulfilled a socio-economic function by providing a dynastic cushion.[38] On the other hand, they served the purpose of the family memoria with its two aspects, "pietas" and "fama".[39] They ensured the preservation and propagation of the family status and helped the souls of the ancestors through the reading of requiem masses. In turn, those requiem masses were the "strongest ritual in the formation of the family identity".[40]

---

36 On this and the following, cf. Weber, Christoph: *Familienkanonikate und Patronatsbistümer. Ein Beitrag zur Geschichte von Adel und Klerus im neuzeitlichen Italien.* (Historische Forschungen 38). Berlin 1988, pp. 34–36. In line with his field of investigation, Weber relies particularly on Italian authors, such as Lucius Ferraris and Giovanni Battista de Luca. On the idea of charity in general, cf. Drossbach, Gisela: "Stiftungen". In: Paravacini, Werner (ed.): *Höfe und Residenzen im spätmittelalterlichen Reich. Bilder und Begriffe. Sub-volume 1: Begriffe.* (Residenzenforschung 15.II). Ostfildern 2005, pp. 342–344, especially p. 343.

37 As they did not confer the "character indelebilis", cf. *Concilium Tridentinum*, sessio XXIII, caput 4 (ed. Alberigo, Giuseppe: Conciliorum oecumenicorum decreta. Freiburg 1962, p. 718): "in sacramento ordinis, sicut in baptismo et confirmatione, character imprimitur, qui nec deleri nec auferri potest"; Engel, Ludwig: *Collegium universi juris canonici […]* Salzburg 1712, I, 16, 1–2 (p. 152; on X. 1.16): "Tria sunt ex Sacramentis, quae *Characterem* invisibilem in anima suscipientis imprimunt, nimirum *Baptismus, Confirmatio, & Ordo*, […] Est autem Character, quem dicta Sacramenta imprimunt, signum *Spirituale & indelebile animae impressum* […]."; Hinschius, Paul: *System des katholischen Kirchenrechts mit besonderer Rücksicht auf Deutschland.* First volume Berlin 1869 (reprint Graz 1959), p. 117.

38 Cf. Weber 1988, p. 37.

39 Cf. Oexle 1995, p. 38.

40 Cf. Weber 1988, pp. 5, 39–40, 291; the quotation on p. 39. For the Middle Ages cf. Angenendt, Arnold: "Theologie und Liturgie der mittelalterlichen Toten-Memoria." In: Schmid, Karl/Wollasch, Joachim (eds.): *Memoria. Der geschichtliche Zeugniswert des liturgischen Gedenkens im Mittelalter.* (Münstersche Mittelalter-Schriften 48). München 1984, pp. 79–199, 171–174.

In the minds of those involved, the decision to found a majorat or capellania was decisively motivated by the need to secure and propagate the family's social status; a need that was expressed in testamentary provisions that were made as precise and long-lasting as possible.[41] In this sense, the aim of the head of every noble family (or of one attempting to obtain a title) was to make his family line perpetual. Economically, they believed that this could be achieved by ring-fencing assets in a majorat; spiritually, by setting up a capellania, which in turn could take on the economic function of providing for a member of the family.

The connection between the family and the capellania could be created by ensuring that it remained in the hands of the family. This is known as a "capellania mercenaria" or "mere laicalis". Church authorities could stake no claim to them. Under church law, the institution was merely a charity, just as a hospital, carried out by a private individual. If there was no suitable cleric within the family and the specific will of the founder did not exclude it, the profits could also be retained by a layperson, a woman or a minor.[42] This form was particularly popular in Spain.[43] It raised no particular legal problems, as it was merely a private matter of the benefactor family that was not subject to canon law and was generally

41 Weber 1988, p. 5: The family members were inspired by the thought "that their own family would be able to retain for ever the status of fame and splendour that had been achieved, and that the actual and ultimately only way to do this that would be effective in the long term was to create their own family church – one could even say a family temple – with a family priest who constantly kept the memory of the forefathers alive and offered them comfort and support in the afterlife by making holy offerings, as well as being a way for the forefathers to help the living […]." Cf. also p. 296: "What de Luca called the 'solita stultitia hominum' showed itself particularly when the focus was on planning for the future rather than on venerating the dead. The idea of grandparents, parents and uncles that, by precise planning, the further advancement of the family for the coming generations could be enforced, had something both presumptuous and ridiculous about it." For Weber's citation cf. Luca, Giovanni Battista de: *Theatrum veritatis & justitiae, […]*. Vol. 10, Venice 1716, XLI, 4 (p. 85): "pro consueta hominum vanitate ac stultitia"; XLVIII, 1 (p. 98): "juxta consueta hominum stultitiam".

42 Gonzales, Hieronymus: *Ad regulam octavam cancellariae*, Rome 1611, gl. 5, no. 26–7: "Item talis Capellania posset obtineri a laico, vel foemina, nisi voluntas fundatoris contrarium declareret. […] Sic etiam, non requiritur aetas 14. annorum requisita ad obtinen. beneficium Ecclesiasticum […]." In the view of some authors, the bishop was unable even to conduct a visitation, ibid. no. 35.

43 Gonzales 1611, gl. 5, 20 (p. 126): "Capellaniae, quae saepe fundari solent, maxime in Hispania, absq. aliqua Episcopi, vel alterius superiori, auctoritate." Barbosa will adopt this formulation, cf. note 45.

transferable.[44] On the other hand, it was also possible for the position created by the capellania to be a normal church benefice, usually to be held by the bishop. This was known as a "capellania collativa". In this case, a financial collapse of the benefactor family had no effect on the capellania.

Finally, there was also a mixed form. In this "capellania gentilitia", the capellania still remained a church benefice, but the family had the patronage of it. The family was then able to nominate an applicant. However, in doing so, they not only had to adhere to the general canon rules, but also to any provisions that had been defined in the deed of foundation. In order to receive the stipend, the applicant had to be admitted to the position by the bishop.[45]

2. Heredity of the right of patronage within the family

The capellania gentilitia required the right of patronage to be hereditary, as only then could it remain in the family permanently. Heredity of rights of patronage

44 Cf. Gonzales 1611, gl. 5, 25: "Sicut etiam pactum factum ratione talis Capellaniae [...], non erit simoniacum." Gonzales goes on to report having compiled an assessment in favour of a "Michaelis Ximenez", who was tried for simony, but was acquitted. If the benefactor of the capellania had stated that only blood relatives of family members should be appointed, in the law governing majorats – that is to say, not canon law – were to be applied, no. 34: "Unde in Capellaniarum quarumque successione, quando vocantur Clerici consanguinei, seu de familia, in causis Hispaniae, dubiae orta diffiniri debent per leges, & iura, de maioratibus loquentia."

45 This tripartite in Weber 1988, pp. 34–5 in accordance with Ferraris, Lucius: *Prompta bibliotheca canonica, juridica, moralis, theologica [...]*, Vol. 2. Frankfurt 1781, p. 95. The principle is also found in Barbosa, Agostinho: *Ius ecclesiasticum universum*. Lyon 1660, III, 5, 2. There, Barbosa repeats Gonzales' remark that in Spain particularly capellaniae mercenariae were founded: "Capellaniae [...] in triplici reperiuntur differentia, [1.] quaedam enim sunt, quae saepe fundari solent, maxime in Hispania, absque alia Episcopi [...] autoritate [...]; [2.] quaedam vero sunt, quae etsi auctoritate Praelati fuerint institutae, tamen ad certum tempus conferuntur, vel ad nutum amovibiles sunt. [3.] Aliae denique sunt perpetuae, auctoritate Apostolica, vel Episcopi erectae [...] & dicuntur Capellaniae collativae." Very similar Pirhing, Ehrenreich: *Jus canonicum in V. libros decretalium distributum [...]*. Vol. 3. Venice 1759, III, 4, 1, No. XII (p. 27): "[3.] Capellaniae in perpetuum auctoritate Episcopi erectae [...] quae dantur Clericis in titulum perpetuum [...]; No. XV (p. 28): [...] [2.] Capellaniae spirituales, & collativae, quae auctoritate Episcopi institutae sunt, sed ad certum tempus conferuntur, vel ad nutum Episcopi, aut Patroni Capellano auferri possunt [...] [1.] Capellaniae temporales, & non collativae, quae a Fundatore, ejusque haeredibus conferuntur, sine ulla Episcopi auctoritate, cui ipsi voluerint, [...] non sunt Beneficia Ecclesiastica, sed mere temporalia stipendium Capellanorum [...]."

was affirmed as far back as the early decretist Rufinus (c. 1164), although he limited the succession to blood heirs, i.e. sons and grandsons.[46] The free heredity of the right of patronage to every heir was advocated from the late 12th century.[47] The latter view asserted itself and was finally recognised in the mid-13th century. The right of patronage was passed on to the heir, regardless of whether or not he was a member of the family.[48] This "juspatronatus haereditarium" presented the risk that the family assets brought together in a majorat and the right of patronage could be separated in the succession, which could not have been the founder's intention, as the idea behind both was to retain the family connection. Instead, the succession with regard to the majorat would have to be permanently identical to that of the right of patronage via the capellania. It could not be allowed to be passed on to just any heir in the form of an inheritable right, but would have to remain within the family and, ideally, remain attached to the majorat as a de facto part of it.[49]

In substance, that was possible if the founder documented his will to this effect.[50] The founder of a capellania could therefore limit the succession to his family or specifically to his own descendants. This made the right of patronage a "juspatronatus gentilitium", also called "juspatronatus familiare". However, if there was no evidence that the benefactor intended only to benefit family members, it was to be assumed that the right of patronage could be freely bequeathed. This produced

46 Cf. Landau, Peter: *Ius patronatus. Studien zur Entwicklung des Patronats im Dekretalenrecht und der Kanonistik des 12. und 13. Jahrhunderts.* (Forschungen zur kirchlichen Rechtsgeschichte und zum Kirchenrecht 12). Köln/Wien 1975, p. 52–3.

47 Namely since Huguccio's Summa (compiled around 1188/90) on the Decretum Gratiani, cf. Landau 1975, p. 54–6. On Huguccio's Summa, cf. in detail Müller, Wolfgang P.: *Huguccio. The life, works, and thought of a twelfth-century jurist.* Washington D.C. 1994 (Studies in medieval and early modern canon law, Vol. 3).

48 Cf. Landau 1975, p. 57.

49 Non-technically formulated by Weber 1988, p. 290: "This is why a foundation also had to belong to the entire body of the family and not to an individual member if the memory of the benefactor was not to be swiftly washed away in the river of time. Specifically, the patronage could not be inherited in the female line, but had to remain the property of the clan."

50 The notion that the will of the testator is not limited to certain heirs fits well into Huguccio's strong emphasis on the will that in Huguccio has precedence over external factors, cf. Müller 1994, p. 136–151, p. 140: "intransigent voluntarism", p. 151: "rigid voluntarism".

a structural rule-exception relationship between the (assumed) free succession and succession only within the family.[51]

In practice, however, the benefactors' need to create a capellania gentilitia was so great that the Italian lawyer Luca called this basic rule unrealistic and less than convincing, as it was obvious that someone who wanted to preserve his own name or the reputation of his descendants would also define the order of succession necessary for this in advance. He believed that this would have to be even more the case for rights of this kind than for other assets and rights, as they conferred so much deference, so many benefits, and reliable verification of a good reputation. Therefore, according to Luca, the rule could already be disproved by very general indications and arguments.[52] Thus, he almost achieves a reversal of the theoretical rule-exception relationship.[53] This interpretation allowed the connection between the succession in the family, the right of patronage and a capellania to be created. A construction was achieved that appeared to fulfil every desire for permanent economic and religious perpetuation of the family.

51 Barbosa 1660, III, 12, 20–1: "iurispatronatus […] haereditarium est, quod transit ad quoscunque haeredes etiam extraneos, […] In dubio enim iuspatronatus est praesumendum haereditarium, & transitorium ad quoscunque haeredes, etiam extraneos; 220: "transit ad haeredes patroni, etiam extraneos"; Luca, Giovanni Battista de: *Theatrum veritatis & justitiae, […]*. Vol. 13, Venice 1716, LX, 1: "Regula est hodie certa, & absoluta, […] ut non constito de diversa explicita, vel implicita fundatoris voluntate deducta ex tenoris fundationis […] ut juspatronatus dicatur haereditarium ad quoscumque, licet extraneos testatos, vel intestatos hęredes […]." The supposition for a juspatronatus haereditarium is reversed if, when filling the position, always the family association and never the free heredity of the right of patronage is stated, or if for 100 years only male successors of the founder have exercised the right of presentation, Barbosa 1660, III, 12, 23.

52 Luca 1716, LX, 3: "etiam ex levibus, ac generalibus coniecturis […] receditur ab hac regula, quae ita potius quodammodo idealis remanere videtur, ex ea nimium convincenti, atque ad naturalem sensum probata ratione, quod qui ambitionem habet, vel ad proprii nominis memoriam conservandam, vel ob ejus posteriatis, seu agnationis decorem, ordinandi hus succedendi necessarium ordinem, quo mediante bona, & jura haereditaria genus vocatum non egrediantur, multo magis id desiderasse censetur in hujusmodi juribus, majorem honorificentiam, ac etiam utilitatem, tutioremque probationem praeseferentibus." Cf. Weber 1988, p. 290 with quotation from Luca 1716, XXII, 14: "Quod de facili admittenda sit qualitas familiaris."

53 Cf. also Weber 1988, p. 290.

IV. Rights of patronage in bankruptcy

As mentioned before, family plans of that kind were often thrown into jeopardy by economic developments. The question arises of how to proceed with a right of patronage in the extreme case of bankruptcy. Did it remain with its insolvent holder entirely unaffected by his bankruptcy? Could a custodian appointed by the court claim the right of presentation? Or could it even be exploited economically?

1. The transferability of the right of patronage during the lifetime of the patron

The possibility of transfer to an administrator or even a creditor first of all depends on the question of whether and how a right of patronage can be transferred in one's lifetime. According to a dictum by Gratian (ca. 1140), a right of patronage is non-tradeable and therefore cannot be transferred through sale.[54] This view can also be found in a decretal of Alexander III (Pope 1159–1181) concerning a case in which someone had coerced the canons of the Augustine priory of Studley in Warwickshire to sell a patronage by threatening that otherwise he would chop off the head of their prior.[55] The permissibility of transfer as a gift was also doubtful.[56] However, this kind of inflexibility would have collided with the legal reality and the predominant ideas of the High Middle Ages. Already the early decretist Rufinus (c. 1164), without committing himself exactly, offers the solution of considering the transfer of an isolated right of patronage as impermissible, while declaring a transfer within an entirety of assets as permissible.[57]

---

54 C. 16 q. 7 dict. post c. 30 (Friedberg, Emil (ed.): *Corpus iuris canonici. Pars pima: Decretum magistri Gratiani.* Leipzig 1879 (reprint Graz 1959), col. 809): "Habent ius providendi, et consulendi, et sacerdotem inveniendi; sed non habent ius vendendi, uel donandi, uel utendi tamquam propriis." Cf. Landau 1975, p. 94. In the 17th century, Salgado will write (Salgado 1651, III, 5, 7): "ius patronatus res est spiritualibus annexa quod nec recipit aestimationem, nec vendi potest, imo quod plus est, ius patronatus non est in bonis nostris [...]".

55 1Comp. 3.33.19 (Friedberg, Emil (ed.): Quinque compilationes antiquae necnon collectio canonum Lipsiensis. Leipzig 1882 (reprint Graz 1956), p. 41–42: "cum ius patronatus annexum sit spirituali, nemini licitum est uendere illud"; Jaffé JL 14158 (Jaffé, Philipp / Löwenfeld, Samuel: Regesta pontificum romanorum II. Leipzig ²1885 (reprint Graz 1956), p. 400). Cf. Landau 1975, p. 95–6.

56 Landau 1975, p. 108.

57 In doing so, he refers to the term "universitas bonorum", together with which even items that cannot be sold alone are transferred, from the Digest (Dig. 23.5.1 and Dig. 41.1.62), cf. Landau 1975, p. 109–110.

This solution was confirmed in two decretals of the aforementioned Alexander III.[58] The result is that a patronage passes over, for example, within an inheritance that is purchased in whole.[59]

2. The transfer of assets in the case of bankruptcy

The problem thus appears to be limited to the question of whether the declaration of the debtor that initiates the concursus creditorum is related to the entirety of the assets. This leads to the core of the bankruptcy process in terms of its development – the cessio bonorum of Roman law, which can be found in the third title of the 42nd Book of the Digest and in the 7th Book of the Codex, Title 71.

In regard to the cessio bonorum in its medieval form, it could be said that despite the relinquishment of all assets, it had no effect on the entirety that could have included the right of patronage.[60] However, in the form developed through Castilian court practice in the first half of the 17th century, which is described by Salgado, the declaration of cessio bonorum did indeed include the assets as a whole.[61] In this

---

58 X. 3.38.13 ('Quum saeculum') and X. 3.38.7 ('Ex litteris') (Friedberg, Emil (ed.): *Corpus iuris canonici. Pars secunda: Decretalium collectiones.* Leipzig 1879 (reprint Graz 1959), col. 613–4, 611). Spanish lawyers could find this solution also in the Siete Partidas, dating from the mid-13th century; cf. *Siete Partidas* I, 15, 8 (ed. Real Academia de la Historia. Madrid 1807, p. 405): "non lo camiando nin lo vendiendo por si apartadamiente mas de vuelta con todas las otras cosas que en el lugar hobiese: et esto aviene porque es ayuntado á la iglesia que es cosa espiritual et non la puede ningungo camiar nin vender por otra cosa temporal ninguna."

59 For the 17th century cf. Salgado 1651, III, 5, 1. Salgado explains that it is not possible to speak of the right of patronage being sold when the entirety is transferred, but that the right is transferred as a necessary consequence: "si cum ea transeat ius patronatus cum de per se non dicatur vendi, sed potius venire in quadam necessariam consequentiam rei venditae inclusae in iure universali" (Salgado 1651, III, 5, 3). In the same way, a right of patronage is transferred automatically when it is attached to an item as its accessory, Salgado 1651, III, 5, 6.

60 Salgado 1651, III, 5, 9, including, among others, a quotation from Covarrubias y Leyva, Diego: Variarum resolutionum libri IIII. In: id.: *Omnia opera.* Vol. 1. Turin 1594, pp. 145–464, here I, 13, 4 (p. 197). There, Covarrubias also quotes the opposite view, but writes: "Verum ex praedictis satis liquet, hanc orationem: Vendo omnia bona mea, esse universale rationem signi: [...]: non autem esse universalem ratione rei, idest, non significare universitatem."

61 Salgado 1651, I, 1, 28: "in eo agatur de quodam iudicio universali, & quasi divisorio universi patrimonii debitoris; I, 3, 1–2: omnia bona omneque patrimonium debitoris cedi, [...] nihil sibi reservato; I, 3, 4: merito dicitur universale, quia omnia debitoris bona, & omne patrimonium exscrutatur, & totum respicit."

sense, the declaration had an universal effect, and by it the entire process became universal. The universality of the process was the core from which Salgado derived the effects for the creditor and the debtor, and especially the exclusive competence of the bankruptcy judge for all actions relevant to the assets. It was not the coming-together – the concursus – of all creditors that generated this universality; instead, it arose directly when the debtor declared cessio bonorum: "universalitas qualitas [...] principaliter, & immediate causatur ab ipsa debitoris cessione."[62]

The question of what happened to the debtor's right of patronage when a concursus was opened thus appears to be answered. The declaration of the debtor which initiated the concursus, always was the declaration of universal relinquishment of assets, including everything, consequently also any right of patronage.[63] However, Salgado immediately drew attention to the fact that the debtor's forfeit of assets put the assets neither in the property of the creditors nor in their possession. The debtor merely loses the administration, i.e. the legal capacity regarding the assets and the power of disposition over them.[64] In Salgado's words, he was considered dead in relation to his assets; he was no longer able to exert any will regarding them that was relevant in law: "nec habet nolle, nec velle, & pro mortuo ad id habetur."[65]

---

62 Salgado 1651, I, 3, 16–7.

63 Salgado 1651, III, 5, 11: "opinio imo quod sub cessione bonorum facta per debitorem in concursu creditorum veniat, & includatur ius patronatus; verior est, facit quia debitor ita bonis suis universaliter cedit [...] ut virtualiter ex natura iudicii comprehendat bona mobilia, & immobilia, iura, & actiones [...] nihil sibi relicto aut reservato"; III, 5, 17: "Ergo verbum in hoc cessio relatum ad concursum creditorum per necesse debet connumerari inter voces significantes universitatem, cum in hanc cessione verificentur omnia requisita, quae iura, & Doctores appetunt, ut aliquid dicatur ius universale." This results either explicitly or by implication from the relevant document of the debtor, Salgado 1651, III, 5, 16: "in memoriali a se exhibito, necnon in libello solet dicere, cedo omnia, & quaecumque bona mea mobilia, & immobilia, iura, & actiones quomodolibet mihi competentia, aut competentes: sive secundum subiectam materiam, & naturam iudicii, etiamsi nihil exprimat; tacite in cessione subintelligitur universaliter omnia, & quaecumque bona sua, & omne patrimonium, seu peculium."

64 Salgado 1651, III, 5, 32–3: "Sed ne decipiaris (prout deceptum vidi doctum quendam virum) primo advertere debes quod ex cessione quam a principio facit debitor in iudicio concursus nullum ius in dominio aut possessione bonorum acquiritur creditoribus suis, nec ipse a se abdicat, sed potius utrumque retinet, usque ad subhastationem bonorum cum effectu celebratam. Sola enim administratio abdicatur."

65 Salgado 1651, I, 14, 18.

The property, however, was passed neither to the creditors nor to the court, but remained with the debtor.[66]

The logical consequence of this appears to be that possession of the assets passed to the administrator appointed by the court, who was entrusted with the assets.[67] Yet this would have terrible consequences. After all, the corresponding right of patronage was transferred simply with possession of an entirety of assets.[68] Even an unlawful owner could exercise the presentation for the patronage position effectively.[69] There is a supposition in favour of the possessor.[70] As the possessor, the bankruptcy administrator could therefore present applicants to the bishop as he pleases. This form of transfer of patronage rights from the noble debtor to the asset administrator would certainly have thwarted any chances of the process presented by Salgado being put into practice.

3. The debtor's possession of his assets

Salgado's solution, which is no longer surprising given this background, was that the debtor himself remained possessor of the entirety of his assets after having declared cessio bonorum.[71] This option was made possible by the difference between two sub-types of sequestration. In voluntarily declared sequestration, the property was transferred to the person with whom the article was deposited. This was not the case in a necessary, court-ordered sequestration,[72] which merely gave

---

66 Salgado 1651, I, 14, 43: "Et huius dominii penes debitorem probatur per argumentum a sufficienti partium enumeratione: non acquiritur nec transit in creditores, [...] non transit in administratorem, non transit in senatum, & curiam: ergo penes debitorem remanet, quia dominia rerum in suspenso esse non possunt."

67 Cf. Salgado 1651, I, 14, 71.

68 Barbosa 1660, III, 12, 221: "transit enim iuspatronatus cum bonorum possessione, quibus inseparabiliter inhaeret."

69 X. 3.38.19 (Alexander III) and X. 3.38.7 (id.) (Friedberg 1879, col. 615, 611). In the Compilatio prima, those decretals were 1Comp. 3.33.23 and 1Comp. 3.33.9 (Friedberg 1882, p. 42; 41). On the complicated contexts, including English law, cf. Landau 1975, p. 195–205.

70 Landau 1975, p. 199 connects it with the development of the supposition of possession for the owner in civil law by Placentinus.

71 Salgado 1651, I, 14, 76: "contrarium verius est, immo ipsum debitorem retinere possessionem [...]; nec in administratorem transire."

72 Barbosa 1660, III, 12, 234: "Intellige procedere in sequestratione voluntaria [...]; in hac enim possessio transit in sequestrem [...] secus autem dicendum in necessaria, quae jubente judice fit, in qua certum est in sequestrum possessionem non transire, nisi id expresse actum sit".

the new owner the "nuda detentio".[73] With the detention, the ius commune refers only to the "actual occupancy, which is not linked to any possession advantages".[74] Salgado thus had the opportunity to keep the exercise of the right of patronage with the debtor by assuming the case of sequestration without transfer of possession during the concursus proceedings. He did this by arguing that, although the debtor must relinquish the administrative authority for the process by definition, this only occurs for the purpose of securing the assets. In a sequestration for this purpose, possession was not transferred.[75] Salgado indicates that the declaration of intent for the forfeit of assets cannot be interpreted more extensively than necessary for the purpose pursued by the declarer.[76]

However, this puts considerable strain on the interpretation of the debtor's declaration. After all, Salgado explained above that the declaration was central to the entire process and must be interpreted in such a way that the debtor intended to declare the universal forfeit of assets of his own accord. The debtor's will to do this was crucial. Now, a declaration was to be interpreted in that way that, through this extensive declaration, his intention was in fact not to trigger a voluntary sequestration, but instead a judicial sequestration to secure the assets in the interests of the creditors. The result appears almost paradoxical: possession remained with the debtor, despite the universally effective forfeit of assets and the fact that the court or administrator holds authority over them. Thus, by virtue of the universality of the process, the right of patronage was incorporated into the bankruptcy, while at the same time remaining with the debtor. The debtor was considered dead in relation to his assets, but nonetheless was able to continue to exercise his rights of patronage and jurisdiction at the same time.

This elaborate legal construction allowed Salgado, by separating administration from possession, to resolve the conflict between the forfeit of assets and the

73 Application in relation to the right of patronage in Barbosa 1660, III, 12, 237: The enforcing creditor receives neither the property not the possession, but only "nuda detentio": "Nam certum est [...] in creditorem iuspatronatus non transire, quia illius juris, sicut & ipsius rei pigneratae, nullum dominium, nullave possessio in illum transfertur, sed solum nuda detentio, donec persolvatur a domino."

74 Kaser, Max: *Das römische Privatrecht, Erster Abschnitt, Das altrömische, das vorklassische und klassische Recht*. München ²1971, p. 389.

75 Salgado 1651, I, 14, 76–78; I, 14, 79: "Et semper, quod ad solam custodiam sit sequestrum, & depositum; in sequestrem non transit possessio"; I, 14, 83: "Et quia licet sequestrum, & administrationis dimissio, & abdicatio sit de essentia, & natura intrinseca iudicii concursus, & legis ipsius praecisa, haec tamen solum tendit ad custodiam, & administrationem bonorum, & ad hoc limitata, ut saepe diximus."

76 Salgado 1651, I, 14, 78.

exercise of both patronage and sovereign rights.[77] He found a clever legal compromise between the requirements of legal doctrine for a rigorously constructed bankruptcy process and the social need for the over-indebted nobility to retain their social position. This consideration confirms that Salgado in his work had an eye on the legal task of managing the excessive debt of noble households and that his consideration for this helped to shape his legal constructions down to the very last detail.[78]

This makes the phenomenon of long-lasting administration – often over multiple generations of noble families – comprehensible as an option for dealing with economic failure. Having one's assets in administration was not overly damaging to one's status, as sovereign and patronage rights could still be exercised. Only when a creditor or a third party acquired the assets as a whole did he also acquire the right of patronage. This occurred through public auction or through a creditor accepting the entirety of assets in place of payment.[79] On the other hand, this allowed a wealthy creditor[80] to acquire everything he needed to improve his social position in one step: seigneuries and annuity securities, i.e. assets on which a majorat could be founded, together with a right of patronage. All that would furthermore be needed was marrying the children favourably to partners of higher social status and developing some creativity concerning the own genealogy.

---

77 This is corroborated by the analysis of the insolvency of the House of Osuna, in which the complete assets were leased, but the sovereign rights still exercised by the Duke, cf. Atienza Hernández 1984, p. 57: "No podemos confundir administración con gobernación. El arrendador debía de emplearse a fondo de la primer función, pero en ningún caso disponía de atribuciones sobre la segunda. El gobierno del señorio con sus facultades correspondientes […] seguían siendo patrimoniales de la Casa de Osuna, y como tales continuaron ejerciéndose."

78 In addition, it is clear that the legal solution must remain incomprehensible without its specific social background. In this case, neither Endemann, Wilhelm: "Die Entwickelung des Konkursverfahrens in der gemeinrechtlichen Lehre bis zu der Deutschen Konkursordnung vom 10. Februar 1877". *Zeitschrift für deutschen Civilprozess* 12 (1888), pp. 24–96, p. 45–6 nor any subsequent author sees the connection between possessio and the sovereign rights. In particular, it is absent in the influential chapter on legal history in Kohler, Josef: *Lehrbuch des Konkursrechts*, Stuttgart 1891, pp. 29, 31.

79 Salgado 1651, III, 5, 35–6. It is also transferred when an individual item to which it is accessorily attached is auctioned, cf. ibid. However, this is not the case where the assets are sold in individual items, Salgado 1651, III, 5, 37–44.

80 Who was involved in the bankruptcy for example with a claim to the return of the basic total of an annuity purchase, cf. Salgado 1651, I, 19, 15.

V. Burial rights in bankruptcy

Closely related to the desire for maintaining the memoria of a family beyond the lifetime of an individual was another legal institution at the crossroads of wealth, social status, church law and economic transaction: the right to a burial place or burial chapel in a church.[81] In the minds of those involved, especially the nobility, having their own burial chapel in which the appropriate requiem masses were read was the material equivalent of the capellania.[82] "Family chapels were the ultimate investment in the redemptive system of the church, both in spiritual and material terms. These private chapels, which were constructed within parish or monastic churches, served a dual purpose. […] First, these niches within the church building served as mausoleums, providing a single, exclusive altar around which entire families could be buried. Second, this private mausoleum with its own altar served as a liturgical centre from which perpetual masses could be offered."[83] For instance, Francisco Gómez de Sandoval y Rojas, Duke of Lerma (1553–1625), the famous "valido" of Philip III, had a burial chapel constructed in the church of San Pablo in Valladolid.[84]

Certainly, according to canon law the right to interment could not be the object of a legal transaction. This ensues from a decretal of Innocent III (Pope 1198–1216), which forbade a local custom of allowing a grave to be dug only after

---

81 For a discussion of the permissibility of burial in a church up to Gratian, cf. Kötting, Bernhard: Die Tradition der Grabkirche. In: Schmid, Karl / Wollasch, Joachim (eds.): *Memoria. Der geschichtliche Zeugniswert des liturgischen Gedenkens im Mittelalter.* München 1984 (= Münstersche Mittelalter-Schriften Vol. 48), 69–78, 76–78. The relevant norms are C. 13 q. 2 c. 15, 18 and 19 <Quod vero>.

82 For the significance of requiem masses cf. above at note 40; for Germany, cf. Heck, Kilian: "Grablegen". In: Werner Paravacini (ed.): *Höfe und Residenzen im spätmittelalterlichen Reich. Bilder und Begriffe. Teilband 1: Begriffe.* Ostfildern 2005 (= Residenzenforschung Vol. 15.II), pp. 273–275, p. 273: "Grablegen gehören im Heiligen Römischen Reich Deutscher Nation vom 11. bis zum 17. Jh. zu den wichtigsten Monumenten dynast. Erinnerungskultur." An Europe-wide treatment can be found in Hengerer, Mark (ed.): *Macht und Memoria. Begräbniskultur europäischer Oberschichten in der Frühen Neuzeit.* Köln/Weimar/Wien 2005.

83 Eire, Carlos M.N.: *From Madrid to purgatory. The art and craft of dying in sixteenth-century Spain.* Cambridge University Press 1995, p. 205–6.

84 Banner, Lisa A.: *The religious patronage of the Duke of Lerma, 1598–1621.* Farnham 2009, p. 25: "The appropriation of San Pablo as his own patronato and site for his burial place can be seen as the use of a venerable, conspicuous church near the palace of the king to enhance Lerma's grandeur."

payment of a fee.[85] Therefore, the right to be buried or interred in a specific place could not be sold.[86]

However, a distinction was made between the illegal sale of a burial place and the adoption of the obligation not to inter anybody else in a particularly honourable place, especially a burial chapel, i.e. to keep the grave free for a specific person or family: "alium est vendere sepulturam, quod prohibetur; aliud vendere obligationem *non sepeliendi alium*."[87] This resulted in a right to a burial place in the form of a right to prevent others from being interred there;[88] in modern terminology, injunctive relief from competitors. This was not a religious but a secular matter centred around honour and social status. A right like this may be subject to pricing: "aestimabile in pecunia est".[89] The church was not forbidden to assign it for money; it can be given a price and sold: "potest pretio aestimari, & vendi".[90] Pertaining to the question of whether it can be deployed as an asset in the case of

85 X. 3.28.13 (Friedberg 1879, col. 553): "Abolendae [...] non prius permittatur effodi sepultura, quam pro terra [...] certum pretium ecclesiae persolvatur."

86 Barbosa, Agostinho: *Pastoralis solicitudinis, sive de officio, et potestate parochi, tripartita descriptio.* Lyon 1688 (first edition: 1632), III, 26, 16: "Pro jure sepulturae, sive ut aliquis in certo loco Ecclesiae, aut coemeterii sepeliri possit, [...] pretium exigere simoniacum est, illa namque vendi non potest, sed gratis praestanda est defunctis."

87 Barbosa 1688, XXVI, 18.

88 Cf. Salgado 1651, III, 5, 48: "ratione usus sepulturae potest alios impedire ne ibi sepeliantur."

89 Barbosa 1688, III, 26, 18. Cf. Banner 2009, p. 47: The Duke of Lerma paid 4.000 ducats for the use of the chapel as his burial place.

90 Barbosa 1688, III, 26, 16: "quasi hoc non videatur concernere spiritualia, sed tantum honorem, & praeeminentiam, quae potest pretio aestimari, & vendi."; Salgado 1651, III, 5, 48: "hoc ius & usus sepulturae sive Capellae est mere temporalis". Barbosa can refer to the moral theology of the Dominican Juan de la Cruz (not the eponymous mystic); Barbosa 1688, III, 26, 16 with reference to Juan de la Cruz: *Directorium conscientiae in duas partes divisum pars prima.* 6th ed. Douai 1631, Pars I, praeceptum 7, quaestio 4, dubitatio 9, conclusio 2: "At non erit simonia accipere pretium pro sepultura in loco honoratiori, aut pro iure perpetuo ad sepulturam; ista enim sunt temporalia, & per accidens unitati sunt spiritualitate sepulturae. Et idem ait D. Th. ad 3. de iure patronatus ad sepulturam, aut capellam. Hoc enim est temporale, & vendibile." Gonzales 1611, gloss. 5 no. 36–7 claims transferability even if someone is already buried there: "si sepulchrum, seu monumentum est factum, non interveniente Episcopi auctoritate, potest vendi, & alienari, quamvis in illo sit aliquis sepultus, [...]." He rejects the argument that burial itself creates an unsellable "locus religiosus", as in canon law a "locus religiosus" cannot come into existence without the permission of a bishop (no. 38–9).

insolvency,[91] Salgado drew the consequence: if the church was not forbidden from granting such a right to a layperson, the layperson must certainly be permitted to transfer it himself. He may sell it; but on the other hand his creditors could also administer it.[92] The debtor's right to his outstanding burial place or a burial chapel thus had a monetary value and could be sold in the case of bankruptcy: "potest pretio aestimari & vendi tanquam mere temporalis".[93] Salgado reports on the bankruptcy of the Marquis of Auñón, a town located east of Madrid in the Guadalajara region. In this case, the royal council decreed the sale of the right to the burial chapel in order to assign the yield to the creditors.[94]

VI. Conclusion

In an environment in which social status, family prestige, and spiritual welfare were inseparable, economic failure threatened not only the prestige of the current head of the family, but also the measures taken to uphold the memoria of the ancestors, which in turn constituted the prestige enjoyed by its living and future

91 Salgado 1651, III, 5, 45.

92 Salgado 1651, III, 5, 49: "si in prima acquisitione licita, & absque labe simoniae ab Ecclesia, potest hoc ius honorificum sepulturae & Capellae vendi, & pretio acquiri tanquam mere profanum & temporale, multo magis poterit, postquam pervenit in potestatem laici, vendi, distrahi, & in executionem capi, pro solutione creditorum, cum sit res pretio aestimabilis, & a iure non prohibitum."

93 Salgado 1651, III, 5, 48. Here, Salgado draws on Diez de Ribadeneyra Noguerol, Pedro: *Allegationes iuris, in quibus [...] quaestiones [...], in suprema Hispaniarum curiae tribunalibus disceptatae, [...] enucleantur*. Lyon 1676 (first printed Madrid 1641), XXXVI, 22f.: "hoc procedit respectu iuris principalis sepulchri [...] non vero respectu eminentiarum, videlicet quod sepulchrum sit privative patrono, & successoribus, & sic in loco praeeminenti Ecclesiae, & quod nullus alius in eo sepeliri possit, qui tunc est mere temporale, & potest vendi absque vitio [...] Et ex hac ratione idem procedit in capella, quae dotatur in Ecclesia, qui ratione huius praeeminentiae est quid mere temporale, & licite potest transferri, & vendi [...] per consequens potest in eis fieri executionem." This argument deals with the enforcement of a judgment that "Maria de Sande & Mesa" had been granted against the heirs "Cardinalis Ducis de Lerma", i.e. the heirs of the Duke of Lerma (cf. above at note 84), who obtained the cardenalate in 1618. Details on Lerma's testaments in Williams 2006, especially pp. 221–226.

94 Salgado 1651, III, 5, 50 quotes Ribadeneyra Noguerol, Allegationes iuris, XXXVI, 24: "Et ita observat praxis Senatus Supremi in multis casibus occurentibus, & fuit decisum in causa creditorum Marchionis de Auñon, ubi patronatus capellae maioris Monasterii Divi Augustini iussus fuit vendi pro debitis fundatoris." Salgado adds: "de quo & nos etiam testamur."

members. As spiritual and secular assets were involved, the legal assessment in this cases had to rely on canon law. While insolvency proceedings often could not be avoided, the Spanish jurists of the 17th century, by deftly applying arguments crafted out of Roman law on problems of canon law, safeguarded the rights of patronage against transfer to the creditors as far as possible. Only in the extreme case of a sell-off of the totality of a debtor's assets, the right of patronage devolved to the buyer as well. This also secured the acceptance of the legal proceedings dealing with insolvency, which, given the immediate access of the highest noble houses to the king, otherwise might have been circumvented by royal intervention.

D. De ruysscher[1]

The Struggle for Voluntary Bankruptcy and Debt Adjustment in Antwerp (*c.* 1520–*c.* 1550)

Legal history concerning early modern insolvency and bankruptcy has often focused on the proverbial "stick". Much attention has been paid to rules that allowed for a swift liquidation of a bankrupt's estate and to penalties for fraud. Solutions that were based on cooperation of the debtor and which facilitated postponements, or a fresh start after the bankruptcy, have unfortunately received less attention. This disparity in the scholarly literature has to do with a focus on normative texts and with a relative neglect of the forensic and mercantile practices surrounding phenomena of indebtedness and insolvency. Legislation tended to be harsh, whereas its implementation was usually less rigid and straightforward. Quite recently economic historians in particular have started analysing statistical data concerning insolvency practices in France in the nineteenth century, which clearly demonstrate many efforts towards negotiation.[2] As a result of their findings, these historians have come to react against the views conventionally proposed in the 'law-and-finance' literature, inclined as these interpretations are to consider liquidation as the most efficient means of tackling persistent payment problems.[3]

---

1 Post-doctoral fellow of the Fund of Scientific Research – Flanders and lecturer at Vrije Universiteit Brussel (VUB). Comments are welcome at dderuyss@vub.ac.be. Preliminary versions of this paper were presented at the seminar "*La responsabilité en justice*" (*École des Hautes Études en Sciences Sociales*) in Paris on 7 March 2013. That conference as well as the meeting of the research group HOST at VUB (Vrije Universiteit Brussel) on 25 March 2014 resulted in the present publication. I would like to thank the participants for their comments and suggestions.

2 Hautcœur, Pierre-Cyrille / Levratto, Nadine: "Bankruptcy law and practice in XIXth-century France". Working paper 2007; Hautcœur, Pierre-Cyrille / Levratto, Nadine: "Petites et grandes entreprises face à la faillite au XIXe siècle en France: du droit à la pratique". Working paper 2007. For Belgium in the first half of the 1800s, comparable data point to a high number of extra-judicial agreements. See De ruysscher, Dave. "Praktijkgerichtheid in de rechtbank van koophandel (19de–21ste eeuw): een uitgeholde traditie opnieuw ingevuld". In: De ruysscher, Dave (ed.): *Rechtspreken en lekenparticipatie: noodzaak of traditie*. Maklu: Antwerp 2013, pp. 148–149.

3 La Porta, Rafael, et al.: "Law and Finance". *Journal of Political Economy* 106-6 (1998), pp. 1113–1155. Authors writing in this tradition commonly build on the assumption

Another reason for the afore-mentioned bias towards tough measures and the liquidation of businesses is a conceptual and even an ideological one, much related to the economic literature belonging to a Schumpeterian tradition. Along these lines legal historians have, for example, labelled the early modern French practice of royal letters (of *répit*, *cession*) as "laxist" remedies preventing creditors from recovering their debts.[4] As such it is a common assumption that firms that go bust are not healthy and that any measure aimed at their recovery is a matter of artificial lenience or inappropriate compassion. In contemporary law, rules regarding payment problems are often framed as being either debtor-friendly or creditor-friendly and, correspondingly, such labels are also quite frequently used for the history of bankruptcy.[5] In addition, it is often thought that judges are not relevant in bankruptcy or insolvency matters, and that an expeditious insolvency proceeding is one that is administered exclusively by creditors.[6]

As this contribution will argue, however, an assessment of insolvency and debt negotiation practices in sixteenth-century Antwerp makes it evident that in that period insolvency for a large part depended on the understanding of creditors. Their involvement did not always result in liquidation, as creditors could accept moratoria and favour a re-integration of a defaulting debtor into their networks. Without official support, though, liquidation remained the default proceeding.

---

that an efficient bankruptcy law is creditor-friendly, which is defined in terms of swiftness (thus preferring liquidation) and a high recovery rate.

4 Hilaire, Jean: *Introduction historique au droit commercial*. PUF: Paris 1986, p. 321 and p. 323. For another perspective, see Deshusses, Frédéric : "Mesurer l'insolvabilité. Usages statistiques des dossiers de faillite (1673–1807)". *Histoire & Mesure* 23/1 (2008), pp. 19–41; Reynard, Pierre Claude: "The Language of Failure: Bankruptcy in Eighteenth-Century France". *The Journal of European Economic History* 30/1 (2001), pp. 355–390.

5 For appraisals of the precursor of contemporary *Chapter 11* arrangements, namely, in the American bankruptcy law of 1898, as (too) "*debtor friendly*", see: Baird, Douglas G. / Rasmussen, Robert K.: "The End of Bankruptcy". *Stanford Law Review* 2002, pp. 751–797; Hotchkiss, Edith: "Postbankruptcy Performance and Management Turnover". *Journal of Finance* 50 (1995), pp. 3–21; Skeel, David A.: "Creditors' Ball: The 'New' New Corporate Governance in Chapter 11". *University of Pennsylvania Law Review* 94 (2003), pp. 1357–1391.

6 At the end of the nineteenth century, this idea was put forward by Josef Kohler. See Kohler, Josef: *Lehrbuch des Konkursrechts*. Enke: Stuttgart 1891, pp. 11–45, and, for an interpretation, Falk, Ulrich: "Die Konkursübel. Forschungsfragen zur Geschichte des Konkursverfahrens in Deutschland". *Zeitschrift der Savigny-Stiftung für europäische Rechtsgeschichte. Germanistische Abteilung* 131 (2014), pp. 277–278 and pp. 317–318.

In an effort to change that process, it became required that the debtor be able to pressure creditors into seeking a compromise. To that end, the authorities of the city of Antwerp and of the princely government cooperated in establishing an institutional framework that facilitated negotiations. By examining the extant material on these talks between debtors and creditors in Antwerp in the second quarter of the sixteenth century, the investigation at hand intends, moreover, to shed greater light on the Antwerp aldermen particularly involved in these proceedings at the local level. As will be demonstrated in what follows, their role was crucial in the diplomacy required to reach the agreements that resolved conflicts surrounding voluntary bankruptcy and debt adjustment.

1. Shifting policies of debt collection and bankruptcy in late fifteenth- and early sixteenth-century Antwerp

Collective and voluntary bankruptcy or insolvency, which became used in Antwerp in the 1520s, grew out of experiences from the preceding decades. These collective features came after a period of generalized individuality in debt collection, and it was only after collectivization of bankruptcy that voluntary bankruptcy/insolvency and debt adjustment could emerge.

Before the later decades of the fifteenth century, namely, Antwerp law and merchant culture had generally labelled debtors with persistent payment problems as frauds. Creditors commonly sought to imprison and expropriate their defaulting debtors, and remedies supporting their recovery were not practised. This practice had to do with the weak status of mercantile debt during most of the 1400s: it was not possible to lay attachment on the basis of non-authenticated documents (i.e. documents other than "aldermen's letters" and certificates) or informal promises and arrangements, except after obtaining a judgment, which was the outcome of a lengthy proceeding before the aldermen of the municipal court in Antwerp. Underlying these rules was the idea that rights of collateral, which were closely related to attachment in this period, had to be checked and approved by the municipal administrators, that is, the aldermen. Mercantile debts were not always put down in writing and if they were, they were usually inserted into private agreements that were not presented to the aldermen for registration. As a result, for most debts of merchants, it was only through a verdict of the municipal court that rights of collateral could be established.[7] Imprisoning a debtor was a swifter method for creditors to collateralize their debts, because detained

7 On certificates and "aldermen's letters", see Asaert, Gustaaf: "De oudste certificatiën van de stad Antwerpen (1468–1482)". *Bulletin de la commission royale d'histoire* 132

debtors could transfer their estate to their creditors in order to be released from prison.[8] In practice, members of chartered merchant organizations could also be arrested and brought to prison.[9] Debtors therefore aimed at avoiding application of the official rules. Compliance inevitably resulted in detention and the demise of their reputation, which would also prevent them from engaging in contracts after imprisonment.[10] Because the practice of re-negotiating debts did not exist, a debtor with permanent insolvency often felt induced to abscond rather than face the defamatory consequences of his creditors' actions.[11] Following payment problems, flight out of jurisdiction or asylum in churches were typical responses of merchants in financial distress for most of the fifteenth century.

Yet over the course of the later fifteenth century, an alternative slowly came to be accepted in Antwerp. Specifically, the new practice concerned private arrangements that had not received the status of official deed from the aldermen, either because the written contract had not been submitted for registration, or because it had not been written down. Such agreements were nonetheless held to encompass collateral rights on the debtor's movable property, even if this had not been expressly stipulated. Creditors could thus lay attachment on assets of a defaulter and start a proceeding before the municipal court in order to be granted

(1966), pp. 261–263; Doehaerd, Renée: *Études anversoises. Documents sur le commerce international à Anvers, 1488–1514*. SEVPEN: Paris 1963, vol. 1, pp. 9–15.

8 Van der Tannerijen, Willem: *Boec van der loopender practijken der raidtcameren van Brabant*. Strubbe, Egied I. (ed.). CAD: Brussels 1952, vol. 1, pp. 262–263.

9 In spite of the charters of their *nations* (as these groups of foreign residents were designated) and the customary safe-conduct ('*saufconduit*') granted by the duke of Brabant for those visiting the fairs in Antwerp, Hanseatic and English merchants were occasionally arrested and detained, in which case the sections of the charters providing for protection were brought up only in the course of proceedings before the municipal court. Arrest and imprisonment were thus feasible methods of debt collection by compulsory means even against privileged traders. See, for example, Antwerp City Archives (Felix Archief) (hereinafter ACA), Vierschaar (hereinafter V), 1231, f. 105 (5 Feb. 1491 ns) and ACA, V, 1233, f. 13v (4 July 1503).

10 This compliance problem is inherent to bankruptcy systems that focus on punishment and imprisonment. For comparable remarks regarding the English bankruptcy system after 1543, see Kadens, Emily: "The Last Bankrupt Hanged: Balancing Incentives in the Development of Bankruptcy Law". *Duke Law Journal* 59 (2010), pp. 1233–1234.

11 For late medieval Italian cities and for sixteenth-century England respectively, see: Santarelli, Umberto: *Mercanti e società tra mercanti*. Giappichelli: Turin 1998, p. 70, and Kadens 2010, pp. 1246–1247.

the right to have that property auctioned.[12] Attachment served as an efficient compulsory instrument. Because seized movable goods could be secured in the city hall and attachments were made public, debtors had incentives to have the ban on their assets lifted as soon as possible. If sureties or additional credit could be offered, creditors commonly withdrew from a proceeding of public sale. During the time period after approximately 1470, attachment gradually became the prime method of debt collection in Antwerp, both during and after the fairs, and among merchants.

Even so, the new principles brought about new problems. An attachment by one creditor could alarm other creditors and result in generalized distrust and subsequent attachments. Furthermore, when many creditors seized assets of the same debtor, debts were then pooled, meaning that they had to be prioritized in one way or another. In this regard, older rules continued to be applied. Privileged debts (hypothecs, and later dowries, too) were compensated according to their date, and priority was given to the oldest debt.[13] For non-privileged debts, the date of the attachment determined the order of the debt. At the payment of proceeds from the debtor's auctioned assets, creditors that had laid attachment first were prioritized over those who had done so at a later stage.[14] This rule had some important negative consequences. Firstly, it resulted in "a run on the debtor". Creditors aimed at quick attachments because, if they hesitated to do so, they risked not receiving a share of their debtor's estate. Secondly, attachment required no preliminary public announcement, though once an attachment was laid, rumours soon spread within the city of Antwerp. All the same, it could take a while before the news reached other locations, thus creating information asymmetries, which put foreigners and others, who often were not aware of a local merchant's insolvency, in a weaker position than locals and resident merchants. When the latter heard of their debtor's situation, they could join in the collective

12 These developments are evident in the transformation of "*marktvrijheid*" (freedom of the market) around 1500. Originally, it was a protection against debt enforcement of all sorts. Around 1500, though, this 'freedom' became restricted to debts that had been agreed outside a fair, whereas for "fair debts" swift attachment and expropriation became optional. See ACA, V, 2, section 141 and f. 35. This rule thus transformed meant that attachment became a popular method of debt recovery during the fairs as well.

13 "Oudt Register, mette berderen, 1336–1439". *Antwerpsch Archievenblad*, 1st series 29 (*s.d.*), pp. 144–146 (26 June 1437); Strubbe, Egied I. / Spillemaeckers, Edward: "De 'Antwerpse rechtsaantekeningen' van Willem de Moelnere". *Bulletin de la Commission royale pour la publication des anciennes lois et ordonnances* 18 (1954), p. 67.

14 ACA, V, 68, f. 12v (around 1508); ACA, V, 1233, f. 281v (20 Oct. 1509).

proceedings already commenced, but because of the municipal code their debts were paid only after those of the creditors that had laid attachments earlier. This situation engendered conflict and litigation with regard to the nature of debts and the date of attachment. In the first years of the 1500s, the exact timing of attachments was a customary point of contention in lawsuits between creditors going after the estate of a communal debtor.[15]

In January 1516, a procedure for collective bankruptcy was instituted by Antwerp's aldermen in an ordinance of the city council,[16] in response to growing credit relationships among resident merchants from different countries, in addition to mounting insolvency cases. According to the ordinance, in case of flight or concealment of assets, a public proclamation was issued notifying creditors to submit claims to the municipal court within forty days. After an audit of the debts was presented to the court, assets of the debtor were sold publicly. Except for privileged debts, which had priority, other debts were paid *pro rata* if all claims could not be compensated in full from the proceeds of the public sale. As a result of the 1516 reform, the rules regarding the collection of arrears became somewhat more equitable, at least for the creditors. The idea behind this mandatory collectivity among creditors was that bankruptcy was a risk that should be shared by all those having contracts with the "perpetrator", so that the market would absorb the shock as effectively as possible. It is evident that the Antwerp aldermen had issued the new law in order to adjust the earlier rules and procedures to suit the international business environment that the Antwerp market had become after 1490. This intention is also clear in a subsequent ordinance dating from 1518, which extended from six weeks to three months the period during which creditors residing outside the Low Countries could submit claims.[17] This measure attempted to facilitate those creditors not having a business agent on location, thereby keeping them well informed about what went on in Antwerp.

The 1516 ordinance thus regulated involuntary bankruptcy; yet it did not detail rules for when the debtor actually wanted to cooperate with his creditors. That is, the 1516 bankruptcy procedure applied only to so-called "fugitives" (*fugitivi*), i.e. those debtors who absconded or had hidden assets. According to the aforementioned ordinance, it was to be presumed that a debtor would attempt to circumvent his creditors' rights. As officer and representative of the duke of Brabant, the *amman* was legally required to seek and retrieve assets that had been brought

15 For example, ACA, V, 1233, f. 67v (23 Jan. 1505 ns).

16 This ordinance was published in *Recueil des ordonnances des Pays-Bas*. 2nd series, vol. 1. Laurent, Charles (ed.). Goemaere: Brussels 1893, pp. 464–466.

17 ACA, V, 4, sections 7–8.

outside the reach of the creditors and stored with relatives, associates or agents. Together with the belongings that had been found with the debtor, they formed a so-called *massa creditorum*, which was the 'mass', or bulk, of all properties available for discharging the debt.[18] Because the 1516 ordinance only envisaged criminal acts, though, its rules still hinged on ideas that had been popular in the fifteenth century. Consequently, deterrence remained the general paradigm in insolvency, whereby the law did not provide for negotiations concerning the payment or postponement of debts. As had been the case before, these rules did not induce debtors to being open about their financial situation and, at the same time, did not make creditors any less impatient to start expropriation proceedings where doubts regarding repayment existed. This state of affairs would soon change.

2. Taking the debtor into consideration (c. 1510–c. 1520)

By the 1510s, more attention was gradually being paid to the honest insolvent who had not committed (criminal) bankruptcy, and whose insolvency was the result of misfortune rather than fraud. In the years before 1510, princely councils such as the Council of Brabant and the Great Council of Mechelen had occasionally granted *lettres de justice* to petitioning debtors. *Lettres de répit*, *de sauvegarde* and other such writs purported to give the debtor an argument in court in a lawsuit against his creditors, in order to have debts postponed or discharged; or they might similarly award protection from imprisonment and expropriation.[19] In the 1510s, central institutions issued such letters only to debtors that were deemed to have been unfortunate. At his "Joyous Entry" as lord of the Habsburg Netherlands in 1515, Charles (later Holy Roman Emperor Charles V) declared that princely letters were to be granted on the condition that applicants had not committed

18 On these topics, see: De ruysscher, Dave: "Designing the limits of creditworthiness: Insolvency in Antwerp bankruptcy legislation and practice (16th–17th centuries)". *The Legal History Review (Tijdschrift voor Rechtsgeschiedenis)* 76 (2008), pp. 309–313.

19 Debtors occasionally petitioned the Council of Brabant for *lettres de répit* (which granted postponement of payments). Other comparable, but (even) less popular remedies were the *lettres de sauvegarde* (protecting the beneficiary from arrest and seizure of his properties, usually without specification of a period of application) and *lettres de saufconduit* (which protected from arrest and attachment during a period of travel). In 1497–98, the Council of Brabant granted 22 *lettres de répit*. This was a maximum; between *c.* 1495 and *c.* 1520, on average between five and ten *lettres de répit* were handed out each year. See Archives of the Realm (Brussels), Account Rolls (*Rekenkamer*), 20784, 20785 and 20786. The earliest found reference to a *lettre de répit* mentioned by an Antwerp resident dates from 1504. See ACA, V, 1233, f. 38 (15 Jan. 1504 ns).

treacherous acts.[20] Furthermore, in the 1510s and thereafter, imprisoned debtors were released from prison upon ceding their estate to the creditors who had locked them away, as had been the case before; now, however, it was further required that the debtor have not attempted to hide assets from his creditors. Even though this "*cessie van goede*" (*cessio bonorum*) entailed that the released debtor lost his rights of citizenship, it was an efficient remedy that kept poor and *bona fide* debtors from a long incarceration.[21] Notably, such "*cessie van goede*" did not bring about a fresh start: if the freed debtor acquired new capital, he still had to repay debts that had not been settled already with the proceeds from the assets that he had transferred.

The ideas mentioned above gained ground properly in the 1520s. In those years, Antwerp insolvents could apply for princely letters that required drawing up negotiations between the debtor and his creditors, which aimed at the postponement of debts. A new focus on the debtor's good faith, in combination with the recent idea of collectivity among creditors, had made talks of this type possible. With these moratoria becoming a real option, many more debtors brought their payment problems to light. Encouraging further cooperation and agreements between creditors and debtors, it consequently became normal practice in the 1530s for an insolvent to file a request with the Council of Brabant to charge the Antwerp aldermen with the task of mediating a compromise with his creditors.[22] Thereupon, the aldermen had to verify the applicant's arguments and detect the causes of his financial problems. If it became clear that the debtor had been deceitful or dishonest in his statements, the request was denied.[23] If the aldermen corroborated the applicant's story, the debtor's properties were inventoried; thereafter the creditors declared the debts owed to them, while submitting evidence of those amounts claimed. In a next phase, negotiations began under the guidance of commissioned Antwerp aldermen and public officers. The case file was then

---

20 *Placcaerten, ordonnantien, edicten … in dese Nederlanden*, Anselmo, Antoon / *et al.* (eds). Vol. 8. Knobbaert: Brussels *s.d.*, p. 136 (26 April 1515, sections 4–5).

21 ACA, V, 1233, f. 85v (1 Oct. 1505), f. 89 (6 Nov. 1505) and f. 110v (9 July 1506); ACA, V, 1235, f. 51 (12 Nov. 1517); ACA, V, 68, f. 33 (1 June 1520). I would like to thank Jeroen Puttevils (University of Antwerp) for bringing the first two references to my attention. See also, in more detail, De ruysscher, Dave: "Reconciling old and new: imprisonment for debts and *cessio bonorum*, in Antwerp and Mechelen (*c.* 1500–*c.* 1530). In: Oosterhuis, Jan Willem / Van Dongen, Emanuel G.D. (eds.): *European Traditions: Integration or Disintegration?* Wolff: Oisterwijk 2012, pp. 35–48.

22 ACA, Privilegiekamer (hereinafter PK), 271, 299 and 312. These files contain many of such forwarded requests.

23 See for example, ACA, PK, 271, 63 and 66.

returned to the Council of Brabant, which confirmed and registered the contract, or took other measures if no compromise had been reached.[24]

This development towards a collective and voluntary debt adjustment was closely linked to the financial and economic crisis that was triggered by the Frisian War (from 1517 onwards) and the Italian Wars (resumed in 1521).[25] Rising prices and interest rates shook the economy of the Low Countries and of Antwerp in particular. In 1518 and 1523, two large Florentine banking firms with agents in Antwerp were wound up (the Frescobaldi and Gualterotti houses, respectively).[26] The Frescobaldi failure was the first international bankruptcy case that caused disturbance in the Antwerp market, and it left many traces in the archives of the Antwerp municipal government.[27] The general economic crisis brought about liquidity and credit problems for many, subsequently setting developments in motion that resulted in an adjustment of the "stick"-approach in Antwerp insolvency law. The sheer rise in numbers of petitions brought about a systematization of the previously "exceptional" procedure of acquiring *lettres de justice*. The earlier existing differences between types of *lettres de justice* were harmonized and all of them henceforth required the mandatory summoning of creditors.[28] The municipal and princely governments cooperated in dealing with the many more demands from debtors for exemptions and protection. The Council of Brabant did not want to pass over the Antwerp aldermen, who were considered to be the ordinary judges in the Antwerp market. The practice of negotiations in the case of petitions was thus municipal and princely

---

24 This practice was formalized by means of a 1536 princely law. See *Recueil des ordonnances des Pays-Bas*. 2nd series vol. 4. Lameere, Jean (ed.). Goemaere: Brussels 1907, p. 328 (30 Aug. 1536).

25 Van der Wee, Herman: *The Growth of the Antwerp Market*. Nijhoff: The Hague 1963, vol. 2, pp. 141–153.

26 Ehrenberg, Richard: *Das Zeitalter der Fugger. Geldkapital und Creditverkehr im 16. Jahrhundert. Erster Band: die Geldmächte des 16. Jahrhunderts*. Fischer: Jena 1922, pp. 280–281.

27 For example ACA, V, 1235, f. 92 (23 June 1518), f. 99 (20 July 1518) and f. 106v (19 July 1518).

28 It seems that in the early decades of the sixteenth century, *inductie* or compulsory summoning of all creditors was systematically applied only for *lettres de répit*. For the first traces of mandatory summoning, see *Recueil des Ordonnances des Pays-Bas*. 2nd series, vol. 3. Lameere, Jean (ed.). Goemaere: Brussels 1902, pp. 134–135 (section 547 and section 552) (princely ordinance on the procedure in the Council of Brabant, 20 March 1531 ns).

at the same time.[29] The change in Antwerp and princely policies vis-à-vis insolvency, from an involuntary system to an attention for voluntary bankruptcy, followed from a new appreciation of moratoria as a means to overcome financial problems.

3. Negotiations in cases of insolvency: the aim for relief, protected by the Antwerp aldermen (c. 1530–c. 1550)

For the 1530s and 1540s, some hints of negotiations between a debtor and his creditors could still be found in the historical record. 59 files from the period between 1527 and 1549 have been preserved in the archives. They were drawn up by commissioned Antwerp officials following petitions to the princely Council of Brabant, from debtors applying for terms of payment and debt adjustment. Most of these 59 files are incomplete: the majority contain a copy of the request and of the commissioning letter from the Council of Brabant to the Antwerp aldermen. In thirteen of these files, there are also notes referring to the negotiations, and most of these files contain a draft letter from the commissioners to the Council of Brabant including a summary of the talks as well as advice on further measures.[30]

The materials mentioned provide a glimpse into the Antwerp practices of voluntary bankruptcy, and – even though one has to be cautious in this respect – into the profile of applicants. Three applicants were women (two widows and one wife in business with her husband); the other 56 were men. Not all of the 59 files mention what the profession of the debtor in distress was. In 24 of them, the petition refers to the type of trade or the occupation. From the descriptions of their activities, it seems that even though many applicants described themselves as "merchants" ("*coopman*", "*marchant*"), most of them were in fact small-scale mercers, stallholders and craftsmen. This status is also suggested by the size and number of their debts, since compared to some liquidation cases of the period mentioned, the debts of applicants (which are detailed in eleven files) were indeed

---

29 In this respect, my views differ from those of Oscar Gelderblom, who has emphasized that the Antwerp municipal government acted in the absence of princely policies. See Gelderblom, Oscar: *Cities of commerce: the institutional foundations of international trade in the Low Countries, 1250–1650*. Princeton University Press: Princeton, 2013. Yet even though in practice there was cooperation with the Council of Brabant, the Antwerp aldermen remained nostalgic for the times when they had autonomous jurisdiction in the matter of *cessie van goede*. See De ruysscher, Dave: "Lobbyen, vleien en herinneren: vergeefs onderhandelen om privileges bij de Blijde Inkomst van Filips in Antwerpen (1549)". *Noord-Brabants Historisch Jaarboek* 29 (2012), p. 69 and p. 74.

30 ACA, PK, 271, 299 and 312. Unfortunately, to my knowledge, the files that were sent to the Council of Brabant have not survived.

modest.[31] Furthermore, from the documents mentioned, it appears that the practice of petitioning for postponements of payment as a measure of debt negotiation mostly concerned local and indigenous members of the urban community; foreign merchants, even resident ones, did not often seek a remedy of this sort.[32] It is probable that in the period of the 1530s and 1540s, high-flying businessmen more often resorted to informal talks with creditors, under the direction of arbiters, or that they opted for mediation within the framework of a debt recovery proceeding. In any case, it seems to have been a practice for prominent merchants not to apply for *lettres de justice* when soliciting debt adjustment from their creditors.[33]

Most of the debts in the afore-mentioned files were private or informal; annuities or other debts encompassed in deeds (i.e. aldermen's letters or certificates) were exceptional. This situation might explain the profile of applicants, as well as the rather limited size of debt that was involved in applications for debt negotiations. If formal and authenticated debts could not be paid, there was no use in notifying all creditors. Because these debts comprised outright collateral, the creditors for these debts were privileged to expropriations and they could easily seek compensation alone, without having to take into account the actions and views of colleagues having non-privileged debts. Their collateralized debt had priority in any case.[34] Therefore, debtors with persistent financial problems only used the remedy of applying for a negotiation if there was a chance that it would have effect, which occurred when debts were non-privileged.

---

31 The highest debt, which was an exceptionally high amount, was some £ 2,500 groat Flemish (hereafter gr. Fl.). See ACA, PK, 271, 48 (request, ap. 15 Febr. 1545 ns). A total debt of over £ 1,000 gr. Fl. was not common (see for two examples, ACA, PK, 299, file of Denys Platynmakere (*c.* 1540) and ACA, PK, 312, 126–130 and 299, file of Jacob van Wijnrecht (1549)). See, for some liquidation cases in the 1520s and 1530s in which more than £ 1,500 gr. Fl. was claimed, Puttevils, Jeroen: *The Ascent of Merchants from the Southern Low Countries. From Antwerp to Europe, 1480–1585.* Unpublished doctoral dissertation, University of Antwerp 2012, p. 291.

32 Of the 59 files, only two were drawn up for foreign traders: ACA, PK, 271, 48, file of Arnoult del Plano (request, apostil of 15 Febr. 1545 ns) (this file concerned a total debt of some £ 2,500 gr. Fl., see also above in footnote 31) and ACA, PK, 299, file of Alberto Pinelli, "merchant of Genoa" (request, ap. of 7 June 1542).

33 See the examples in Puttevils 2012, pp. 292–297.

34 For *lettres de cession*, see *Recueil des ordonnances des Pays-Bas.* 2nd series, vol. 5. Lameere, Jean and Simont, Henri (eds.). Goemaere: Brussels 1910, p. 56 (section 37) (19 May 1544). For *lettres de répit*, this seems to have been the practice as well. See *Coutumes de la ville d'Anvers.* De Longé, Guillaume (ed.). Vol. 4, Gobbaerts: Antwerp 1874, p. 430 (part 4, chapter 17, section 14).

The requests of debtors contain many similar and even stereotypical arguments. They insist on their "falling into insolvency", thus hinting at the exteriority of the event, and the applicants complained about economic conditions. Personal statements relate to the needs of children and wife, and to the applicant's young age.[35] However, this depiction of a miserable state went hand in hand with references to the capability of the debtor and the size of his network. Many requests stress the fact that the insolvency had resulted from the defaulting of debtors and not from risk-taking or mistakes.[36] In fact, most requests underscored that debtors of the applicants themselves had gone "bankrupt" or had fled.[37] When describing their own financial situation, petitioning debtors used milder terms ("insolvency", "poverty", "bad fortune"). When *vis maior* was identified as the cause of the indebtedness (e.g., loss at sea,[38] war,[39] debtors residing in Protestant countries[40]), then the request commonly listed the actions that had been taken in response, even though they had failed.[41] Another frequent motive was that the creditors of the debtor were "rich and powerful" and that it was to be feared that they would destroy a viable business and/or the debtor's reputation by means of attachments.[42] Some petitions referred to a liquidity problem, as the debtor made it clear that he possessed immovable property but that if his creditors pursued expropriation these assets would be sold at too low a price.[43] This argument could also refer to merchandise.[44]

---

35 E.g. ACA, PK, 312, request, ap. of 21 Aug. 1536. One has to be cautious as to the veracity of such remarks. This need is evident from an example of a standardized request containing the formula "N [i.e. *nomen nescio*], a poor man, who became insolvent due to the hard times and having the responsibility for his wife and small children". See ACA, PK, 228.

36 For example, ACA, PK, 312, 21–25 (request, ap. Febr. 1536).

37 E.g. ACA, PK, 312, 1–2 (request, ap. 16 Nov. 1534) and 312, 113–115 (request, ap. 28 Jan. 1546 ns).

38 E.g. ACA, PK, 271, 48 (request, ap. 15 Febr. 1545 ns) and ACA, 312, 5–6 (request, ap. 17 Febr. 1535 ns).

39 E.g. ACA, PK, 312, 9–17 (request, ap. 19 April 1536).

40 E.g. ACA, PK, 312, 3–4 (request, ap. 17 Febr. 1535 ns).

41 ACA, PK, 312, 28 (request, ap. Oct. 1540). Pieter Stevens had organized transport by ship of a precious belt, which had slipped into the river at Dordrecht. Stevens detailed how much he had paid for searches for the belt, which unfortunately remained lost.

42 ACA, PK, 312, 5–6 (request, ap. 15 Febr. 1535 ns) and 1–2 (request, ap. 16 Nov. 1534).

43 ACA, PK, 312, 9–17 (request, ap. 19 Apr. 1536) and 126.

44 ACA, PK, 312, 1–2 (request, ap. 16 Nov. 1534).

The measures that were requested varied. It was not uncommon to specify terms of payment, which was either for a few months or for a longer period (three or four years). A partial discharge was sometimes granted, but never explicitly petitioned.[45] Exceptionally, the request and compromise stated a five-year term.[46] Yet many requests were rather vague in what was demanded: often only an "*inductie*" (i.e. an invitation of all or some creditors) was requested or a "reasonable" compromise ("*appointement*").[47] In every request, commissioners were solicited, and sometimes *nominatim*. In some cases, the request targeted "unwilling" creditors; asking for commissioners then served the purpose of pressuring such creditors into accepting an agreement that had been signed by a number of other creditors of the applicant.[48]

When receiving an invitation of the princely council to which a petition for a *lettre de justice* was attached, the Antwerp aldermen appointed one or two aldermen or another official (usually one of the two commissioners was the city secretary), who then supervised the negotiations and who represented the debtor in meetings of creditors. It was typical for sixteenth-century Antwerp that merchants were only appointed to become aldermen as an exception.[49] Because the supervision of debt negotiations in the case of a princely request was considered a privilege of aldermen in the city council, commissioners were members of this council or they worked for it as public officer. Merchants were thus not invited to preside over the talks. Upon their appointment, the commissioners either went to the homes of creditors or they could summon some of them to the city hall. It seems that there was no public announcement attached to these actions: no proclamations or public statements were made. Visits and invitations were discreet and also swift, even though this depended on the number of creditors and on their presence in the city. Even in complex cases, with multiple sessions of negotiations, it took no more than three weeks for the commissioners to inform the Council of Brabant of the results.[50] The debtor himself was usually not present at the talks,[51]

---

45 See for some examples of modest discharges: Puttevils 2012, pp. 292–297.

46 ACA, PK, 271, 43 (*s.d.*, *c.* 1544).

47 E.g. ACA, PK, 312, 5–6 (request, ap. Oct. 1540).

48 E.g. ACA, PK, 312, 28 (request, ap. 12 Oct. 1540).

49 Marnef, Guido: *Antwerp in the Age of Reformation: Underground Protestantism in a Commercial Metropolis, 1550–1577*. Johns Hopkins University Press: Baltimore (MD), 1996, 17.

50 E.g. ACA, PK, 271, 5 (Oct. 1535).

51 Exceptions are ACA, PK, 271, 6 (12 Nov. 1535). However, in this case only one creditor was invited, because he was the only one being "unwilling" to grant postponements.

although he could give instructions to the commissioners.[52] In preparation for the meetings, a *bilan* (also called "*presentatie*") was made, containing an overview of assets, debts and claims of the debtor, dividing the latter into good and bad debts.[53]

4. Defamation and rent-seeking strategies

The tactics of creditors could differ. When being confronted with invitations regarding debt adjustment, creditors faced the dilemma of accepting postponements or executing their debt through individual actions. An initial constraint for preventing invited creditors from attempting to cash in on their debts individually could be the belief that an agreed-upon solution would in the end result in higher rewards than a quick liquidation. Peer pressure from creditors sharing this view could reinforce such ideas. All thirteen files containing evidence of negotiations refer to multiple creditors accepting the terms proposed by the debtor. In only one case did all invited creditors consent to an agreement of postponed payments.[54] Yet it seems that in most cases coalitions could be formed in favour of the debtor's position.

However, not every creditor was easy-going or convinced of potential higher returns. In those cases, the authority of the Antwerp aldermen and their commissioners was a second constraint that resulted in a negotiated solution on many occasions. Commissioners made active use of their powers to persuade creditors. They could single out stubborn creditors, by calling them to the city hall for a private conversation.[55] Moreover, when creditors refused to comply with the proposals, the commissioners insisted that they submitted "reasons of refusal" in written form, to which the debtor was allowed to reply.[56] For a creditor who refused, this process brought about additional costs since it was common practice that such documents were drawn up by legal professionals. Also, this method resulted in protracted talks, thus increasing the pressure on all creditors. The involvement of the Antwerp aldermen often resulted in creditors being more or less obliged to comply with a proposed settlement.[57] If all invited creditors agreed, a contract was signed.[58]

---

52 ACA, PK, 312, 9–17 (request, ap. 19 April 1536). One of the two brothers who applied for a compromise suggested to the commissioners what they could offer to the creditors.
53 E.g. ACA, PK, 312, request and file (1536).
54 ACA, PK, 312, 9–17 (see footnote 52).
55 ACA, PK, 312, 9–17 (1536).
56 ACA, PK, 271, 6 (letter of commissioners 24 Oct. 1535).
57 E.g. ACA, PK, 271, 19 (July 1535).
58 ACA, PK, 271, 43 (*s.d.*, *c.* 1544).

When efforts toward convincing did not bear fruit, the commissioners usually advised the Council of Brabant to grant the postponements petitioned for. In a letter, they then argued why dissident creditors should be ignored, because the majority of creditors had reached an agreement,[59] for example, because of the limited amount owed to the rejecting party, and/or in view of the modesty of what was solicited.[60] The conclusions of the commissioners were important: in no less than eleven of the above-mentioned thirteen files containing the advice of the commissioners, these aldermen argued in favour of granting what had been asked, even though in ten of these eleven files, not all creditors accepted the debtor's offer.

These actions, for a large part, resulted from the more or less realistic requests of applicants. When occasionally excessive demands were made, the commissioners could easily brush them aside. In 1545, Jan Matthijs filed for re-negotiation of his debts, which comprised several hundred pounds groat Flemish (the exact numbers are not mentioned in the documents). He asked for postponement for eight years. Given the amount of debt and the number of creditors (around forty), the commissioners did not put much effort into soliciting approval from the creditors. Instead, they simply mentioned the latter's refusal to accept the proposed terms, and then argued that the applicant was a man of good faith, but since it was unlikely that debts would be repaid, *cessie van goede* was advisable.[61]

The constraints mentioned here were not any guarantee of success. Creditors could leave the negotiating table and go to the municipal court on their own behalf. The exemptions that were associated with the (provisional) granting of *lettres de justice* were not absolute. Petitioners commonly demanded protection against arrest and attachment during the talks ("*sûreté de corps [et de biens]*"), but even if *lettres de justice* conferred such benefits, creditors could start a proceeding for recovery of their debt. This was a viable option if the *lettre de justice* had a limited scope, which meant that it did not apply to the creditor. In one case, English merchants proceeded against a debtor who had applied for a *lettre de justice*, stating that such a *lettre* did not correspond with the privileges of the English *nation* in Antwerp and that it thus had no effect with regard to their debt.[62] But even when *sûreté de corps et de biens* had been granted in an applicable princely letter, a regular debt proceeding remained an option. Lawsuits for debts could be filed since the protection of *sûreté de corps et de biens* only concerned attachments of assets and personal arrest and detention, and it did not rule out ordinary

59 ACA, PK, 312, 126–130 (letter of commissioners Febr. 1549 ns).

60 ACA, PK, 271, 20 (letter of commissioners 13 Jan. 1545 ns).

61 ACA, PK, 271, 54 (letter of commissioners 15 Dec. 1545).

62 ACA, PK, 312, 9–17 (1536).

proceedings. There are examples of creditors bringing a lawsuit on their debts while deliberately attacking princely letters before the Antwerp aldermen, with arguments as to the fraudulent statements of the applicant.[63] Allegations that the debtor was "a bankrupt" were common.[64] This label encompassed connotations of fraud, and such defamatory practices could serve several purposes. Assertions could be directed against the granted *lettre de justice*, for which the condition was that the applicant could not be reproached for malicious acts. Another goal could be to push the decisions of negotiating creditors towards not accepting an agreement. A possible side-effect was that spectacular accusations could incite others who had claims against the debtor but had not been invited to the talks.[65] In lawsuits and negotiations, debtors could easily be branded as bankrupts, if their creditors choose to do so, and it seems that such labelling could be unfounded. A certain Peter van Leemputten, for example, who had applied for debt negotiations in 1537, was mentioned in a 1545 file as "a bankrupt" in reference to the 1537 facts, even though this label had never been used during the negotiations from that earlier time.[66]

If the debtor had filed for re-negotiation of his debts first, any charge of bankruptcy could be discussed during the talks supervised by the commissioners, and eventually these aldermen decided whether or not they were true.[67] However, if a creditor's proceedings had been initiated after the negotiations had begun, it was not possible for the commissioners to halt or suspend the proceedings. This move would have gone against the powers of the litigating parties, as well as the overall passive attitude and reluctance of judges, which was a typical feature of procedural principles during this time period. Commissioned officials could try to pressure a creditor into abandoning or suspending his actions, though. In one case, the commissioners advised the Council of Brabant to compel that a trial be stopped, even though this was technically not possible.[68]

63 ACA, V, 1233, f. 38 (15 Jan. 1504 ns).

64 ACA, V, 144, f. 18v (27 Jan. 1542 ns).

65 The complex debt relations in the Antwerp market meant that the list of invited creditors was largely written in accordance with the debtor's statements, especially when he did not keep books.

66 ACA, PK, 271, 13 (1537) and ACA, PK, 271, 54 (letter of commissioners of 15 Dec. 1545).

67 In one file, they proved to be true: ACA, PK, 271, 63 (letter of commissioners 16 Dec. 1544)

68 ACA, PK, 312, 9–17 (1536). It is unclear what the outcome was. The advice is remarkable since it was not allowed for a judge or court to call an end to an ongoing proceeding, and certainly not on the basis of policy considerations.

The lack of procedural threats also regarded payment plans that were signed by creditors. Even when an agreement had been reached, any creditor that did not sign it was not bound by its terms. It was only at the beginning of the seventeenth century that moratoria and compromises among the majority of creditors had to be honoured by other creditors as well.[69] In his *Descrittione di tutti I Paesi Bassi* (1567), Guicciardini mentions the fact that in Antwerp creditors could only be bound if they had consented with the provisions of the agreement.[70]

All in all, the constraints mentioned were rather weak. An efficient procedural framework forcing creditors into talks and agreements was lacking for the most part. If, by proceeding against the debtor, creditors wanted to challenge the aim of the Antwerp administrators in seeking a compromise, they could do so. One creditor alone could seriously damage the negotiations by starting a proceeding and thereby raising doubts among those who remained at the negotiating table. Yet in so doing, such dissenting "free riders" seriously challenged the authority of the municipal government, and a decision of this kind was probably not taken too lightly.[71]

What the new mindset for re-negotiation of debts allowed, then, was the buying of time. The debtor could continue his business at least during the talks as well as for a short period of time afterwards, for example, of a few months (which was the period that was most common). Lawsuits that had been started by unwilling creditors usually lasted longer than this limited period of relief. Thereafter persistent creditors could lay attachment and even apply for arrest. Since exemptions such as *sûreté de corps et de biens* and also terms agreed on in a settlement were temporary, creditors not wanting to be lenient could await their opportunity. A procedural framework that enshrined agency for litigants likewise ensured the persistence of the fifteenth-century mentality of defamation and culpability in many respects.

Conclusion

The Antwerp example shows that, after a period of transition, a procedure for voluntary bankruptcy was implemented that focused on cooperation between the debtor and his creditors and aimed at drawing up agreements of postponement

69 This was detailed in the 1608 Antwerp law book.

70 Guicciardini, Lodovico: *La Description de tous les Pais-Bas, autrement appellés la Germanie inférieure, ou Basse Allemagne*. Plantin: Antwerp 1582, pp. 108–109.

71 Unfortunately, how many persistent creditors that left the negotiations started proceedings while the talks were ongoing could not be checked. This is due to lacunae in the series of judgments of the municipal court of Antwerp for the period 1533 until 1541.

of debt. This new practice came to be applied in the 1520s, and it followed from an earlier collectivity in bankruptcy among creditors, not to mention from a new attention towards "good bankrupts". The control enjoyed by Antwerp aldermen over the negotiations was crucial, for as commissioners they could attempt to persuade creditors into accepting a compromise, even though this action was not always successful. It seems from the Antwerp evidence that creditors were not *per se* averse to moratoria, and it can be presumed that they understood that under some circumstances leniency was also to their advantage. In this regard, a dichotomy between creditor-friendly and debtor-friendly measures and systems is not demonstrated in the Antwerp source material. At the same time, however, it seems that individual actions of creditors jeopardized the voluntary insolvency approach and that its best result was temporary relief. Liquidation remained the default proceeding in the long run. Even though creditors could in principle be convinced of the necessity of postponements, some of them were not. As independent agents, those free riders had the tools to depict the debtor as a fraud, and thus undermine his possibilities of definitive recovery. They could wait until the short-term exemptions expired.

The struggle between a compromise-oriented municipal government and free-acting individuals in debt collection, which could hamper negotiated solutions, went on throughout the sixteenth century. Near the end of the 1500s, the legal framework had integrated the negotiation strategy, but in practice defamation and a search for individual expropriation were still common, as had been the case in the 1400s. It seems that after around 1540 settlements became more practised than before, which is reflected in declining numbers of public announcements of liquidation proceedings and of summons for creditors to present their claims, as well as in several princely laws of the 1540s prohibiting debt settlements for criminal bankrupts.[72] Negotiations could start following a request to the Council of Brabant, they could remain extra-judicial, or they could be initiated even after allegations of criminal bankruptcy and the start of liquidation proceedings. High-level merchants commonly evaded official proceedings by organizing informal talks, but they still might be accused of bankruptcy and drawn into a trial. It was fairly typical of the new attitude towards debt negotiations that even under such circumstances creditor meetings were organized. The example of John Over is telling. He was the governor of the English Company of Merchant Adventurers.

72 De ruysscher 2008, pp. 325–326 and De ruysscher, Dave: 'Naer het Romeinsch recht alsmede den stiel mercantiel'. *Handel en recht in de Antwerpse rechtbank (16de–17de eeuw)*. UGA: Kortrijk 2009, pp. 320–327.

He owed considerable sums to his creditors and was publicly denounced as a bankrupt in January 1540, with an ordinance that invited creditors to present their debts. The correspondence of the agent of the Van der Molen house, which was one of the creditors, shows that in the course of February 1540 there had been a creditor meeting at which the debtor had offered to repay his debts to Van der Molen in kerseys and English cloth.[73] However, in spite of a tendency towards negotiations pursuant to financial problems or bankruptcy, liquidation was the proceeding that remained the easiest to prosecute. The only collectivization with lasting effects that was legally enforceable concerned the expropriation and distribution of proceeds from a public sale of assets. A request to the Council of Brabant could enforce talks, but the outcome was uncertain and mostly temporary. This situation did not change after 1540, either. As a consequence, the solutions of both these laws from 1516 and 1518 continued to prevail over the entire period of the Golden Age of Antwerp, lasting until the middle of the 1560s.[74] The result of innovations in the 1520s and 1530s was therefore a modest two-branched bankruptcy system for *bona fide* debtors, providing but temporary protection from actions of expropriation and detention.

73 Puttevils 2012, p. 295.

74 See for the second half of the sixteenth century, De ruysscher 2008, pp. 325–326 and De ruysscher, Dave: 'Naer het Romeinsch recht alsmede den stiel mercantiel'. *Handel en recht in de Antwerpse rechtbank (16de–17de eeuw)*. UGA: Kortrijk 2009, pp. 320–327.

Klas Nyberg & Håkan Jakobsson

Stockholm University

Negotiations, credit and trust in Northern Europe: institutional efficiency in the handling of bankruptcies in late eighteenth-century Stockholm

Introduction

To minimise the damage from personal bankruptcies, an institutional administration of the bankruptcy procedure was introduced in many places in medieval and early-modern Europe. One of the key aims of the administration was to secure the assets and divide them between the creditors, and to remove the possibility for creditors to profit from a bankruptcy through compulsion and manipulation.[1] A substantial body of research has shown that the bankruptcy-institution was further improved and enlarged in Europe and in the United States during the period of modernization and industrialization in the eighteenth- and early nineteenth century.[2] The advances were important for the creation of a more stable financial

1 Fryde, Edmund: "The Bankruptcy of the Scali of Florence in England 1326–1328". In: Britnell, R. / Hatcher, J. (eds.): *Progress and problems in medieval England: Essays in honour of Edward Miller.* Cambridge University Press: Cambridge, 1996, pp. 107–120; Jones, William John: "The Foundations of English Bankruptcy. Statutes and Commissions in the Early Modern Period". *Transactions of the American Philosophical Society* 69(3), 1979; Muldrew, Craig: *The Economy of Obligation: The Culture of Credit and Social Relations in Early Modern England.* Macmillan: Basingstoke 1998; Agge, Ivar: "Några drag av det svenska konkursförfarandets utveckling". In: *Minnesskrift ägnad 1734 års lag av jurister i Sverige och Finland.* Stockholm 1934; Safley, Thomas Max: "Bankruptcy: Family and Finance in Early Modern Augsburg". *The Journal of European Economic History* 29(1), 2000. Safley, Thomas Max (ed.): *The history of bankruptcy. Economic, social and cultural implications in early modern Europe.* Routledge: New York 2013.

2 Finn, Margot C.: *The character of credit. Personal debt in English culture, 1740–1914.* Cambridge University Press: Cambridge 2003; Markham, Lester V.: *Victorian Insolvency. Bankruptcy, Imprisonment for Debt, and Company Winding-Up in Nineteenth-Century England.* Clarendon Press: Oxford 1995; Mann, Bruce H.: *Republic of debtors: Bankruptcy in the age of American Independence.* Harvard University Press: Cambridge

platform for entrepreneurs and merchants who depended on credits when conducting normal business-operations.

This article examines the function of the institutional administration of bankruptcies in late eighteenth-century Stockholm, and in particular the role of the various individuals that were entrusted to handle the bankruptcy-process, including local civil servants, state officials, administrative trustees, creditors and their proxies. An underlying aim of the analysis is to show that concepts such as credit, security and insolvency, in the early-modern period were considered in more than strictly economic terms. Financial relations between individuals and companies based on promissory notes, cheques and bills of exchange, were embedded in different types of networks based on social and professional relations, kinship, gender, ethnicity and confession.

It is well known that financial survival for merchants and entrepreneurs in the early-modern period required a raft of different strategies.[3] A career as a merchant was often begun after a long period of training as a trade apprentice and commercial clerk. When a former clerk was accepted to operate as an independent merchant or wholesaler, his solvency was guaranteed by sponsors, normally two established traders of good repute. The earlier training in this scenario was not just a learning period, but also a period when the future merchant built up his creditworthiness. Established merchants and entrepreneurs used other strategies, for example by making sure that financing was secured through many smaller, instead

2002; Hansen, Bradley: "Commercial Associations and the Creation of a national Economy: The Demand for Federal Bankruptcy Law". *Business History Review* 72(1), 1998, pp. 86–113; Balleisen, Edward J.: *Navigating failure: Bancruptcy and commercial society in antebellum America*. University of North Carolina Press: Chapel Hill 2001; Skeel, David A.: *Debt's dominion: A history of bankruptcy law in America*. Princeton University Press: Princeton 2001; Welamson, Lars, *Konkursrätt*, Norstedt: Stockholm 1961; Gratzer, Karl / Sjögren, Hans (eds.): *Konkursinstitutets betydelse i svensk ekonomi*. Gidlund: Hedemora 1999. Marriner, Sheila: "English bankruptcy records and statistics before 1850". *Economic History Review* 33(3), 1980, pp. 351–366; Hoppit, Julian: *Risk and failure in English Business 1700–1800*. Cambridge University Press: Cambridge 1987.

3 Mathias, Peter: "Strategies for Reducing Risk by Entrepreneurs in the Early Modern Period". In: Lesger, C. / Noordegraaf, L. (eds): *Entrepreneurs and entrepreneurship in early modern times: merchants and industrialists within the orbit of the Dutch staple market*. Stichting Hollandse Historische Reeks: Den Haag 1995, pp. 5–24; Spufford, Peter: "Access to credit and capital in the commercial centres of Europe". In: Davids, Karel / Lucassen, Jan: *A Miracle Mirrored: The Dutch Republic in European Perspective*. Cambridge University Press: Cambridge 1995, pp. 303–337.

of a few large creditors. In Stockholm during the eighteenth-century prominent financiers regularly monitored bankruptcies that involved fairly small amounts. Still, the chance of surviving a bankruptcy where the debt was held by numerous creditors, appears to have been greater than if the debt was held by few creditors, where each had a greater vested interest.[4]

Earlier research has indicated that the bankruptcy law of 1767 served as an important first step in the establishment of a modern bankruptcy-legislation in Sweden.[5] In this article we build on this assumption, when discussing the impact of a number of further laws and regulations introduced in the time-period between 1766 and 1773. While the changes in the legal system serve as a point of departure, much of the analysis and the results are based on empirical information and statistical data taken from actual bankruptcies. This huge, but previously little used source-material, enables us to show how the bankruptcy-system evolved practically in the period after the introduction of the new legislation. We suggest that the legal system was designed to safeguard credit networks and companies with the aim of reducing losses. In the end it led to a faster and more efficient administration of bankruptcies.[6]

---

4 Nyberg, Klas: *Säljes: Ull, Köpes: Kläde. Yllemanufakturens företagsformer i 1780-talets Stockholm*. Uppsala 1992, p. 175. For further discussions on credits, financing, bankruptcies and similar issues in Sweden during the eighteenth-century see: Nyberg, Klas / Jakobsson, Håkan: "Financial networks, migration and the transformation of the merchant elite in 18th century Stockholm". In: Safley 2013; Nyberg, Klas: "The early modern financial system and the informal credit market". In: Ögren, A. (ed.): *The Swedish Financial Revolution*. Palgrave: Basingstoke 2010, pp. 15–40; Nyberg, Klas: "Risk, tillit och kreditvärdighet: finansiella nätverk i 1700- och 1800-talets Stockholm". In: Nyberg, Klas (ed.) *Handel och risk. Fyra uppsatser från Ekonomisk-historiska mötet vid Umeå universitet 2005*. Uppsala 2007, pp. 57–85; Nyberg, Klas: "Finansiella nätverk – kredit- och egendomsförhållanden". In: Nyberg, Klas (ed.): *Kopparkungen. Handelshuset Björkman i Stockholm 1782–1824*. Stockholmia Förlag: Stockholm 2006, pp. 155–180; Nyberg, Klas: ""Jag existerar endast genom att äga kredit". Tillit, kreditvärdighet och finansiella nätverk i 1700-talets och det tidiga 1800-talets Stockholm". In: Berglund, Mats (ed.): *Sakta vi gå genom stan. Stadshistoriska studier tillägnade Lars Nilsson*. Stockholmia Förlag: Stockholm 2005, pp. 184–211; Nyberg, Klas: "Riksens ständers Manufakturkontor och dess förhistoria 1727–1766". In: *It all began in Old Town. A Swedish Banking History*. Sveriges riksbank: Stockholm 2002.

5 Welamson, pp. 7–17.

6 Some of the underlying ideas presented here have been previously discussed in: Nyberg, Klas / Hayen, Mats / Jakobsson, Håkan: *Credit, Trust and Financial Networks in 18th and 19th Century Stockholm*. (Unpublished paper, presented at the 9th European Social Science History Conference in Glasgow, 2012); Nyberg, Klas / Hayen, Mats /

Bankruptcy-cases at the Stockholm Court of Justice

All bankruptcy-cases studied as part of our investigation were filed in the Stockholm Court of Justice, the district court for the capital. Today the various archival series related to the bankruptcy-processes at the court can be found in the Stockholm City Archives.[7]

The material is highly diverse, covering bankruptcies from a broad spectrum of individuals, ranging from the least affluent to some of the wealthiest and highest-ranking members of society with vested interests in commerce and industry. The bankruptcy-files are still structurally similar, not least following from the fact that all bankruptcies were viewed and hence administered as personal, and not corporate bankruptcies. Though technically a second instance court, in cases of bankruptcies, the Stockholm Court of Justice functioned as a first instance court in the judicial system. When a verdict was appealed, the case was referred to the Svea Court of Appeal, one of several High Courts.[8]

The total number of cases of bankruptcies registered by the Stockholm Court of Justice between 1750 and 1849 was 16,588 (Figure 1). While fluctuating, the general picture is that of a long-term increase, from rather small numbers, with few long-lasting ruptures. Between 1750 and the middle of the 1760s the number of bankruptcy-cases hovered slightly below or around 50 per year. This shifted markedly from the end of the 1760s, when the annual number of cases suddenly rose to more than 100. From the 1780s until 1809, when a state-coup severely

---

Jakobsson, Håkan: *Analyzing industrial, commercial and financial bankruptcies in Stockholm, 1750–1850. The background, main sources and methods of a project at the Stockholm City Archives.* (Unpublished paper, presented at the XVIth World Economic History Congress in Stellenbosch, 2012).

7 Stockholms stadsarkiv (SSA), Stockholms magistrat och rådhusrätt, various series, principally including A3a, A4a, C5a, C11 and F6a. Most of the statistical, and much of the empirical data is also available in an on-line database at: www.tidigmodernakonkurser.se, compiled as part of a project funded by the Bank of Sweden Tercentenary Foundation.

8 A good introduction to the Stockholm Court of Justice during this period is Johanson, Ulla: "Stockholms magistrats och rådhusrätts arkiv 1720–1849. Ärendenas handläggning samt arkivets bestånd". *Stockholms stads arkivnämnd och stadsarkiv årsberättelse*, 1970, pp. 39–123; For the history and function of the Svea Court of Appeals see: Petrén, Sture / Jägerskiöld, Stig / O:son Nordberg, Tord: *Svea hovrätt: studier till 350-årsminnet.* Norstedt: Stockholm 1964; Wersäll, Fredrik et al. (eds.), *Svea hovrätt 400 år*. Norstedt: Stockholm 2014.

affected political life and the Swedish economy, the number of bankruptcy-cases generally stayed on a stable level, only rarely dropping below 150 per year. In 1811, for the first time since 1770 less than 100 bankruptcies were registered. Thereafter however, there was a steady growth, to a level of around 250 cases per year in the middle of the nineteenth-century.

Figure 1: Annual number of bankruptcy applications in Stockholm 1750–1849

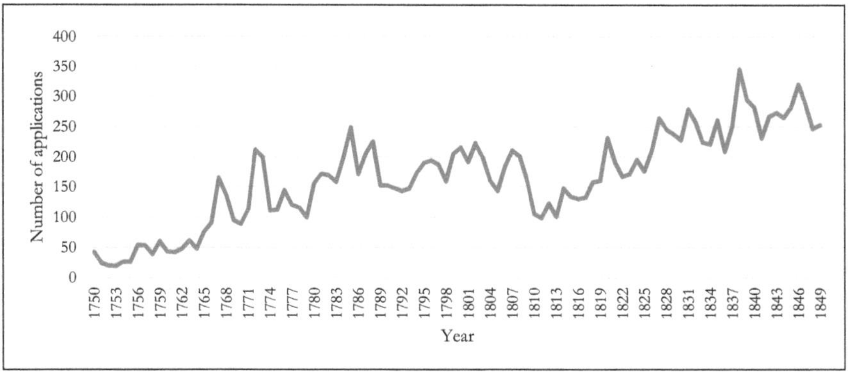

Source: SSA, Stockholms magistrat och rådhusrätt, C5a, Konkursdiarier, 1750–1849.

The long-term increase in the number of bankruptcies could possibly be considered as a natural by-product of a growing population. During the period Stockholm grew slowly, from a population of approximately 59,400 in 1750 to 91,545 in 1849 (Figure 2). While statistically an upward movement, the growth was clearly very modest. While it cannot be ruled out that the growth in population played some part in the increasing number of bankruptcies, we see limited correlation between the growth and most short-term fluctuations. The fluctuations must instead be considered in the light of external factors that affected the financial climate. The unruly domestic situation in and around 1809 has been mentioned, a development triggered by the toppling of the ruling monarch Gustav IV Adolf (r. 1792–1809) and the introduction of a new liberal constitution. Interestingly, and perhaps somewhat surprisingly the situation seems to have led to fewer bankruptcies. The same can be said for the low numbers in 1786, 1789 and 1790, which coincided with the first instances of absolute rule by Gustav III (r. 1771–1792), and the Russo-Swedish war of 1788–1790 respectively. Peaks, such as 1772 and 1773, each with more than 200 registered bankruptcy-applications on the other hand can be viewed in connection to the change in government following a coup d'état in the summer of 1772.

Figure 2: Population-growth in Stockholm 1750–1849

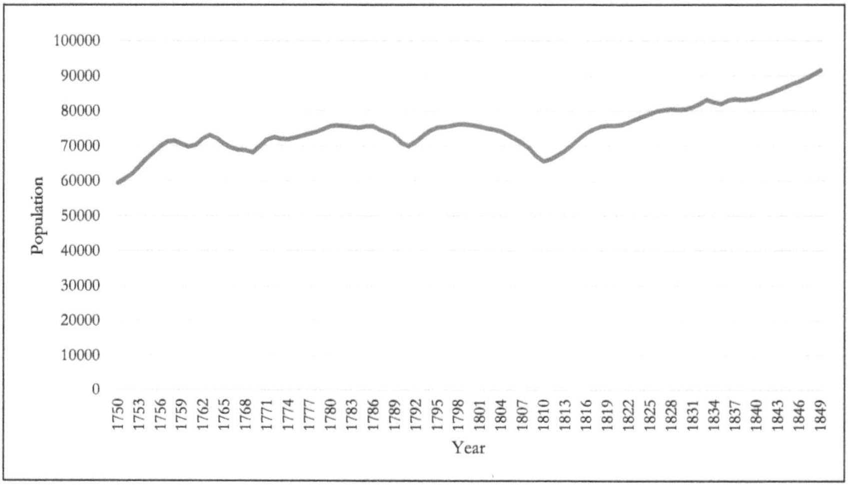

Source: *Statistisk årsbok för Stockholms stad för år 1905.* K. L. Beckman: Stockholm 1907, pp. 67–68.

The lack of progression in the local economy, and the effect which this situation had on artisans and the lower middle classes has been considered important reasons for the very fact that bankruptcies continued to plague the economy during the period. Söderberg, Jonsson and Persson have argued that: The series [of bankruptcy-cases] is to be regarded primarily as a general handicrafts and petty bourgeois business index. The majority of bankruptcies stemmed from handicraft masters, small dealers, and other individuals who were not engaged in medium-sized or large manufacturing.[9] A classification of the total number of bankruptcies according to occupational activities and titles supports this interpretation.[10] Throughout the period individuals involved in handicraft, including workers and laborers together constituted the largest group that applied for bankruptcy. The lack of development and the difficult conditions for workers and artisans still only partly explains the general trend of a growing number of bankruptcies. Over time

9 Söderberg, Johan / Jonsson, Ulf / Persson, Christer: *A Stagnating Metropolis. The Economy and Demography of Stockholm, 1750–1850.* Cambridge University Press: Cambridge 1991, pp. 152–153.

10 The classification (not presented here) is based on the so-called HISCO-system: Leeuwen, Marco H. D. van / Maas, Ineke / Miles, Andrew: *HISCO: historical international standard classification of occupations.* Leuven University Press: Leuven 2002.

an increasing number of individuals applied for bankruptcy in all occupational groups.

In the following we will turn our attention to the period in the late 1760s when the annual number of cases rose from a relatively stable low of around 50 to a level of more than 100 bankruptcy-cases per year. We have chosen to stress the impact of a new legislation, and in particular the improved handling of the bankruptcy-process that was introduced during this period. In our view, the improvement in the bankruptcy-process meant that it became easier to declare bankruptcy. Arguably, the improved efficiency in the handling of bankruptcies even created a positive incentive for individuals to declare bankruptcy.

The bankruptcy-process

A bankruptcy-process at the Stockholm Court of Justice was typically initiated after an individual approached the court with a request to enter into a state of bankruptcy and be protected from all creditors. In the bankruptcy-legislation that developed from the late 1760s, the court normally accepted the request, if certain procedures were followed correctly, and as long as the individual agreed to certain set terms and conditions. These conditions included providing a true account of all assets and credits, agreeing to surrender all property to the court and accepting a restriction of freedom of movement. The case was closed with the final ruling of the court, which established how the assets of the debtor should be distributed among the creditors.

All bankruptcy-cases, evolved along relatively similar lines, with set check-points, and meetings that had to be passed, in order for the next steps in the process to take place, or to be considered legitimate. The objective was to ensure that all documents were correct and all assets were accounted for, and that all creditors were informed and thus in a position to file their claims.

The first definition of the bankruptcy-process was made in the General Law of 1734. The treatment was brief, even though certain aspects were well-covered. This included the order in which creditors would regain the possession from a debtor, information that would remain more or less unchanged throughout the period of investigation. One major limitation in the 1734 law was the almost complete lack of details on the procedure and organization of a bankruptcy-case.[11]

11 *Sweriges Rikes Lag. Gillad och antagen på Riksdagen Åhr 1734.*

The first detailed rule of procedure for bankruptcy-proceedings was only published in the Bankruptcy Law of 1767. In the intervening years the Stockholm Court of Justice made use of odd paragraphs retrieved from other sections of the general law to define the process. The specifics of a bankruptcy, however meant that this left most aspects of the procedure uncovered, effectively leaving the scene open to indiscriminate and inefficient proceedings. The 1767 law and two additions with further clarifications published in 1768 and 1770, improved this situation, by laying down a complete procedure, covering all the various steps in the process. The changes and additions were incorporated and published in the Bankruptcy Law of 1773.[12]

The legal framework of the new regulation was not groundbreaking insofar as to provide an entirely new way to handle a bankruptcy-case. Indeed, as far as can be told, bankruptcy-cases also before the 1760s proceeded in roughly the same basic way as they did following the publication of the new law. The main novelty was the fact that the new regulations detailed how possible issues that could arise in the various meetings during the proceedings should be handled. The new decree in effect created a model for a more efficient court-procedure.[13]

That the new codification did little to change the basic structure of the process can be established when reviewing the multitude of documents and papers that were produced during a bankruptcy. Today this material exists in the form of bankruptcy-files. They remain structurally fairly similar both before and after the introduction of the new regulation. The documents in a bankruptcy-file were originally collected by the court during the ongoing process, and were subsequently bound together as a case-specific dossier.[14]

Practically all bankruptcy files include the application provided by the debtor, as well as the copy of the official declaration of a Day of Proclamation that was originally posted on the door of the court-building. Both documents were crucial

12 *Kongl. Maj:ts nådiga Förklaring, om hwad wid Fallisementer samt Cessions- och Concours twister hädanefter bör i akt-tagas. Gifwen i Stockholm i Råd-Cammaren then 8 Maji 1767*; *Kongl. Maj:ts Ytterligare Nådige Förklaring, Til i agt tagande wid Cessions- och Concours-twister. Gifwen Stockholm i Råd-Cammaren then 24 Martii 1768*; *Kongl. Maj:ts Nådige Förklaring, Om hwad wid Fallissemens- samt Cessions- och Concours-Twister hädanefter bör i akt tagas. Gifwen Stockholm i Råd-Kammaren then 23 Martii 1770*; *Kungl. Maj:ts Förnyade Nådiga Stadga, Angående Afträdes- och Förmons- samt Boskilnads- och Urarfwa mål. Gifwen Gripsholms Slott then 26 Augusti 1773.*

13 Jakobsson, Håkan: *Konkursens papper* (Unpublished paper, Stockholm 2012).

14 SSA, Stockholms magistrat och rådhusrätt, F6a, Konkursakter, huvudserie.

for the bankruptcy. Without a correct application and without a set date for the Day of Proclamation, a bankruptcy-case could not proceed, and was cancelled.

To a modern observer, the application undoubtedly stands out as one of the more interesting documents in the bankruptcy-file. Not only does it show personal reasoning and the general argumentation that the debtor provided to the court to support the request to declare bankruptcy. It also includes two further elements required by the court, namely a list of all assets, as well as a list of all creditors. Both the list of assets and the list of creditors were based on information provided by the debtor. The list of creditors is of particular interest. On its own it relates important information about the credit-networks of the debtor at the time of the application. More exactly it provides information on how the debtor viewed and reported the credit-network at the time of the application. As will be discussed later, it can however also be compared with a later list of the creditors, who actually registered their claims in person, taken down by the court at the Day of Proclamation.

A number of procedures existed to ensure that the list provided by the debtor at the Day of Application and the list compiled by the court at the Day of Proclamation provided the most correct representation of the credit-network. The list provided by the debtor at the Day of Application was for example required to be signed and was as a result viewed as a sworn statement. A subsequent preparatory meeting, held within a week of the application, made it possible for the court to assess the accuracy of the information. Only after having reached a conclusion about the validity of the application at the preparatory meeting, did the court set a date for the Day of Proclamation.

At the Day of Proclamation, all creditors with an interest in the bankruptcy, or their proxies were required to come before the court, and present their claims in writing, in double copies, before 12:00 noon. The meeting commenced with a general call, with all the names of the creditors taken down in a roll book. The creditors were thereafter required to take an extensive oath, with one hand on the bible, certifying before God that their respective claims were just and correct. Only thereafter were their claims accepted.

The procedures in connection to the Day of Application and on the Day of Proclamation were in our opinion designed to prevent fraud on the part of the debtor, and get rid of any opportunistic behavior on the part of the creditors. The true importance of the lists however lies in the time-span that they cover. Indeed, a comparison of the two lists almost always shows shifts in the credit-network between the Day of Application and the Day of Proclamation. The changes can often be further highlighted when reading the various documents, typically unpaid bills or other financial agreements that the creditors lodged to back their claims at the Day of Proclamation. We will come back to this later.

The role of the preparatory meeting

As discussed, a key meeting in the bankruptcy-process was held on the so-called Day of Proclamation, a day to which the creditors were called to lodge their claims against the debtor. Failing to appear at this point meant that a creditor was precluded from the final proceedings leading up to the verdict and the distribution of the assets.

As mentioned above, the Day of Proclamation had been preceded by a preparatory meeting, in our minds an equally important step in the process. The preparatory meeting was in all essentials a checkpoint introduced by the court to be able to judge the validity of the bankruptcy-application. To this preparatory meeting, the court called all creditors who were immediately available. The purpose was to have them verify that the financial statement and other information given by the debtor, was correct.[15]

The preparatory meeting suggests that the bankruptcy-process was constructed, not solely as a process decided and presided over by appointed professionals, but as a process that also involved and relied on respected members of the local community. The nature of the process, with the call for the immediately available creditors, meant that the creditors that appeared at the first meeting almost exclusively were individuals who resided in Stockholm. They were furthermore individuals with a position that enabled them to leave their normal day-to-day business to attend the meeting. This in effect meant that the meeting gathered a local business-elite, self-employed individuals who both had knowledge of the bankruptcy-applicant as a person and a good understanding of the role and function of the applicant in the local economy.

Interestingly, the meeting could also lead to the conclusion of the entire bankruptcy-process. The cancellation was ultimately in the hands of the court. The information on which the court based its decision was however provided by the creditors that showed up at the meeting. Our main point is that the meeting often functioned as a way for the creditors and debtors to find common ground, and

15 The date of the preparatory meeting can normally be found in the diary in which the court recorded the different steps in ongoing bankruptcy-proceedings. The diary exists from the first years of the eighteenth-century, but only includes the full range of information from the 1770s. The date of the meeting before this point can often be found by reviewing the bankruptcy-files and the general session-protocols of the Court of Justice. The bankruptcy-diaries can be found in SSA, Stockholms magistrat och rådhusrätt, C5a, Konkursdiarier. The diaries have been scanned and manually registered, and are searchable on-line as well as available as downloadable PDF-documents at www.tidigmodernakonkurser.se.

potentially control and settle the economic situation before it was made public in connection to the Day of Proclamation. The meeting was an opportunity for members of societies, guilds and other religious- or language-based groups, individuals who often appeared as creditors to an applicant, and were members of the same institutions, to avoid a costly and damaging process.

Investigations of bankruptcy-proceedings in cases of bankruptcies in the period between 1782 and 1810, involving Jewish members of the Stockholm community, show that a substantial number of the bankruptcy-applications never led to a bankruptcy. Out of 74 applications, only 41 led to an actual bankruptcy. Closer investigation reveals that a majority of the bankruptcies that were cancelled, were stopped in the context of the preparatory meeting, after settlements involving other members of the Jewish community.[16] We believe this pattern was similar in other close-knit groups with a common background and mutual reliance, at least in the pre-industrial society that dominated in Stockholm in the late eighteenth and early nineteenth century. With the advent of a less close-knit community, this tendency probably gradually disappeared.[17]

Further regulations

In December 1766, half a year before the publication of the Bankruptcy Law of 1767, and hence before the legislation which clarified the different steps in the

---

16 Jakobsson, Håkan: *Konkurser bland judiska handelsmän i Stockholm 1780–1810.* (Unpublished paper presented at the Swedish Economic-history Conference in Uppsala, 2009).

17 Such close-knit groups included the trade-societies that were formed in the late 1730s and early 1740s, to administer the interests and affairs of merchants, industrialists and artisans in Stockholm. The role of the society of wholesalers, the largest and most important of the societies has been extensively discussed in Nyberg, Klas / Jakobsson, Håkan: *Storköpmän som samhällskraft: Borgerskap och Grosshandelssocietet i Stockholm,* I (1736–1850). Informationsförlaget: Stockholm 2012. Next to the Jewish religious group, a strong common religious bond also existed in the French and German congregations. For the French community see: Bedoire, Fredric: *Hugenotternas värld: från religionskrigens Frankrike till skeppsbroadelns Stockholm.* Bonnier: Stockholm 2009, also available in French as: *Le monde des huguenots: de la France des guerres de religion au Stockholm de la noblesse marchande.* H. Champion: Paris 2013. A short overview of the history of the German congregation in Stockholm: Schieche, Emil: *400 Jahre Deutsche St. Gertruds Gemeinde in Stockholm 1571–1971: Festschrift.* Stockholm 1971. The standard-work on the Jewish congregation in Stockholm during this period is: Valentin, Hugo: *Judarnas historia i Sverige.* Bonnier: Stockholm 1924 and by the same author: *Urkunder till judarnas historia i Sverige.* Bonnier: Stockholm 1924.

bankruptcy-procedure, a decree was introduced that improved the security and stability in the bankruptcy-process by addressing the questions of distraint and debtors' prison.[18]

Before 1766, when a debtor failed to pay a debt, a creditor could do one of two things, either extend the debt-time-period, or protest and take the matter to the office of the Stockholm governor. If the claim was deemed legitimate, the debtor's belongings were placed under the threat of distraint, that is to say, under the threat of possible seizure. If the debtor had no money or objects of value, he or she would be placed in debtors' prison, until the debt was settled.[19] The right of the creditors to use distraint or debtors' prison was sanctioned in the General Law of 1734 and subsequently explained in several decrees and official letters from the Court of Appeals.[20]

The only way for a debtor to escape the threat of distraint or debtors' prison was to travel to another country (typically Copenhagen or Christiania (Oslo) in Denmark-Norway), and then send an application of free passage to the Swedish king. The nature of the situation made the process laborious. If the request was granted, the king's letter made it possible for the debtor to return to Sweden and try to settle the matter. If necessary the debtor could then declare bankruptcy, with the option to voluntarily surrender all goods to the creditors, and thus avoid arrest. Until the Court of Justice ruled in the matter, the debtor could use the king's letter to ward off possible threats of distraint and debtors' prison.

Before 1766, if the debtor chose to stay in Sweden and opted to declare bankruptcy, the threat of distraint or debtors' prison still did not disappear. At any time

---

18 *Kongl. Maj:ts Nådige Förordning Angående Rymmande för Gäld. Gifwen Stockholm i Råd-Cammaren then 11. Decembr. 1766.* We are grateful to Mats Hayen for drawing our attention to this decree. It has been discussed more extensively in Nyberg / Hayen / Jakobsson (Stellenbosch, 2012).

19 On debtors' prison and associated issues see: Gratzer, Karl: "Default and Imprisonment for Debt in Sweden: From the Lost Chances of a Ruined Life to the Lost Capital of a Bankrupt Company". In: Gratzer, Karl / Stiefel, Dieter (eds.): *History of Insolvency and Bankruptcy from an International Perspective*. Södertörn Academic Studies: Huddinge 2008, pp. 34–43.

20 See for example: *Kongl. Maj:ts nådige Förklaring, angående Lagens rätta förstånd uti 5. Cap. 10. §. Utsöknings-Balken, om Gäldenärs bysättning. Dat. 19 October 1750*; *Kongl. Maj:ts Förklaring, huru i anledning af Förordningen then 19 Maji 1756 med owilkorliga förskrifningar, hwilka Gardes- och andre Soldater samt Ryttare och Dragoner af the wäfwade och indelte Regementer och Båtsmän kunna utgifwa, bör förhållas. Dat. 12 October 1757*; *Kongl. Swea Håf-Rätts Bref, angående beswär i mål, rörande bysättning å then, hwilke hos Domaren sökt cessionem bonorum. Dat. 20 Decemb 1757.*

during the bankruptcy-process the creditors could try to seize money or belongings from the debtor. Following the issue of the new decree, the creditors' right to seize the property, or call for the placement of the debtor in debtors' prison was removed, for the entire time-period from the initiation of a bankruptcy-process to the verdict. From this point onwards every bankruptcy-application, if accepted by the Court of Justice, was given the same status as a letter of free passage issued by the king, protecting the debtor from distraint and debtors' prison. As most cases of bankruptcy continued for at least 18 months or more, the protection was a substantial and important development.

The official reason for the issue of the new decree was the significant rise in bankruptcy-cases that began in 1763 and continued up until 1766. The background was an international banking crisis, with its origin in Amsterdam that quickly spread to Hamburg and other financial markets across Europe.[21] Between 1763 and 1766 an alarming number of Swedes fled abroad because of debt, with potentially highly damaging effects on the economy. Protection against distraint and debtors' prison during cases of bankruptcy was further sanctioned in a new decree issued in 1767 and also in the bankruptcy-law of 1773.[22]

It is likely that the rise in the annual number of bankruptcy-applications from the end of the 1760s, can be explained not only as an effect of a stagnating economy, but also because of the fact that a larger number of individuals every year, actively chose to apply for bankruptcy, instead of as before flee the country. The new legislation turned the prospect of bankruptcy into something that the debtor, to a much higher degree than before, could benefit from. After the 1760s, a bankruptcy was not necessarily an unwanted last resort for the debtor. In many cases it was a rational, conscious choice that made efficient use of the protection offered by the legal system.

---

21 The literature on the crisis is fairly extensive. Some of the classic treatments include: Dillen, J. G. van: "De beurscrisis te Amsterdam in 1763". *Tijdschrift voor geschiedenis* 37, 1922; Jong-Keesing, Elisabeth Emmy de: *De Economische crisis van 1763 te Amsterdam*. N.V. Intern. Uitgevers en h. Mij: Amsterdam 1939 and Skalweit, Stephan: *Die Berliner Wirtschaftskrise von 1763 und ihre Hintergründe*. W. Kohlhammer: Stuttgart 1937. For a modern treatment, with a bearing on the financial turmoil in the early 21st century see: Schnabel, Isabel / Shin, Hyun Song: "Liquidity and contagion: the crisis of 1763". *Journal of the European Economic Association* 2(6), 2004, pp. 929–968.

22 *Kongl. Maj:ts nådiga Förklaring, om hwad wid Fallisementer samt Cessions- och Concours twister hädanefter bör i akt tagas. Dat. Then 8 Maji 1767; Kongl. Maj:ts förnyade Stadga, angående Afträdes- och Förmåns- samt Boskilnads och Urarfwa mål. Dat. then 26 Augusti 1773.*

The rule of preclusion

In May 1767 another important decree was issued. It introduced the concept of preclusion to the Day of Proclamation.[23] Preclusion meant that creditors, who failed to show up on the Day of Proclamation, either in person or by proxy, lost all further rights in the case.[24]

The decree further underlined the Day of Proclamation as a very important day in the entire bankruptcy-process. Before 1767 it was possible for creditors to present their claims after the Day of Proclamation, and in many cases add claims to an ongoing case. After 1767 this was not possible anymore. Another consequence was that creditors only could be removed from the network after the Day of Proclamation, not added to it. This is interesting from a methodological perspective as it makes it possible to analyze how the Day of Proclamation affected the creditors. This can be done by comparing the network presented by the debtor on the Day of Application with the network at the end of the Day of Proclamation. The impact has been studied as part of an analysis of bankruptcies by employees at the Royal Opera in Stockholm between 1773 and 1792. During this period a total of 34 applications by opera-employees were accepted by the Stockholm Court of Justice. It is clear that the Day of Proclamation had an important effect on the networks. In total 328 creditors appeared in the 34 applications before the Day of Proclamation. Only 68 percent, or 223 creditors, remained after the Day of Proclamation.[25]

Available data suggests that the rule of preclusion worked differently for different groups of creditors. The new legislation created a new kind of economic arena, a kind of bankruptcy-process arena. This arena was utilized by certain groups to their advantage, but worked negatively for other groups. It was clearly better suited for persons who were accustomed to the workings of the financial and judicial world than for people that appeared as creditors based on unpaid services or goods. Wholesalers, merchants and accountants, as well as members of the law, including notaries, clerks and similar occupations typically negotiated the market more efficiently than shoemakers, general dealers, or owners of drinking establishments.

---

23 *Kongl. Maj:ts nådiga Förklaring, om hwad wid Fallisementer samt Cessions- och Concours twister hädanefter bör i akt tagas. Dat. Then 8 Maji. [1767].*

24 On preclusion see Agge, pp. 931–933.

25 Hayen, Mats: "*Bakom kulisserna på Gustav III:s opera. Konkurser för personal vid Kungliga Teatern, 1773–1792*", (forthcoming article).

The interesting thing however is that the situation not only affected the creditors, insofar as to ensure that creditors with good connections, a good information-network and time on their hands, were in a position to secure outstanding capital, and vice versa that creditors with none of these opportunities, and abilities, had limited possibility to do the same. Indeed, the new system also made it possible for the debtor to use a bankruptcy as a way to improve a financial position before the final verdict of the court. Calculations suggest that some 15–35 percent of the total sum of claims disappeared on the Day of Proclamation, leaving the debtor in a much better position when the bankruptcy-process entered its latter stages.

A more efficient process

One important result of the new legislation was a new emphasis on the need to limit the duration of the bankruptcy-process. A call to ensure a swift handling of the bankruptcy-applications was already included in the 1767 bankruptcy law. In 1768 the Svea Court of Appeals followed up on this when issuing a letter that instructed all second-tier courts to handle cases of bankruptcy with promptness. It also requested the courts to deliver lists of all cases that had been brought to a successful end, or otherwise risk fines.[26] The call was an effort to bring old unfinished cases to conclusion. It should however also be viewed as a response to the new protection against distraint and debtors' prison that guarded the debtor during the bankruptcy-process. While the 1766 decree protected the debtor, the Svea Court of Appeal came to the protection of the creditors, by trying to limit the duration of the process and hence the period during which the protection would remain in place. In reality the focus was on the final step in the process, or the actual verdict. While the debtor and the creditors could influence the duration of a bankruptcy-case, the court and more specifically the presiding judge had the most important influence on the timeframe of a bankruptcy, as the sole provider of a verdict.[27] The immediate effect of the call is difficult to analyze due to the lack of sufficient information for the period immediately after 1768. For the period after 1785, however, available data shows an ongoing clear downward trend, and long-term a drastic reduction in the duration of bankruptcy-cases handled by the Stockholm Court of Justice (Figure 3).

---

26 Johanson, p. 73; *Kongl. Swea Hofrätts Bref til derunder hörande domstolar om skyndesamt afgörande af cessions och concurs twister, 31 oktober 1768.*

27 Agge, pp. 915–937.

Figure 3: Average number of days from application to verdict for cases of bankruptcy begun in a given year 1785–1849

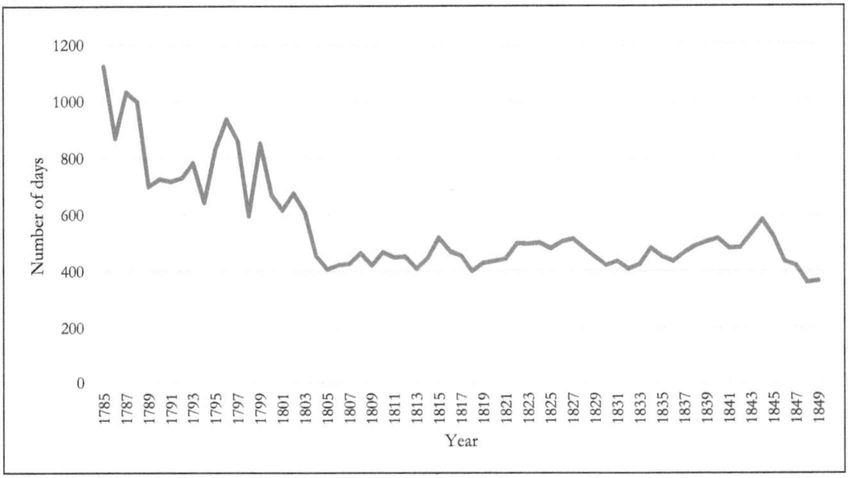

Source: SSA, Stockholms magistrat och rådhusrätt, C5a, Konkursdiarier, 1785–1849.

Importantly, the trend cannot be seen as a result of new legislation introduced after 1773. While three further bankruptcy-laws were published after the 1773 bankruptcy-law, namely in 1798, 1818 and 1830, few changes to the bankruptcy-process that would have affected the duration of the process were introduced.[28] The increased efficiency was instead most likely the result of the factors that were established in the time-frame between 1767 and 1773, including the improved practical handling of the bankruptcy-process, but also the principle that processes had to be concluded as quickly as possible.

Conclusions

In this article we have highlighted the role of the modernization of bankruptcy laws and procedures and the interplay between private and public administrators in the administration of the bankruptcy-process in late eighteenth-century

28 *Kungl. Maj:ts Förnyade Nådiga Stadga, Angående Afträdes- och Förmons- samt Boskilnads- och Urarfwa-Mål. Gifwen Stockholms Slott den 28 Junii 1798; Concurs-Lag; Gifwen Stockholms Slott å Rikssalen den 13 Julii 1818; Concurs-Lag gifwen Stockholms Slott å Rikssalen d. 12 Mars 1830. Med sedermera deri skedda förändringar.* Stockholm 1849.

Sweden. In Stockholm, civil servants, appointed by the city administrated the bankruptcy, in collaboration with key members of organizations such as guilds and societies. Specially appointed trustees with a strong position in the local economy, with links to industry, good personal credit, and with thorough knowledge of the debtor's business, played key roles in the proceedings. The same can be said of municipal, state and private representatives, typically with a high level of trust, who acted for the state, for local institutions or for absent or foreign claimants.

In the period between 1766 and 1773 the Swedish state and the court-system combined to bring about a comprehensive overhaul of the entire bankruptcy-regulation. The results were in many ways impressive. In a few years, a better organized and structured bankruptcy-process was presented and implemented. Old inefficient procedures that threatened not only the workings of the bankruptcy-system, but also theoretically the underpinnings of society were removed. New check-points were introduced to diminish the possibility that single bankruptcies could damage society and individual creditors. The system opened up the possibility to negotiate settlements, before the bankruptcy was made public. The involvement of private actors in the bankruptcy-process, also improved the possibility that unnecessary bankruptcies could be avoided.

Overall the entire bankruptcy-process at the Stockholm Court of Justice became much more time-efficient following a range of attempts to speed up the process in 1767 and 1768. Most noticeably this can be seen in the dramatic drop in the average length of bankruptcy-cases from application to verdict. Between 1785 and 1805, the duration of this process almost halved from on average around 1000 days to around 500 days, and thereafter remained relatively unchanged throughout the rest of the period.[29]

In studies of the Paris credit market between 1690 and 1840 Philip Hoffman and colleagues have shown the significance of public notaries in ensuring the working and function of the private credit market.[30] The notaries helped, among

---

29 A bankruptcy-process in Sweden today has a typical duration of 2 years. *Doing Business 2012: Doing Business in a More Transparent World*. The World Bank: Washington 2012, p. 129.

30 Hoffman, Philip T. / Postel–Vinay, Gilles / Rosenthal, Jean–Laurent: *Priceless Markets. The Political Economy of Credit in Paris 1660–1870*. The University of Chicago Press: Chicago 2000; Hoffman, Philip T. / Postel–Vinay, Gilles / Rosenthal, Jean–Laurent: "Private Credit Markets in Paris, 1690–1840". *The Journal of Economic History*, 1992, pp. 293–306; Hoffman, Philip T. / Postel–Vinay, Gilles / Rosenthal, Jean–Laurent: "*Redistribution and Long-Term Private Debt in Paris, 1660–1726*". *Journal of Economic History*, 1995, pp. 256–284. See also Grantham, George: "Review of: Priceless markets:

other things, to stabilize the credit networks by applying strict regulations governing public loans. The institution of notary underlines the important role played by trusted public actors and institutions in ensuring the function of credit in business undertakings and in the general economy. In this article we have built further on this idea, when suggesting that the interplay between public and private actors in the handling of claimants in bankruptcy proceedings should be viewed as an important aspect of the history of the credit market.

The political economy of credit in Paris, 1660–1870". *Journal of Economic Literature* 40, 2002, pp. 559–561; Arrunada, B.: "The economics of notaries". *European Journal of Law and Economics* 3(1), 1996.

Magnus Ressel

Norms and Practice of Handling Complex and International Insolvencies in Early Modern Venice

Introduction

The "German Nation" (*Nazione Alemanna*) in eighteenth century Venice was an important and privileged group of merchants and even merchant dynasties that had a substantial stake in most of the transalpine trade routes between northeastern Italy and Upper Germany. Dense family links to the imperial cities and towns of southwestern Germany and the secret upholding of an officially prohibited Lutheran church characterized this community.[1] The Republic had consciously decided to retain the *Nazione Alemanna* in the seventeenth and eighteenth century and to give it significant support in the form of commercial privileges, since its members connected Venice not only via the transalpine routes to the central European markets but also via the sea lanes to the wider north European world, namely London, Amsterdam and Hamburg.[2] The intense trade connections to the more advanced centers of Western capitalism made this group particularly

1 On the strong family relations to southwestern Germany, especially Swabia, cf.: Simonsfeld, Henry: *Der Fondaco dei Tedeschi in Venedig und die deutsch-venetianischen Handelsbeziehungen, Vol. 2*, Stuttgart 1887, pp. 164–217; Kellenbenz, Hermann: "Die Wirtschaft der schwäbischen Reichsstädte zwischen 1648 und 1740". *Jahrbuch für Geschichte der oberdeutschen Reichsstädte* 11, 1965, pp. 128–165; on the secret upholding of the Lutheran confession by the Germans in eighteenth century Venice cf. esp.: Oswald, Stephan: *Die Inquisition, die Lebenden und die Toten. Venedigs deutsche Protestanten*, Sigmaringen 1989.

2 It is interesting to note that after 1720 many Dutch merchants left Italy alongside an overall retreat from Mediterranean markets. German merchants in Venice and Livorno, coming in the former case mostly from southern and in the latter case mostly from northern Germany, replaced the Dutch, cf.: Beutin, Ludwig: *Der deutsche Seehandel im Mittelmeergebiet bis zu den napoleonischen Kriegen*, Neumünster 1933, pp. 51–72; Wood, Alfred: *A History of the Levant Company*, London 1935, pp. 136–178; Georgelin, Jean: *Venise au siècle des lumières*, Paris 1978, pp. 667–684; Israel, Jonathan: "The Phases of the Dutch straatvaart (1590–1713)". *Tijdschrift voor Geschiedenis*, 99(1), 1986, pp. 1–30, here pp. 28–30; Schulte Beerbühl, Margrit: "Zwischen England, Deutschland und Italien. Protestantische Handels- und Familiennetze im 18. Jahrhundert". In:

vulnerable to international economic crises. Thus, every case of failure of a German merchant inevitably affected not only Venetian businesses but also foreign partners far away in countries with diverse languages. The handling of insolvencies of Germans was therefore a complicated affair. Merchants from diverse countries had to be contacted and involved in procedures that should in the end lead to a settlement accord between all parties concerned. Venetian norms and regulations for insolvencies could conflict with different international regulations and some compromise along the lines of international commercial custom had to be sought and formed via the inevitably slow postal communication. The strong preference of the legislators for an "accord" and the corresponding aim of avoiding a "trial" is reflected by the fact that all the cases of German insolvencies in eighteenth century Venice that I have hitherto found in the archives (altogether 17 are documented for the eighteenth century) were solved by a composition between creditors and the insolvent merchant. Such an outcome was fairly typical for the city of Venice; perhaps only five percent of all cases of insolvency (irrespective of the home countries of the individual merchants) were not resolved by an "accord".[3]

In the following paper, a short description of the Republic's insolvency laws as well as a case study on the failure of a big German merchant house will be presented in order to highlight the essentially "Venetian" characteristics of the normative system and its capacity to achieve a solution that satisfied most interests in theory and in practice. For this purpose, the paper will be divided into two parts: Firstly, the normative regulations that had emerged in Venice during the Middle Ages and which remained largely unchanged from the fifteenth century until the end of the Republic shall be described. In the second part, an insolvency case will be presented in detail to show how such a case was worked out with all its complications and particular problems. Finally, a conclusion will bring the findings together and attempt to reach a comparative and balanced judgment on the Venetian way of handling insolvencies.

Part I – Norms for cases of insolvency in early modern Venice

In Italian the words "fallimento" and "bancarotta" originally (i.e. in the Middle Ages) described different concepts. The former was the overarching one; it could

---

Matheus, Michael / Israel, Uwe (eds.): *Protestanten zwischen Venedig und Rom in der Frühen Neuzeit*, Berlin 2013, pp. 203–230.

3 This is the impression one gets from the overview of the insolvencies of eighteenth century Venice: Archivio di Stato di Venezia (henceforth: ASV), Sopraconsoli dei Mercanti, No. 177.

potentially apply to everybody, not only merchants, while the latter one was reserved for bankers. From the sixteenth century onwards both terms became in many regards overlapping and often were used indiscriminately for cases where merchants were no longer able to pay.[4] In the French commercial ordinance of 1673 the terms "banqueroutes" and "faillites" were used synonymously.[5] This was still the case in the edition of 1762.[6] However, in the edition of 1767 *faillite* and *banqueroute* were, for the first time, carefully distinguished. While a case of "faillite" happened because of bad luck in business and the resulting inability to repay debts, the term "banqueroute" had a negative connotation that implied some immoral or even illegal behavior on the part of the debtor before the downturn of the business.[7] This terminological change has never turned out to become international but it reflects a particular early modern attempt from the side of the French legislators to mark a *principal and timeless* distinction in this area of business law.[8] Therefore in the following paper I will use the term "insolvency" in order to emphasize that I am referring to ordinary cases rather than criminal ones. This usage finds support in the normative regulations of the Republic of Venice where the word "bancarotta" never appears throughout its entire history, while "insolventi" or "falliti" are synonymously and frequently used. The use of "bankrupt" in the following paper reflects an explicit reference to criminal cases, which in medieval and early modern Venice were mostly called "fallimenti fraudulenti".

According to several legal and economic historians, in the early modern age continental Europe knew of two principal modes of dealing with the failure of a business. Either the "privatrechtliches" (here translated as: *private-law*) or "publizistisches" (here translated as: *public-law*) principle formed the basis of the respective legislation. According to the private-law principle, an insolvency was an affair between private individuals and was left mostly to them. From that point

---

4 Lattes, Alessandro: *Il diritto commerciale nella legislazione statutaria delle città italiane*, Milan 1884, p. 313.

5 *Ordonnances de Louis XIV Roy de France et de Navarre. Données à Saint Germain en Laye au mois de Mars 1673*, Paris 1673, pp. 42–46.

6 *Ordonnance de Louis XIV, Roy de France et de Navarre, pour le commerce. Donnée à S. Germain en Laye, au mois de Mars 1673*, Paris 1762, pp. 40–44.

7 Bornier, Philippe: *Ordonnance de Louis XIV sur le Commerce. Enrichi d'annotation et de décisions importantes*, Paris 1767, pp. 452–453.

8 The distinction between the fraudulent and non fraudulent within the group of entrepreneurs or businesses no longer able to pay their debts is still a fundamental principle in present-day legislation, c.f.: Schlüchter, Ellen: *Der Grenzbereich zwischen Bankrottdelikten und unternehmerischen Fehlentscheidungen*, Tübingen 1977, pp. 31–35.

of view a case of insolvency belonged to the world of commerce and the state was only marginally involved. According to the public-law principle, however, an insolvency was regarded as an affair to be handled by the state and dealt with exclusively by the courts. This dichotomous juxtaposition has become rather popular in research due to the classic account on insolvency by Josef Kohler, professor of commercial law at the University of Berlin.[9] Kohler had a very partisan view of the two principles; he strongly preferred the private-law principle. According to him, the handling of insolvencies by merchants instilled a certain degree of pragmatism and realism into the dealings and thus was the preferable legislation for the world of business. If the state-controlled courts were the principal addressees responsible for solving an insolvency, this led, according to Kohler, to protracted proceedings and endless complications. Kohler sees the private-law principle as the prevailing one in medieval and early modern Italy, France, Belgium, the Netherlands and most other European states, while he regards Spain and Germany as primary examples for the public-law principle. Both countries had, according to him, followed the ideas of the mid-seventeenth-century Spanish jurist Francisco Salgado de Somoza, with his strong emphasis on a state-controlled procedure.[10] In England, Kohler identifies a mixture of both principles: he sees the private-law principle prevailing among businesses belonging to individuals, but in the event of insolvency of a trading company the state intervened quite heavily.[11]

Kohler's findings have always been criticized by experts. Already in 1917, Alfredo Rocco, an Italian legal historian pointed out that Kohler's juxtaposition was highly flawed in his allegation that the private-law principle had been dominating in early modern Italy. Rocco instead identified a strong tendency towards a state-centered procedure all over medieval and early modern Italy, which was first and foremost demanded by the merchants.[12] Recently, Wolfgang Forster has called the dichotomous and judgmental juxtaposition of the two principles patently absurd. He was able to identify a confusion of diverse concepts and definitions in Kohler's model, which hardly gives us an accurate description of the early modern practice of insolvency cases. Early modern insolvency legislation was much more diverse, refined and, most important of all, nuanced. A case of insolvency was in

---

9 Kohler, Josef: *Lehrbuch des Konkursrecht*, Stuttgart 1891.

10 de Somoza, Francisco Salgado: *Labyrinthus creditorum concurrentium ad litem per debitorem communem inter illos causatam*, Lyon 1645.

11 Kohler (1891, pp. 10, 57).

12 Rocco, Alfredo: *Il Fallimento. Teoria Generale e Origine Storica*, Milan 1917, p. 200.

most European countries handled in a complex but pragmatic manner in which state and creditors were alike involved.[13]

The Republic of Venice is an excellent example to demonstrate the rather sophisticated medieval and early modern procedures of dealing with insolvencies. The lagoon city had been a commercial hub of great importance since the Middle Ages. According to Kohler the Republic belonged to the Italian norm system, i.e. the proceedings were nominally handled by the merchants themselves or by some trustee nominated by them. In fact, a state-controlled institution – the magistrate of the *Sopraconsoli dei Mercanti* – was, from its foundation in 1301 until the end of the Republic, charged with overseeing and supervising most cases of insolvency in Venice, and after 1425 practically all cases.[14]

The entire legislation and the competencies of the Sopraconsoli were laid down in the *Novissimum Statutorum ac Venetarum Legum*, a compilation of Venetian statutory law from 1242 onwards.[15] The average merchant must have had difficulties to cope with the book, as the diverse statutes and ordinances were scattered throughout the volume and the contradictions between older and newer ordinances could only be discerned and solved with good legal training. The fact that many parts of the text are in Latin may have reduced its understandability even further for common merchants.[16] It is perhaps for this reason that the Venetian lawyer Marco Ferro published his ten-volume *Dizionario del diritto comune e Veneto* in Italian between 1778 and 1781. It is mainly a comment on and an explanation of how Venetian civil, canonical, commercial and criminal law worked in practice. The work was written in Italian, it was well ordered with a table of contents, a detailed register and in focusing on the practice it was easy to understand.[17] Under the entry "Sopra-consoli" is a description on the handling

---

13 Forster, Wolfgang: *Konkurs als Verfahren. Francisco Salgado de Somoza in der Geschichte des Insolvenzrechts*, Cologne 2009.

14 A brief and rather unsatisfying overview of the Venetian insolvency legislation and official procedure is given by: Fuchs, Carl: *Das Concursverfahren*, Marburg 1863, pp. 19–21. Fuchs misses crucial aspects of the Venetian legislation, especially the fundamental differentiation between "fuggitivo" and "aggravato dei debiti".

15 *Novissimum Statutorum ac Venetarum Legum Volumen duabus in partibus divisum*, Venice 1729.

16 That book may be seen as a typical example of the early modern Italian practise of compiling diverse and contradictory laws and statutes which go back to the Middle Ages, cf. Ortalli, Gherardo: "L'outil normatif et sa durée. Le droit statutaire dans l'Italie de tradition communale". *Cahiers de recherches médiévales* 4, 1997, pp. 163–173.

17 On the work and its author: Vedova, Giuseppe: *Biografia degli Scrittori Padovani, vol. 1*, Padua 1832, p. 403.

of insolvencies in the Republic.[18] It is interesting to note that Ferro supported his description with extensive quotations from international literature on the subject, irrespective of its author or place of publication.[19] Even if the concept of the *Lex mercatoria* or *Law merchant* is nowadays widely rejected by research, the fact that in legal literature the authors cited each other all over Europe irrespective of individual traditions or confessional or national boundaries shows us that the lawyers tried to see common patterns in the international legal handling of commercial litigation.[20] Yet, mostly these citations served to highlight and emphasize the superior legal and institutional fabric of the Venetian Republic. This aspect is particularly apparent in Ferro's account on insolvencies.

A merchant turned insolvent when he was no longer able to pay for the daily obligations relative to his business, the reason being the "scompiglio" (disarray) of his affairs. Ferro distinguishes three possible cases of insolvency categorized by the reason for the downturn. The first sort of insolvency is caused by misfortune (e.g. loss of a ship) or poor running of the business even though the merchant had not worked with any "mala fede". The second sort is the bankruptcy "per malizia", meaning the attempt of a merchant to flee and thereby to cancel out his debts. The third case is an insolvency (bordering sometimes on bankruptcy) due to pure mismanagement of the business. In Ferro's eyes only the first category of merchants was "worthy of compassion since against any adverse fortune neither council nor prudence were of use".[21] Against the insolvent of the second class, called "criminal cases", the full brunt of the law had to be used, whilst the third was not worthy of compassion but still should not be treated as criminal. Implicitly Ferro thus admits that, legally speaking, there were just two categories of insolvencies – one criminal and one ordinary.

Ferro continues explaining the usual procedures for the innocent fallito and the ones who went insolvent partly by their own fault. In contrast to the "inhuman rigor of the barbarian laws", which left the debtor entirely at the mercy of the creditors, Venetian law ensured his protection. According to Ferro, one of the

---

18 Ferro, Marco: *Dizionario del diritto comune e Veneto, vol. IX*, Venice 1781, pp. 89–91.

19 Ferro cited e.g. Johann Marquard, *Tractatus Politico-Juridicus De Iure Mercatorum et Commercium singulari*, Frankfurt/M 1662. On this author and his work cf.: Mohnhaupt, Heinz: "Jura mercatorum durch Privilegien". In: Köbler, Gerhard (ed.): *Wege europäischer Rechtsgeschichte*, Frankfurt/M 1987, pp. 308–323.

20 Baker, John: "The Law Merchant and the Common Law Before 1700". *The Cambridge Law Journal* 38(2), 1979, pp. 295–322; Kadens, Emily: "Myth of the Customary Law Merchant". *Texas Law Review* 905, 2012, pp. 1153–1206.

21 Transl. from Italian: Ferro (1781, p. 89).

underlying aims of creating the institution of the Magistrate of the Sopraconsoli dei Mercanti had been to provide relief to those who had lost their capital or property by misfortune. Thus, anybody who went insolvent could turn to the magistrate of the Sopraconsoli and from that moment onwards depended completely on it. He had the duty to submit to the magistrate all his papers, books, credits and debts, so that the Sopraconsoli could protect him from the "invasioni dei creditori". He obtained a passport (called *fida* or *salvacondotto*) that gave him some time to come to an accord with his creditors.

The system is rather peculiar in its strong centralization of the cases at one magistrate. From the legislation emerges the aim of the Venetian government to impose a rather neutral arbiter in order to satisfy all affected parties. The Italian historian Alessandro Lattes identified here a procedure that favored those who went insolvent:

> From the statuary legislation of the Middle Ages the Venetian distinguishes itself by its thoroughly deplorable and over time always increasing mildness while in the other Italian communes the rigor of the punishment of the insolvent always increased.[22]

Lattes refers to the fact that the debtor was presupposed not to have acted fraudulently, that it was very difficult to have him considered as a criminal even if this was rather clearly the case and, most important to Lattes, that there was no possibility for the creditors to have their claims satisfied immediately by a direct confiscation of the debtor's goods.[23] The cornerstone of Venetian legislation was for Lattes the *fida* or *salvacondotto*, the passport that protected the debtor from his creditors. The paper usually had a validity of two months; the duration could be prolonged to up to four months in order to allow the debtor to submit all his papers to the magistrate of the Sopraconsoli. This time span was extended regularly to four months during the sixteenth century, probably since it had become more complicated with the geographical expansion of trade and the accompanying settlement of more foreign merchants at the lagoon city to bring together all necessary commercial papers.[24]

It is worthwhile to follow the legal evolution of this system. In 1244 the magistrate of the *Giudici di Petizion* had been founded in Venice; initially this institution

---

22 Transl. from Italian: Lattes, Alessandro: *Il fallimento nel diritto comune e nella legislazione bancaria della Republica di Venezia*, Venice 1880, pp. 9–10.

23 Lattes (1880, pp. 10–11).

24 Lattes (1880, pp. 20, 32). This time-span was more or less usual in early modern Italy: Lattes (1884, p. 320); Santarelli, Umberto: *Per la storia del fallimento nelle legislazioni dell'età intermedia*, Padua 1964, pp. 262–263.

had the exclusive right to handle insolvency cases.[25] The establishment and empowerment of the *Sopraconsoli dei Mercanti* in 1301 originated from the necessity to find and imprison fugitive bankrupts.[26] A Venetian peculiarity was the separation of insolvent debtors into *fuggitivi*, debtors who had fled the spot, and *aggravati di debiti*, debtors who remained; for the latter the *Giudizi di Petizion* remained responsible until 1425.[27] Even though the origin of this distinction had been actual attempts of flight, it became a mere legal concept already during the fourteenth and especially the fifteenth century.[28] While the *aggravati* were able to pay off their debts in full within two years, the *fuggitivi* were merchants who mostly stayed in Venice and who had to ask for an overall reduction and a term for payment beyond two years.[29] The need to flee became therefore much less pronounced in the later Middle Ages, since Venetian legislation explicitly aimed at protecting the debtor.[30] That was stated by the Sopraconsoli themselves in 1457:

> The office of sopraconsul was created on the principle and for the sole purpose of making certain that our citizens, when reduced to insolvency by adverse fortune, would be able to carry on their business and not be forced to leave their families and wander about like idle beggars.[31]

Thus, since the distinction between insolvent debtors had turned into a mere conceptual one because of the explicit aim to instill mildness into the procedure, in 1425 the Sopraconsoli obtained the complete authority to handle all cases of insolvency.[32]

---

25 Lattes (1880, pp. 8–9).

26 Cassandro, Giovanni: *Le rappresaglie e il fallimento a Venezia nei secoli XIII–XVI: con documenti inediti*, Turni 1938, pp. 96, 102.

27 Cassandro (1938, pp. 95–96); Lattes (1884, p. 313). Incorrectly described by Santarelli (1964, p. 315), who sees the Sopraconsoli as being completely responsible from 1301 onwards.

28 Cassandro (1938, p. 126).

29 Lattes (1880, pp. 20–21).

30 The hypothesis of Reinhold Müller that most "fuggitivi" had actually attempted to flee may have been true in the fourteenth century; this was hardly any longer the case in the fifteenth century, even though a definite judgment will in all likelihood never be possible: Müller, Reinhold: *The Venetian Money Market: Banks, Panics, and the Public Debt, 1200–1500*, Baltimore/London 1997, p. 123.

31 Lattes (1884, p. 347) The translation is taken from Trieman, Israel: "The Law and the Insolvent Debtor". *Washington University Law Review* 12(3), 1927, pp. 189–195, here: p. 194.

32 Lattes (1880, pp. 15, 20); Cassandro (1938, p. 124).

Was this creditor-unfriendly? Not necessarily. From historical evidence we find that it had been mostly the merchants who had demanded during the 13th century the installation and furthermore the empowerment of a state institution as an arbiter in order to avert unjust repartition of the mass of the outstanding debts. Contrary to Lattes, Giovanni Cassandro sees the Venetian legislation and institutionalization of the procedures not as too mild towards the debtors but as resulting from the demands and necessities that conflicts among the creditors had caused.[33] Flights of the insolvent merchants were probably seen as potentially more damaging to the creditors and thus the debtors had been given such a surprising degree of protection.

Once the Sopraconsoli had registered a debtor, it was officially proclaimed that all his creditors had to register their claims within three days.[34] Thus, in an ideal case all claims and debts of the debtor and his creditors were known by the office of the Sopraconsoli within either a few days or, if it took a lot of time for the debtor to collect his papers, within a maximum of four months. Afterwards an attempt was made to bring in the debt claims of the debtor. Of course, this took some time and usually some of his claims turned out to be irretrievable. In the end, a compromise had to be found that was determined by the expectations of the creditors as to what they could get within a specific time span from the debtor who was ideally continuously collecting his debt claims. As soon as two thirds of the creditors gave their consent, the accord was concluded.[35] This procedure could be accelerated by the Sopraconsoli in several ways, mostly by overseeing that the involved parties complied with the time limits or with the threat of punishments in case of non-compliance.[36] For that reason, the ultimate authority for the process always remained, at least theoretically, with the office of the *Quarantia criminale*, the Venetian high court. In practice, its assent was usually a mere formality. The *Quarantia* had to sanction the accord and it was the tribunal for cases of insolvencies in which it had not been possible to come to an understanding between creditors and debtors.[37]

On 12 March 1611 the last piece of legislation on the insolvency procedures in the history of the Republic of Venice was enacted. It again emphasized that

---

33 Cassandro (1938, p. 93).

34 Cassandro (1938, pp. 130–131).

35 Rocco, Alfredo: *Il Concordato nel Fallimento e Prima del Fallimento*, Turin 1902, p. 41; Manzini, Vincenzo: "La bancarotta e la procedura fallimentare nel diritto veneziano, con cenni sui grandi fallimenti del sec. XV". *Atti del Reale Istituto Veneto di scienze, lettere ed arti* 85, 1925/1926, pp. 1091-1135, here: p. 1117.

36 Cassandro (1938, pp. 121–122); Sciumè, Alberto: *Ricerche sul fallimento nel diritto moderno. Il momento settecentesco*, Milan 1985, pp. 71–73.

37 Lattes (1880, pp. 14, 31–36); Cassandro (1938, pp. 115, 136).

the debtor had to give the Sopraconsoli all his books, balances, testaments etc. so that the Sopraconsoli were able to obtain a picture of "tutti li effetti del debitore". The new element here was the empowerment of the Sopraconsoli to seize the documents of the debtor "da sé" (on their own) without his consent. A number (usually three) of *capi* should be elected by ballot from the creditors and these should represent the case on behalf of their group. However, they did not have special privileges to lead the procedure but only to supervise it, give opinions and oppose any prejudicial moves from the side of the Sopraconsoli.[38] Fixed time limits to hand in claims or complaints were again emphasized in order to assure a regular proceeding of the case. Provisions for the wives of the insolvent were also given. These could insure parts of their capital against the claims of the creditors.[39]

Cassandro criticizes the Venetian system for several deficiencies. In contrast to Lattes, he does not regard it as particularly debtor-friendly but rather as well directed in its endeavor for impartiality and fair treatment of the parties involved.[40] The problems he saw were a juridical overlap of competences between the magistracies involved and some imprecision in the legislation with ramifications for the practice. He found cases dating from the fourteenth and fifteenth century where several magistracies (*Consoli dei Mercanti, Sopraconsoli dei Mercanti, Giudici di Petizion*) were played off against each other by the debtors since each of them had a certain power to give out salvacondotti that protected the debtors. Furthermore, he mentions cases where debtors had been able to continue their businesses after the beginning of the insolvency process and thus acquired new debts and debt claims outside of the process. Also, he found examples where creditors who had not registered themselves at the Sopraconsoli remained outside of the process and thus their claims had been untouched by the accord.[41]

It remains unclear to what extent these problems continued to affect insolvency cases in the early modern age. It is even unclear what the consequences had been in the Middle Ages, Cassandro gives no clear picture in this regard.[42] We may presume that a routine had established itself and that these problems no longer

38 Three "capi" were usually elected: Cassandro (1938, pp. 109–110); Santarelli (1964, p. 323).

39 *Novissimum Statutorum ac Venetarum Legum Volumen duabus in partibus divisum*, Venice 1729, pp. 278–280; Lattes (1880, p. 29); Lattes (1884, p. 337); Cassandro (1938, p. 106).

40 Cassandro (1938, pp. 98–100).

41 Cassandro (1938, pp. 127–136).

42 Cassandro hints subtly that in cases of conflicts between different magistracies the Consiglio Minore intervened and often decided that the full authority lay with the Sopraconsoli dei Mercanti: Cassandro (1938, pp. 135–136).

effectively hampered the proceedings. From the practice of the early modern age, we see the following solutions emerging in regards to these problems:

1. Any debts that the debtor had incurred within the last six months before his declaration of insolvency at the Sopraconsoli were not protected by the salvacondotto; they could, depending on the individual case, even be taken as a sign of "mala fede", i.e. as bordering on a criminal act.[43] Needless to say, this was even more valid for the time after the registration at the Sopraconsoli.
2. The creditors who did not register themselves in time lost all their claims with the conclusion of an accord.[44]

That this was the usual procedure emerges from the contemporary literature. The Florentine Girolamo Bardi described to his readers in 1587 how the Venetian system worked in practice. Like a typical jurist, he presented an ideal case where the debtor was called "Giuliano da Roma". Giuliano was considered a "fuggitivo" and the Sopraconsoli publicly proclaimed that he had eight days to appear before them with all his books and goods. As soon as the eight days were over and he had not appeared before the Sopraconsoli (i.e. he was a real fugitive), it was proclaimed that all his creditors should come forward to register at the Sopraconsoli in order to elect some capi. The chosen representatives then went with the police to the house of Giuliano in order to sequester his belongings. Exempt from this sequestration were goods belonging to other merchants which had simply been deposited in the house of the debtor and the dowries of the debtor's wife. If the debtor was merely a legal "fuggitivo", he had four months of immunity from his creditors in order to bring his books together, a time span that could be extended if the Quarantia gave its consent. Afterwards, he had up to two years to come to an accord with his debtors.[45]

Ideally an insolvency case in Venice ended with the remaining capital of the debtor being redistributed in exact proportion to the respective claims of the creditors. Usually all creditors obtained a specific percentage of their claims. The absolute equality of creditors in Venice (at least on the normative side) stands in stark contrast to most other commercial centers of early modern Italy.[46]

---

43 Ferro, Marco: *Dizionario del Diritto Comune e Veneto, Seconda Edizione*, vol. I, Venice 1845, p. 56.

44 Lattes (1884, pp. 338–340).

45 Bardi, Girolamo: *Delle cose notabili della città di Venetia*, Venice 1587, pp. 143–146.

46 Mauro Ferro explicitly stated that debts in Venice were only numerically valued, not – as in most other Italian cities – according to "anzianità, ipoteche, privilegii ecc.": Ferro (1845, p. 379).

After the final acceptance of the accord the debtor was allowed to start anew. That system seems to our eyes rather streamlined, yet in essence it had been in existence since the beginning of the fourteenth century. The "mildness" of Venetian legislation towards the debtor is also reflected by the fact that torture was unknown in insolvency proceedings in the Republic and that the ultimate aim of the entire system was a quick but just conclusion in the best interest of all parties.[47]

A glimpse beyond may strengthen the argument that the normative and institutional regulation of insolvencies at work in Venice were comparatively "modern". Only Genoa had a similar institution, the *Magistrato dei rotti*, which was only installed here in 1474.[48] The procedures of the *Insolvente Boedelskamer* in Antwerp, institutionalized in 1518, were similar to the *Sopraconsoli dei Mercanti* in Venice. Before its establishment, the principle that the first claimant was prioritized in the redistribution of the insolvent party's capital had been at work in Antwerp. The new institution very much resembled the Venetian model.[49] The *Insolvente Boedelskamer* was even copied in Amsterdam where the *Desolate Boedelkamer* was founded in 1643.[50] Venice may thus safely be called the cradle of a model for handling insolvency cases in early modern Europe. The fact that the legislative measures of Venice were enacted in a period of Venetian trade dominance in the Mediterranean (1244–1611) supports the conclusion that the institutionalization

47 Lattes (1884, p. 311); Marrella, Fabrizio / Mozzato, Andrea: *Alle Origini dell'arbitrato commerciale internazionale. L'arbitrato a Venezia tra Medioevo ed Età Moderna*, Milan 2001, p. 20.

48 Forcheri, Giovanni: *Doge, governatori, procuratori, consigli e magistrati della Repubblica di Genova*, Genoa 1968, pp. 153–155.

49 De Ruysscher, Dave: "Designing the limits of creditworthiness. Insolvency in Antwerp bankruptcy legislation and practice (16th–17th centuries)". *The Legal History Review* 76, 2008, pp. 307–327.

50 De Ruysscher, Dave: "Antwerp commercial legislation in Amsterdam in the 17th century: legal transplant or jumping board?". *The Legal History Review* 77, 2009, pp. 459–479, here: p. 475. It is interesting to note that this model was not taken up in Hamburg, even though at that time the city on the river Elbe copied a lot of commercial and other institutions from Amsterdam, e.g. the bank or the insurance legislation, cf.: Sieveking, Heinrich: "Die Hamburger Bank". In: van Dillen, Johannes G. (ed.): *History of the principal public banks*, London 1964, pp. 125–160, here: p. 125; Kiesselbach, Arnold: *Die wirtschafts- und rechtsgeschichtliche Entwickelung der Seeversicherung in Hamburg*, Hamburg 1901, pp. 12–17. Its *Falliten-Ordnung* of 1647, however, was based on the legislation of Nuremberg and Augsburg and thus rather debtor-unfriendly and in several aspects unpractical: Baumeister, Hermann: *Blicke auf einzelne Gegenstände des Hamburgischen Rechts*, Hamburg 1852, pp. 267–275.

was very much appropriate for a commercially powerful and active place where the constant striving for the economically best-fitting solution dominated the aims of the legislators.

Part II – An example of insolvency of a German merchant house

In order to see how an insolvency process worked in practice and what trajectory it took in Venice, an example shall now be presented. Insolvencies of foreign business houses were probably the most complicated cases that came before the Sopraconsoli. In principle, the handling of such failures did not differ: Foreigners who resided in the city enjoyed the same rights as Venetian citizens. This was explicitly also the case when it came to insolvencies.[51] That was again a specifically Venetian exception on the Italian peninsula, where foreigners were usually excluded from the benefits of the insolvency legislation.[52] Venice, by contrast, traditionally tried to actively attract foreign merchants by granting them privileges, among others equal treatment before the law.[53]

Regardless of their equality before the law, the cases involving foreigners residing in Venice were among the more difficult to deal with. Foreign merchants usually had strong commercial connections with other countries and therefore their debts and debt claims involved merchants who resided far away and probably neither knew Italian nor were acquainted with Venetian legislation.[54]

We shall now look at a complex insolvency of a German merchant house. One of the most famous and entrepreneurial German merchants, George Frederic Faber, declared his insolvency in 1773 and concluded a valid accord with most of his creditors several months later. At that time he was the only owner of a factory in the town of Follina on the Venetian terraferma. This factory produced, by a rather modern method, what was known as *Londrine*, a type of cloth based on the famous and much sought-after French or English style (hence the name, even for thus fabricated French cloth). Faber's factory has received some attention in recent historiographical literature; a brief account of its history shall now be given.[55]

---

51 Lattes (1880 p. 17); Cassandro (1938, pp. 117–122).

52 Lattes (1884, p. 311).

53 On this phenomenon in general: Ravid, Benjamin: "Venice and its Minorities". In: Dursteler, Eric (ed.), *A Companion to Venetian History, 1400–1797*, Brill 2013, pp. 449–485.

54 Santarelli (1964, pp. 305–307).

55 Especially Walter Panciera has studied this enterprise in detail and published intensely on it: Panciera, Walter: *I lanifici dell'alto Vicentino nel XVIII secolo*, Vicenza 1988,

At its beginning, the factory did not start as a German but as a Venetian enterprise. The idea behind its foundation had been to copy and apply proto-industrial techniques that had been developed in Great Britain around the turn of the seventeenth and eighteenth century. One of the more entrepreneurial Venetian nobles, Nicolò Tron (1685–1772) had spent two years in Great Britain on a diplomatic mission from 1715 to 1717 where he was inspired by the new production methods of the economically vibrant country. When he returned home, he at first embarked on a political career for some time. After his failure of pushing through a reform agenda, he eventually decided to enter a business career.[56] In 1719 he founded a wool mill at Schio at the foot of the Alps, where he employed British and French experts.[57] His enterprise laid the foundation for a substantial and long-lasting development of the regional economy.[58] In 1739, Tron entered into business relations with John George Stahl (died 1759), a German merchant from the *Nazione Alemana*, who was registered in the *Fondaco dei Tedeschi*.[59] Stahl's part in the business was henceforth to oversee and promote the selling of the Londrine in Venice and on foreign markets.[60]

Why had Tron chosen a German to do the retail selling in the city of Venice? Although we cannot answer this question from the sources, recent literature has emphasized the strength of the international connections of the Germans

pp. 25–32, 39–44; Panciera, Walter: "Vent'anni di bilanci di un'impresa laniera nel secondo Settecento". *Studi Veneziani N.S.* 19, 1990, pp. 125–170.

56 Gullino, Giuseppe / Linussio, Jacopo: "Nicolò Tron ed una possibile manovra di politica economica agli inizi della protoindustria veneta". In: Bertoli, Bruno (ed.): *Chiesa, società e Stato a Venezia. Miscellanea di studi in onore di Silvio Tramontin*, Venice 1994, pp. 197–206.

57 For an overview of proto-industrialization in the alpine regions of seventeenth and eighteenth century Veneto cf.: Nützenadel, Alexander: "Coping with Decline. Commercial Networks, Merchants and the Regionalization of Trade in Eighteenth Century Venice". In: Schulte Beerbühl, Margrit / Vögele, Jörg (eds.): *Spinning the Commercial Web. International Trade, Merchants and Commercial Cities, c. 1640–1939*, Frankfurt/M 2004, pp. 27–42.

58 Panciera (1988 pp. 33–35).

59 The Fondaco was the German factory. All German merchants had to register as members and tenants in order to enjoy the privileges of the German nation in Venice. The most recent contribution based on intensive archival research, is: Backmann, Sybille: "Le Fondaco dei Tedeschi. Pratiques marchandes des compagnies allemandes à Venise (1550–1650)". In: Wolfgang Kaiser (ed.): *La loge et le fondouk. Les dimensions spatiales des pratiques marchandes en Méditerranée. Moyen Âge – Époque moderne*, Paris 2014, pp. 113–141.

60 Panciera (1988, p. 39).

in Venice.[61] We can therefore assume that Tron, who was aiming for a factory to operate on an international level, needed a well-connected merchant at the commercial center of the Republic as a partner. Of Stahl we do not know very much. He came from Stuttgart and was admitted as a young apprentice in 1717 to the merchant Svajer in Venice.[62] In 1722 he founded his own business and soon became rather successful.[63] We know that he was associated with another German merchant, Georg Matthias König, from 1736 to 1744.[64] This was fairly typical; the Germans usually preferred joint partnerships with other German merchants on the spot.[65] In 1753 Stahl became consul of the German nation in Venice and held this position until his death in 1759.[66] We can thus legitimately conclude that he had been one of the more successful German merchants of Venice.

In the mid-1740s Tron moved his business to Follina, 80 kilometers further east of Vincenza. The hostility of the inhabitants of Vincenza towards his business, who feared the competition, had induced him to this step.[67] In Follina, local knowledge of textile production was substantial as similar businesses existed already at the time of the relocation.[68] Here Tron wanted to build up a grand enterprise that should compete with the best French and British cloth directly in the Levantine markets. The Venetian state, anything but averse to such examples of proto-industrialization and trade expansion, subsidized his business with

---

61 Georgelin, Jean: *Venise au siecle des lumieres*, Paris 1978, p. 674; Ressel, Magnus: "Venice and the redemption of Northern European slaves (seventeenth and eighteenth centuries)". *Cahiers de la Méditerranée* 87, 2013, pp. 131–145.

62 The Svajer family, originally from Nuremberg, had moved to Venice in the late seventeenth century. At the end of the eighteenth century, Amadeo Svajer was probably the richest of all German merchants residing in the city: Ferrari, Stefano: "Amadeo Svaier (1727–1791): un mercante erudito nella Venezia del Settecento". In: Bonazza, Marcello (ed.): *I buoni ingegni della Patria. L'Accademia, la cultura e la città nelle biografie di alcuni Agiati tra Settecento e Novecento*, Rovereto 2002, pp. 51–85.

63 Elze, Theodor: *Geschichte der Protestantischen Bewegungen und der Deutschen Evangelischen Gemeinde in Venedig*, Bielefeld 1883, p. 63.

64 Simonsfeld (1887, p. 191).

65 Cf. the printed lists of admitted members of the Nazione Alemanna in: ASV, Cinque Savi alla Mercanzia, Ser. I, Nr. 966, 12 Feb. 1780 (in the sources 1779, following the Venetian calendar) & 27 Feb. 1787 (in the sources 1786, following the Venetian calendar). These prove that the great majority of German merchants had themselves registered as partnerships in cooperation with other Germans.

66 Simonsfeld (1887, pp. 211–212); Elze (1883, p. 82). As a consul, Stahl represented the Nazione Alemana and spoke on their behalf to the Venetian authorities.

67 Panciera (1988, pp. 39–43).

68 Panciera (1990, pp. 127–128).

export premiums.[69] In 1755 Tron convinced Stahl to enlarge his investment in the enterprise. From 1755 onwards both co-owned the business, which had a capital stock of 60 000 D.; thus each nominally owned 30 000 D.[70] At the factory at Follina between 20 and 30 looms were constantly in use. It was thus one of the largest textile-producing factories of the Venetian Republic in these years.[71]

In 1755, George Frederic Faber, a native of the city of Colmar in Alsace, entered into Stahl's business as a young apprentice.[72] As it was the same year that Stahl went into partnership with Tron, we may assume that it was in Venice that Faber acquired the necessary knowledge to manage the day-to-day affairs connected to the factory at Follina. The reason why Stahl, at a relatively advanced age, had decided to invest in Tron's business in 1755 remains obscure. Since Tron stemmed from a powerful family of the Venetian aristocracy, we may assume that Stahl, at the summit of his career and success, had deemed the step of entering into direct business with a highly respected Venetian partner at this time not too risky.

Stahl oversaw a profitable enterprise in the last four years of his life. Only after his death in 1759 a slow decline set in. 1762 was a particularly bad year, followed by continuous losses after the end of the Seven Years War. The enterprise held on for another decade on a very low level but already after 1765 the business was marginalized and the official closure some years afterwards could no longer be averted. Even though the company has been studied in detail, we find that its problems have been presented with a partly misleading emphasis. Walter Panciera sees the French competition as the basic problem of the Tron-Stahl-Faber business. According to Panciera, French dominance in the Levantine markets had

69 This involvement on the part of the Republic of Venice stands in latent contrast to the picture painted by Caizzi, who accused the ruling elites of having been averse to industrial development: Caizzi, Bruno: *Industria e commercio della Repubblica Veneta nel XVIII secolo*, Milan 1965, pp. 10–12, 31–32; on the support for Tron cf.: Panciera (1990, p. 129).

70 In eighteenth century Venice, several currencies were used simultaneously. The most widespread currencies mentioned in the sources are ducats and lire. The abbreviations used here are "D." and "L.", respectively. One ducat was worth 24 grossi; these are stated after the comma. One Venetian lira was worth 20 soldi; these are stated after the comma. One ducat equaled 124 soldi or 6 1/5 lire in the eighteenth century. On the Venetian currencies in the eighteenth century: Ludovici, Carl Günther: *Grosses vollständiges Universal-Lexicon aller Wissenschafften und Künste, Vol. 46*, Leipzig/Halle 1745, pp. 1303–1305.

71 Panciera (1990, pp. 131–132).

72 Elze (1883, p. 64). Even though Faber came from territory that belonged to the French monarchy, he was still considered a German in the eighteenth century and therefore his admission to the Nazione Alemana did not cause a problem.

always remained insurmountable in the middle decades of the eighteenth century. Already at the beginning of the Seven Years War, the French conquest of Minorca in June 1756 allegedly sealed the fate of the Venetian cloth exports towards the Ottoman Empire. The French were able to dominate the Ottoman markets of Londrines and the factory faced constant losses. The failure of the business had therefore not been caused by a momentary crisis. It had been a structural problem that the company had not been able to solve in the nearly 20 years of its running.[73]

Panciera's account is correct, overall. However, looking at the losses of the company in the years after 1759, one discovers a rather high number of defaults of payment from the Turkish side. Several Turkish merchants in Venice obviously had an explicit preference for Venetian Londrines. Some spectacular insolvencies or flights of very important Turkish clients caused high losses for the enterprise.[74] It is therefore legitimate to conclude that the Venetians had the potential to compete with the French on the Levantine markets and that the failure of this specific enterprise was caused more by bad luck with the Turkish partners or perhaps by a certain negligence on the part of the Europeans in Venice in their dealings with Ottoman merchants.

The insolvency case shall now be described based on the available archival material. On 5 October 1773 Faber went to the Sopraconsoli dei Mercanti to declare his inability to continue his business and pay off his debts. Thus began the process, which lasted until 14 May 1774. Afterwards he had to enact all the payments and the case was officially closed on 30 May 1775. 48 860.12 D. remained as *debiti* after having settled and ordered all of Faber's outstanding debts and debt claims. Faber's process is a typical example of the proceedings of the Venetian authorities when dealing with cases of insolvency. Nearly 200 pages of archival documentation on his case allow us a rather detailed look into the workings of an insolvency case.

Most of the records originate from the year 1774. On the first four pages, Faber summarized his situation in order to convince the Sopraconsoli that he had not brought the failure upon himself by his bad conduct in business but that instead he had been a hardworking and diligent merchant who was struck, through no fault of his own, by misfortune. He wrote that he had been in Venice for 13 years,[75] and had lived "senza scialacquii" (without squander, fraud or embezzlement).

73 Panciera (1990, pp. 134–138).

74 Faber himself stated that the losses caused by "crediti erreditoti verso Turchi" had cost him more than 25 000 D., an enormous sum that is confirmed by his balances: ASV, Sopraconsoli 133, fol. 1r, 34r, 35r–36r.

75 This is in strictly legal terms correct; he had been admitted to the Fondaco dei Tedeschi, the factory of the German merchants on 18 February 1759, cf.: ASV, Cinque Savi alla

However, the unthinkable "fatalità" (misfortunes) had ultimately become so many that he was finally forced with extreme shame and grief, to stop his business in order to avert the ultimate desolation of the interest of his creditors.[76] He continued that he had taken over the business of his former principal, John Frederic Stahl, in 1759 with only 746.18 D. capital and the obligation to pay off some debts of Stahl's business with 600 D. annually until 1767. The business had consisted principally of the factory at Follina. In the first years after his takeover the factory had continued rather smoothly. Grave problems began when he had to write off credits he had given to Turkish merchants to the amount of 5 000 D. and a fire in the factory on 21 August 1762. The damage amounted to 46 711.4 L. Faber and Tron had afterwards obtained a generous credit from the state of 15 000 D., to be paid back in 15 years, yet this support had obviously not been enough. In 1771 Nicolò Tron had left the business in accordance with Faber. He was to receive 20 000 D. of his originally invested 41 000 D., to be paid in 16 half-yearly rates. A wave of insolvencies of his clients between 1764 and 1773 had caused Faber further losses of 32 518.7 D. Some credits that he had taken with high interest caused additional losses on his side that amounted to 25 975.5 D. Even though Faber had encountered a lot of "disgrazie e fatalità" he had tried until the last day to meet his payments. When he could no longer save any money or pay any debts, he went to the Sopraconsoli, the magistrate created as "relief of the afflicted and innocently oppressed by fortuitous accidents".[77] He asked the magistrate to bring his creditors to accept the accord proposed by him, which "surpassed the two thirds prescribed by the law".[78] He explicitly expressed the hope that the magistrate would force also the "discontent" to accept the conditions of the accord. In order to achieve it, he explicitly wanted to prove eleven points, all either signed by several merchants or otherwise certified:

Firstly, that he had always managed his business with maximal punctuality and without any shadow of fraud. Secondly, that he had in 1759 inherited Stahl's share in the factory on Follina. Thirdly, that the factory had been co-owned by Nicolò Tron. Fourthly, that he had had to pay and actually paid certain debts of Stahl until 1767. Fifthly, that he had inherited 43 091.12 D. from Stahl, as liquid

---

Mercanzia, Seconda serie, 966, Nr. 79. However, he had been living in Venice since 1755, when he had arrived at the city as a young apprentice: Elze (1883, p. 64).

76 All of the following: ASV, Sopraconsoli 133, fol. 1r–4r.

77 In the Italian original: "ho risolto di getarmi in seno alla Clemenza di quest'ecc^{mo} Mag^{to} destinato dalle Leggi al sollieuo degli affliti, ed inocenti oppressi dà disgrazie fortuite".

78 On the necessity to obtain the consent of more than two thirds of the creditors see Fn. 35.

capital, and 42 344.18 D. of debts, so that he had in fact inherited only 746.18 D. Sixthly, that Nicolò Tron's share had been ceded to Faber for 20 000 D. Seventhly, that between 1759 and 1772 he had lost 32 518.7 D. through defaulting Turkish merchants and debtors that had gone bankrupt. Eighthly, that in 1762 a fire in the factory in Follina had caused a loss of 46 706.4 L. Ninthly, that he had afterwards obtained an interest-free credit from the public side of 15 000 D. to be repaid in 15 years with 1 000 D. annually.[79] Tenthly, that he had taken loans, which had cost him altogether 25 975.5 D. of interest. Eleventh, that from 18 January 1772 until 24 July 1773, i.e. until two months before the declaration of his insolvency, he had paid back the sum of 52 262.10 D. to all his creditors.

The Sopraconsoli registered Faber's case on 5 October 1773. Only some aspects of the detailed documentation can be outlined here. At the beginning, many statements from diverse, and mostly Venetian, merchants were collected and more or less all emphasized that Faber had been an honest, trustworthy, moderate, "illibato" (uncorrupt) and punctual merchant of "buon umore".[80] These proofs of an impeccable reputation were probably the most important part of the documentation. Having assured the magistrate of the solidity of his conduct and character, the creditors elected two procurators: the German merchant Johann Jakob Gutterman and the Venetian merchant Giovanni Battista Andrioli.[81]

In the following documentation, the above shortly outlined business trajectory is mostly proven. Some details are worth mentioning: Already in 1770, Nicolò Tron mentioned the losses he had met in the business with the Turks as his reason for leaving the company, thus again blaming Ottoman merchants for the downturn the company had taken.[82] His statement is confirmed by a look at the balance sheets, which reveal that losses through failures of payments by Muslim merchants were often huge, one even with the comment "murdered in Tripoli".[83] In 1768 alone Faber claimed to have lost 55 196.18 L. to Turkish merchants.[84] From Faber's statements we get the impression that more than 95 percent of his losses stemmed from transactions with Turkish clients but this may have been somewhat

79 In the credit certificate, we can read that the reason for this generous intervention was the aim of protecting employment for many subjects and thus food for their families as well as of safeguarding market shares in the Eastern and Western Mediterranean markets: ASV, Sopraconsoli 133, fol. 47r–47v.
80 ASV, Sopraconsoli 133, fol. 6r–7v.
81 ASV, Sopraconsoli 133, fol. 103r.
82 ASV, Sopraconsoli 133, fol. 27r.
83 ASV, Sopraconsoli 133, fol. 34r.
84 ASV, Sopraconsoli 133, fol. 35r.

exaggerated in order to strengthen his defense.[85] The documentation of the 10th chapter is rather interesting. Here we find a list of all creditors of Faber after 1759. Mostly the German merchants of Venice had given him the highest sums.[86] Tron had evidently found in Faber a partner who had access to a rather large amount of credits from his fellow Germans. In the 11th chapter we see a list of all transactions of money and of merchandise Faber had enacted in the last two years of his business. The recipients of his merchandise (and sometimes of his money) were mostly Venetians and only some Germans.[87] This structure reflects the fact that Faber operated with less frequency but in quantitatively larger dimensions, i.e. as a wholesale trader with German partners and on an intense frequency but with smaller single payments, i.e. as a retail trader, with Venetians.[88] In his letter to his creditors Faber explained again in detail why he failed, emphasizing that even "moderation, restraint and fidelity" could not save humans from the vicissitudes of life. Here he also mentioned the high price of wool and low price of Londrine as structural problems of his company.[89] Eventually being faced with insurmountable debts, he was left with no other option but "la miserabile libertà della Persona".[90]

How was the case being actually handled? With creditors and debtors all over Europe, how could they be involved in the proceedings and justice be done to all parties within a reasonable time span? The list of signed creditors shows that German and (though rarely) other merchants on the spot acted as procurators for merchants from places far away. They signed a document demanding their "crediti legittimi e reali" in accordance with the laws.[91] A precise balance sheet was drawn

---

85 It should be added that the Turkish merchant community at Venice was an established and rather respected group and we may suppose that the extraordinary number of insolvencies and non-payments that haunted Faber may have been the result of adverse economic conditions within the Ottoman empire after the beginning of its war against Russia in 1768, cf. on the Turkish community in Venice: Arbel, Benjamin: *Trading Nations, Jews and Venetians in the Early Modern Eastern Mediterranean*, Leiden 1995, S. 67–68.

86 ASV, Sopraconsoli 133, fol. 49r–62v.

87 ASV, Sopraconsoli 133, fol. 64r–81v.

88 The pattern is not dissimilar to Jewish traders in Livorno at the same time: Trivellato, Francesca: *The Familiarity of Strangers. The Sephardic Diaspora, Livorno, and Cross-Cultural Trade in the Early Modern Period*, New Haven 2009, pp. 132–152.

89 ASV, Sopraconsoli 133, fol. 83r.

90 ASV, Sopraconsoli 133, fol. 83v.

91 ASV, Sopraconsoli 133, fol. 83v- 84v. The typical formulation was e.g.: "Michiele Vagner come Procurator del Sig. Godifredo Federico Ammann d'Augusta aff(er)mo per il suo Credito". The Germans did also act as representatives for Italians, e.g.: "Gio. Giacomo

up three days after Faber's registration at the Sopraconsoli on 8 October 1773, with all creditors and debtors listed with exact sums.[92] His debtors and creditors came mostly from Upper Italy and Upper Germany with Vienna, Augsburg and Zurich as important centers but he had also had some important business relations with Great Britain, the Netherlands and northern Germany. Turks are not mentioned; obviously any credit claims on these were already written off. The fact that the goal was to sum up in this document all possible financial means still available to him is reflected in the first entry on the list that should actually contain only his debtors: "Mobili et Utensili del Negozio e Conto de' Mobili nelle mie Camere" – 682.4 D."[93]

The negotiations leading to an accord took some months; we may assume that Faber used the time to claim and get back as many arrears and debts as possible. On 22 April 1774 he presented an accord to his creditors. He offered to cede all of his fortune to be redistributed among these.[94] Within three weeks the two representatives of the creditors convinced more than two thirds of their representees, who owned more than two thirds of the debt claims (34 020.11 D. were their debt claims, 14 840.1 D. were the debt claims of the "non contenanti"), to sign the accord. Most of the "non contenanti" merchants came from places as far as Hamburg. Evidently it had not been possible to inform them in time but the fact that they did not sign did not necessarily lead to a rejection of the accord. In any case, their acceptance of the accord was not necessary; they were simply confronted with the result. On 14 May 1774 the balance was officially approved by the Sopraconsoli.[95]

The approval allowed Faber to start business again, just over seven months after the announcement of his insolvency. In the following year the payments to his creditors were enacted. On 30 May 1775 his case was finally closed when the representative of the Quarantia di Criminal officially proclaimed their consent with a publication at the stairs of St. Marco.[96]

Even though his further fate remains as sketchy as his origins, Faber does not seem to have suffered too badly after his insolvency in Venice. His name appears

---

Gutermann di Comissione del Sig(no)re Domenico Basire di Napoli affermo per il suo Credito".

92 ASV, Sopraconsoli 133, fol. 98r–101v.

93 ASV, Sopraconsoli 133, fol. 98v.

94 ASV, Sopraconsoli 133, fol. 102r–102v.

95 ASV, Sopraconsoli 133, fol. 103r–111v.

96 ASV, Sopraconsoli 133, fol. 112r. This formality seems to have been always necessary to close an insolvency case, see Fn. 37.

in a list of creditors of an Austrian iron mine in 1782; its owner owed Faber 2 828.57 Austrian guilders.[97] It seems likely that Faber had moved to Austria after his insolvency in Venice and had become a rather successful merchant. Theoretically it would have been possible for him to start anew in Venice; especially, if we remember how emphatically his trustworthiness and good conduct had been praised by his partners.[98] Faber's factory at Follina was not closed down when he left the business. After having reduced the number of looms and following several changes of ownership, the factory was still running in 1819.[99]

Conclusion

The Venetian bankruptcy regime and the handling of Faber's failure suggest a rather debtor-friendly environment. However, even the most debtor-friendly system cannot make up for the many pitfalls and problems that any insolvency necessarily caused for a debtor. A letter written by a German merchant in 1711 from Venice to a friend in Helmstedt describes drastically what had happened within the German community when one of the partners had turned insolvent:

> The good Matthias Lauber[100] died on 26 December last and, sadly, his brother[101] followed him this year on 26 June. … The evil and uncalm man Alexio Schorer has had good part in his death since he came after the Matthias' death in his house to sanctimoniously give his condolences, the next day he let citations and sequesters run on the inheritance … [After the death of Johann Christoph Lauber] Schorer has even shown more his grim and evilness and given the greatest affront in the world to the house of Lauber by sending his son with Comandatori and Fanti[102] into the house to let all [possessions and goods] be counted and inventarised. Yet this was soon redeemed and declared invalid by the justice. Even though he [Schorer] does not abate to torment this house [Lauber], a Palace, he has already lost two cases in the Quarantia.[103]

---

97 Müllner, Alfons: *Geschichte des Eisens in Inner-Österreich von der Urzeit bis zum Anfange des 19. Jahrhunderts mit besonderer Berücksichtigung der ökonomischen, sozialen und handelspolitischen Verhältnisse sowie des Eisenhandels nach sämtlichen europäischen Ländern, der Levante und Nordafrika*, Vienna 1909, p. 427.

98 See Fn. 80. It was fairly common to start anew in Venice after a bankruptcy, cf.: Maier, Johann Christoph: *Beschreibung von Venedig, Zweiter Theil. Zweite, durchaus verbesserte und vermehrte Auflage*, Leipzig 1795 pp. 227–229.

99 Panciera (1990, p. 138).

100 Matthias Lauber of Laubenfeld, born 1627, on him: Simonsfeld (1887, p. 183).

101 Johann Christoph Lauber, born 1641, on him: Ibid.

102 These were servants of Schorer, not state officials.

103 Royal Library of Denmark, Copenhagen, Ms. Thott 1235, Letters from Pommer to Fabricius, 1.7.1711.

This letter is of great interest to us. The German merchant Schorer was used to the harsh systems of Augsburg and thus tried to sequester the goods of the German debtor Lauber and treat him as a criminal. The Venetian system, however, did not allow for such treatment and stopped the creditor in such proceedings. This did not avert the death of one of the two elder Laubers due to age and grief but it decisively hindered such attempts, to the strong disadvantage of the creditor who now had to face losses in the courts.

Thus: The handling of insolvencies in eighteenth century Venice does not seem to have been, from the institutional point of view, a biased or particularly pre-modern affair. The merchants here faced a magistracy that explicitly aimed at balancing the interests of all the affected parties to come to a viable solution. Viewing the Venetian insolvency laws and practice, it can be concluded that they do not support Kohler's dichotomous model of private law vs public law in insolvency. On the one hand, the actual negotiations were left to the merchants while the court's task was to supervise and assist. On the other hand, the magistrate had executive power to force unwilling creditors and the debtor to accept the verdict. The combination of a principal protection of the debtor, several rather clear steps prescribed by the law, their potential enforcement by a stately institution, and yet the respect for the sphere of the merchants and their internal handling of the case, was the result of a learning process of several centuries. Therefore we find here a rather balanced way of dealing with cases of insolvency.

We find this confirmed in the insolvency case of George Frederic Faber, an entrepreneurial German merchant in Venice. His factory produced cloth in the English and French style, which was competitive on the Levantine markets. Handling the production and the export of the merchandise obviously impressed the Venetian government, which subsidized the business with export premiums and an interest-free loan when a fire caused some severe damage. The problems of the business, however, were not so much internal to the Republic but lay elsewhere. Some cases of non-payment of high sums on the part of the Ottomans, the mentioned fire and strong French competition on the Levantine markets weakened the enterprise severely and finally caused its ultimate downturn. When this happened, Faber, as destitute and despaired as he must have been, received the protection of the Venetian legal and administrative institutions. From the day of his approaching the Sopraconsoli dei mercanti until the final accord, he had to wait just over seven months. Afterwards he enacted the payments, which took him a few more months. Being declared a man free of debts and any further legal prosecutions, he was able to make a fresh start one and a half years after the registration of his case at the latest. That he was not unsuccessful in his future endeavors has been indicated.

We may thus conclude that the Venetian procedure of handling insolvencies was an element of "good governance", especially in comparison to other European commercial centers. Having a fine-tuned institutional and legal system for tackling the pitfalls of businesses probably played a not insignificant role in keeping the place attractive for foreign merchants who wanted to settle here; and it can certainly be counted among the more impressive aspects of the early modern Republic of Venice.[104]

104 Current research emphasizes that "well-functioning corporate governance and bankruptcy laws are generally believed to be critical to investment and growth, they are particularly important in emerging market economies". In: Berglof, Erik et al., *Government and Market Failures in Emerging Market Economies: Implications for Corporate Governance and Bankruptcy*, working paper, URL: http://siteresources.worldbank.org/DEC/Resources/84797-1251813753820/6415739-1257192350745/ErikBerglof.PDF (last visited: 4.10.2014). This aspect is rarely highlighted in research on bankruptcy but it seems to have been a non-negligible part of the Venetian institutional fabric designed to ensure a healthy investment climate.

Viera Rebolledo-Dhuin

Below and Beyond Bankruptcy: Credit in the Parisian Book Trade in the Nineteenth Century[1]

"What does it mean to go bankrupt?" asked Eugénie [Grandet]. "To go bankrupt", replied her father, "is to commit the most dishonourable of all the acts that can dishonor a man." [...] "Bankruptcy, Eugénie, is a kind of theft which is unfortunately protected by the law. People entrusted their property to Guillaume Grandet on the strength of his reputation for honor and integrity, then he took everything and left them only their eyes to weep with. A bankrupt is worse than a highway robber: with the robber attacks you, you can defend yourself, he risks his life; but the bankrupt... In short, Eugénie, Charles is dishonoured."[2]

Honoré de Balzac, *Eugénie Grandet*, trans. by Lowell Bair, New York, Bantam Classic, 1959.

The increase in the number of commercial bankruptcies is proportional to the increase in the number of commercial businesses, and is rather an indicator of prosperity than distress.[3]

Augustin-Charles Renouard, *Traité des faillites et des banqueroutes*, Paris, Librairie Guillaumin et Cie, 1857, vol. I, p. 196.

---

1 I am very thankful to Eric Lequesne, Marion Pic, Stéphane Onillon and Geneviève Chrétien-Vernicos for their precious help in translating my French text, but above all to Christine Haynes for her invaluable critical reading.

2 « Qu'est-ce que c'est, mon père, que faire faillite ? demanda Eugénie [Grandet]. Faire faillite, [expliqua] le père, c'est commettre l'action la plus déshonorante entre toutes celles qui peuvent déshonorer l'homme. [...] Faire faillite, Eugénie, reprit-il, est un vol que la loi prend malheureusement sous sa protection. Des gens ont donné leurs denrées à Guillaume Grandet sur sa réputation d'honneur et de probité, puis il a tout pris, et ne leur laisse que les yeux pour pleurer. Le voleur de grand chemin est préférable au banqueroutier : celui-là vous attaque, vous pouvez vous défendre, il risque sa tête ; mais l'autre... Enfin Charles est déshonoré. » H. de Balzac, *Comédie Humaine*, Paris, Gallimard, (Bibliothèque de la Pléiade), 1976 vol. III, p. 1094.

3 « L'augmentation du nombre des faillites se proportionne à l'accroissement des affaires commerciales, et est un signe de prospérité plutôt que de détresse. »

Charles Renouard's statement seems to disagree with the common view of his contemporaries, who usually considered business failure in negative terms. Etymologically, the French word for bankruptcy, *faillite,* is related to fall and dishonour. As Grandet taught his daughter in his lectures on moral education, bankruptcy is tantamount to fraud and avoidance: the bankrupt is a potential runaway because he could pocket millions if he escaped, and since he does not fulfil his obligations in order to get rich, he is worse than a robber. That is why bankrupts were to be denounced and exposed to the public. Like the medieval custom that compelled a debtor to wear a green hat – a diabolical colour, that predominate too the portraits of the usurers in the Balzac's novels, who was inspired himself of the Flemish painting –, so in nineteenth century France, the bankrupt was still discredited: he was immediately put in jail, his possessions were seized, and he was legally unable to acquire new property. The insolvent merchant could neither vote nor be elected, he was banned from the Stock Exchange and was, to quote Balzac, "civilly dead".

Credit, as a necessary financial mechanism and a cornerstone of trust for traders' activities, is thus the core issue of any legal procedure. It was the decisive *criterion*, so to speak, for codifying commercial law. Contrary to what Balzac claimed for literary reasons, commercial bankruptcy, manifested by suspension of payments, was a specific procedure defined in the *Code de Commerce* of 1807 and differed from "civil bankruptcy" or ruin (*déconfiture*), or "negligent" or "fraudulent" bankruptcy (*banqueroute simple* or *frauduleuse*). In French law, *déconfiture* – from *decoctor*, for somebody who has "consumed" all his assets[4] – implicated all defaulting debtors, who were tried in an ordinary court. Negligent or fraudulent bankruptcy was punished in a correctional court, and fraud, e.g. a crime, in an assize court; while commercial bankruptcy or insolvency (*faillite*) led to a collective procedure against the insolvent traders in a Commercial Court. Directly derived from commercial customs followed by tradespeople before the French Revolution, bankruptcy law was included in the process of codification started by Napoleon in the beginning of the nineteenth century. Later, following various criticisms, it was gradually "de-codified", leading to what historians mostly consider was a softening of the procedure on economic failure. The drafting of a bankruptcy law took place in the context of the standardization of practices, with due respect for both the fundamental rights of individuals, and the strong centralizing push of the State advocated since the French Revolution and manifest in the *Code civil* in 1804. The economic outrage of the French people in such crises as

4 É. Richard (ed.), *Droit des affaires : questions actuelles et perspectives historiques*, Rennes, Presses Universitaires de Rennes, 2005, p. 549.

the bankruptcy of John Law (1720), the 1805 crisis and the Panama scandal from 1889 to 1903, also had a strong influence on bankruptcy law.

Chart 1: Types of insolvency trials in French Law

Déconfiture « civil bankruptcy »/« ruin »		all debtors common jurisdiction
Faillite **« Insolvency »/« commercial bankruptcy »**		**insolvent traders** **commercial court**
Banqueroute « bankruptcy »	↗ *Banqueroute simple* « negligent bankruptcy »	negligent debtors correctional court
	↘ *Banqueroute frauduleuse* « fraudulent bankruptcy »	fraudulent debtors assize court

The purpose of this paper is to show that bankruptcy law, defined empirically and based on the practices of non-professional judges with a view to imposing the rule of law over practices, was part of the effort to raise the moral standards of trade while serving the social and economic ambitions of all parties involved in the legal procedure. The importance of bankruptcy in economic life is well known and some historians of economy have already studied the economic impact of the legal changes on the practices, at the macroeconomic scale.[5] Nevertheless, your study intends link the different scales to understand how the evolution of the law and the jurisdictional practices change as the commercial's as the credit's uses. More generally, I intend to link on the one hand the enterprises history and the

5 See for example : P.-C. Hautcœur et N. Levratto, « Petites et grandes entreprises face à la faillite au XIXe siècle en France : du droit à la pratique », dans *Le capitalisme au futur antérieur. Crédit et spéculation en France, fin XVIIIe–début XXe siècles*, N. Levratto et A. Stanziani (ed.), Bruxelles, Éditions Bruylant, (Droit et économie, n° 2), 2011, p. 199–266 ; and from the sames: « Does the law alone explain the rise in bankruptcies in XIXth century France? », https://halshs.archives-ouvertes.fr/halshs-00589125/document, accessed July 15, 2015.

book history, both dominated yet by the monographical studies, and on the other hand the macroanalysis of the economists and the micro-historians' interests, to study the relations that characterise the credit's structures of the life of the book's enterprises. Also, I ambition to participate in the history of the financials' practices of the 19th-Century's firms, which permit understand the construction of an urban socio-economical elite.

This paper is based on an exhaustive analysis of 141 bankruptcy files of nineteenth century Parisian book traders and publishers, amounting to about 75% of all samples available today for the said period.[6] In fact, in the nineteenth century France, the booksellers and the publishers are confounded under the *libraire* term. In its prosopographical analysis, it also echoes more recent projects that deal with the development of urban elites in the nineteenth century.[7]

The particularities and motivation of the judicial procedure in France will be outlined infra in the section about the evolution of bankruptcy law as a way to highlight the problems it addresses, the roles of all the parties involved in a bankruptcy, and the specificities of bankruptcy in the Parisian book trade in the nineteenth century.

Commercial Bankruptcy, a law in progress

Roman law granted each creditor the right to sue their debtor (debt bondage[8]) individually, but it also allowed a rudimentary collective procedure – *venditio bonorum*, called later on during the Early Empire, *distractio bonorum*. Nevertheless, it was only in medieval Italy, in a growing commercial environment, that a strong legislation emerged – relying on a consular jurisdiction.[9] In France, the drafting

---

6 V. Rebolledo-Dhuin, *La librairie et le crédit. Réseaux et métiers du livre à Paris (1830–1870)*, PhD in History, University of Versailles-Saint-Quentin-en-Yvelines, 2011. More specifically, this article is the core of the first part of my book, drawn from my updated thesis, to be published by the *Éditions du Comité des Travaux Historiques et Scientifiques*.

7 V. Rebolledo-Dhuin, « De la circulation du papier dans la librairie à Paris au XIXe siècle ou les dynamiques du crédit inter-entreprises dans le secteur du livre », *Entreprises et histoire*, vol. 4, n° 77, 2014, p. 59–73.

8 N. Levratto, « Abolition de la contrainte par corps et évolution du capitalisme au 19ème siècle », *Économie et Institutions*, n° 10–11, et 2ème semestre 2007, p. 221–249 ; D. Desurvire, *Histoire de la banqueroute et faillite contemporaine*, Paris, L'Harmattan, (Logiques juridiques), 1993.

9 J. Hilaire, *Introduction historique au droit commercial*, Paris, Presses universitaires de France, (Droit fondamental), 1986, p. 306–313.

of bankruptcy law did not begin before the sixteenth century – when customs were officially written down and consular courts created. This movement gained momentum at the end of the seventeenth century, in the wake of the strengthening of royal power, concomitant with the development of trade and of the concept of a French law initiated by the humanists, but it found its concrete application with Colbertism after 1664.[10] Although it challenged the pre-eminence of Roman law and assimilated to common law, this French law nonetheless followed the same path, through Italian law and customs from Lyon.[11]

The spirit and paradoxes of Book III of the Commercial Code of 1807

The Ordinance of 1673, frequently called "Code Savary" – after the influential Parisian trader who drafted it – laid the foundation of bankruptcy legislation and fully corresponded with a quest for more stability and uniformity dominant in France after the Revolution. Even if the distinction between *déconfiture* and bankruptcy derived from Italian law, the Ordinance and the following legislation were strongly influenced by the conception of Roman bankruptcy law.[12] The *Code* of 1807 resulted directly from those two traditions. The legislation was part of civil justice but also dealt with public order, and was therefore subject to police and monarchical power. So even if the law still pushed for amicable settlements between the parties, early modern bankruptcy law – and particularly a strict reading of it – was at the core of legislation on economic failure until 1838, or even 1889.

The conditions of the drafting of the Code and the spirit of the law

The 1807 *Code* reformed the Savary Code. The idea of further reforms already emerged as early as the 1680s, as is apparent by the 1681 Ordinance on maritime trade. Miromesnil (1723–1796, Louis XVI's minister of justice from 1774 to 1787) started to draft a new bankruptcy law in the 1770s but his project failed – it was still under study when the French Revolution started, so that only with the codification of Napoleon did commercial law[13] appear. Several points of the drafting of

10 P. Baubeau, *Les « cathédrales de papier » ou la foi dans le crédit. Naissance et subversion du système de l'escompte en France : fin XVIII*[e] *– premier XX*[e] *siècle*, PhD in History, University of Paris Ouest Nanterre La Défense, France, 2004, p. 83–107.

11 *Ibid.* ; J. Hilaire, *Introduction historique*, p. 317–318.

12 J. Hilaire, *Introduction historique*, p. 317–320.

13 *Ibid.*, p. 81–82.

the *Code de commerce* seem paradoxical but are fully typical of Napoleonic governance, based on the reconciliation of two incompatible pasts: customary law and revolutionary law.[14] The text remains in line with both the work of reformers of the *Ancien Régime* and the revolutionary reconstruction. The apparent dichotomy can be attributed to the shifting balance of power between public and civil law experts as the legislation was written, before and after the 1805 crisis.[15] In accordance with the revolutionary legalism reversing the legal system – henceforward statute law prevailed over customs –, the *Code de commerce* aimed at shaping practices. But after 1805, this was done with great "subservience to the Ordinance" of 1673.[16] The Commercial Code strengthened the French idea of a specialized and hierarchical legal system, dominated by the *Civil Code* of 1804, raising private ownership to the status of a natural right and asserting the pre-eminence of the individual over the group. Thus the 1807 trade law was an exception to the civil law on which it was based, and it was designed as a way able to enforce probity in customs.[17]

Furthermore, despite remaining consistent with the individualistic mindset started with the Allarde decree and the Le Chapelier law,[18] the Commercial code nevertheless favoured the reconstitution of a community of traders – actually born in 1563 and recreated in 1790. In fact, commercial courts represented an exceptional jurisdiction and judges, chosen by their peers, were experts focused on "an implicit ethics of the trades".[19] Like the members of the Chambers of Commerce and of the Prud'hommes, the judges of the Commercial Court, particularly willing to spread proper standards of conduct, were focused on imposing a better code of practice which might justify their representing a "legal world" of their own, while preserving their independence, the basis of their credibility in the eyes of the persons under their jurisdiction. To defend the traders' honour, the judges, who

---

14 About the double legacy of Napoleon's policy on religion, see: J.-O. Boudon, *Napoléon et les cultes. Les religions en Europe à l'aube du XIXe siècle : 1800–1815*, Paris, Fayard, 2002.

15 J. Hilaire, *Introduction historique*, p. 83–91.

16 « servilité à l'ordonnance » *Ibid.*, p. 89.

17 *Ibid.*, p. 86 ; P. Baubeau, *Les « cathédrales de papier »*, p. 93–107.

18 N. Praquin, « Les faillites au XIXe siècle. Le droit, le chiffre et les pratiques comptables », *Revue française de gestion*, vol. 34, n° 188–189, 2008, p. 359–382.

19 « *une éthique implicite des affaires* » C. Lemercier, « Juges du commerce et conseillers des prud'hommes face à l'ordre judiciaire (1800–1880 », in *La justice au risque des profanes*, H. Michel et L. Willemez (ed.), Paris, Presses Universitaires de France, 2007, p. 116–117.

rejected the idea of a full power for civil justice, reinvented community traditions and some forms of self-regulation among traders.[20]

In short, the power conferred to commercial courts allowed the State to "combine social individualism and parliamentarian legicentrism[21]" and, as far as bankruptcy was concerned, to make procedures more public, in order to render trade more moral and to stop amicable settlements, until then frequently signed "in notary offices beyond all legal control".[22] Therefore bankruptcy trustees frequently condemned the odious effect of procrastination in order to highlight the benefits of liquidation, which was fairer to the creditors, the debtor's financial health and the ethics of trade.

The strict measures included in the text

Book III – entitled "Of insolvency and bankruptcy" – is a good illustration of the effort to improve early modern legislation, and of the repressive approach adopted in the *Code de commerce*. Economic failure, only one heading with 13 clauses in the 1673 Ordinance, was now a real organization of commercial law with an entire book comprising 178 clauses. The section on the bill of exchange aside, the heading on bankruptcy was the most detailed in the *Code*, with 126 clauses. The general principles remained unchanged (the collective procedure, the distinction between civil, commercial insolvencies and bankruptcies, the methods of dispute resolution, etc.) but some new ones were introduced,[23] and the conditions of the procedures were clarified. Therefore, the opening of a bankruptcy procedure now required a statement by the Commercial Court, although the day of suspension was not generally fixed: to protect the creditors' dividend in the case of liquidation, the court can declare the bankruptcy before the payment suspension of the debtor; also all the commercial operations are cancelled at the benefit of the creditors. On

---

20 C. Lemercier, « Juges du commerce » ; « Discipliner le commerce sans corporations. La loi, le juge, l'arbitre et le commerçant à Paris au XIXe siècle », *Le Mouvement Social*, vol. 224, n° 3, 2008, p. 61–74.

21 « *combin[er] individualisme social et légicentrisme parlementaire* » P. Minard, « Le métier sans institution: les lois d'Allarde-Le Chapelier de 1791 et leur impact au début du XIXe siècle », *La France, malade du corporatisme? XVIIIe–XXe siècles*, Paris, Berlin,? (Socio-histoires), 2004, p. 81–95.

22 J. Hilaire, *Introduction historique*, p. 76. On this point see too : N. Praquin, « Les faillites au XIXe siècle », p. 361–362 ; N. Coquery, « Les faillites boutiquières sous l'Ancien Régime. Une gestion de l'échec mi-juridique mi-pragmatique (fin XVIIe–fin XVIIIe siècle) », *Revue française de gestion*, vol. 34, n° 188–189, 30 décembre 2008, p. 341–358.

23 J. Hilaire, *Introduction historique*, p. 326–330.

the other hand, an arrangement between creditors (or *concordat*[24]) was now only possible on the basis of a majority of three-quarters of the checked and asserted amounts. Moreover, what creditors could do was limited by the increased power of the commercial judge who named officers, supervised them until liquidation of the bankrupt was pronounced, and selected – from a list approved by the creditors – a temporary trustee to be replaced by a permanent one in case of a *union* between the creditors.[25] In addition, the creditors' *union* was not possible until their claims had been checked. The judge supervised the whole procedure and ensured that no agreement between the parties was made.

Finally, the 1807 *Code* established a strongly repressive jurisdiction against the bankrupt and his family. The matrimonial assets and the legacy to his children were placed under judiciary control, while the bankrupt was jailed as a preventive measure and had his civil and commercial rights revoked, not only to ensure he would participate in the procedure, but also to make him a scandalous figure. At the beginning of the nineteenth century, people still had in mind John Law's bankruptcy and the 1805 crisis revived their anxiety. The imprisonment of insolvent debtors, abolished in civil cases on March 9th, 1793 and reinstituted four years later (on Ventôse 24th, year V of the French Revolution),[26] ensured that society would be protected. During the review of Book III by the *Conseil d'État* before the Emperor himself, the latter allegedly said:

> Given the present habits, severity is a necessity; bankrupts gain fortunes without losing their honour, and this is what we have to reverse. A bankrupt can no longer look triumphant or indifferent; he must at least appear in public as a man beset with great misery. As habits have taken a different course, we must change them. Putting the bankrupt in jail will see to that.[27]

---

24 A *concordat* represents an agreement between the debtor and the creditors. Usually it includes a reduction and new schedule for the debts. But it requires a majority of the creditors in number (50%) and in claims (75%).

25 Before 1838, there were two bankruptcy procedures: the composition (*concordat*)or the liquidation of the assets (*union*) of the creditors. In the first case, the creditors authorized their debtor to pursue his trade and they granted him a remission of debts. When this agreement was not possible, the creditors united themselves against the debtor, who had to stop trading and was a "civilly dead" until his rehabilitation. When a bankrupt cannot obtain a *concordat*, the *union* of the creditors is meaning that the debtor continues to be pursued individually for his debts.

26 N. Levratto, « Abolition de la contrainte » ; P.-C. Hautcœur, « La statistique et la lutte contre la contrainte par corps », *Histoire & mesure*, XXIII, n° 1, 2008, p. 167–189.

27 « Dans les mœurs actuelles, la sévérité devient nécessaire ; les banqueroutes servent la fortune sans faire perdre l'honneur, et voilà ce qu'il importe de détruire. Qu'un

The debtors were then brought to Sainte-Pélagie prison where they were detained *à la pistole* (they had to pay hefty sums for the cell) or, after 1834, to the prison in Clichy.

Still this "barbaric law, which only aims at the unfortunate, and never the criminal[28]", was rarely enforced and the prisoner's life was apparently not too unpleasant. According to Moreau-Christophe, rich prisoners found in their "cell all the luxurious comforts of [a] hotel" and "rich or poor [...] all receive[d], from visitors, the solace of love or of friendship.[29]" Through a *topos* widely used by his contemporaries,[30] the author of this physiology of prisoners denounced the imprisonment of insolvent debtors as inefficient. Indeed only four out of the 141 bankrupts whose files we analysed were clearly detained in the *hostel of debt*.[31] Before as well as after the 1832 text, a lot of them probably benefited from safe-conducts liberally granted to those whose probity was beyond doubt.

Beyond insolvency (*faillite*), negligent and fraudulent bankruptcies (*banqueroutes simple et frauduleuse*) proceeded from the same distinction between the good and the bad trader: the jurisdiction drew a clear line between the inexperienced

failli n'affecte plus un air de triomphe ou du moins d'indifférence ; qu'il se présente du moins en public avec l'abattement d'un homme auquel il est arrivé un grand malheur ; et puisque les habitudes de la vie ont pris une direction différente, il faut les changer. L'incarcération du failli opérera cet effet. » Quoted by A.-C. Renouard, *Traité des faillites et banqueroutes*, 3e ed., Paris, Guillaumin, 1857, vol. 1, p. 135–136.

28 « [Cette] loi barbare, qui n'atteint que le malheur et jamais le crime. » H. de Balzac, *Œuvres diverses*, Paris, Gallimard, (Bibliothèque de la Pléiade), 1996, vol. II, p. 209.

29 « [Les riches détenus retrouvent dans] leur cellule toutes le[s] habitudes luxueuse de [leur hotel] [...] [et] riches ou pauvres, [...] tous reçoivent, des visitants et visitantes qui les viennent voir, les consolations de l'amour ou celles de l'amitié. » Moreau-Christophe, « Les détenus », in *Les Français peints par eux-mêmes: encyclopédie morale du dix-neuvième siècle*, L. Curmer (ed.), 1st ed. L. Curmer, 1840–1842, 10 vol., Paris, La Découverte, (Omnibus), 2004, vol. 2, p. 589–590. We have lightly modificated the ponctuation.

30 See : M. Croisy, *La question pénitentiaire vue par les romanciers : l'écrivain et la prison, les représentations de la prison dans les récits de 1830 à 1900*, PhD in History, University of Paris 3, work in progress.

31 *Archives départementales de Paris* (then AdP) : D11U3/93, file n° 7215, Joseph Opigez (1847) ; D11U3/176, file n° 11537, Charles Désiré Videcoq (1855) ; D11U3/261, file n° 14818, Amable Combette (1858) ; D11U3/531, file n° 6499, Benoît Dumont (1866). One should probably add : Auguste Poulet-Malassis, whose bankruptcy file (D11U3/399, file n° 606) does not say anything about his imprisonment mentioned by C. Baudelaire, *Correspondance*, Paris, Gallimard, (Bibliothèque de la Pléiade), 1973, vol. I, p. 793 note 2 and p. 808–809 note 1.

trader, who did not keep his ledger book up to date, and the dishonest man who had willingly hid his accounts from the judges.[32] To answer its numerous critics, the insolvency statute was gradually adapted, beginning in the 1830s, by establishing a distinction between traders, based on their morality.

The 1838 and 1889 reforms distinguished the unfortunate trader and the dishonest man

Criticism arose soon after the promulgation of the *Code* but it grew more vocal in the 1820s.[33] Three major criticisms were levelled at the bankruptcy procedure: the cost and the duration of the procedure and its harshness, which drove some traders in difficulty to unlawfully close their businesses. In a memorandum dated May 22nd, 1827, Count Peyronnet (Minister of Justice from 1821 to 1828, opposed to Napoleon's Empire) took into account the requests for reform and consulted the royal courts, as well as the chambers of commerce and courts. However, the work was delayed by the July Revolution of 1830 and only resumed in November 1833.[34] The examination of the project was lengthy and the text was only promulgated on May 28th, 1838. Although the principles of moralization, standardization, and legalization remained, the whole Book III of the *Code du commerce* was deeply modified, the procedure was reorganized and less harsh. Meanwhile, other laws suppressed stamps on trading books,[35] therefore cancelling the 500-franc fine imposed for each non-stamped book; registration fees were lowered,[36] and the Act dated April 17th, 1832, reduced the duration of imprisonment for insolvent debtors.[37]

---

32 Let us recall that the former is heard in a civil court and subject to one month to two years of prison, while the latter is heard in a court of assize and might be subject to several years of forced labour.

33 Good examples : J.-G. Locré, *Esprit du Code de commerce ou Commentaire puisé dans les procès-verbaux du Conseil d'État, les exposés de motifs et discours, les observations du Tribunal*, Paris, s.n., 1807 ; É. Vincens, *Exposition raisonnée de la législation commerciale, et examen critique du code de commerce*, Paris, Barrois l'aîné, 1821. Let us note that this author's remarks were used for the drafting of the law dated May 28th, 1838.

34 A.-C. Renouard, *Traité des faillites, vol. 1*, p. 176–180.

35 The *Code* imposes a control on the commercial books and the traders have must pay this control by a stamp.

36 A.-C. Renouard, *Traité des faillites, vol. 1*, p. 180 ; J. Hilaire, *Introduction historique*, p. 329–331.

37 N. Levratto, « Abolition de la contrainte ».

The May 28th, 1838, Statute

The 1838 text had the same goal of cutting the cost and reducing the length of the procedure. Several measures were instituted to simplify it. The complex handover between officers, the temporary and permanent trustees – who were often one and the same person[38] – was discontinued: the officers disappeared and, in an effort to prevent fraud, the creditors no longer named their own representatives, but the judge appointed one or more trustees after consulting the creditors (art. 462). As indicated by N. Coquery and N. Praquin, this led to trustees becoming more professional,[39] which influenced the way the disputes were settled. Furthermore, in order to hasten the end of the procedure, in case it was proven that creditors could not receive enough compensation from the benefits of the trial, the 1838 text defined a new kind of resolution: closure for lack of assets (art. 527 and 528).[40] The benefit of the new law obviously lay in facilitating the procedure, for both debtors and creditors. On the one hand, commercial insolvency was declared not at the time of the suspension of payment but when insolvency was decreed (art. 441), allowing the trader to administer his assets until he was condemned. In order for this freedom not to harm the creditors, several dispositions were enacted in their favour by creating a ""nuanced system of invalidity" or more precisely of unenforceability on the mass [of all the creditors together]".[41] On the other hand, the imprisonment of the insolvent merchant was now restricted: it was mandatory when bankruptcy was declared by a court or requested by the creditors, it became optional if the business was put into liquidation within three days after the judgment (art. 456), and the debtor who exceeded the statutory period could receive a temporary safe-conduct from the judge (art. 472). Furthermore, the insolvent merchant and his family could have access to some form of "alimentary" aid (art. 473). Thus some insolvent book traders were allowed to keep their

38 J. Hilaire, *Introduction historique*, p. 327.

39 N. Coquery et N. Praquin, « Règlement des faillites et pratiques judiciaires. De l'entre-soi à l'expertise du syndic (1673–1899) », *Histoire & mesure*, XXIII, n° 1, 2008, p. 43–83.

40 Imagined since 1838 this modality of bankrupt closing is effective with the 1856's law. The *concordat par abandon d'actif* "gave the possibility to the bankrupt who benefited it to restart a new business without having to fear that his new assets could be seized in order to compensate his creditors." (P.-C. Hautcoeur et N. Levratto, « Does the law alone explain the rise in bankruptcies in XIXth century France? », p. 4.)

41 J. Hilaire, *Introduction historique*, p. 331. The period labelled as dubious, prior to the ruling, during which some operation might be deemed as void, could not be extended at the creditors request before the time of verification and claim of the debts. (art. 446 à 449).

furniture or part of their industrial equipment; others received money not only during the bankruptcy but also after the creditors' union. These lenient measures were in tradition with the repressive logic of the legislation. On July 22th, 1867 imprisonment for debt was finally abolished.

Chart 2: Classical and new outcomes of the commercial bankruptcy in the nineteenth century

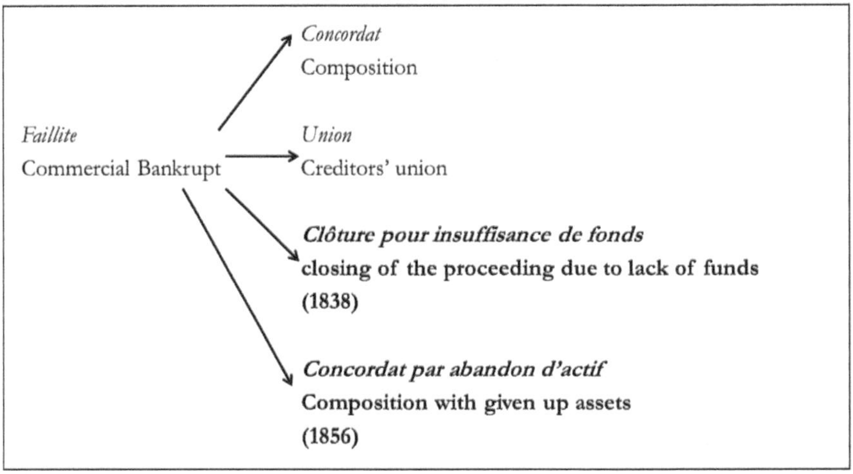

The road to the 1889 Act

However, the limits of the 1838 text were once again quickly denounced but the criticisms, which peaked in the 1860s, did not lead to an essential reform of the system until the end of the nineteenth century. The criticisms focused on three aspects: amicable settlements under the supervision of the court, the abolition of the imprisonment of insolvent debtors and the need for different procedures to differentiate the unfortunate debtor from the dishonest trader. Such distinction was not properly achieved until the 1889 reform.

The unrest in the 1840s was particularly strong and peaked with the 1848 revolutions. The temporary government made decisions (the decree dated March 19th, 1848), which satisfied no one.[42] Some jurists, like Jules Favre, wanted to have the amicable settlements adopted by the majority of creditors automatically approved, while others like Pierre Bravard-Veyrières wanted to defend the interests

42 A.-C. Renouard, *Traité des faillites, vol. 1*, p. 180–185.

of creditors with harsh laws against debtors,[43] in keeping with the *Code* of 1807. On August 22th, 1848, five months after the first decree, the government promulgated a second decree that matched Jules Favre's proposition.[44] This only increased the debate: as the second decree had suppressed the first, François Dabeaux (then MP for Haute-Garonne until 1851, when he became, for supporting the coup, master of requests to the State Council) immediately requested the abrogation of the first decree, which took place in November 1849. Bravard-Veyrières and others – the literary critic Sainte-Beuve among them –, saw that the second decree was contradictory with the 1838 law and asked for its abolition. These laws revealed the instability of the bankruptcy system as well as the abundance of reform proposals. Some projects were abandoned – notably those in favour of workers – but other proposals were more fruitful. Bravard-Veyrières proposed to implement a composition with given assets in 1850. A growing number of debtors had apparently taken to offering assignment of their assets in order to return to business as soon as possible.[45] To ensure the legality of the bankruptcy, Bravard-Veyrières suggested a new meaning of the amicable settlement to both fight the "de-codification" promoted by the 1838 law, and stop debtors from embezzling or concealing assets.[46] It came into force with the text of July 17th, 1856, and became a solution that included the advantages of suspension of payment.[47]

43 P.-C.-J.-B. Bravard-Veyrières, *Traité des faillites et des banqueroutes : extrait du cours professé à la Faculté de droit de Paris*, Paris, A. Marescq, 1864.

44 "Art. 2. The Commercial Court has the right, in case an amicable settlement is already agreed between the debtor and at least half of the number of creditors representing three-quarter of the amount, to exempt the debtor from the seal procedure and from the judicial inventory." [*Art. 2. Le tribunal de commerce aura la faculté, si un arrangement amiable est déjà consenti entre le débiteur et la moitié en nombre de ses créanciers, représentant les trois quarts en somme, de dispenser le débiteur de l'apposition des scellés et de l'inventaire judiciaire*] A.-C. Renouard, *Traité des faillites, vol. 1*, p. 185.

45 *Ibid.*, p. 187.

46 Y. Guyot et A. Raffalovich (ed.), « Entrepreneur et entreprise », dans *Dictionnaire du commerce, de l'industrie et de la banque*, Y. Guyot et A. Raffalovich (ed.), Paris, Guillaumin et Cie, 1901, vol. II, p. 130.

47 N. Levratto, « Abolition de la contrainte », p. 241–244.

Chart 3: Classical and new opening modalities of commercial insolvency trial

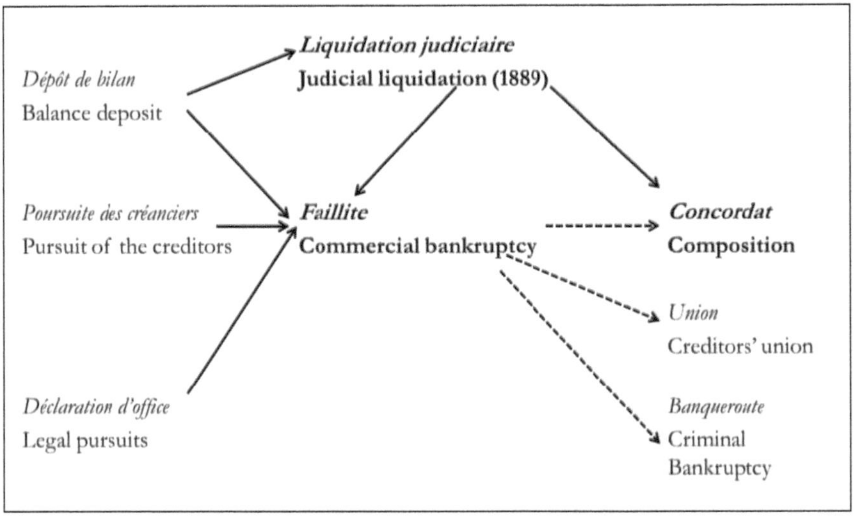

Perception of bankruptcy kept on changing throughout the 1840s, with even quicker change in the 1860s, probably the effect of the previous reflections on it. The literary production on commercial law in general, and on commercial insolvency in particular, are good proof of it. One of the criticisms levelled at the 1807 *Code* and the 1838 law remained unanswered even after the suppression of the imprisonment of insolvent debtors, a measure which hit "imprudence, misfortune and crime indiscriminately[48]". Hippolyte François Mascret indirectly became its most vocal supporter in the preamble of his famous *Dictionnaire des faillites* (1863) when he distinguished the unfortunate good trader from the scheming crook[49]

48 J.-B. Bayle-Mouillard, *De l'emprisonnement pour dettes, considérations sur son origine, ses rapports avec la morale publique et les intérêts du commerce, etc.*, Paris, Impr. royale, 1836, p. 127 ; cité par P.-C. Hautcœur, « La statistique et la lutte », p. 174.

49 "In short, for the honest man hit by misfortune and accepting the consequences of unearned tragedies, our society should not add another misfortune. But it should be different, at least we hope, for those it would upset, without remorse, in their disrespectful luxury, and for those whom golden insolvency would reveal and stigmatise" [*En résumé, pour l'homme honnête frappé dans sa fortune et résigné aux conséquences de catastrophes imméritées, notre publicité ne peut être un malheur nouveau. Mais il n'en sera pas de même, nous l'espérons du moins, pour ceux qu'elle troublerait, à défaut de remords, dans leur luxe insolent, pour ceux encore dont elle démasquerait et stigmatiserait l'insolvabilité dorée.*] H.-F. Mascret, *Dictionnaire en tableaux synoptiques d'après*

while advocating for giving bankruptcy more publicity. The push for making bankruptcy more public testifies to the important economic transformations of the period, with the expansion of credit and the development of new corporate structures, both instrumental in the evolution of insolvency statutes.[50]

But, just as in 1848, the political environment hastened changes in the legal treatment of economic failure. In fact, the statute dated March 4th 1889, was partly inherited from the special jurisdiction set into place after the 1870' war.[51] These limited measures based on "customary liquidations" reignited the debate in the late 1870s and early 1880s.[52] Building on the experience of 1871 and on different models abroad – especially Belgium and the United Kingdom[53] –, the March 4th, 1889 Statute altered significantly the spirit of the *Code de commerce* while softening the treatment of the debtor. Liquidation, granted to the trader or the company filing for insolvency within fifteen days after suspension of payment, allowed the debtor to carry on with his business. This new procedure did not prescribe a publication of the bankruptcy in order to protect the trader's reputation. It was designed to lead to a simple composition (with part of the debt forgiven) or a composition with assigned assets.[54] Only if the debtor did not get a composition would he have to go through the traditional insolvency procedure. The creation of a specific protocol led to the Béranger law of December 30th, 1903 facilitating the full redemption of the honest trader after suspension of payment.[55] Liquidation paradoxically strengthened the repressive dimension of insolvency procedures in the late nineteenth century or even early twentieth century.[56]

---

les journaux judiciaires des faillites, séparations de biens, nominations de conseils judiciaires, interdictions et réhabilitations prononcées par les tribunaux de Paris, depuis le 24 février 1848…, Paris, Chez l'auteur, 1863, vol. I, p. VI–VII.

50 P.-C. Hautcœur et N. Levratto, « Faillite », in *Dictionnaire historique de l'économie-droit, XVIIIe–XXe siècles*, A. Stanziani (ed.), Paris, LGDJ, (Droit et société, n° 17), 2007, p. 162–163.

51 J. Hilaire, *Introduction historique*, p. 333. And which has been extended beyond March 13th, 1872 by some courts.

52 J. Lefort, « La réforme de la législation des faillites », *Journal des Economistes. Revue de la science économique et de la statistique*, vol. 46, avril-juin, 1889, p. 3–16. At the end of the 1870s, several study groups were set up; the first proposals were introduced in the Parliament as early as April 1879 followed by one after the other until the law was enacted on March 4th, 1889.

53 *Ibid.*, p. 10.

54 J. Hilaire, *Introduction historique*, p. 333 ; N. Praquin, « Les faillites au XIXe siècle », p. 364.

55 N. Praquin, « Les faillites au XIXe siècle », p. 364 ; P.-C. Hautcœur et N. Levratto, « Faillite », p. 163–164.

56 J. Hilaire, *Introduction historique*, p. 336–339.

Slowly but surely, bankruptcy law took shape during the nineteenth century. Procedures of economic failure became more complex, and due to the growing number of companies, the judicial system was enriched. Although the system was still repressive, several procedures for insolvency were instituted in order to soften the fate of honest debtors. Furthermore, particularly so with the imprisonment of insolvent debtors, there seem to have been discrepancies between the judicial texts and the actual handling of bankruptcy, making research into the behaviour and relations of the involved parties particularly important, as they set the tone of the moral treatment of trade.

The *Code* and honour: bankruptcy, a matter of trust

Raising the moral standard of trade

The importance of bankruptcy files for historians was highlighted quite late in France.[57] Those files often contain pieces from three separate stages of the procedure (the beginning, the investigations concerning the debtor's solvency, the outcome) during which three actors (the bankrupt, the creditors, the court officers) took a more or less important part, all willing to raise the moral standard of trade.

Chart 4: Heuristic schema of the insolvency procedure's steps

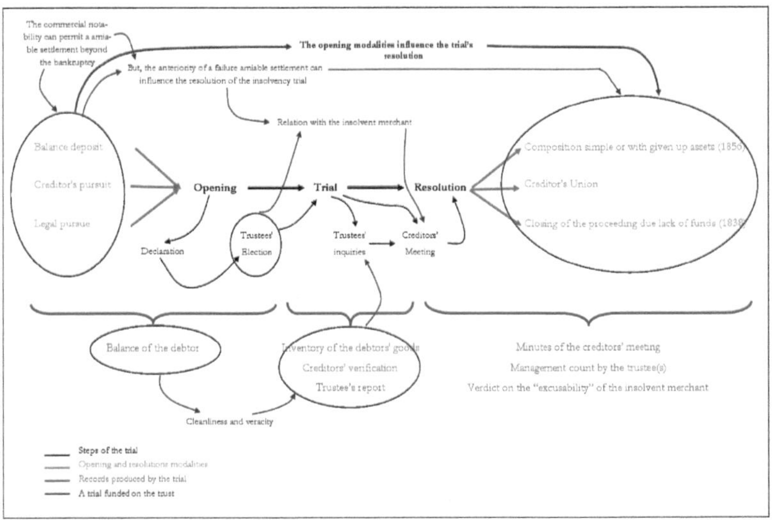

57 H. Hauser, « Une source de l'histoire du commerce et des banques : le fonds des faillites », *Annales d'histoire économique et sociale*, vol. 3, n° 12, 1931, p. 542–550.

Filing for bankruptcy

The procedure began at the request of the debtor, at that of his creditors, or imposed by a judicial authority. After that the trader had to liquidate his business within three days after suspension of payment had been proven. Despite what Jacques Savary des Bruslons, the 1807 *Code* (art. 471) and legal and commercial textbooks[58] strongly prescribed, nineteenth-century bankruptcy statements bear a lot of resemblance to those of the early modern era. Short and heterogeneous[59] in form, they rarely followed the legal instructions on presentation. Four pages at most, book traders' bankruptcy statements generally separated assets and liabilities, displayed at best on a double page with amounts opposite each other, or with successive titles in a single column. The description of the assets often followed the recommended order, first detailing the movable then the immovable property, and logically from the more public to the more private items: the assessment of cash on hand, goods and industrial equipment, then personal furniture or non-industrial real estate property. Then the outstanding debts were listed, usually separating the good from the doubtful ones. However when determining the assets, debts unlikely to be recovered were mixed up with the rest. As for liabilities, they usually appeared as a list of individual names with sometimes their status and addresses, in alphabetical order or order of importance, or according to some other logic like the day when they had entered the ledger book – though no chronological information was indicated– or even, but rarely so, according to the creditor's occupation. Making the presentation of the bankrupt's accounts as clean, exact and truthful as possible was a proof of credibility.

Once appointed, the officers or temporary trustees were in charge of checking whether the bankrupt was solvent and in good faith. Unless it had already been done, they drew up the bankrupt's balance sheet or corrected it; then made an inventory of the bankrupt's assets and took part in the examination of the creditors' debt obligations under supervision of the judge from the Commercial Court.

58 J. Savary Des Bruslons, *Dictionnaire universel de commerce: contenant tout ce qui concerne le commerce qui se fait dans les quatre parties du monde… Ouvrage posthume du Sr Jacques Savary Des Bruslons… continué… et donné au public, par Philémon-Louis Savary, … Nouvelle édition*, Paris, Vve Estienne, 1741 ; *Code du commerce*, 1807 (art. 471 confirmé par l'art. 439 de la loi de 1838) ; P.-C.-J.-B. Bravard-Veyrières, *Traité des faillites*, en particulier p. 44–47.

59 N. Coquery, « Les faillites boutiquières ».

The inventory

The inventory often took several days of work for the trustees, assisted by the local justice officer. Items were examined individually in the presence of the trader, his wife or one of his employees; the examination helped to get a very precise idea not only of his home and workplace, but also of all the "everyday things"[60] in the debtor's life. For example, after the industrial, commercial and personal assets of Joseph Bry, the inventory of which had required the trustee to go to Meudon where the debtor lived,[61] there followed the list of books, papers and declarations of the bankrupt and his relatives.

Those documents revealed part of the debtors' private life, commercial strategy, and legal strategy, as well as the credit practices of the troubled book traders. Like a lot of women, working-class or not, Madame Dupuich used pawnshops as savings banks,[62] thus protecting what property was vital for the household, the essential furniture for example. Furthermore, separation as to property, requested when the first troubles occurred, was an economic strategy, in the case of bankruptcy, which elevated the debtor's wife to the rank of a primary creditor, thus shifting the balance of power against the mass of unsecured creditors. These strategies of trying to preserve a minimal property could account for some incoherence between the lists of creditors established by the bankrupts themselves and that checked by the trustees.

The verification of creditors

Soon after the inventory, the verification of creditors was performed under the supervision of a court judge. When officially summoned, they had to present their claims in person or through a proxyholder within the period of time set by law.[63] The more numerous the creditors, or the later their claims were made, the longer the checking took. Those registers, though sometimes difficult to read

60 D. Roche, *Histoire des choses banales: naissance de la consommation dans les sociétés traditionnelles (XVII*[e]*–XIX*[e] *siècle)*, Paris, Fayard, 1997.

61 AdP : D11U3/389, file n° 211.

62 L. Fontaine, *L'Économie morale. Pauvreté, crédit et confiance dans l'Europe préindustrielle*, Paris, Gallimard, (NRF essais), 2008, p. 164–189.

63 The periods for the presentation of the creditor's claims were fixed by the *Code* of 1807 to forty days (art. 502), but to twenty-three days by the 1838 Act (art. 492). Moreover, and in order to reduce the length of the proceedings, the additional periods decreased further: one day for three myriameters in 1807 (art. 511), lowered to one day for five myriameters in 1838 (art. 492).

because written by tired hard-pressed court clerks, still abound in information. They reveal the credit network built by traders in their activity, and are telling of the life of each individual company. We must keep in mind that both the inventory of the bankrupt's assets and the verification of creditors allowed the judge to determine whether the declarations of the trader were truthful, thus getting to know his honesty, an important factor for the continuation of the procedure.

The report of the trustees and the meeting of the creditors

The trustees listed the main items of their investigation and made a report which was read during the creditors' meeting – just before the vote for the outcome of the procedure. These reports reveal that examining the bankrupt's solvency was in fact an investigation into his lifestyle: trustees were in charge of screening the trader's past – public and private – for elements which could truly enlighten his credit and credibility. Most reports kept at the Commercial Court of the Seine and the Paris Departmental Archives[64] review the bankrupts' personal situations and the companies' histories from creation to fall. They amount to letters between different ministries, or services of a ministry. As far as book trading is concerned, we often see cross-checkings between what information was given by book trade inspectors or the prefectural services dedicated to the Direction of Book Trade, attached to the Ministry of Interior, and what was later presented by the trustees. Likewise, some trustees corresponded with other jurisdictions to get additional information.[65] Despite some extraordinary cases, after the 1838 law, reports written by trustees gradually evolved into real accounting documents with less qualitative information. From then on, quantitative information formerly a small chapter at the end, prevailed. This did not necessarily help troubled traders, as proven by the increase of creditors' unions.

During the creditors' meeting, after reading his report, the trustee – successively acting for the different parties – allowed the debtor to make proposals for the creditors to decide upon. The bankruptcy settlement, reached with a double *quorum* – of the number of creditors and the amounts due – as set by law (1807,

64 We could see, for example, in the Yvelines Departmental Archives different methods of conservation: only the bankrupts' statements and the trustees' verifications remain in the bankruptcy files.

65 See the case of Paul Valentin Dupray de la Mahérie, developed in my PhD or in the article: V. Rebolledo-Dhuin, « Paul Valentin Dupray de la Mahérie (1828–1911), « marchand de salade » ou escroc au long cours. Un libraire en quête de sociabilité », *Criminocorpus, revue hypermédia. Histoire de la justice, des crimes et des peines*, 2012.

art. 519; 1838, art. 507), sometimes provoked extraordinary meetings, where tensions prevailed on the day of the verdict. For instance, during the trial of the medical bookseller Joseph Gabon, on November 15th, 1830, at the peak of the crisis of the book trade, the bankrupt's proxyholder, the lawyer Delattre, left the meeting and fetched his client when the court refused to hear him. Gabon then interrupted the trustee as he was reading his report, refused to let him resume and denied the report, reciting the "observation he had written himself [...] [but] overwhelmed by emotion, he could not go through with his reading". Although his offer was to pay the full amount (principal, interest and fees) of his debts within eight years, it was turned down. Poor Gabon did not get his creditors' agreement – essentially because he and "the girl Caroline Cleppé", with whom he had eloped to Brussels when he suspended payment of his debt, were living unmarried; and because a composition granted by creditors had to be approved by the court.[66]

The court sometimes vetoed the decision voted by creditors, mostly because the traders had already gone bankrupt before. So it was for the popular publishers Pierre Henri Krabbe in 1860 or Ernest Glaeser two years later, whose creditors were forced into a union.[67] What could have been a marital mistake, or a financial one, eventually came to affect the credibility of a book trader in trouble. The judge had to decide whether the bankrupt could be excused, after setting up an individual record including his civil status and all previous convictions –determining whether he could be rehabilitated or was beyond excuse, or was to be preventively imprisoned for negligent or fraudulent bankruptcy. The trustee had to report on the progress of his operation during the liquidation. Thus, he could be under suspicion of collusion with the parties, or even of dishonesty. Balzac often voiced the same accusations, especially when he had the narrator of his great novel about bankruptcy say:

> The agent, instead of being the creditors' man, may play into the debtor's hands. [...] The agent can make something out of both sides, [...] and in this way can hold with the hare and run with the hounds. [...] The agent turns to the best furnished crib [...]. In nine hundred and ninety-nine cases out of a thousand, the agent is for the debtor. [...] Moral: Let the debtor choose his trustees, verify the claims, and arrange the amount of composition himself.[68]

---

66 AdP : D11U3/66, file n° 6232, creditors' meeting and union contract, November 15th, 1830.

67 AdP : D11U3/307, file n° 16633 ; D11U3/386, file n° 120.

68 « L'agent, au lieu d'être l'homme des créanciers, peut devenir l'homme du débiteur. [...] Il ménage la chèvre et le chou [...], se tourne vers le râtelier le mieux garni [...] Sur une moyenne de mille faillites, l'agent est neuf cent cinquante fois l'homme du

The influence of the different parties on the outcome of the settlement

Although the aim of the law was to intervene between the parties in conflict, reducing their scope for action to prevent insidious agreements, the bankruptcy procedure was in itself deeply contractual. Even if starting the bankruptcy procedure broke the trust between the parties – since the impossible amicable settlement publicly made the Commercial Court the arbiter – it mainly challenged the previous agreement between the parties, judging of the possibility of its renewal through the assessment of the bankrupt's honesty. The bankrupt, the creditors and the court officers (judges and trustees) all held prime roles in this "drama of commerce". The bankrupt showed his good will, his honesty and his solvency by performing the liquidation as expected by the other parties in order to gain his creditors' leniency. The creditors aimed at recovering as much of their credit as possible but, because of their respective status and relation to the bankrupt, their calculations differed, which might lead to disputes. Finally, judges and trustees were linked with both groups. The point of the meeting between the parties was to try to reconcile everyone's best interests.

Beyond the trial: notability enables private settlement?

Before filing for bankruptcy, unfortunate traders sometimes tried to avoid the misery of a trial and the dishonour attached to it by some procrastinating proposals and amicable remittances before the procedure started. Although sometimes generous, the proposals were not always unanimously accepted. For example, although Hector Bossange offered to pay 40% of his debts, with an up-front of 15% so as "to avoid liquidation he knew would be lethal to the interests of his creditors", as well as to his own honour; and although his proposal was accepted by "a large number of his [creditors] [...], a few third parties refused it, in the hope they might gain some specific benefit[69]". Hector Bossange was thus forced to liquidation, which was detrimental not so much to his own business as to his creditors, who were only granted a 15% pay-out in three years. Furthermore, when bankruptcy was declared, previous settlements leading to a disagreement between the creditors and their debtor or between the creditors themselves partly influenced the opinion of the Commercial Court. The judges

failli. [...] Morale : Le débiteur nomme ses syndics, vérifie ses créances et arrange son concordat lui-même. », H. de Balzac, *CH*, t. VI, p. 273–276. (trans. *The Rise and Fall of César Birotteau. The Secret of a Princess*, London, Forgotten Books, 1906, p. 280–284).

69 AdP : D11U3/87, file n° 6948, trustee's report, July, 16th 1831, we underline.

of the Commercial Court, as well as the trustees, seemed particularly anxious to preserve their legitimacy because they had been co-opted, and they had become public figures.[70] As traders who were elected by their fellow traders and as non-professional members of the judicial system, judges and trustees insisted on showing their attachment to the "rule of law"[71] by assuming a neutral position and air of distance, which gave them more credibility and made them closer to magistrates. In their reports trustees often denounced amicable settlements signed outside of the procedures as pointless, or even odious. So "Monsieur Johanneau uselessly attempted to reach an amicable settlement"[72] before going to court; as well, "in the grip of great troubles did Monsieur Faure, after pointlessly fighting and trying to reach an amicable settlement, decided on March 14th [1868] to file for bankruptcy, with regard for society".[73] Trustees sometimes indicated the damaging effects of such external schemes",[74] for both creditors and future bankrupt book traders. Still, such settlements aimed at controlling and ensuring ethics as well as coherence in the traders' community. Johanneau, Faure and Pétion were actually granted their compositions.

The traders' community wielded a lot of power in the procedure

In practice, the attitude of judges and trustees matched the will of the legislator as they tried to avoid creditors' unions, as testified by the successive changes in the bankruptcy law.

Studying the occupations of the judicial actors is of great interest. When insolvent book traders' trials were arbitrated by book trade people, the result often favoured them. In the Commercial Court there were few publishers or book

---

70 C. Lemercier, « Les carrières des membres des institutions consulaires parisiennes au XIXe siècle », *Histoire & mesure*, XX, n° 1/2, 2005, p. 59–95 ; « Discipliner le commerce », p. 68 ; *Un modèle français de jugement des pairs. Les tribunaux de commerce, 1790–1880*, HDR, University of Paris VIII Vincennes-Saint Denis, 2012, in particular chap. II ; S. Humbert, « À l'instar de "César Birotteau", des juges honnêtes et de loyaux commerçants à Lille aux XVIIIe et XIXe siècle? », *Revue d'histoire de la Justice*, 17, Les Tribunaux de commerce. Genèse et enjeux d'une institution, 2007, p. 145–152.

71 P. Bourdieu, « La force du droit. Éléments pour une sociologie du champ juridique », *Actes de la recherche en sciences sociales*, vol. 64, n° 1, 1986, p. 3–19.

72 AdP : D11U3/64, file n° 6134, trustee's report, June, 26th 1830.

73 AdP : D11U3/591, file n° 9291, trustee's report August, 18th, 1868.

74 AdP : D11U3/169, file n° 11243, November, 28th 1853. We borrow from the trustee Thiébault his phrase in his report dated March 14th, 1854: "The man Pilon thought he could save [his] situation by an external scheme (*combinaison en dehors*), but it aborted."

traders[75] but those few never failed to favour their fellow book traders in trouble. Between 1825 and 1870, 50% to 70% of book traders' bankruptcy procedures over which they presided ended up with a composition.[76] However, according to Balzac or to the jurist Raymond Serville, the "bankruptcy judge [was] often a sluggish character" on whom the "trustee often succeed[ed] in making a positive impression.[77]" The percentage of compositions reached by trustees coming from the book trade was even more impressive: until the 1838 Act bankruptcy officers belonging to the book trade managed close to 40% of all procedures between 1825 and 1839, and more than 80% of those ended up with a composition between the parties.

Generally speaking, creditors' unions seemed to be particularly unfavourable to the bankrupt as well as to the unsecured creditors, not only because the procedure tended to drag on and the legal fees were high, but also because liquidation, especially for books in stock – often auctioned by weight – contributed to reduce the dividend the creditors could expect. Indeed, while a composition was granted within two years if assets had not been assigned[78] –, a creditors' union took as long as four years and a half. Assessing how much dividend could be recovered by creditors was particularly harmful to this type of procedure. Although trustees

75 Around 5% according to C. Lemercier, *Un modèle français.*, annexe 8 who counts 8 people from the book trade among the 156 judges in the Commercial Court between 1832 and 1847. We thank Claire Lemercier for sending us her more extended database covering the whole century, which accounts for 22 book trader and publishers among 426 judges.

76 AdP : D10U3, 1825–1870. We note that of 474 bankruptcies filed, 78 (16%) were presided over people from the book trade (print salers, printers, book traders, papermaker) and 53 (68%) of those end up with a composition signed between the debtor and his creditors. Book traders were more generous than printers: the latter took part in 10 bankruptcies and only granted five compositions, while the former were in favour of the parties in 34 of the 49 cases.

77 R. Serville, « Étude sur les syndics de faillites (réformes qui pourraient être introduites dans l'organisation de leurs pouvoirs et de leurs fonctions, d'après l'examen des principales législations étrangères) », *Bulletin de la société de législation comparée*, vol. 17, n° 5, 5 mai 1888, p. 441.

78 É. Richard (ed.), *Droit des affaires*, p. 562–563. The author notes that liquidation with assignment of assets, created by the law dated July 17th, 1856, can be performed in two ways : either "the bankrupt gives up his properties to his creditors in payment of his debts and the creditors become undivided owners before sharing some time afterward » ; or the bankrupt keeps the formal ownership of the property in order to only transmit the useful possession to the creditors along with the right to sell them." We then understand that in both cases, the liquidation with assignment of assets take as much time as the creditors union.

were more attached to the debtors' moral credibility, before 1838 they edited the bankrupt's book shop balance sheet, applying a hefty depreciation to the goods in warehouse.[79] "Newer trustees" were more interested than their predecessors in using accounting as a tool for measuring and estimating the ethic of the business. They often evaluated the stock of the bankrupt book shop and depreciated it in order to offer a realistic dividend. For example, Louis Janet' widow said she had 126.554,41 francs worth of books in her shops. The trustee estimated the lot, after a "10% depreciation rate[80]", at 58.290,30 francs, that is to say a real depreciation rate of 54%. While bankrupt traders estimated their goods based on their selling prices, trustees evaluated possible earnings in an auction – through judicial and/ or professional newspapers, like *Bibliographie de la France* – or by weight on retail prices depending on the popularity of the books, of their authors or of the authors of the autographs inside. Some book traders got their supply from auction houses such as Hôtel Drouot. Ambroise Firmin-Didot already noted in 1831 that it took around ten years for an edition to be sold out. So, due to the usual markdowns, book prices continuously decreased as years went by.[81] Yet, when the bankrupt did not sell off his stocks himself in order to honour the composition, the stocks were auctioned by weight. It is quite logical that a longer procedure should have decreased the benefits creditors could expect. Dividends, rarely evaluated at the beginning of the century,[82] were higher in case of a composition than with a creditor's union.[83] The trustees presented the different stages of the bankrupt assets and liabilities and played a major role in evaluating how much creditors could get. For their estimation, their premise was that a composition would be signed, so

79 Our study strengthen N. Praquin's one, « Les faillites au XIXe siècle », p. 376, since the trustees say they estimate the books in store with a depreciation rate of 10 to 90% compared to the bankrupt's declarations.

80 AdP: D11U3/169, file n° 11250, declaration dated December 1st, 1853, inventory done from December 5th, 1853 and balance sheet presented by the bankrupt on November 30th, 1853.

81 A.-F. Didot, *Réponses aux questions soumises par MM. les membres de la Chambre Commerce de Paris, sur la situation de la Librairie, de l'Imprimerie, de la Fonderie de caractères, et de la Papeterie*, Paris, impr. Ambroise Firmin Didot, 1831.

82 AdP: D11U3 : 21 of the 48 trustees reports (among the 141 studied bankruptcy files) not mentioning any pay-out are dated 1830.

83 P.-C. Hautcœur et N. Levratto, « Les défaillances d'entreprises au 19ème siècle en France: du droit à la pratique », Seminar EHESS, Paris, 2006 ; P. Labardin, « Comprendre le comportement des acteurs dans les faillites à partir de l'évaluation comptable. Une étude dans le département de la Seine (1847–1887) », Journées d'histoire de la comptabilité et du management, Lille III, IRHIS, 2010.

they often reduced the dividends to next to nothing. Moreover their estimations would be lower, compared to what the bankrupt had offered, so the creditors tended consequently to agree with the latter.

The importance of judicial ethics was not specific to bankruptcies in the Parisian book trade, and it supported the intentions of the authorities, which made sure that union was an extraordinary outcome across the country, or at least that it was less appealing than composition. With the *Compte général de l'administration de la justice civile et commerciale,*[84] the legislator became aware of some malfunctions and tried to correct them. The Statute of July 17th, 1856, instituting the liquidation with assignment of assets, clearly tried to reduce the number of bankruptcies ending in union, which had been increasing continuously from the beginning of the century. This trend worried the minister of justice who observed in 1880 that legislation had failed.[85] Indeed, the new 1856 procedure was so slow that it did not appeal to creditors. Although the dividends (apart from the legal procedure costs) granted – or hoped – after unions were usually lower than those granted in compositions, they were safer and more quickly obtained – and since the 1870s, it had been easier to get more than 50% of the amount of debts with a union than with a composition. Thus the minister of justice widely publicized his request that statistics about the dividends obtained through assignment of assets be published from 1877, because he wanted to highlight that in case of a disagreement, the medium way was the most profitable.

Every actor of the legal system tried to preserve and support judicial procedure, seeing it as the most conducive way to settle disputes. Judges and trustees were especially anxious to fulfil this mission, both to legitimate their functions and preserve the cohesion of the traders' community. Contrary to Raymond Serville's

84 *Compte général de l'administration de la justice civile et commerciale*: General accounting of civil and commercial justice administration. This annual and official publication is part of the state's willingness to evaluate the efficiency of the different courts. Published from 1840, the *Comptes* include several thousand pages of statistics every year, based on a collection of the data produced by each Commercial Court.

85 "We are dumbfounded by the diminution of the number of compositions which, since 1846–50, did not stop, even if we take into account the compositions by assignment of assets. The increase in the number of bankruptcies closed by lack of assets is very high, so that the interests in commercial business are less and less safe." Ministère de la Justice, *Compte général de l'administration de la justice civile et commerciale en France*, Paris, Imprimerie royale, 1831, during the year 1880, p. XXXVII ; quoted in part by P.-C. Hautcœur, « Produire des statistiques : pour quoi faire ? L'échec de la statistique des faillites en France au XIXe siècle », *Histoire & mesure*, XXIII, n° 1, 2008, p. 122.

thoughts, it seems that, across the whole period, trustees mostly aimed at balancing the social and material desires of the involved parties and making bankruptcy a conciliation procedure.

Starting the bankruptcy procedure represented a breaking point in a relationship based on trust since the amicable settlement required the Commercial Court to be the arbiter. It mainly put to the test the agreement previously reached between the parties, judging whether renewing it was possible, based on the study of the bankrupt's honesty. The declaration of bankruptcy, the process and the outcome was a moment when the parties' credibility was assessed, so that the trial resembled an investigation into the debtor's morality and honour. Beyond the study of the legal process of bankruptcy to which it was central, the more general question of credit in the book trade at large is a point to consider.

Bankruptcy and credit in the Parisian book trade

For economists bankruptcies are synonymous of a break of trust, a sign of crisis, and are useful tools for business demographers who follow Alfred Marshall and study companies' life-cycles. The corpus we studied shows results differing from those found by previous analysis. More generally, book traders, often lacking credit can make the economic and social context of the legal procedure of bankruptcy more understandable.

Book traders going bankrupt: a French exception?

Business demographers rely on the constitutive instruments of businesses, considered their birth, as well as on bankruptcies, their death, to study business flows and stocks in order to better understand how fast and where industrialization took place,[86] or how the industrial fabric evolved.[87]

As far as the number of business bankruptcies is concerned, Luc Marco's reference study shows that French bankruptcies followed a rising trend for almost

86 P. Jobert et J.-C. Chevaillier, « La démographie des entreprises en France au XIXe siècle. Quelques pistes », *Histoire, économie et société*, vol. 2, 1986, p. 233–264 ; A. Strauss et P. Verley, « Parisian industries and national capitalism in the first half of the nineteeth century (1830–1850) », in *The birth and death of companies. An historical perspective*, P. Jobert et M. Moss (ed.), Carnfoth/Park Ridge, The Parthenon Publishing Group, 1990, p. 89–103.

87 M. Lescure, *PME et croissance économique. L'expérience française des années 1920*, Paris, Économica, (Collection Économies et sociétés contemporaines), 1996.

two centuries (1820–1988).[88] According to the author, an inflection point occurred around 1840, when the flow of bankruptcies was below this trend. The rising number of bankruptcies can be related to the increasing pace of industrialization.

The curve representing bankruptcies in the Parisian book trade, established from the bankruptcy registers of the Seine department Commercial Court, generally follows that of the national bankruptcies which concerns all businesses as established in the *Compte Général* for this period.[89] Among all bankrupt traders, people from the book trade represented a minority with no statistical significance: they accounted for less than 2% of all national as well as Parisian bankruptcies.[90] Within this ill-defined business, bookseller-publishers and printers were the bulk of the working companies, and logically of the bankrupt businesses. However, a major difference can be noted: while the flow of the bankruptcies of Parisian printers contributed to the increase in the general number of bankruptcies in the book trade, the number of Parisian bookseller-publishers going bankrupt decreased during the whole period, as shown in the chart below.

88 L. Marco, *La montée des faillites en France, XIXe-XXe siècles*, Paris, L'Harmattan, (Logiques économiques), 1989.

89 Our census, based on the bankruptcy registers (AdP: D10U3), takes into account the bookseller-publishers, the printers, the papermakers, the engravers, the bookbinders and the writers. However, because we checked the registers according to the files of trades in bankruptcy – created by the archives centre – from the book trade and short of entering the full list, our census is probably undervalued, especially relatively to "secondary" trades: founders, etc.

90 1,85 % on average both on the national scale (between 1886 and 1913) as on that of Paris (between 1848 and 1863, under an analysis of a sample of the Mascret's *Dictionnaire des faillites*, built from one page on five – 1, 6, 11, 16, etc. – of the first volume of the periodical publication).

Chart 5: Development of bankruptcies among Parisian bookseller-publishers, 1820–1913

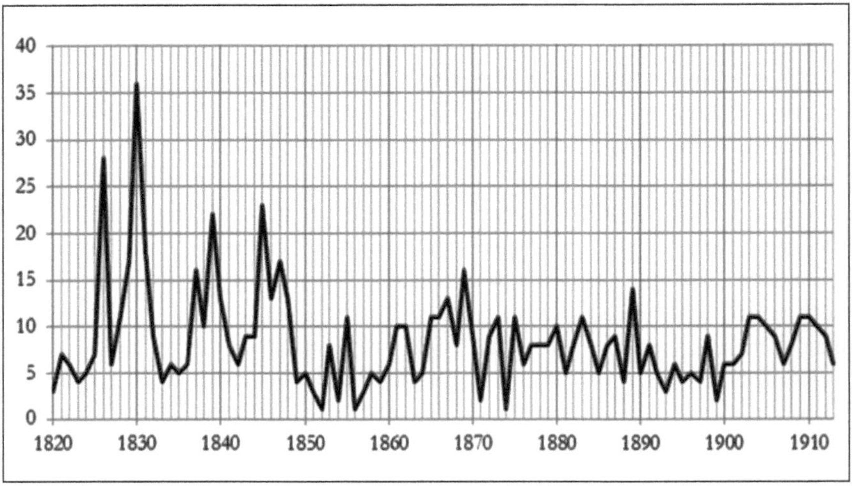

Source: AdP : D10U3, 1820–1913.

Around the middle of the century, the graph takes a different development. Two peaks are clearly visible in 1826 and 1830, with 28 and 36 bookseller-publishers going bankrupt. Up to 1847 more than fifteen bankruptcies a year are usually recorded. After that date they declined to about ten per year or even less. A slight increase appears in the 1860s: 16 book traders were driven to bankruptcy before 1870. The one-off rise in 1889 is related to the introduction of liquidation. At the beginning of the twentieth century the level seems to stabilize.

All in all the number of book traders-publishers going bankrupt showed an atypical trend compared to the general trend of failures between 1827 and 1847.

When comparing constitutive instruments and businesses bankruptcies, most business demographers, agree that small and medium businesses are more likely to 'die' early. Stana Nenadic, who studied the lifetime of companies based on the Edinburg registers between 1862 and 1890, reveals that 34% of them died within their first year of existence, and 78% within their first five years.[91] In a different context, Jean-Marie Bouvaist and Jean-Guy Boin also noticed that close to 60% of all French publishing companies created between 1974 and 1988, and over 50%

91 S. Nenadic, « The life-cycle of firms in late nineteenth century Britain », in *The birth and death of companies. An historical perspective*, P. Jobert et M. Moss (ed.), Carnfoth/ Park Ridge, The Parthenon Publishing Group, 1990, p. 181–195.

of those created between 1988 and 2005, disappeared before they had reached the fateful five-year threshold.[92]

In the nineteenth century, contrary to others industries, very few book traders were organised as corporations and most of the *Actes de creation de société* don't reveal the formation of a new company but only editorial enterprises, of variable geometry and more and less simultaneous. Prosopographical research is necessary in order to find when bankrupt traders had opened their shops, which leads to a nominative demography of book companies. Thanks to the study of trustees' reports, patents granted to book traders, commercial calendar books and the works of book historians, the dates of opening of 408 individual shops could be traced out of the 511 book traders' and publishers' bankruptcies between 1815 and 1870.[93] The compilation of the data reveal that the failures in the trade follow the general econometric trend[94]: the vast majority of the bankruptcies occurred soon after the business had started. One-fifth of Parisian book traders went bankrupt within their first three years of activity, 35% within their first five years, two-thirds before the tenth; while only slightly more than 15% of bankruptcies happened after 20 years of activity.[95]

---

92 In the opinion of J.-M. Bouvaist, *Pratiques et métiers de l'édition*, Paris, Promodis, 1986, p. 32 : 50% of the 150 small enterprises funded each year in the 1980's, disapear before their third birthdays and less than 30% of them dead before their 7 years. See too: J.-M. Bouvaist et J.-G. Boin, *Du printemps des éditeurs à l'âge de raison. Les nouveaux éditeurs en France 1974–1988*, Paris, La Documentation française, 1989 ; B. Legendre et C. Abensour, France, *Regards sur l'édition. II. Les nouveaux éditeurs (1988–2005)*, Paris, La Documentation française, (Questions de culture), 2007.

93 AdP : D10U3.

94 L. Marco et M. Rainelli, « Les disparitions de firmes industrielles en France : un modèle économétrique », *Revue d'économie industrielle*, n° 36, 1986, p. 1–13.

95 Respectively: 88 book traders in bankruptcy (21,57 %), 150 (36,76 %), 247 (60,54 %), 65 (15,93 %).

Chart 6: Bankrupt Parisian book trades lifetime between 1815 and 1870

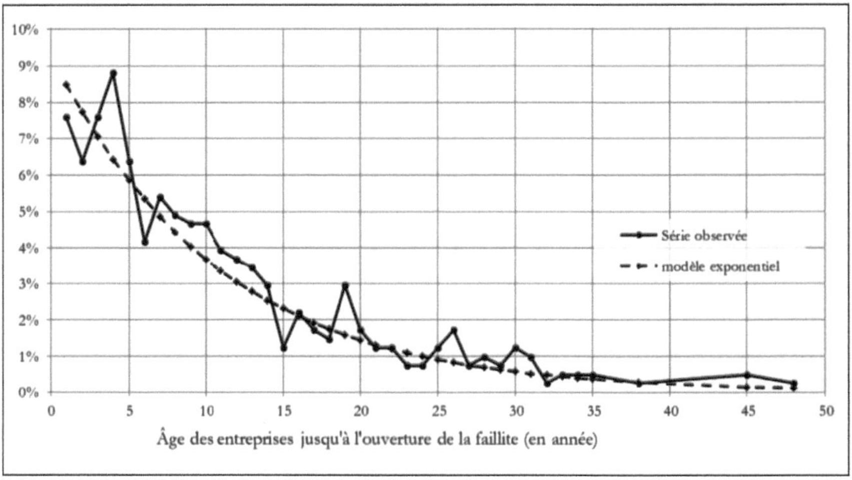

Sources: Bottins ; AN : Libredit ; G.-A. Vuaroqueaux, *Édition populaire*, vol. 3, p. 46–81 ; AdP : d10U3.

However, unlike as in Stana Nenadic's study,[96] the median lifetime of the bankrupt Parisian book traders between 1815 and 1870 is eight years, and it tends to increase from seven to 11.5 years over this period. In fact, if the axis of reference is not the date of the bankruptcy but that of the assumed start of activity, the median lifetime tends to decrease. Two paradoxical but complementary remarks come to mind: book traders opening a shop at the beginning of the century went bankrupt later than others, whereas the most experienced book traders were most likely to go bankrupt at the end of the period.

The flow of Parisian book traders' bankruptcies does not exactly follow the trend of national bankruptcies. It also differs from the general trend of Parisian bankruptcies. This questions the idea that younger business are more likely to 'die'. The social role that the commercial jurisdiction played is also a point to consider, since the whole judicial procedure revolved around the question of credibility.

The question of credit: in the trial and beyond

More than any other trade, the book trade lacked access to credit. To obtain a patent, book traders had to produce witnesses vouching for their morality and

96 S. Nenadic, « The life-cycle ».

they also had to deal with big fixed assets; in spite of this, they were not trusted by bankers. In other words, the book trade was expensive and not held in high regard.

In the *Envers de l'histoire contemporaine*, Madame de la Chanterie explains that although the book trade is "one of the most beautiful trades, it is badly made...", and she adds:

> How many excellent books have remained two or three years without achieving the success they deserved. [...] And, as I know, publishers have ways of driving bargains and taking their charges, which make the business one of the most risky and the most difficult to disentangle of all in Paris. Monsieur Nicolas can tell you about these difficulties, inherent in the nature of bookmaking.[97]

In fact, selling out a whole edition took an average of ten years. If the purchase of a business was sometimes heavy to bear, the working capital necessary to day-to-day business weighed the most in the accounts of book traders, who were also publishers at that time. Indeed, while a Parisian butcher spent an average of 3,500 francs a year,[98] a book trader needed three to six times as much in his daily business. And the rise of "publishing capitalism",[99] as well as the democratisation of the trade, pushed up the price of the investments necessary for mass production, while newcomers with limited financial resources were entering the market. The daily costs were all the harder to endure as traders could not get credit from banking institutions. People of the book, and especially book traders, suffered from the institutionalization of credit. Balzac, a connoisseur of this trade, had in Madame de la Chanterie say: "We know that the *Banque de France* is constantly suspicious of the book trade, even though it is one of the finest trades".[100]

Indeed, the *Banque de France* credit rating of 1804 was particularly unfavourable to the book trade, let alone the book sellers. According to the study of Emmanuel Prunaux, who highlights the extent of bad credit as well as the differences between the different trades in this sector, at the beginning of the century, 25%

---

97 « Combien d'excellents livres sont restés un, deux ou trois ans sans avoir le succès qu'ils méritent ! [...] Et je sais que les libraires ont des façons de traiter, de réaliser, qui font de leur commerce le plus chanceux et le plus difficile à débrouiller de tous les commerces parisiens. M. Nicolas vous parlera de ces difficultés, inhérentes à la nature des livres », H. de Balzac, *CH*, t. VIII, p. 381–382. (trans. by Bell, Clara, *The Seamy Side of History*, London, Forgotten Books, 1897, pp. 196–197).

98 A. Daumard, *La bourgeoisie parisienne de 1815 à 1848*, 2e ed., Paris, Albin Michel, (Bibliothèque de l'Évolution de l'humanité, n° 21), 1996, p. 451.

99 J.-Y. Mollier, *L'Argent et les lettres. Histoire du capitalisme d'édition, 1880–1920*, Paris, Fayard, 1988.

100 H. de Balzac, *CH*, t. VIII, p. 382.

of papermakers had good credit rating, while one-fifth of book traders were not even rated.[101] Out of the 141 bankruptcy files on which our corpus is based, only 13 book traders declared owing money to the *Banque de France*, most of them ran their businesses during the second half of the century. As Gaston Roulleau noted, before the *Banque de France* developed branches in 1836, "being granted a loan was an honour bestowed upon a privileged few".[102] During the first half of the century, only few renowned book traders held a current account in the *Banque*, with or without discount facility. Neither the decision of the *Banque de France* to establish branches in 1836 nor the 1848 crisis, produced a democratization of credit beneficially for the book traders; it led only to a geographical diffusion of the discount, that is consist in a means of payment used as a credit tool following since the merchants to the bankers.[103] In short, during the second half of the nineteenth century too, only some booksellers could benefit from the *Banque de France*'s credit, and probably only through the support of colleague involved in the institution, as with the famous medical bookseller Jean-Baptiste Baillière who had entered the credit committee of the *Banque*.

Book traders were granted few loans even if we include other lenders, such as big merchants and brokers, goldsmiths and jewellers, as well as landlords and pensioners. All together they all only amounted to 20% of the creditors of book traders in our corpus. Although the sums they had lent were considerable compared to the other creditors,[104] two-thirds of them were not declared by the bankrupt. If we look at the names of recurring lenders, the ranking obtained in the number of occurrences and the amounts lent, these only partly correspond to the Parisian or French financial elite.[105] No Rothschild, Pereire or Fould, very few Laffittes, Ganneron or Lehideux were registered. Some individuals from high finance were present but disappeared after the 1830 crisis, although some were still active after this date, such as Charles Vernes or Garçon Jacob Goudchaux's

101 E. Prunaux, « La classification des crédits et le renseignement économique à la Banque de France à l'époque napoléonienne », IHMC, 2008, p. 18.

102 G. Roulleau, *Les règlements par effets de commerce en France et à l'étranger*, Paris, Impr. Dubreuil, Frèrebeau et Cie, 1914, p. 40.

103 P. Baubeau et V. Rebolledo-Dhuin, « Escompte. L'évolution d'une pratique d'origine marchande aux XIXe et XXe siècles », in *Dictionnaire historique, analytique et critique de la comptabilité des entreprises*, D. Bensadon, N. Praquin et B. Touchelay (ed.), Villeneuve d'Ascq, Presses universitaires du Septentrion, 2015.

104 They altogether represent over 40% of the credits granted to the book traders.

105 For the list of the 19 first recurring bankers creditors, we refer to our PhD : *La librairie et le crédit*, p. 628.

sons. Only renowned book traders, such as Bossange, or bookseller-discounters, like Depélafol who owed 450,000 francs to 19 bankers – i.e. 70% of his debts –, had the trust of 'money men' during the July Monarchy.

The lack of credit worthiness of book traders stemmed from the structure of the business. Insufficient funds affecting some small publishing houses, as well as the lack of cash, led book traders to use promissory notes. As they could not sell off their production, book traders kept on delaying the previously due date. We understand why "the Parisian trade hated the notes signed by book traders", which were only accepted by usurers. The circulation of those notes led to the establishment of a large number of local credit go-betweens.

In order to get their supply and produce their editions, book traders, because they lacked funds, ran into debt with their providers, some of whom became discount specialists or speculated on their debtors' future bankruptcy.

Probably two-thirds, or at least two-fifths, of the traders in our corpus who went to the Commercial Court, had previously tried, with varying success, to appeal to their creditors.[106] As we already noted, an agreement before bankruptcy was a solution preferred by both debtors and creditors: the debtor to keep his reputation, the creditor to obtain as much commercial or financial dividend as possible from the agreement. Not all debtors succeeded, whether in the short or the long term. In fact, the success of such a negotiation outside the rule of law depended on the credibility of the insolvent trader but also on that of one of his creditors, and on his ability to convince the plaintiff who had trusted the trader's reputation. This is how Louis-Ludovic Tenré, a book trader-banker and member of the well-known and influential *Banque de France*, succeeded in convincing the co-creditors of the bankrupt Charles Desiré Videcoq, a publisher at the Commercial Court, to sign an agreement in 1850. If, the insolvent book trader wanted to create solidarity between his creditors in order to be granted a composition and a debt remittance, he had not expected the schemes of Tenré, who had bought the claims of some creditors to make a composition fail, for his own advantage.

As creditors individually aimed at limiting their loss, debtors who might be sued again by each one of them, sometimes thought it preferable to file for bankruptcy to protect themselves and recreate *de facto* solidarity between their creditors. Not all creditors were as malevolent as Tenré. Famous book trader Gervais Hélène Charpentier, who initiated a revolution in book format, had one of his

106 Of the 141 bankruptcy files studied, only 41 individuals did not clearly try to get a preliminary amicable agreement, while 74 files do not mention such a move, the *factums* available at the BnF or the dispute files of the BdF fill the holes in the bankruptcy files.

renowned fellow book traders and creditors cancel his bankruptcy. Henri Claude Fabre, partners with the Desfossés who founded the *Tribune Desfossés*, and with Dalloz, succeeded in ending his bankruptcy procedure one month after it had begun: the lack of funds was replaced by credit. In order to clean the family's reputation, Madame Fabre had her husband's bankruptcy file re-opened forty years later in 1906 and "offered [although they were separated as to property] the assignment of assets with money coming from [her] own funds only".[107]

A bankruptcy can have two outcomes: either the creditors agree with the debtor to grant him time and remittances, or they unite against him and he might be sued by each one and every one of them.

Due to the lack of sources enabling us to estimate when cessation of activity occurred for small businesses, business demographers consider the date of bankruptcy as the death of the company. Luc Marco adds that fewer than 3% of companies survived bankruptcy in the long term, but for how long he does not say precisely.[108] The results obtained from the bankruptcy registers for the 511 book traders filing for bankruptcy at the Seine Court between 1815 and 1870 are different. Naturally almost half of them ceased their activity just after their trial, or at least did not leave any trace. But given the gaps in the corpus and excluding the 234 book traders of whom we do not know anything after their bankruptcy, more than half got back on their feet and remained in the book trade for over 10 years.[109] The book traders that disappeared – if only from the archives – soon after going bankrupt had mostly had very young businesses (44.27%). Premature death only concerned 58 businesses, representing less than 15% of our sample.[110] Among the 150 businesses going bankrupt during the first six years, 47 companies

107 AdP : D11U3/580, file n° 8723, declaration date November 16th, 1867, closing of the proceeding on December 26th, 1867, reopening on January 30th, 1906.

108 Proposals change along the pages in L. Marco, *La montée des faillites*, p. 7 et 46–46: « less than 3% of the bankruptcies (and other procedures) lead to a lasting survival of the failing companies »; « bankruptcies can lead to the full firm assets liquidation, as well as to its merger-absorption. But the statistical reality shifts the balance in favour of full disappearance, the bankruptcies leading to a long term survival for only 1% of the failing businesses ».

109 Among the 277 book traders for which we found the date of cessation of activity, 153 (55 %) continued their business after their bankruptcy for at least 10 years.

110 Among the 234 bankrupt above mentioned, 58 (44,27 %) filed for bankruptcy before their 6th year of business, but for 103 of them, we do not know their business opening date. Considering or excluding these, the early over-mortality *stricto sensu*, thus affected 58 of the 511 (11,35 %) of the 408 (14,22 %) bankrupt book traders between 1815 and 1870.

(31.33%) went on for over 10 years. Only in 16 out of 408 failures did the founder leave business definitely, amounting to less than 5%.[111]

Like in *Splendeurs et misères des courtisanes*, where Nucingen got richer soon after his commercial insolvency, rather than experiencing some form of death, bankruptcy was a commercial stepping stone for book traders and their heirs, as so nicely illustrated by Sophie Grandjean with Fayard.[112] Indeed, the founder, Arthème Fayard, went bankrupt twice before leaving his growing business to his son Arthème II, who in 1904–1905 initiated the second revolution in the book prices. Bankruptcies were also a way for creditors to rebound. Also, the medical publishers Baillière and Méquignon favoured the union of Gabon's creditors in order to appropriate his stock in trade supplied and the Baillères became masters in such speculations: Baillière's son, a councillor at the discount committee at the *Banque de France*, "harshly denounce[d] [the company] Bachelin-Deflorenne, [and] decide[d] its bankruptcy as well as the sale of its ancient books, some of which were bought by some of Monsieur B[aillière]'s friends[113]".

Given the credit crunch and the major role played by book traders specialized in commercial discount – or bookseller-discounters –, bankruptcy reveals the social dynamic of the commercial discount system. Two examples are particularly noteworthy. Louis Joseph Tenré was born in Douai where his father traded in earthenware. He applied in 1816 in Paris to obtain a book trader patent along with his partner Étienne Ledoux, with whom he published *curiosa*. The company crashed when Depélafol, with whom Étienne Ledoux was committed, ran away. At the end of the 1830s, Tenré gave up the book trade for banking. In 1836, with the Delatouche brothers – directors of the famous *Papeteries du Marais* –, Tenré created a bank. Afterwards Tenré invested in real estate in *Saint-Germain-en-Laye*, where he purchased several estates that had been left as collateral by his debtors and multiplied his financial investisments. His son, Louis-Ludovic, followed in his steps. During the 1860s, Louis-Ludovic bought shares in promising enterprises: French railway and mines in Latin America. He became Consul in Paraguay, took part in the major investigation of the discount rate launched by the *Banque de France* and represented American interests during the 1867 World Exhibition. In

111 Here we take into account the businesses going bankrupt between their 10th and 21th year of activity and not surviving more than 6 years after their bankruptcy. This globally corresponds to one generation.

112 S. Grandjean-Hogg, *L'évolution de la librairie Athème Fayard (1857–1936)*, PhD in History, University of Versailles-Saint-Quentin-en-Yvelines, France, 1996.

113 Banque de France : censor file.

the third generation, Charles-Henri Tenré, a painter, who regularly appeared in social magazines during the 1920s, celebrated his marriage in 1894 with Émilie Aguado, great-grand-daughter of the King of Spain's banker and the niece of Adalbert de Talleyrand-Périgord, the last duke of Montmorency. Aguado's dowry was estimated at 120,000 francs. Within three generations, the Tenré had entered the European nobility.[114]

The case of the Ledoux family is equally interesting. Louis Thomas Romain Ledoux was born in 1767 in l'Aigle (dept of Orne, Normandie's region), where his father was a wheelwright. In 1796, in Paris he married Anne-Marie Collenberg, whose parents, of Swiss origins, worked at the Mint (hôtel de la Monnaie). At this time, Louis Thomas Romain Ledoux ran a paper business (wallpaper and printing paper) in rue Saint-André-des-Arts and later, at n° 10 rue de Buci. As early as the 1810s he provided discounts, under mortgage, to his fellow upholsterers and book traders. Like the above-mentioned example, Ledoux secured his assets and built a real estate empire. Between 1814 and the mid-1820s, he successively obtained some buildings in Paris from his debtor and purchased 90% of the lands in the town of Vaires-sur-Marne. This gave Ledoux some notoriety: he was the first mayor of Vaires and was soon appointed as a judge at the Seine Commercial Court, and as a censor at the *Banque de France* Paris discount committee. His son Roch Romain Ledoux, who succeeded him in the same offices, died early.

Bankruptcy law evolved from traditional commercial law and underwent deep changes during the nineteenth century. Due to a procedure considered degrading for a long time, the trader in debt was still dishonoured during the nineteenth century. Eventually punishments were reduced and softened even before the codification – introducing the distinction between misfortune and fraud – and then the abolition of the imprisonment of insolvent debtors. Judges and trustees, creditors and bankrupts were the main actors in modernizing the procedure, irrespective of the current law. These practices reveal the inner nature of bankruptcy as a collective and contractual procedure. The involved parties aimed at bringing ethics to trade practices, and the credibility of each of them determined how the procedure started, unfolded and ended. The bankruptcies of book traders, discredited by banking institutions, are a vantage point from which to consider the dynamics set in motion by judicial legislation. Far from marking a commercial death, bankruptcy represented a crucial crossroad for debtors and creditors alike on a path that sometimes took them to extraordinary success.

---

114 N. Stoskopf, *Banquiers et financiers parisiens*, Paris/Le Mans, Picard/Cénomane, (Les patrons du second Empire, n° 7), 2002.

Erika Vause

The Ties that Bind?: An Analysis of the Debt Imprisonment Records in Lyon 1835–1840

In an 1845 petition addressed to the French Chamber of Deputies, the debtors of Lyon's Saint Joseph prison denounced the injustice of debt imprisonment. Condemning debt imprisonment as a 'residue of barbarism', they described themselves as individuals 'completely foreign to true commerce'.[1] Yet they nonetheless attributed their predicament to 'commercial selfishness, which, seeking to reduce everything to a negotiable value, includes a man's own liberty in the capital he can traffic'.[2] For these inmates, debtors' prison represented a kind of double exploitation: not merely the victims of a vestigial and backward institution rooted in a traditional personal economy, they were also collateral of capitalism's excesses. In concluding their petition, the debtors urged the deputies to ease the rigors of a law that allowed creditors to privately detain their debtors.

Few institutions better exemplified the ambiguities of the transition to a modern credit economy or the problematic nature of defaulted promises in the so-called 'golden age of contract' as the debtors' prison. In nineteenth-century France, the law of debt imprisonment, called *contrainte par corps,* allowed a creditor to seize and hold his debtor in prison to enforce payment. Largely designed to aid commerce, the debtors' prison gave rise to all sorts of fanciful stories and narratives of creditor motives. It purportedly housed thousands of victims of personal vendettas, sordid schemes, and perverse romantic intrigues. Financial debts masked secret stories of vengeance and hatred. In such tales, the debtors' prison awaited those who felt awry of an all too personal economy. Yet debt imprisonment also represented the cash nexus par excellence: usurers, bankers, bill discounters and third-party holders of bills with little or no direct relationship to the debtor, threw him (or, less frequently, her) in prison to regain their precious lucre. Like contemporary observers, historians have also debated the true character of the nineteenth-century debtors' prison. They have called upon competing and

1 Debt prisoners of Lyon: "Les Detenus pour dettes à Lyon aux prises avec la contrainte par corps en presence de la representation nationale et de leur concitoyens". Imprimerie de Th. Lépagnez: Lyon 1845, p. 10.

2 Ibid. p. 12.

sometimes directly opposing ideas of how debt imprisonment functioned within the making of the industrial economy, some characterizing it as an old-fashioned vestige of an interpersonal economy while others perceiving it as a disciplinary tool for the working class.[3]

Departing from analyses of debt imprisonment, which have largely concentrated on its legal, cultural, or political meanings, this paper looks at how debt imprisonment was really used by creditors and debtors by examining both specific cases and the actual demographics of debtor's prison. This paper considers debt imprisonment as a strategy in certain debtor-creditor relations. It attempts to understand who got imprisoned and who imprisoned as well as to speculate as to how this institution functioned for both lenders and borrowers in an early nineteenth century credit economy. This paper begins by situating *contrainte par corps*in the context of the larger credit economy and in relation to other forms of debt settlement, both those tightly regulated by French law (such as the process of *faillite,* or bankruptcy) and those often settled informally, such as the *cession des biens* (roughly equivalent to consumer insolvency) and private arrangements. Viewed within this legal landscape, debt imprisonment provided one possible card among many to be played in a complicated game between debtors and creditors, a game inextricably linking the social, legal, and financial meanings of capital. Subsequent analysis of the internment records over the course of five years at Lyon's Saint-Joseph prison suggests the types of creditor-debtor relations in which these multiple logics of debt imprisonment may have come into play. In so doing, we can see why the debtors' prison – a lightning rod for controversy throughout the early decades of the nineteenth century – shows the often uneasy relationship between a legal framework that governed commercial activity and the realities of an economic world where the need for credit was rapidly expanding.

Historians who have examined the nature of credit and discredit in this period have argued for the inextricably interwove nature of the social and financial meanings of the word. In a seminal article on business failure in the French town of Niort, for example, Jean-Clément Martin used court dossiers spanning several decades of the nineteenth century to demonstrate that bankruptcy depended neither on

3 See in particular Mann, Bruce: *Republic of Debtors: Bankruptcy in the Age of American Independence.* Harvard University Press: Cambridge, MA 2002; Finn, Margot: *The Character of Credit: Debt and English Culture, 1740–1914.* Cambridge University Press: Cambridge 2003; Cohen, Jay: 'The history of imprisonment for debt and its relation to the development of discharge for bankruptcy'. *Journal of Legal History* vol. 3, no. 2 (1982), pp. 153–171.

macroeconomic trends nor on the personal failings of individual debtors.[4] Rather, the likelihood of bankruptcy rested largely on the social connections of the debtor and the industry in which he or she worked. Martin showed that there were some industries – established and central to the regional economy – where individuals almost never appeared in dossiers as either debtors or creditors in bankruptcies. In other lines of work, meanwhile, individuals appeared as creditors but rarely as bankrupts and in still others they appeared as both creditors and debtors. From these facts, Martin argues that bankruptcy largely befell those peripheral to the commercial community as a whole or those who sought to promote their rise within this community too rapidly. Debtors more firmly embedded in the commercial community may have heavily indebted themselves, but lenders tended to overlook their failings whereas creditors pounced on interlopers quickly. Martin's persuasive work on the discredit of bankruptcy leads us to similarly examine debt imprisonment. If bankruptcy could be seen as a sort of "punishment" for individuals who defied commercial norms, where might debt imprisonment have fit into such an economy? Were incarcerating lenders and incarcerated borrowers also from certain marginal professional groups? If so, what can this tell us about the way that credit was extended during this time period?

The Legal Uses of Debt Imprisonment

To answer these questions we must first situate *contrainte par corps* within the legal landscape of nineteenth-century France. Debt laws restricted imprisonment to certain kinds of debts, and many of these fell outside the realm of business or consumer failure (although this paper will be principally concerned with commercial debt imprisonment). Other applications of imprisonment included debts owed for fines, customs violations, and court compensation, as well as all debts owed by foreigners and debts where a temporary property-holder refused to return property with which he had been entrusted. Indeed, many of these uses exist today in France under the appellation of *contrainte judiciare*. However, in nineteenth-century France commercial debt imprisonment was by far the most common form of *contrainte pour corps*. *Contrainte pour corps pour dettes commerciales* could be invoked for debts contracted between professional merchants – as defined by the 1807 Code of Commerce – or debts involving financial instruments such as bills of exchange. A bankrupt also faced imprisonment if he could not obtain a safe conduct pass from his creditors. Creditors granted this pass to the

4 Martin, Jean-Clément: 'Le commerçant, la faillite et l'historien'. *Annales. Économies, Sociétés, Civilisations* vol. 6, no. 35 (1980), pp. 1251–1268.

majority of bankrupts and withheld it only when they had considerable doubt about the bankrupt's conduct.[5]

Obtaining an arrest for commercial debt required an audience before the local commercial court, which generally ruled in favor of the creditor. The jurisdiction of such courts, however, theoretically extended only to those who were merchants – defined by the 1807 Code of Commerce as individuals who made buying and selling their regular profession. Given the looseness of this definition, the exact nature of a commercial profession remained largely dependent on custom and judicial discretion. Commercial debt imprisonment was enforced by special commercial courts and arrests made by bailiffs *(huissiers)* or, in Paris, by commercial guards specially designated for the task. Creditors then paid an advance to keep the debtor in prison for the length of his stay – with the expenses added to the amount of the outstanding debt. The state nevertheless mandated limits on the maximum prison stay according to the amount of debt owed. Certain individuals were also excluded from arrest – women and minors, for instance, could only be arrested for commercial debts if they were officially registered as merchants with the commercial courts while those over sixty-nine were released from any *contrainte par corps*. Such restrictions help account for the rather low number of debt prisoners in France. Annual arrests nation-wide fluctuated between 1000 and 3000 individuals in France each year.[6]

Nevertheless, despite such numbers, debt imprisonment, after being abolished during the French Revolution in 1793 and reestablished in 1797, evoked considerable controversy throughout the first decades of the nineteenth century, both inside and outside the halls of government. Following five attempts to reform debtors' prison between 1816 and 1832, a new law enacted in April of 1832 mandated some significant changes to debt imprisonment, setting a minimum amount for arrest and restricting further the kinds of individuals who could be incarcerated. More profound critiques emerged in popular culture and in the many pamphlets – largely hostile to the practice – written about imprisonment. In the novels of Balzac and Eugène Sue, debt imprisonment inevitably served as a tool of blackmail, intrigue and revenge that had nothing to do with "real

5 See Chapter 4 of my dissertation "In the Red and in the Black: Bankruptcy, Debt Imprisonment, and the Culture of Credit in Post-Revolutionary France" (PhD thesis, University of Chicago, 2012).

6 Bayle-Mouillard, Jean-Baptiste: *De l'Emprisonnement pour dettes: considération sur son origine, ses rapports avec la morale publique et les intérêts du commerce, des familles, de la société; suivies de la Statistique de la contrainte par corps*. Imprimerie royale: Paris 1836.

merchants" or even with genuine financial distress. The famous 1840s panorama of French society, *Les Français peints par eux-mêmes*, described the jails as full of 'land-owners, literary men, military officers, law or medical students, *rentiers*, water carriers, charcoal peddlers… and other individuals also foreign to commerce, for whom urgent need or a pressing momentary necessity, forced them to enter into an obligation improperly called an act of commerce'.[7] The eclectic group that crowded debt prisons reflected what many saw as the institution's greatest irony; namely that debtors' prison disproportionately affected those who were not commercial people at all.

Debt imprisonment appeared all the more bizarre because fully developed legal proceedings existed for managing failure, in the form of bankruptcy, reserved for "commercial individuals," and *cessions des biens*, intended for those who were not businessmen or merchants. The existence of these alternatives undoubtedly reinforced the impression that particularly ferocious creditors used the debtors' prison in order to punish errant borrowers rather than to recuperate financial losses. Yet in reality most creditors seem to have used the debt imprisonment as a complement to these mechanisms rather than as unique means of enforcement. Indeed, creditors made use of the reality or threat of imprisonment at various junctures in the lending process and with various goals. The first way that debt imprisonment could enter into legal proceedings for bankruptcy was as an initiation of bankruptcy or *cession des biens*. In this, *contrainte par corps* compelled a debtor to arrange with his creditors. If a debtor obtained a *cession des biens* or filed for *faillite*, he would be released from debtor's prison. Thus the possibility or reality of imprisonment incentivized such arrangements, which were, at the time, generally debtor-initiated. *Faillite* was available only to those deemed to be merchants by the commercial courts. Key to understanding the role played by debt imprisonment in this process is that debtors themselves generally chose to file for bankruptcy at least through the first half of the nineteenth century. Repeated orders of *contrainte par corps*, particularly coupled with confiscation of property, were often sufficient to compel a merchant into bankruptcy.

Cession des biens provided similar safety from pursuits for non-commercial debtors. A civil court granted a judicial *cession des biens* upon presentation of the debtor's balance sheet and proof that he was "good faith" and merely "unfortunate" rather than attempting to abuse his creditors' trust. *Cession* was available to debtors

---

7 Moreau-Christophe, Louis-Mathurin: "Les detenus pour dettes". in : Cumier, Léon (ed.): *Les français peints par eux-mêmes: encyclopédie morale du dix-neuvième siècle*. L. Curmier: Paris 1840–1842, vol. 4, p. 45.

who were unable to pay debts on merchants' instruments – most prominently bills of exchange – but who were not merchants. *Contrainte par corps* probably played a prominent role here in compelling debtors to ask for official settlement. One M. Fleury pled for a *cession*, arguing that, having fallen into the grasp of usurers at a young age, he 'barely 27… found [himself] under several orders of *contrainte par corps* and menaced with being committed to the debtors' prison, which would have prevented [him] from utilizing [his] instruction and [his] knowledge and freely exercising [his] industry in the interest of [his] creditors'.[8] Such an appeal nevertheless failed to convince his judges and his creditors. Indeed, numbers of court-granted *cession des biens* were small throughout and supporters of debtors prison often pointed to the small number of debtors judged capable of making use of *cession des biens* as 'non-commercial debtors of good faith'.[9]

A second function of *contrainte par corps* in the legal landscape of failure was to mobilize alternative credit resources. The reality or threat of *contrainte par corps* evoked the sympathy of the debtor's solvent friends or family in ways that the mere menace of property confiscation might not. These people might pay some or all of the debt to release a loved one. Some creditors apparently relied more or less openly on this 'speculation on human affection.' The creditors of a certain Jaubert, unable to achieve any satisfaction through seizures, arrested him in the hopes that 'his powerful family would surely have come to his assistance'.[10] The judges at the Royal Court in Paris reproved them for such assumption saying that 'one should not pay the debt of ones' relatives, above all not when they are bad subject, one should leave them in prison. It does them good'.[11] A creditor could also hope, in marital regimes of separated property, that a wife would alienate portions of her dowry in order to free her husband from prison, one of the few events for which the Civil Code Article 1558 allowed such an act. When Sieur Gontier of Caen was imprisoned and recommended by a Sieur Fromage (not, alas, a cheesemonger) for a 6000 franc debt, Gontier's wife obtained notarial authorization to use some property from her dowry to satisfy Sieur Fromage and free her husband.[12] So widespread was this practice that critics even charged that unscrupulous husbands used debt imprisonment to gain control of their wives' property.[13]

8 *Gazette des Tribunaux* 3.1.1840, p. 225.
9 *Le Moniteur Universel* 25.3.1867, p. 359.
10 *Gazette des Tribunaux* 6.4.1841, p. 559.
11 Ibid.
12 *Gazette des Tribunaux* 26.1.1840, p. 303.
13 Bayle-Mouillard, p. 151.

It is essential to keep in mind, however, that while *contrainte par corps* played an important role both as a means of compelling debtors to settle with their creditors and of punishing those who could not pay, a stay in debtors' prison did not necessarily mean that a debtor was insolvent or had ceased payments to all his creditors. Indeed, the well-known prison stays of certain fabulously wealthy men, in the first decades of the nineteenth century demonstrated how affluent debtors used prison to avoid payment. Indeed, the speculator James Swan, an American arrested under slightly different terms as a foreigner, became a legend by his refusal to pay his debt to a former business partner named Hermann Lubbert proclaiming that 'considerations much superior to interest' provoked his otherwise unconscionable decision to prefer 22 years in Paris's Sainte-Pélagie prison to paying back a creditor to whom he insisted he owed nothing.[14]

The Internment Records of Saint-Joseph Prison, Lyon

As helpful as particular cases can be in revealing the possibilities of debt imprisonment, we can truly understand its function in the topography of failure and obligation only by moving beyond anecdotal evidence to study the relationships between debtors and creditors quantitatively. One useful source for obtaining such information comes from the prison internment records, a legal necessity for each debtor's entry into prison. These entries included the name, profession and address of the debtor, the name, profession, and address of the incarcerating creditor, the arresting bailiff, and the amount of the debt and the way in which it was contracted. I have analyzed 318 of these entries from Lyon between 1835 and 1840, beginning three years after the passage of the law of 17 April 1832 but coinciding with the tail end of a decades' long controversy about the debtors' prison, which seems to have largely quieted down by the mid-1840s.

A few words should be said about the choice of this archive for an analysis of debtor-creditor relationships. For, in fact, Paris would seem the best place to study debtors' prison in nineteenth-century France. Indeed, only the capital had a true debtors' prison reserved exclusively for debtors (the Maison de Clichy, dedicated to this purpose in 1834), and contemporary reports generally placed Paris's share of all imprisoned debtors as somewhere around one third of all debtors.[15] Sadly, however, internment records for Sainte-Pélagie and Clichy prisons in Paris do not appear to exist. Although the absence of Parisian data is disappointing, Lyon nevertheless serves as a logical replacement. As France's second largest city

14 James Swan, "A Messieurs de la Chambre des Députés" Paris: Chez l'auteur, 1817, p. 4.
15 Bayle-Mouillard, p. 206.

during the time period with a population of some 340,000 inhabitants, Lyon was at the forefront of the industrial production of textiles – as much as one half of the labor force was involved with silk production in some fashion. It was also home to a precociously politicized working class, as was made abundantly clear by the urban upheavals of the 1830s.[16] After the Seine and the Seine-Inferieure, the Rhône, the department in which Lyon was situated, had the most litigation placed before its commercial courts.[17] The dominant role played by one single industry in Lyon's economy – as well as Lyon's relatively representative nature as a large French city of the time – make Lyon an ideal site for understanding general trends about the debtors' prison and the economy throughout France.

Moreover, Lyon imprisoned a substantial number of debtors in comparison to other French cities. When Jean-Baptiste Bayle-Mouillard, the lawyer who compiled the most comprehensive statistical overview of imprisonment of the French debtors' prison, tabulated incarceration rates between 1824 and 1833, he counted 22 women and 781 men imprisoned for private debts in the department of the Rhône.[18] These figures helped place the department of the Rhône fourth in per capita debt imprisonment rates, directly below the Seine, the Seine-Inferieure and Cantal. Bayle-Mouillard insisted that the Rhône's relatively high ranking could not be merely attributed to its urbanization; the Haut-Rhin, including Strasbourg, and the Bouches-du-Rhône, including Marseille, ranked middling to last in terms of per capita incarceration rates.[19] Rather, the Rhône, like much of southern France, had higher rates of incarceration than comparable provinces in the north.

The evidence in the Saint-Joseph prison internment records provide valuable clues both to understanding the particularities of the situation in Lyon and to speculating about how debt imprisonment functioned more generally. The first important fact revealed by the analysis of the internment records is the amount of money for which the debtors were arrested. In interpreting this data, we can probably assume that large debts implied a debtor had access to a large credit in the first place and was therefore generally of a more affluent social position whereas the prevalence of more small debts suggests the use of debt imprisonment by a lower socioeconomic class, both in terms of the creditors and debtors involved. On the other hand, an important factor to consider here is legal limitations: the law of April 17 1832 had fixed 200 francs as the minimum debt occasioning imprisonment. To put this sum

16 McDougall, Mary Lynn: "Consciousness and Community: The Workers of Lyon, 1830–1850". *Journal of Social History* vol. 12, no. 1 (1978), pp. 129–145.
17 Bayle-Mouillard, p. 356.
18 Bayle-Mouillard, p. 332; 336.
19 See Bayle-Mouillard, p. 345–346.

in perspective, according to Louis-René Villermé's 1839 statistics, 200 francs equaled roughly 4 months' labor for a male textile weaver.[20] Of the 318 records analyzed, forty-one were for debts under 300 francs (with 8 debtors arrested for 200 francs exactly). The Law of 17 April 1832 also ordered that debts under 500 francs could result in a maximum of one year in prison – the prison records reveal that 143 of the 318 arrests were for debts under 500 francs and ten were at 500 francs exactly. Thus the majority of debtors were imprisoned for sums that were considered relatively low. On the other hand, some debtors owed very large amounts of money to their creditors. Two debtors, Antoine Ferlat, a merchant, and Pierre Ferrier, a businessman, were each arrested for 10,000 francs in running accounts owed to two different businessmen.[21]

Chart 1: Amount of Debt (Number in Francs)

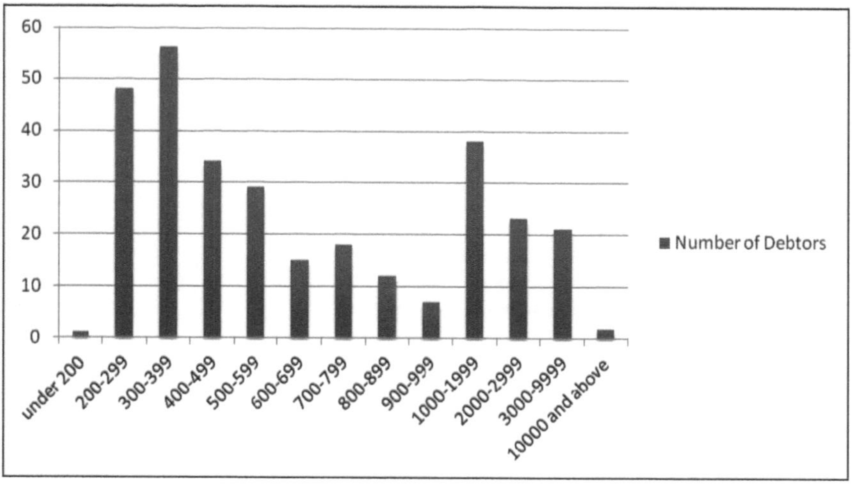

In regards to understanding how imprisonment worked as a social strategy, perhaps the most interesting information revealed by these internment records involves the respective professions of debtors and creditors.Yet making definite conclusions in this regard can be difficult. While some debtors were given almost

20 Villermé, Louis-René: *Rapport à l'academie des sciences morales et politiques sur l'état physique et moral des ouvriers, employés dans les fabriques de soie, de coton et de laine.* Mémoires de l'Académie des sciences morales et politiques: Paris 1839, p. 349.

21 Archives départementales du Rhône (ADR) 2 Y 284 Entry 20.7.1836 and ADR 2 Y 285 8.11.1837.

impossibly specific professions – for example one debtor was listed as a "merchant of lithographic stones" – thirty-one incarcerated debtors were unhelpfully called "merchant" and sixteen were called "négociant" [businessman]. Careful observers like Bayle-Mouillard suspected that the application of such general terms to describe a debtor's profession revealed the anxieties of creditors, particularly after the laws of April 1832, which had restricted even arrests for bills of exchange to those who actually "performed acts of commerce and made of these their profession".[22] Indeed, Bayle-Mouillard openly doubted the commercial activity of most of these so-called merchants.[23] Furthermore, a significant number of debtors were listed as having two careers – sometimes fairly complementary, such as "grocer" and "wine merchant," while others are quite detached from each other, such as "baker" and "joiner." It is unclear whether the debtor rotated from one career to another – many debtors are described as "former baker" or "former notary" – or whether he – or she- scraped together a living performing multiple tasks. In such cases, I have chosen to consider the debtors by their first listed profession.

Chart 2: Professions of Incarcerated Debtors

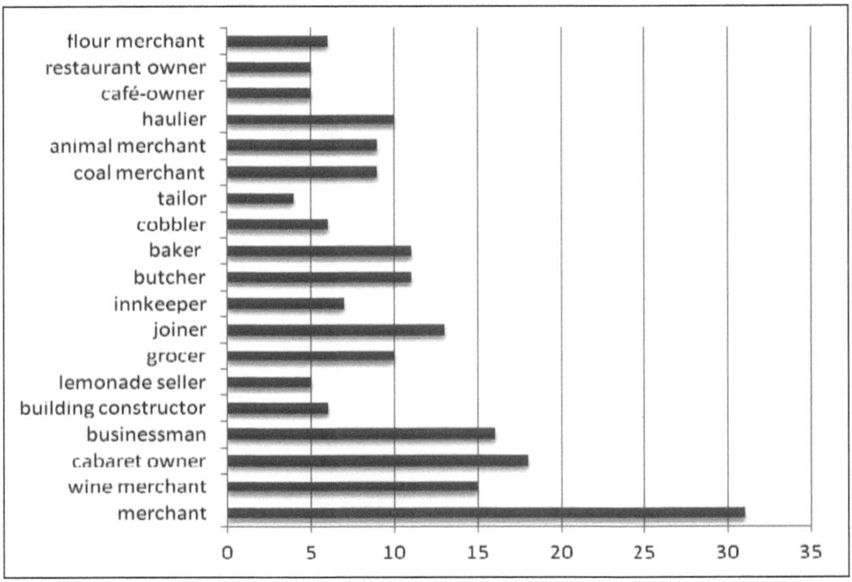

22 Code of Commerce 1807 Book 1 Article 1.
23 Bayle-Mouillard, p. 222.

Despite these problems, some clear patterns emerge from the data. For example, eighteen debtors were listed as cabaret owners [*cabaretier*]. Another five appeared as restaurant-owners [*restauraunter*], five as café owners [*cafétier*] and five as lemonade sellers [*limonadier]*. A total of fifteen debtors were considered wine merchants. Given the frequently porous boundaries between these professions, it seems that a substantial number of debtors (totally 48 in all) fell into what might be called the hospitality and catering sector. Butchers and bakers – the given profession of eleven debtors each – also made up sizeable numbers of inmates, but probably not disproportionate to their percentage in the general population. Haulers [*voituriers*] on the other hand – numbering ten – do seem overrepresented, and perhaps were specifically targeted by their creditors because of the flight risk they may have posed. The number of artisans – including joiners – is notable as is the number of coal peddlers and livestock or horse dealers. Forty-eight of the debtors provided a residence outside of Lyon or the surrounding communes (namely Perrache and Guillotière), but most of these were from towns in the Rhône or neighboring departments like the Isère. Only nineteen debtors were female, and of these nineteen six were widows and four were 'desmoiselles' (unmarried women). Considering that women had to be officially registered as merchants with the commercial court to be arrested for debt and that the law of 17 April 1832 had forbidden the arrest of husband and wife for the same debt, their small number in the prison population of Lyon is to be expected.

An analysis of the creditors' professions is perhaps even more revealing, although it again poses similar problems in terms of generalization. Nevertheless, a sizeable portion of creditors – here some eighty-nine of the total 296 different creditors – describe themselves as 'négociants' rather than 'marchands' or 'commerçants' While 'négociant' could signify an ordinary merchant, it more typically referred to a wholesale dealer who bought merchandise from smaller suppliers, and thus generally implied a superior socioeconomic class.[24] Of those creditors providing more specific careers, only one described himself as a banker. Meanwhile, for transactions that were supposedly commercial in nature, the number of creditors who gave their professions as either annuity-holder or property-owner is striking; they tie for the second most listed career at twenty-six creditors each. It is probable that these people, whose titles would imply that they were not commercial at all, in fact ran informal banking practices as was common practice at the

24 Amalia Kessler, '"A 'Question of Name": Merchant-Court Jurisdiction and the Origins of the Noblesse Commerçante,' in Mary Jane Parrine (ed.), *A Vast and Useful Art: The Gustave Gimon Collection on French Political Economy*. Stanford University Press: Stanford 2004.

time.[25] Wine merchants and animal merchants –abundantly represented among debtors- are also represented among incarcerating creditors. While innkeepers and tavern-keepers were not as well-represented among creditors as among debtors, brewers appeared on creditor occupations but not on those of debtors. Overall, and probably not surprisingly, these connections between creditors and debtors seem to have largely been vertical rather than horizontal: creditors overall generally appear to have represented superior socioeconomic classes and debtors inferior ones. This is even more apparent in some of the individual relationships between creditors and debtors. When the debtor and creditor are in the same line of work, we often see the creditor holding a position of power– such as that of iron merchant – and the debtor as a blacksmith.

Chart 3: Creditor Professions

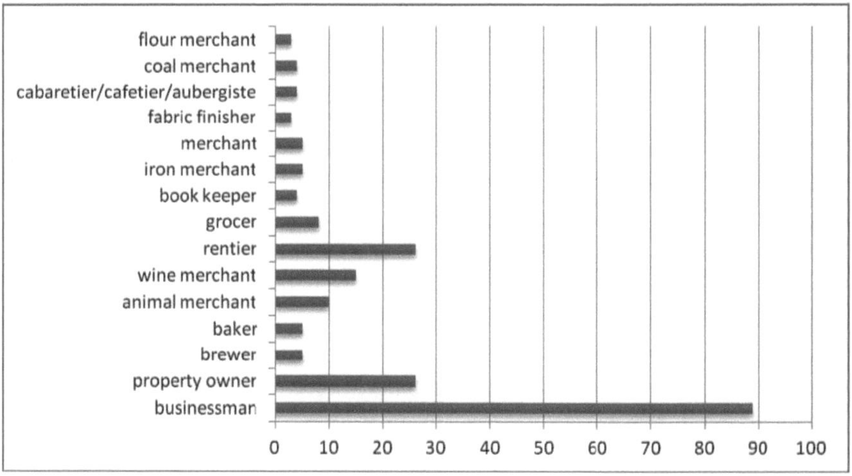

Strikingly, forty-five of the total creditors provided their names in the arrest records as part of a company or a partnership. Most typically, these took the form of two individuals or "So and So and Company," although on occasion debtors were arrested by a "father and son," "brothers" or, less commonly, "husband and wife." Lastly, creditors were much more likely than debtors to a primary residence outside of Lyon or the Guillotière. Fifty-four creditors were from surrounding

25 Plessis, Alain: 'Les banques locales, de l'essor du Second Empire à la « crise » de la Belle Epoque'. in: Lescure, Michel / Plessis, Alain (eds.): *Banques locales et banques régionales en France au XIXe siècle.* Albin Michel: Paris 1999, p. 204.

towns in the Rhône or from other departments. Five claimed residence in Paris. Despite frequently publicized fears of women imprisoning men, only nine arresting creditors were women, not counting the two women who arrested a debtor in tandem with their husbands.

A few preliminary steps can next be taken towards analyzing the social and professional proximity of debtors and creditors. From the data in the internment records, what might we be able to say about the relationship between creditors and debtors? Some debtors and creditors appeared to be connected by more or less explicit professional ties where the creditor probably supplied some sort of good or service to the debtor for which the latter owed reimbursement. Indeed, sometimes the merchandise in question is noted in the internment record. One example would be the arrest of Charles Luquet, a tanner, by one Sieur Ronnaud, a leather merchant.[26] On the other hand, there is no straightforward business relationship in others. While the debtor in such cases may have been borrowing money for his practice from a creditor, the two are not part of the same or interrelated trades. An example of such a transaction would be the arrest of Claude Bailly, a merchant mechanic, by one Jean Pierre Beard, an annuity-holder who arrested two other debtors within the period from 1835 to 1840.[27] A third group exists where the relationship is particularly ambiguous – for example the arrest of one Sieur Beaume, a finisher of shawls, by Sieur Tifrot and Company, coal merchants. Sieur Beaume may have been behind in paying his heating bills, but Sieur Tifrot and Company may not have supplied any such product to the finisher at all.[28] The conclusions drawn from this data must of course be cautious ones. Merely noting that a business relationship involving the actual purchase of goods or services could have existed does not mean it necessarily did. Moreover, there are many types of social relations – for example kinship lines and common membership in associational groups that may have been as important as professional connections – that cannot be ascertained or even hypothesized by the available data. Despite these caveats, the prison records nevertheless reveal certain patterns of possible business relationships. The majority of these of creditor-debtor relationships – some 142 out of a total 318- remain unclear largely because of the vagueness of the professional titles provided for either the debtor or creditor. Of those where creditor and debtor provided more specific information, eighty-one

26 ADR 2 Y 285 Entry 14.9.1839.
27 ADR 2 Y 284 Entry 23.4.1835.
28 ADR 2 Y 285 Entry 29.11.1836.

indicated no clear business relation whatsoever while ninety-one could be potentially have been part of a business relationship.

Another aspect of imprisonment visible in the records is that of 'recommendation' – a process that allowed multiple creditors to extend the length of a debtor's prison sentence. Since the 'recommended' debtors were obviously incapable or unwilling to pay a number of debts, it begs the question of why these individuals did not file for bankruptcy protection. Of the debtors, twenty-four were recommended. The majority of these twenty-four were recommended by one or two additional creditors usually within a month of the first arrest but sometimes by as many as four or five creditors independently over the space of several months. Many of these arrests seem to have been made in lieu of or perhaps in order to compel a declaration of bankruptcy. One particularly egregious case is that of Jean-Marie Cote fils, a merchant butcher who was arrested on March 9 1838 and recommended within the month of March alone by four other creditors.[29] Three of these creditors were livestock sellers from surrounding areas (indeed two of these animal sellers from different regions outside of Lyon had him arrested on the same day). The other two creditors were listed as a landowner and a wine merchant. While these careers suggest no clear link with Cote fils, they may well have supplied him some sort of service or merchandise. Similarly, a merchant named Jean-Marie Merney, arrested and recommended five times in 1837, owed money in round sums to everyone from business partnerships to a draper and a wine merchant.[30] Antoine Naphaeli, a straw merchant arrested and recommended several times over the months of November and December 1837 by creditors who had had judgments from the commercial court for over a year, owed the whopping sum of 8044 francs to a Sieur Guy whose occupation was listed as an annuity-holder.[31] Why did these individuals languish in prison rather than filing for bankruptcy immediately? Although we will never know the particularities of each case, these debtors may not have actually been merchants or they may not have kept books in an orderly fashion to prove their status as merchants. On the other hand, the relatively sizeable sums these individuals could borrow, seems to indicate that someone had judged them trustworthy enough to advance money in the first place.

The existence of so-called habitual creditors is equally revelatory of the uses of debt imprisonment.The Lyonnais debt prisoners in the 1830s articulated concerns

29 ADR 2 Y 285 Entries 9.3.1838 [two]; 16.3.1838; 21.3.1838; 23.3.1838.

30 ADR 2 Y 285 Entries 3.8.1837 [three]; 14.8.1837; 18.8.1837.

31 ADR 2 Y 285 Entries 30.11.1837; 5.12.1837 [two]; 13.12.1837; 14.12.1837.

about creditors who regularly relied upon incarceration, an abuse that they linked to the Martin Bequest, a 12,000 franc annuity left in 1824 by one Major Jean-Marie Martin ironically intended to help out imprisoned debtors.[32] The debtors charged that the prison administration had chosen to allot 100 francs to all debtors, regardless of their provenance, good character, or the amount of the debt, and in so doing had not only ended up favoring debtors of dubious character from abroad over Lyonnais natives but also had encouraged usurers to exploit Martin's largesse for their own ends. In December 1830, for example, a short-lived journal called *Le Pauvre Jacques Lyonnais* written and published by debtors within the prison recorded how one cloth merchant, a 'habitual incarcerator', arrested a woman in her eighth month of pregnancy for a sum of 312 franc telling neighbors that he had bet on her pregnancy to get him the money quickly.[33] He was not disappointed. Indeed, such abuses caused the debtors themselves to protest not only against the administration of the bequest, but the nature of the bequest itself. In the petition mentioned earlier, Lyon's debt prisoners estimated that the Don Martin had increased the number of imprisoned debtors tenfold.[34] Indeed, they argued that the money would better be dispensed to help out the families of those imprisoned rather than on freeing debtors from prison as this only increased the use of debt imprisonment.

Is there any evidence of this among the lists of creditors? Without exit records it is difficult to discern. Although the recording of names tends to be somewhat less precise with creditors than with debtors – many individuals with relatively common last names are identified as 'Sieur' or only by their last name and sometimes their address is not listed – at least 9 creditors seem to have held multiple debtors in prison. Most of these 'habitual incarcerators', however, held only two debtors in jail – a far cry from the predatory ilk depicted in the Martin Bequest legends. Indeed creditors who routinely relied on debt imprisonment seem to have been the exception rather than the rule. Probably the most egregious of these creditors was one Claude Pemeret, an animal merchant whose residence was alternatively listed as the Guillotière and the Vaise, and who arrested or recommended four debtors (including the aforementioned Cote fils) between 1836 and 1838. Three of these debtors were butchers.[35] The last of his debtors, a 'Dame Liaubert', does not have any profession at all provided for her, and was arrested by Pemeret for the minimum possible sum of 200 francs.[36]

32 ADR 1 Y 42 dossier: Legs Martin.
33 *Pauvre Jacques Lyonnais*, 5.12.1830, p. 4.
34 Debt prisoners of Lyon, p. 12.
35 ADR 2 Y 285 Entries 9.3.1838; 24.11.1836, 2.3.1838.
36 ADR 2 Y 285 Entry 5.4.1837.

Conclusion

The preliminary conclusions I have drawn from this data seem to confirm Bayle-Mouillard's nation-wide statistics and provide additional insights concerning Martin's analysis of bankruptcy. In his analysis of national statistics on debt imprisonment, Bayle-Mouillard noted the disproportionate number of men who listed their professions as "rentier" or "property-owner" among the lists of creditors. My evidence also suggests that creditors often belonged to the moneyed classes, whether in the form of "businessmen" – often working as partnerships or companies – or as annuity-holders or landowners. It seems likely that these individuals had lent money to their debtors rather than having accepted credit in return for supplying merchandise, a speculation confirmed by the registry entries that discuss the nature of the transactions involved. Nevertheless, as in Martin's findings about professions involved in bankruptcies either as debtors or as creditors, very few of these incarcerating creditors called themselves "bankers". Again paralleling Martin's findings, those described as "négociants" lacked any direct connection with the primary industry of the town – namely silk. It appears that these incarcerators were men – and occasionally women – who sought the potential of investing their extra income with the largely under-banked population of small producers and consumers. In this, they resembled the "négociants" who appear on the balance sheets of bankrupts – operators at the peripheries of the credit market, they functioned as lenders of last resort for those in monetary difficulty.

Again paralleling Martin and Bayle-Mouillard's studies, debtors tended not to be members of the more well-established professions – or those with higher entry barriers. In Lyon, incarcerated debtors were substantially clustered in the hospitality industry – whether as tavern-keepers of some form or as wine merchants. In this, they differed from Martin's list of professions that tended to be overwhelmingly debtors rather than creditors. Indeed, professions such as "cabaretier" and "limonadier" do not even appear in Martin's study, which may indicate that these professions were often "below" the bankruptcy threshold – practiced by individuals whose lack of proper book keeping or full establishment made them more likely to be imprisoned than to immediately declare bankruptcy. There was also a not insignificant contingent of artisans among imprisoned debtors. Commercial courts may not have considered these individuals eligible to declare bankruptcy given that they not "merchants." Although these groups would have been relatively minor players in a commercial economy, they do seem to have been largely "commercial individuals." However, for the large number of debtors simply listed as "merchant" or "trader" it is hard to know what realities may have lurked behind such titles or to what degree they actually participated in commercial activity.

Among the most striking facts in the data is the almost total absence on the internment records of debtors or creditors involved in Lyon's principle industry, silk production. This is indeed stunning, given the figures we have cited above. Jean-Clément Martin noted the disproportionately low likelihood for failure among those tied to the principal industries of Niort. For Martin, this was because those in established industries were less likely to be outsiders or "nouveau riche." This meant that when problems arose, they had stronger social connections that insulated them from the worst of the panic. A similar dynamic seems to have been at play with debtors. Bayle-Mouillard observed that nation-wide debtors and creditors drew from the same classes – wine merchants, coal peddlers, innkeepers and the like – rather than from the principle trades of any given town. In Lyon, however, it would seem that most creditors were either wholesalers or actual money-lenders. Overall, these debtor-creditor relationships seem to have been vertical rather than horizontal across social class. Furthermore, there seems to be little proof that usurers habitually relied on debt imprisonment as a means of reimbursement for their debt, although many of the creditors in question were more than likely lending money outside formal channels of credit.

What can these findings, however preliminary, tell us about both the practice of debt imprisonment and the place of the debtors' prison within the industrializing economy of the early nineteenth century? We may never be able to know the details of the transactions that eventually led each of these debtors to prison – or what profit their creditors sought by incarcerating them. Yet we can place this demographic analysis in conversation with the uses of debt imprisonment encountered in individual anecdotes, where *contrainte par corps* functioned as a means of both a form of collateral and a means of collecting upon it. The combined evidence suggests an alternative answer to the dichotomy generally posed between a moral economy based on interpersonal relationships and a cash nexus based on informal ones. By taking into account the role that debt imprisonment played in complementing rather than replacing legal and informal procedures for settling failure, such as bankruptcy and cession of property, it demonstrates the importance of law in regulating markets that were poorly equipped to deal with risk. Lenders – such as annuity holders and landowners – used the laws of debt imprisonment to enforce the reimbursement of money often loaned to those whose precarious financial status made bankruptcy perhaps impossible and at the very least impractical.

Jasper Kunstreich

Bankruptcy Laws as *Standortpolitik* – The Case of Hamburg 1850 to 1870

Introduction

Standortpolitik is one of those typically German compound nouns. The notion captures the practices and strategies by which governments try to attract business to their political jurisdiction. Calls for a more efficient *Standortpolitik* frequently occur in the press whenever companies announce the relocation of their production sites to a country with cheaper labour costs and lower tax rates.

Standortpolitik, or location politics, is by no means a phenomenon of our modern age. This article argues that we can trace it back in history and that bankruptcy laws played a vital role in it. The cities of the Hanseatic League have traditionally been places to which location policies played an essential role – probably because it was the *only* meaningful measures they had. Though the Hanseatic League was long gone by the nineteenth century, these places still contained a spirit of their former status. Three of the four sovereign cities in the German Confederation were Hanseatic towns: Bremen, Lubeck, and Hamburg. The latter and its bankruptcy code (*Fallitenordnung*) will be the subject of this article.[1]

It is the nature of case-studies to rely on the uniqueness of a particular place. Focusing on Hamburg between 1850 and 1866 nevertheless also serves as a prism through which German economic history can be analysed: between the revolution and the unification wars, the German economy underwent fundamental changes while the legal landscape remained fragmented. This makes Germany a

---

Author's note: This chapter is part of my doctoral-research in economic and social history at the University of Oxford. I am enormously grateful for the help and support of my supervisors, Professor Avner Offer and Professor Joshua Getzler. I also owe thanks to Professor Margrit Schulte-Beerbühl, Anthony Hotson, and Konrad Duden for helpful feedback and proofreading. This research was possible thanks to the enthusiastic help from the archivists at the Hamburg *Commerzbibliothek* and thanks to funding from the Economic and Social Research Council and the Scatcherd European Scholarship. All errors are mine.

1 *Der Stadt Hamburg Neue Falliten-Ordnung auf Befehl E. Hochedl. Raths publicirt den 31. Aug. 1753 nebst den Additional-Artikeln und den das Fallitwesen betreffenden neueren Conclusis und Verordnungen,* Hamburg 1823, henceforth "Neue Fallitenordnung".

fascinating "laboratory" for studying bankruptcy laws as the outcome of a society's underlying normative and behavioural beliefs.

This article is structured as follows: section I explains the notion of *Standortpolitik* and elaborates how bankruptcy laws fit into it. This is followed by a brief appraisal of the Hamburg bankruptcy regime in section II. Section III moves on to an empirical study of how these rules worked in reality. To this end two datasets are exploited for qualitative and quantitative evidence. The datasets have been compiled from the records of the Hamburg *Staatsarchiv* and the Hamburg *Commerzbibliothek*, the former containing some 1,016 bankruptcy files from the city's commercial court, the latter containing 4,145 cases of defaults registered in the records of the *Commerzdeputation*. Before the conclusions, section IV turns to the economic crisis of 1857 and shows how Hamburg responded to an external shock by changing its bankruptcy law.

Lastly, the reader should be reminded of some caveats that apply to court cases as a source for historians. First and foremost, the sample is self-selected. Going to court is costly and time-intensive. Whether or not a case was fought out in court depended on the parties' resources. Furthermore, very few archives kept court files: war, water and the need to make space in the shelves for new material have thinned out the material.

I. Bankruptcy as Standortpolitik

Standortpolitik refers to the practice of using tax incentives, investments in infrastructure, and commercial law in order to attract businessmen.[2] The US state of Delaware became a synonym for this kind of policies: more than fifty per cent of all American publicly traded companies are incorporated in Delaware and not in places like New York City, Chicago, or Los Angeles.[3] The "doing-business-index", constructed and provided by the world bank, gives an impression of the range of issues for policy makers to take into account. They range from dealing with

---

2 See Oatley, Thomas: *International Political Economy. Interests and Institutions in the Global Economy*, New York 2010, Chapter 9.

3 Delaware Division of Corporations, *Why Corporations Choose Delaware*, retrieved 07.01.2015 from: http://corp.delaware.gov/pdfs/whycorporations_english.pdf; Bebchuk, Lucian Arye / Bar-Gill, Oren / Barzuza, Michal: "The Market for Corporative Law". *Zeitschrift für die gesamte Staatswissenschaft/Journal of institutional and Theoretical Economics* 162(1), 2006, pp. 134–160.

construction permits to protection of minority investors.[4] Globalization has put enormous pressure on individual countries to "behave" in a business friendly way or else see increasingly mobile companies depart to other places.

Globalization and international competition are no new phenomena, however. History is full of rulers, who attempted to bring trade and commerce to their places by way of making concessions to merchants.[5] Pre-unification Germany is particularly interesting since it provides a sample of states, which were reasonably close to each other and cooperated in the German Confederation, but simultaneously employed different legal systems autonomously. Between 1815 and 1870 the German states also faced, to varying degrees, the challenges of industrialisation as well as the pressures to democratic reform and political unification.[6] What was the role of bankruptcy laws in all this?

Bankruptcy laws were important because they could help building a business friendly reputation. They are designed to provide a solution for situations in which a debtor cannot honour his obligations as they become due. The law intervenes and prevents the debtor's assets from being torn apart by each creditor trying to enforce his claims individually.[7] Instead, the assets are being kept together in order to achieve a higher dividend on their liquidation, which is then distributed to all creditors according to some distributional principle. Every regulation on bankruptcy generally tries to achieve multiple goals simultaneously: discourage fraudulent behaviour, maximise returns for the creditors and limit the costs for the community that stem from a bankruptcy, such as unemployment or consequences for other businesses.[8] Governments always had an interest in keeping a modicum of control over the winding-up process of individuals and firms. After all, the assets of a bankrupt could include land, shops, buildings, and factories

4 World Bank Group: *Doing Business. Measuring Business Regulations*, retrieved 07.01.2015 from http://www.doingbusiness.org/rankings.

5 De Long, Bradford / Schleifer, Andrei: "Princes and Merchants. European City Growth Before the Industrial Revolution". *The Journal of Law and Economics* 36(2), 1993, pp. 671–702.; Greif, Avner / Milgrom, Paul / Weingast, Barry R.: "Coordination, Commitment and Enforcement. The Case of the Merchant Gild". *Journal of Political Economy* 102 (4), 1994, pp. 745–776.

6 Breuilly, John: "Urbanization and the Social Transformation 1800–1914", in: Sheilagh Ogilvie and Richard Overy (eds.): *Germany, A New Social and Economic History*, Vol. 3, London 2003, pp. 192–225.

7 Foerste, Ulrich: *Insolvenzrecht*, Munich 2004.

8 Goode, Roy: *Principles of Corporate Insolvency Law* London 2008.

within their territory.[9] Furthermore, enforcing the rights and claims of creditors and punishing fraudulent debtors while simultaneously maintaining social peace was an important task and seen as the public duty of authorities. Mayors, merchants, civil servants and legislators had to take bankruptcy laws into account if they wanted a fully functioning market place.[10]

However, the question of what exactly constitutes a business friendly environment is much harder to tackle than the "doing-business-index" suggests. When is a bankruptcy law business friendly? Should it embrace a lenient stance towards debtors or should it focus on creditor protection? Are businessmen not usually both debtors and creditors at the same time? We should better view the two perspectives as the endpoints of a continuum. Which balance between the two goals is achieved is ultimately a normative decision, subject to the discretion of a legislator.[11] In the case of the US bankruptcy regimes, for example, it has been argued that the pendulum between debtor- and creditor-protection swang back and forth over time, depending on a mix of path-dependence and political influence of interest groups.[12] Aside from balancing creditors' and debtors' interests, one must not forget that the legislator might pursue interests of its own. In addition to the creditor vs. debtor dimension there is the dimension of the community.[13]

Bringing the many different perspectives and goals in line with each other was a challenge to the authorities and law-makers. Each of the nineteenth century German states sought its own way of employing some sort of *Standortpolitik*.[14]

---

9 Baird, Douglas: "Bankruptcy's Uncontested Axioms". *Yale Law Journal* 108, 1998, pp. 573–599.

10 Häberlein, Mark: "Merchant's bankruptcies, economic development and social relations in German cities during the long 16th century", in: Thomas Max Safley (ed.): *The History of Bankruptcy: Economic, Social and Cultural Implications in Early Modern Europe*, London 2013, pp. 19–33.

11 Sgard, Jérôme: "Do Legal Origins Matter? The Case of Bankruptcy Laws in Europe 1808–1914". *European Review of Economic History* 10, 2006, pp. 389–419.

12 Coleman, Peter: *Debtors and Creditors in America: Insolvency, Imprisonment for Debt, and Bankruptcy, 1607–1900*, Madison 1974; Hansen, Bradley / Eschelbach-Hansen, Mary: "Crisis and Bankruptcy: the mediating role of state law 1920–1932". *The Journal of Economic History* 72(2), 2012, pp. 448–468.

13 Sullivan, Teresa / Warren, Elizabeth / Westbrook, Jay Lawrence: *As We Forgive Our Debtors: Bankruptcy and Consumer Credit in America*, New York, Oxford 1989; Skeel, David: *Debt's dominion. A history of bankruptcy law in America*, Princeton, Oxford 2001.

14 Meier, Anke: *Die Geschichte des deutschen Konkursrechts, insbesondere die Entstehung der Reichkonkursordnung von 1877*, Frankfurt am Main et al. 2003; Falk, Ulrich: „Die

One way out of the dilemma could have been "diversification": having more than one possible option for winding-up firms, distinguishing between business cases and private cases, discriminating according to class and status. In fact, modern insolvency law does contain these elements. A private actor files for bankruptcy under a completely different procedure than a company. Although the company as an entity had not yet fully evolved by the middle of the nineteenth century, contemporaries agreed that the case of a merchant-banker should be treated differently from that of a small craftsman.[15]

It is possible to think of at least three ways in which this diversification could be achieved: first, by establishing different jurisdictions with access restricted to a clearly defined membership. All cases under a certain jurisdiction would be reasonably homogenous, which in turn meant that the parties involved were more likely to agree to a given set of rules and norms. A second option was for the law itself to distinguish between different types of cases, for example with reference to their size. And finally, those in charge of applying the law could discriminate in their application even if the law itself did not contain any explicitly discriminating provisions. The following paragraphs venture to show that people in Hamburg combined all three options of diversification in their bankruptcy regime.

II. The bankruptcy regime in a free city

One of the most important traits of German towns and cities was its corporatist structure – a fact that must be reiterated before delving into details, for it applies to the four free cities (Frankfurt, Lubeck, Hamburg, and Bremen) as well as individual towns in other German states. It is often thought of as an early modern phenomenon while the prevalent conceptualizations of the nineteenth century emphasize state-formation and nation building. Yet, politics and the law in German towns were always embedded in a complex nexus of relationships between different corporate bodies.[16] The stability of the system ultimately rested on the fact that none

---

Konkursübel. Forschungsfragen zur Geschichte des Konkursverfahrens in Deutschland". *Zeitschrift der Savigny-Stiftung für Rechtsgeschichte, Germanistische Abteilung* 131, 2014, pp. 266–324.

15 Getzler, Joshua / Macnair, Mike: "The Firm as an Entity Before the Companies Act", in: P. Brand, K. Costello and W. N. Osborough (eds.): *Adventures of the Law: Proceedings of the Sixteenth British Legal History Conference, Dublin, 2003*, Dublin 2005, pp. 267–288.; Guinnane, Timothy / Rosenthal, Jean-Laurent / Harris, Ron / Lamoreaux, Naomi: "Putting the Corporation in its Place". *Enterprise & Society* 8(3), 2007, pp. 687–729.

16 Schmidt, Manfred G.: "Germany: The Grand Coalition State", in: Joseph Maria Colomer (ed.): *Political Institutions in Europe*, London 1996, pp. 57–94.

of the bodies could ever dominate it.[17] So deeply rooted was this system that most towns returned to it even after a brief interval of French occupation, during which Napoleon had abolished many of these old bodies.[18]

In Hamburg, just like in any other German town, corporatist groups rather than a central government in our modern sense regulated many policy fields. Craftsmen and artisans were organised in guilds, which dominated the city's economic life.[19] Most important for this paper is the organization of merchants: all merchants, including religious minorities and merchants without citizenship, formed the *Ehrbare Kaufmann* (honourable merchant) or *Kaufmannschaft*, a corporatist body and distinct legal entity. It was governed by a committee, the *Commerzdeputation*, which was in charge of the Hamburg Bourse and also controlled seven seats in the civic assembly.[20] The *Commerzdeputation* furthermore named four members of the *Kaufmannschaft* who would serve as lay-judges together with one trained lawyer at the Hamburg commercial court.[21]

Those two bodies – the *Commerzdeputation* and the commercial court – essentially administered Hamburg's bankruptcy regime. It is no surprise that the code appears to be tailor-made for merchants in many respects. The preface to the *Neue Fallitenordnung* reads:

> "[...] to prevent as much as possible the formal insolvency with its multiple and extensive procedures in court [...]. To this end we have prescribed first and foremost the accelleration of out-of-court settlements [...] and have directed our aiming and doing partly to the service of the credit and partly to the advantage and flourishment of our commerce so that [...] nobody shall be left out alone with respect to the others."[22]

---

17 Walker, Mack: *German Home Towns: Community, State, and General Estate, 1648–1871*, Ithaca, London 1971, p. 55.

18 Dölemeyer, Barbara: „Frans Recht in Noord-Duitsland: De Inlijving van de Noordwestelijke Gebieden van Duitsland bij het Franse Keizerrijk". *Pro Memorie* 13(2), 2011, pp. 186–202.

19 Gelderblom, Oscar / Grafe, Regina: "The Rise and Fall of the Merchant Guilds: Rethinking the Comparative Study of Commercial Institutions in Premodern Europe". *Journal of Interdisciplinary History* 40(4), 2010, pp. 477–511.; Ogilvie, Sheilagh: *State corporatism and proto-industry. The Württemberg Black Forest, 1580–1797*, Cambridge 1997.

20 Handelskammer Hamburg (ed.): *Dokumente zur Geschichte der Handelskammer Hamburg*, Hamburg 1965.

21 Ibid., 77–84.

22 Neue Fallitenordnung, 1753, pp. 1–4, own translation, German original: *[...] die bisher über die Maasse vervielfältigten und ausgedehnten gerichtlichen Processe, so viel immer möglich, zu vermindern [...] Wir haben des Endes zuförderst die Beschleunigung eines*

The quoted passages describe the division of the bankruptcy procedure into two distinct paths: the code's first objective is to lead to a friendly agreement between creditors and debtors. An informal insolvency procedure in court was only seen as subsidiary remedy. According to the code, a commission of members of the city council was installed immediately after a merchant had petitioned for bankruptcy to monitor all the proceedings. The commission also named the administrator from among the creditors. His task was to compile a coherent inventory of the debtor's assets, continue his firm, start negotiations with creditors for a friendly agreement, and prepare monthly reports to the commercial court. The case was conferred to a formal insolvency procedure only if these negotiations failed, and this procedure usually meant liquidation.[23]

This division into a settlement-procedure and a liquidation procedure is a pattern that can be found in the other free cities, too. Bremen's bankruptcy law[24] distinguished between a *Moratorialverfahren* (moratorium negotiations) and the *Konkursverfahren* (bankruptcy proceedings). The aim of the *Moratorialverfahren* was a formal contract between debtor and creditors that would end the procedure either through a debt discharge or through other means.[25] In Lubeck merchants could avoid going to court by petitioning at the city council for an out-of-court procedure, called *Debitverfahren*. Again, the objective of this procedure was to facilitate a settlement between creditors and debtor and to resolve the issue quickly.[26] Until 1862 Lubeck also lacked a written bankruptcy code that would specify the procedure in court.[27] Before this time the formal insolvency procedure probably followed German customary law and Prussian law with their elaborate rank order

solchen Accords […] anempfohlen, […] und dabey unsere Absicht, vereinigtermassen, theils auf den Nutzen des Credits, und theils auf den wahren Vortheil und Flor der Handlung solchergestalt gerichtet, daß […] niemand vor dem anderen […] allein leer ausgehen […] möge.

23 Baumeister, H.: *Blicke auf einzelne Gegenstände des Hamburgischen Rechts*, Hamburg 1852, p. 265.

24 Senat der freien Hansestadt Bremen, "Verordnung für Debit- und Nachlaßsachen vom 24. Mai, publiziert 5. Juni 1843", in: *Sammlung der Verordnungen und Proclame des Senats* (1846), p. 30.

25 Deutscher Reichstag, "Motive zu dem Entwurf einer Konkursordnung und dem Entwurf des Einführungsgesetzes", in: Deutscher Reichstag, *2. Legislatur-Periode, 2. Session 1874, zu No. 200*, p. 55.

26 Hach, Johannes Friedrich: Gedanken über das Fallitwesen in Lübeck, 05.11.1822, in: Archiv der Hansestadt Lübeck, Gemeinnützige Gesellschaft, Vorträge Nr. 330.

27 Deutscher Reichstag, 1874, p. 46.

of creditors and two administrators.[28] Frankfurt, the most southern of the free cities, had a similar situation: the court procedure followed German customary law, while older city statutes such as the city's *Reformacion* from 1509, the statute against fraudulent bankruptcies in 1708 and the law on bills of exchange in 1739 made special provisions for the insolvency of merchants.[29] Contemporary authors report that moratorium-contracts to prevent a case from going into court happened so regularly that they were considered the natural starting point for every bankruptcy case.[30]

The emphasis on out of court settlements could be linked back to the abovementioned corporatist structure of German towns. In Hamburg, the *Commerzdeputation* got involved with almost every bankruptcy case. In the first place, the public notification of an insolvency case was made at the boards of the Hamburg Bourse. It prompted creditors to bring their claims before the appointed commission that oversaw the case. It also marked the debtor, who was henceforth excluded from trading at the Bourse until his case was resolved. If the appointed administrator wanted to sell the bankrupt's assets, officially certified brokers first had to estimate their value. Again, it was the *Commerzdeputation* that appointed these brokers. Furthermore, all merchants in Hamburg were usually members of the *Kaufmannschaft*, just like the lay-judges at the commercial court, who were appointed by the *Commerzdeputation*. In essence, an association of members of the same profession administered most of the case, particularly if it was settled entirely out of court.

Art. 109 of the bankruptcy code declared that the law should be applied to all citizens and city dwellers as well as the adjacent territories under Hamburg law. This inclusive scope is remarkable: no distinction was made between citizens and non-citizens, between foreigners and Hamburgers. Whoever declared insolvency *in* Hamburg, had to follow the provisions of this code.

Yet, it did not follow from this that all debtors were treated equally. The same Article 109 prescribed that not everyone in Hamburg had equal access to its courts. Only debtors who owed more than 4,000 Mark Banco could petition for the procedure according to the code. Cases, which fell below that threshold, faced considerable obstacles, above all because they were proscribed from entering into

28 Meier, 2003, p. 62–77.

29 Coing, Helmut: *Die Rezeption des römischen Rechts in Frankfurt am Main*, Frankfurt 1939.

30 Bender, Johann Heinrich: Handbuch des Frankfurter Civilprocesses, Frankfurt am Main 1854, p. 203; Adlerflycht, Justinian von: *Der Civilproceß der freien Stadt Frankfurt*, Frankfurt am Main, 1832, p. 1326.

court for official insolvency procedures and judicial liquidation. These cases were usually administered by one of the *Praetors*, an official of the lower city court and were subject to his discretion.

Contemporary lawyers in Hamburg criticized this practice not because they thought it was discrimination against small debtors, but because they thought it discriminated too little. Some lawyers saw it as too strong a concession to ordinary people if a bankruptcy code was not exclusive to merchants. Johann Georg Büsch, in his handbook for merchants,[31] opined that the "privilege" of bankruptcy should be denied to anyone outside the mercantile community and those debtors be left to the doings of their creditors.

> It is a major mistake of those statutes, that they not only admit the helpers of merchants, for example brokers and accountants, but also craftsmen and people of all sorts, who live from a stable or occasional income, into an orderly bankruptcy procedure, and that it grants them those advantages, which had been introduced into the statutes only with respect to the issues of the merchants' trade.[32]

"Ordinary persons" usually had a steady income, on which creditors could count for their compensation, or lived of occasional jobs and alms, in which case Büsch deemed it perfectly fine if creditors grabbed "whatever they can get hold of". Merchants on the other hand often made a living from buying and selling on credit. Seizing all their assets and destroying the relationship to their creditors would cut them off from their source of income, which in turn made the debtor's recovery unlikely. Theodor Hasche, who wrote the most extensive commentary on the Hamburg bankruptcy law, agreed that a merchant's business was substantially different in quality. Nevertheless, he argued, refusing a proper bankruptcy procedure to non-merchants could have detrimental effects on the civic community as a whole. Instead, a separate bankruptcy-code for non-merchants would have been desirable.[33]

---

31 Büsch, Johann Georg: *Theoretisch-Praktische Darstellung der Handlung in deren mannigfaltigen Geschäften*, Vol. II, Hamburg 1792, p. 165.

32 Ibid, p. 165, own translation, German original: *Dieß ist aber ein wesentlicher Fehler mancher solcher Verordnungen, daß man nicht nur Hülfspersonen der Handlung, wie z.E. Maklern und Buchhaltern, sondern auch Handwerkern und Leuten aller Art, die von festgesetztem oder zufälligen Verdienste leben, ein ordentliches Fallissement erlaubt, und ihnen mehr oder weniger die Vorteile angedeihen läßt, welche nur die billige Rücksicht auf die Unfälle der Handlung in diese Verordnungen gebracht hat.*

33 Hasche, Theodor: *Erläuterung der Hamburgischen Falliten-Ordnung*, Vol. III. Friedrich Perthes: Hamburg 1805, p. 275.

The debate about the question whether ordinary people should be able to petition for bankruptcy should be contrasted with how the Hamburg law answered another important question: when is a debtor insolvent and when is he illiquid? The law of 1753 did not specify these terms. In fact, a debtor who petitioned for bankruptcy did not have to prove his insolvency or undergo a special pre-bankruptcy procedure to assess his situation.[34] According to Art. 1 of the code, someone was insolvent if he declared himself to be insolvent or if he stopped his payments, a provision comparable to Art. 437 and 441 in the French *Code de Commerce*.[35] From the perspective of Hamburg merchant-bankers, this provision was desirable because it avoided a static distinction between illiquidity and insolvency. Since liquidity problems could occur easily in all businesses that were heavily reliant on credit and debt, having a remedy at hand to summon one's creditors and negotiate a respite or a settlement was vital.

III. The Bankruptcy Code as a Filtering Device

The characteristics of the law, as described above, could be seen as mechanisms of "diversification": they regulated the entry to the bankruptcy procedure and ensured that each case was directed to the right channel.[36] Small debtors – and possibly also non-merchants – were separated from the rest by virtue of article 109. The procedure itself was split in two stages, with the first stage aiming at a friendly agreement between debtor and creditors. Finally, bankruptcy was embedded in an institutional setting that was dominated by mercantile interests, manifest in the role played by the *Commerzdeputation*.

This filtering function of the bankruptcy law can already be observed from the collection of some simple frequencies. Figure 1 shows the number of bankruptcy cases as recorded in the books of the *Commerzdeputation* (Fig. 1.a, straight line). These record books counted all cases that were made public at the Hamburg Bourse, regardless of whether they were petty cases or not.

---

34 Deutscher Reichstag, 1874, p. 50.

35 Bédarride, Jassuda: *Traité des Faillites et Banqueroutes ou Commentaire de la Loi du 28 Mai 1838*, Vol. 1, Paris 1838.

36 For a "grammar" of rules and the importance of entry- or boundary-rules see Ostrom, Elinor: *Understanding Institutional Diversity*, Princeton 2005 and Crawford, S. / Ostrom, Elinor: "A Grammar of Institutions". *American Political Review* 89(3), 1995, pp. 582–600.

Figure 1: Frequencies of bankruptcy cases according to a) type of procedure and b) jurisdiction, Source: Stiftung Hanseatisches Wirtschaftsarchiv, Safebestand der Commerzbibliothek, *S/599 122 c–d blau*

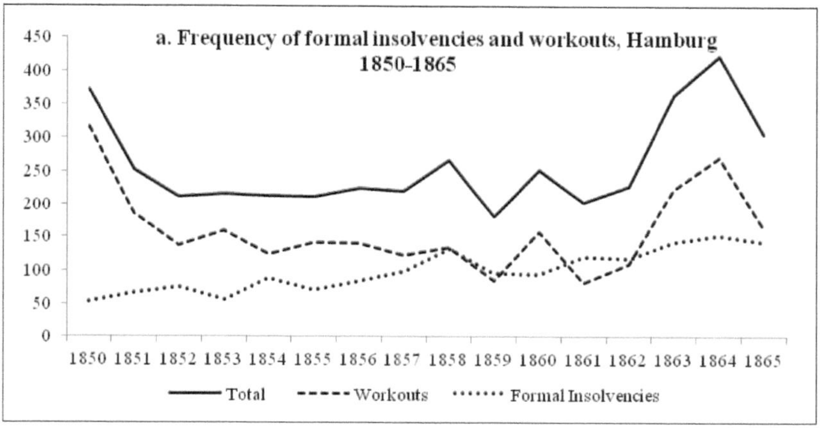

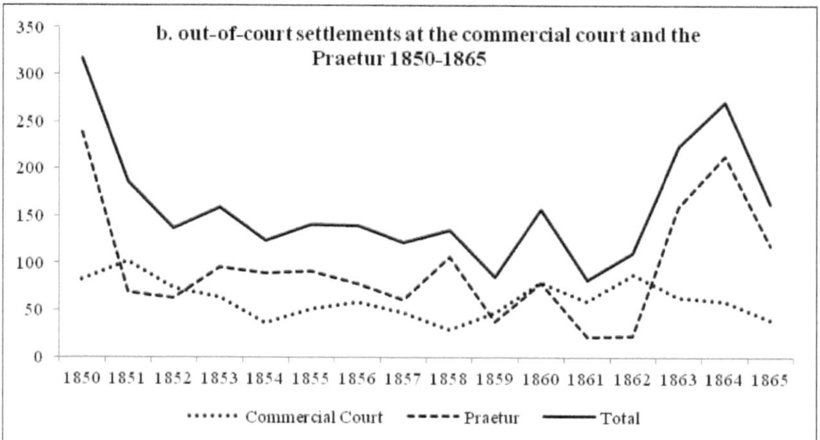

The overall number of bankruptcy cases in the period 1850 to 1865 was rather large. Even if we exclude the peaks in 1850 and 1864, the average number of cases per inhabitant in Hamburg exceeded that of other German states for which data is available. In Hamburg, per one thousand inhabitants 1.2 to 1.5 bankruptcy cases were filed.[37] Comparable statistics for the Prussian kingdom reveal a rate of 0.5

37 Population Data from Viebahn, Georg Wilhelm von: *Statistik des zollvereinten und nördlichen Deutschlands,* Vol. 2. Berlin 1862.

to 0.7 cases per one thousand inhabitants. The Rhineland, where the supposedly more "business-friendly" French law was applied,[38] achieved similar rates to those in Hamburg; their statistics recorded between 1.1 and 1.4 cases per thousand inhabitants for the 1840s.[39] The pattern even continued after legal unification. In the German bankruptcy statistics of the 1880s, Hamburg still features as one of the cities with the highest frequency of bankruptcies per head.[40]

Figure 1.a. furthermore distinguishes two subcategories. The dotted line depicts those cases that were sent to the commercial court for a formal insolvency procedure. The number of these cases seems to have risen constantly over the 1850s and 1860s. The dashed line represents those cases that were dealt with out of court, either through settlements between creditors and debtors or by the *Praetor*. This latter sample is further dissected in figure 1.b. in order to show how many of those out-of-court procedures came under the jurisdiction of the *Praetor* and how many cases came under the jurisdiction of the commercial court. The latter category comprises the cases that actually enjoyed the privileges of Hamburg bankruptcy code that attempted to facilitate a settlement between creditors and debtors. They are depicted by the dotted line in Figure 1.b. The dashed line in the same figure refers to cases that were channelled to the fast track procedure for petty cases.

Two lessons can be learned from this exercise. Firstly, the high frequency of bankruptcy cases in Hamburg is noteworthy and indicates that the bankruptcy code made it indeed easy to petition for the procedure. Yet, secondly, it did not automatically follow that everyone had an equal chance to reach a debt discharge. The number of settlements was in fact decreasing while formal insolvencies became more frequent. And even within this decreasing sample of cases that were handled out of court, only a smaller subpart actually came under the jurisdiction of the commercial court. The rest was dispatched as petty cases. The system appears much less accessible; the Hamburg institutions made spare of the "privilege" of bankruptcy. Unfortunately, it is only the sample of formal insolvencies for

38 Acemoglu, Daron / Cantoni, David / Johnson, Simon / Robinson, James: "The Consequences of Radical Reform. The French Revolution". *The American Economic Review* 101(7), 2011, pp. 3286–3307.

39 Data on Prussia and the Rhineland for the time period between 1812 and 1842 is reported in Kamptz, Karl Albrecht von: *Jahrbücher für Preussische Gesetzgebung*. Berlin 1815–1843; after 1843 see *Justiz-Ministerialblatt der Preußischen Monarchie*. Berlin 1850 and *Jahrbuch der Preußischen Gerichtsverfassung*. Berlin 1853.

40 Reichsjustizamt: *Deutsche Justizstatistik*, Vol. 1–4. Berlin 1883–1889.

which we can obtain more detailed information from court files.[41] Information about the outcome of the settlements is few and far between and we know virtually nothing about the petty cases.

The strong emphasis on the out-of-court-settlement represents the normative decision of the Hamburg government that the bankruptcy law should help keep viable firms as going concern. Swift liquidation would harm this prospect and even lower the proceeds realized on the values. The underlying rationale was that firms could suffer short-term liquidity problems without necessarily being insolvent. Whether or not a firm could honour its obligations as they became due could also be a question of how many of their assets were fixed in long-term investments. In some cases, a maturity mismatch between long-term fixed assets and short-term obligations could bring a firm in financial distress. In the Hamburg bankruptcy code it becomes apparent that the legislator did not want to leave the decision about a firm's viability to the judges. It is possible to conjecture that these provisions for debtor-creditor settlements were designed with the aim to support credit networks in the merchant town.

Figure 2: Frequency of Bankruptcy cases reported to the Commerzdeputation *and at the commercial court grouped by month of declaration; the vertical axis to the left applies to the columns, depicting formal bankruptcies in court, the vertical axis to the right to the line representing bankruptcy declarations at the Hamburg Bourse. November 1857 to June 1858 are excluded because Hamburg applied a special bankruptcy law during the economic crisis of these months*

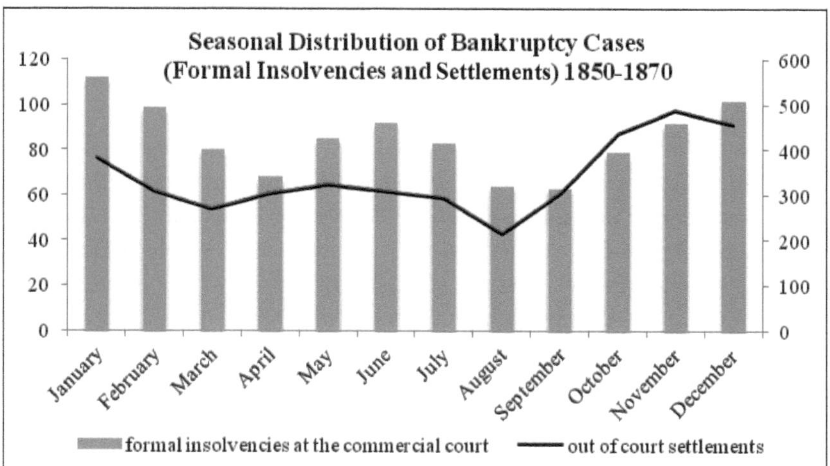

41 Staatsarchiv Hamburg (StAHH), *Bestand Handelsgericht* 222–3 B1, B2.

Another piece of evidence in support of this conjecture is presented in figure 2. It groups all cases according to the month in which they were brought to court or to the attention of the *Commerzdeputation*, excluding the time between November 1857 and June 1858, when Hamburg was hit by a worldwide economic crisis. Each column represents the cumulative frequency of formal insolvencies filed at the commercial court in the respective month for the time period between 1850 and 1870 (values on the vertical axis to the left). Peak months were January and June. The line depicts the corresponding frequencies for out-of-court procedures (values on the vertical axis to the right), with a peak in November. The pattern seems to indicate a veritable cycle of bankruptcies of the course of a year. Most bankruptcy cases, both out-of-court procedures and formal insolvencies, where filed between November and January.

The end of the year and beginning of winter was a critical phase in the yearly business cycle. After the harvest period and with the cold season approaching, the more weather dependent businesses would come to a halt. As the year drew to a close, merchants examined their books and tried to bring in any arrears. The six-month-rhythm that can be observed in the figure furthermore corresponds to the typical maturity of bills of exchange, most of which had a so-called tenor of either three or six months.

It follows that bankruptcy in Hamburg must have been something else than just the inevitable answer to economic failure. The institutions in Hamburg handled bankruptcies with a certain regularity and routine. In many cases, troubled merchants possibly sought the protection of the prescribed procedure to summon their creditors to renegotiate the terms of their loans or find an amicable solution for a firm in financial distress. Cases in which this was impossible would then be conferred to the court shortly thereafter.

Although this observation suggests an almost natural bankruptcy-rhythm in the Hamburg legal system, we must also consider the fact that the number of formal insolvencies was constantly rising during the 1850s and 60s. This latter finding seems to indicate that the system was not as stable as it looks in figure 2 and raises the question whether the Hamburg bankruptcy code from 1753 was in need of reform by the middle of the nineteenth century. As it has been shown that the bankruptcy code mirrored the corporatist structure of the city, it should be asked to which extent this was still the case in the 1850s. Figure 3 shows the relative share of different occupational groups in the sample of 1,016 bankruptcy cases at the commercial court between 1850 and 1870. It does not come as a surprise that merchants were by far the most numerous group in our sample. Nor did we expect to find many ordinary labourers and servants, since their cases were most likely to end up as petty cases. Yet the picture also reveals a decreasing merchant-dominance. Correspondingly the cohort of craftsmen in formal insolvency slowly increased.

Figure 3: Occupations of debtors in a sample of cases at the Hamburg commercial court between 1850 and 1870. The figure reports the share of each occupational group in the overall sample. Data collected from Staatsarchiv Hamburg, Bestand Handelsgericht *222–3 B1, B2*

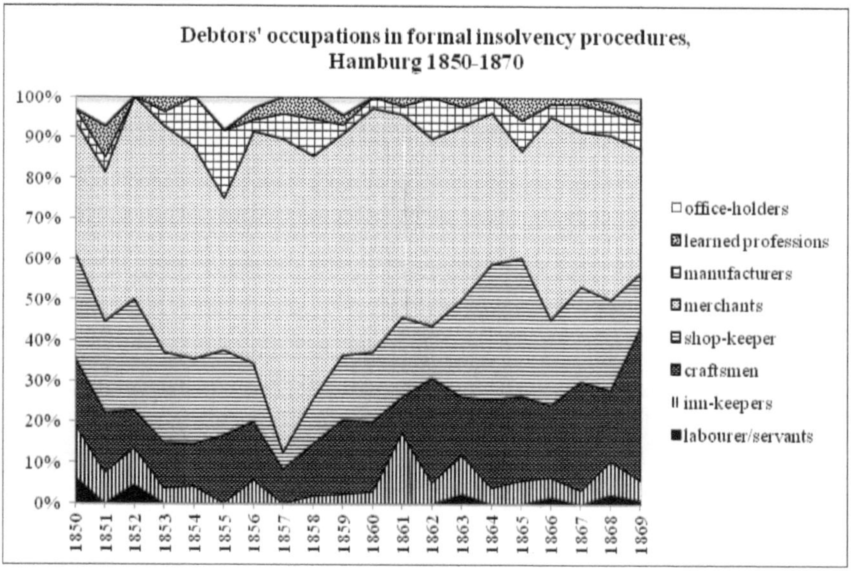

There are several possible explanations for this change. It is quite likely that by 1850 the threshold of 4,000 Mark Banco to bring a case under the jurisdiction of the commercial court was no longer high enough to keep out all non-merchants. In addition, a small new category of "manufacturers" appeared, who often pursued business models that were new and alien to the traditional logic of merchant-bankers in Hamburg. Economic change and industrialisation, which gave the nineteenth century its dynamic, might have rendered those old social distinctions porous.

A closer look into the court files also reveals that different occupational groups received different treatments. Table 1 reports the mean and the median for a number of variables.[42] The amount of debt is reported in the local currency, Mark

42 While the mean reports a weighted average, the median specifies the point that divides the sample in exactly two halves. Both measures are given here, since the sample is not normally distributed.

Banco. The duration of a case is measured in months. A merchant case took on average half a year longer to conclude compared to cases concerning office-holders, rentiers, or labourer. Across the entire sample of cases, the compensation for creditors was well below forty per cent, which was a legal threshold stipulated in the bankruptcy code for debtors wanting a full discharge. But the recovery rate was substantially lower for merchants than for anyone else. Additionally the number of cases in which nothing was distributed to creditors at all, while debtors were nonetheless able to walk away after the end of procedure without being penalized is the highest among merchants.

Table 1: Distribution of occupations in the sample of court cases from the Hamburg commercial court 1850–1870 and descriptive statistics.

	N	debt		creditors		recovery rate		duration	
		mean	Median	mean	median	mean	median	mean	median
labourer, servant	10	5,056	4,508	24	22			24.32	21.14
Inn-keeper	52	8,211	6,709	45	37	31.05	30	32.02	27.37
craftsmen	168	15,259	6,668	66	28	19.07	11.4	30.57	22.31
shop-keeper/ dealer	250	19,006	8,017	42	35	17.66	10	30.67	25.3
merchants	354	46,536	13,585	37	30	17.91	8	35.45	27.99
Manufacturer	72	28,126	9,848	37	32	19.19	12.38	35.33	27.09
learned professions	22	16,609	7,556	60	39	27.09	8.9	33.3	27.63
office-holder/ rentiers	13	8,774	5,241	36	36	36.67	40	19.78	19.81

Does this suggest that the Hamburg bankruptcy regime was more lenient towards merchants? Reading through some of these court files suggests that, yes, merchants did not have to fear bankruptcy per se. To begin with, in the subsample of merchant-cases at the commercial court, many debtors petitioned for bankruptcy several times. The *Commerzdeputation*'s record book lists 4,145 cases, but only 2,298 different names. Not a single one of these "reoffenders" qualified as a petty case.[43] Sometimes a debtor showed up three or four times in the records, sometimes entire families, one after another, including wives and in-laws.

43 A debtor was counted as recurrent debtor if his surname as well as the combination of his forenames was the same as in a previous entry. We have no means to inquire whether some people might have carried both the same family name and the same forename.

One of those reoffenders was Adolph Cohn, from a family of Jewish merchants, who filed for bankruptcy first in November 1852 together with his brother Eduard Cohn. They reached a settlement with their creditors by recovering 7.75 per cent of the debts. Only two years later, Adolph Cohn petitioned again for bankruptcy, this time alone. He could settle the case without formal insolvency but also without any of his creditors being compensated. The fact that the Cohns appeared frequently in the record books seems to suggest that going bankrupt did not bring the family-name into disrepute per se. Benjamin Cohn, a cousin of Adolph, went bankrupt in 1854 and fled to the US and left behind two adult sons, who later established themselves as merchants and real estate agents.[44] They in turn filed for bankruptcy, the oldest already in 1859, the youngest in 1869.[45] It should also be noted that Cohn was Jewish family name.[46] Even though Hamburg denied its Jewish inhabitants citizenship until 1863, the bankruptcy regime might have worked perfectly well in their favour, as long as they qualified as merchants.

We know most about those cases that entered formal insolvency because a family decided not to rescue one of its members. This shows the role family networks played in credit relations. Simon Heckscher's case is illustrative in this respect. We know about this case because here the negotiations for a settlement failed and the case went to a court.[47] Heckscher wrote to the judges in 1855:

> Because my application to my creditors, intended to relieve me from some of the burden of debt through an accord mediated by my relatives, ended without avail, I feel compelled to submit my declaration of insolvency.[48]

Heckscher's list of creditors is like a family reunion. The biggest creditor was his father in law, followed by two cousins, another brother in law, and his wife.[49] Their final report of the administrators mentioned that Heckscher's problems

---

44 StAHH, 222–3 B1 No. 3044, Cohen.

45 StAHH, 222–3 B1 No. 3483 & 4554.

46 We cannot be sure, though, that all these debtors belonged to the same family clan or whether they all just happened to bear the same, admittedly very common Jewish surname. See the index of the *Neue Deutsche Biographie,* digitalised for the database of German biographies, on 24.102014 retrieved from http://www.deutsche-biographie.de/index.html.

47 StAHH, 741–4 Ka 538 (Mikrofiche), Nr. 3118 Heckscher, Simon.

48 Ibid., own translation, German original: *Da meine Vorstellung an meine Creditoren mich durch einen mittels meiner Verwandten zu Stande zu bringenden Accord von meiner Schuldenlast zu liberieren, vergebens gewesen ist, so sehe ich mich genöthigt, meine Insolvenzerklärung zu überreichen.*

49 Ibid., Designatio Creditorum, No. 2.

stemmed from the fact that he himself was creditor to a number of defaulting debtors. Heckscher had transferred a number of securities to father in law prior to bankruptcy, and the administrators had no objections to validating these transfers. With regard to Heckscher's wife, the administrators even went so far as to allow her to take out wedding presents and precious items from the bankrupt's assets.[50] Heckscher experienced financial difficulties because some of his own clients had petitioned for bankruptcy. But he only entered formal insolvency proceedings because his extended family was reluctant – for whatever reason – to support him in that situation.

Craftsmen, on the other side, had a much harder time to raise additional funds if they came into financial difficulties. Transfer of title prior to bankruptcy and family help was quickly seen as attempt to fraud in their case. Money had to come either from merchants or professional money-lenders. In case of financial distress, those parties were reluctant to agree on any settlement.

The stonemason and bricklayer Krienke may serve as an example. Krienke went into liquidation in 1869, quite at the end of our period of observation. But his story already started in 1853, the year when he bought his first house and then made a little fortune from selling it quickly afterwards.[51] Around 1861 a merchant talked him into a deal where he would invest all his savings into this merchant's business and become a partner. This ended in huge losses for Krienke. Unperturbed by his misfortune and "avidly looking for new sources of revenues" – as it is written in the court files – he eventually fell prey to a real estate agent in 1866. Krienke bought two parcels of land from this agent and received a loan from him in order to finance the construction of two houses. There was a time period specified in the contract within which Krienke should have finished the houses. As it became clear that he would fail, he sought help from his family. His son in law gave him another loan, in exchange for which he mortgaged the unfinished houses to his relative.[52] When one of his suppliers got notice of that loan, he sued Krienke in court for fraudulent bankruptcy.[53] The case is quoted here because it points to a different attitude to family help with non-merchants. While the help of family members probably solved the majority of merchant-cases, this immediately triggered suspicions of fraudulent behaviour with non-merchants. Krienke was eventually discharged of the accusations, but his entire business and all his assets

50 This is unusual as one reads in other bankruptcy codes, cf. the Prussian Bankruptcy Law in *Allgemeine Gerichtsordnung,* Theil 1, Titel 50, §§ 269–294, 592.

51 StAHH, Ka 570 (Mikrofiche), 4643, No. 17 "Bericht der Curatores".

52 Ibid., No. 40 "Schlussbericht".

53 Ibid., No. 1 "Antrag auf Universalarrest".

had gone into liquidation in order to cover the costs of the procedure. His experience was probably similar to that of many other smaller craftsmen.

IV. The Crisis of 1857

Hamburg's bankruptcy law from 1753 had established a system that provided an important legal remedy to merchants in financial distress while simultaneously limiting access to its jurisdiction. Yet by the 1850s, economic change had seized most of Germany, particularly its urban areas. While this triggered legal reform in a number of German states, merchants and the city council in Hamburg seemed to cling to this system. When in 1857 a major economic crisis hit the city, one of the responses, a special bankruptcy policy, only reinforced the existing system.

Historians usually link the outbreak of the 1857 crisis to the bankruptcy of the Ohio Life and Trust Insurance Company in the U.S. on August 24th. This event brought an abrupt end to a decade of relatively prosperous years in the world. Economic historians differ over the question of what exactly caused the crisis.[54] Whatever the exact causes may have been, the crisis soon reached Europe. In relation to other German cities, Hamburg suffered most from the slump. In fact, it preoccupied the city's politics well beyond the 1857 and left a mark in the collective memory of citizens and merchants.[55] The fact, that Hamburg decreed a special insolvency procedure in 1857 as a remedy to the crisis is maybe the best example for our *Standortpolitik*-Hypothesis.

The bill-market was at the heart of all concerns in the crisis since bills of exchange functioned as a surrogate for money. A shock like the one that happened in 1857 could be exacerbated through chain effects in the bill market. If the bill market froze in response to a shock, an important source of short-term liquidity was lost.[56] In the absence of other sources of credit, even economically viable firms became endangered. Table 2 gives an overview of all the rescue measures adopted by the Hamburg city council in 1857. As shown, these measures fall into broadly two groups. The *Belehungskommission* and the *Diskonto-Kasse* both tried to solve

54 This chapter cannot engage with this debate in full detail. A good summary of the arguments in that debate in Temin, Peter: "Review of The Panic of 1857 and the Coming of the Civil War by James L Huston". *The Business History Review* 62(4), 1989, pp. 704–705. ; Calomiris, Charles / Schweikhart, Larry: "The Panic of 1857: Origins, Transmission, and Containment". *The Journal of Economic History* 51(4), 1991, pp. 807–834.

55 Ahrens, Gerhard: *Krisenmanagement 1857. Staat und Kaufmannschaft in Hamburg während der ersten Weltwirtschaftskrise*, Hamburg 1996.

56 Rosenberg, Hans: *Die Weltwirtschaftskrise von 1857–1859*, Suttgart 1934 p. 106.

the liquidity crisis at the bill market by supplying new paper money. The other two measures, *Vertrauenskommission* and *Administrationsverfahren*, were designed to explicitly help troubled firms.

Table 2: Rescue Measures taken by the Hamburg Government in November/December 1857

Title	Enacted	Official Start	Target
Belehungskommisions	26.11.1857	01.12.1857	Credit, Commodities
Administrationsverfahren	30.11.1857	05.12.1857	Merchants
Diskonto-Kasse	06.12.1857	07.12.1857	Bill Market
Vertrauenskommission	08.12.1857	08.12.1857	Support for five largest merchant-bankers

The *Administrationsverfahren* was a de facto temporary suspension of the bankruptcy code. Debtors put their business as well as the control over their assets under the administration of their creditors. How was this different from the ordinary bankruptcy law? To begin with, the petition for an administration could be based on "momentary financial difficulties while the applicant believes his assets to be generally sufficient to pay back all his creditors".[57]

In other words, entry into this sort of procedure was made as easy as possible. The law's definition distinguished between solvency and insolvency and addressed all those firms, which were believed to be viable but experienced liquidity shortages. The legal consequences were the same as in insolvency (individual lawsuits came to an halt, creditors could only act as a collective body), but the case was neither officially declared an insolvency nor did the procedure come under the aegis of a court.

Discerning viable from unviable firms was left to the discretion of the majority of creditors. In a first step, creditors appointed an administrator from their ranks.[58] He was given four weeks to examine the debtor's books and compile a detailed report for the other creditors. After this period, the community of creditors either confirmed their decision of opening an *Administrationsverfahren* or conferred the debtor to the court, in which case it would become an official insolvency case.[59]

This was most likely to happen in cases where creditors could not solve internal disputes. It did not necessarily indicate insufficient funds. If creditors wanted to

57 Amtliche Bekanntmachung: Verordnung wegen zeitweiliger Einführung eines Administrations-Verfahrens im Falle von Zahlungssuspensionen, in: Hamburger Börsenhalle, 03.12.1857, Commerzbibliothek, S 599, No. 55 rot, Zeitungsausschnitte.

58 Verordnung wegen zeitweiliger Einführung eines Administrations-Verfahrens, § 2.

59 Ibid, § 5.

liquidate the debtor's firm, they could easily achieve that under the *Administrationsverfahren*. Articles 9 and 10 of the law stipulated that any sale of goods could happen without obtaining the approval of the court and no detailed inventory was needed. This certainly opened the door for out-of-court liquidations. Moreover, this form of private liquidation was not without benefits for the debtor either. Although he only received a full discharge of all claims if he could serve at least 80 % of his secured debts, Article 8 and 9 of the law decreed that a procedure under this law had no consequences for the debtor's person and the liquidation was not made public.[60] Hence even if his entire business would be torn apart by his creditors, the debtor could still exercise all his citizen rights while the fact that he had been liquidated remained secret – at least as secret as such an event can remain in a merchant city.

It is difficult to assess how efficient the administrative procedure was in avoiding an insolvency crisis. Table 3 summarizes the outcomes of the procedures as far as those were recorded by the *Commerzdeputation*. On first sight, the ratio of successful administrations was much higher than under the normal bankruptcy regime. Out of 118 firms that petitioned for the special procedure, 65 could fully compensate their creditors. 38 cases ended with a settlement between debtors and creditors, with the average rate of recovery being 43,78 per cent. Only fifteen cases actually went into formal bankruptcy and liquidation and still received an average recovery rate of 33,30 per cent.[61]

Table 3: Descriptive Statistics for Administrations in Hamburg

	N	Minimum	Maximum	Mean	Std Dev.
Duration in months	118	2.86	86.74	18.84	16.76
settlements	38	2	96	43.78	18.53
liquidations	15	5	86	33.30	20.80
Full compensation	65	n.a.	n.a.	n.a.	n.a.

V. Conclusions

Bankruptcy laws have multiple functions, some of which might even contradict each other. What exactly determines a "business-friendly" bankruptcy law is difficult to

60 Ibid., §§ 8–9.

61 The numbers are obtained from a table containing all administrations in Hamburg and compiled by the *Commerzdeputation*, "Übersicht Administrationen", in: *Commerzbibliothek Hamburg* S 599 No. 55 rot.

bring to a standardized formula. Hamburg's bankruptcy code from 1753 provides an example that insolvency regulation was a valid policy-instrument to protect or shape the mercantile character of a place. This paper argued that the Hamburg city council and the Commerzdeputation tried to achieve this goal by way of diversifying the bankruptcy procedure. that the city council and the *Commerzdeputation* tried to achieve this goal.

The particularly business-friendly character of Hamburg's law can be seen in the emphasis on out-of-court settlements. A second chance for the debtor was generally regarded as a better solution than tearing his business apart. The formal insolvency procedure that lead to the liquidation of the debtor's assets was only applied subsidiarily. The institutional setting ensured that a merchant's peers handled his bankruptcy. Four elements were decisive: the monitoring commission of councilmen, the administration of the bankrupt's firm by his creditors, the jurisdiction of a specialized court, and the fact that everyone involved was simultaneously a member of the *Kaufmannschaft*. The entire mercantile community was bound together by a network of credit relations and had established institutions that helped overcome coordination problems when things went wrong. The bankruptcy procedure supplied debtors and creditors with a structured procedure to re-negotiate their relationship.

Whoever was not part of that network was also excluded from the benefits of the bankruptcy regime. The jurisdiction of the commercial court and the conditions for a friendly agreement with their creditors were nearly impossible to access for non-merchants. Petty cases were dealt with by one of the lower court-officials like an administrative act. If the debts of a non-merchant were high enough for him to be able to apply before the commercial court, they received a different treatment. Qualitative evidence from the court files shows that almost all those acts that were normal steps for securing an out-of-court settlement in the case of merchants, such as family help and transfer of title, were seen as attempts of fraud in the case of non-merchants.

It is questionable whether this system still worked smoothly in the 1850s. The sample of cases at the commercial court exhibited a growing number of smaller craftsmen. Around the same time-period a number of German states reformed their bankruptcy laws. Yet when in 1857 Hamburg was haunted by the worldwide economic crisis, the immediate response was not a reform but a temporary suspension of the bankruptcy code in order to protect the mercantile community. An overall reform of the bankruptcy regime did not happen until the introduction of the national German bankruptcy code in 1877.

Ulrich Falk & Christoph Kling

The Regulatory Concept of Compulsory Composition in the German Bankruptcy Act[1]

Preliminary note

The text below contains the translation of an initially German edited paper, including a translation of most quotations. One might question, with good reason, the whole endeavour of translating into English an article on German legal history that bases almost all of its argument on German-speaking sources. The particular difficulty of translating a highly condensed technical language like legal terminology stems from the fact that the reader's interpretation of expressions immensely depends on the reader's own cultural and educational background, in contrast to the translation of natural language, where most human beings share a much larger degree of common understanding.[2] Great additional difficulties arise from the character of specifically German legal terminology, which reached a notable level of consensus on the core of many notions notwithstanding numerous, inevitable and partly fundamental controversies. This vocabulary is often being

---

1 The article builds on a cross-epochal paper by Falk, Ulrich: Die Konkursübel. Forschungsfragen zur Geschichte des Konkursverfahrens in Deutschland (The bankruptcy evil. Research questions regarding the history of bankruptcy procedure in Germany), *Zeitschrift der Savigny-Stiftung*, German Section, Vol. 131 (2014), pp. 266–324. The abstract of that paper is as follows: "The paper discusses issues of the development of bankruptcy procedure in Germany from the mid-seventeenth century to the present day. The common theme throughout is criticism of current secondary literature, above all Wolfgang Forster's, Konkurs als Verfahren. Francisco Salgado de Somoza in der Geschichte des Insolvenzrechts (Köln 2009). Another focus is on compulsory composition (*pactum remissorium*, Akkord, Zwangserlassvertrag) as an instrument for solving the structural problems of bankruptcy in a way that meets all interests, as well as on Wolfgang H. Puchta, the undervalued father of Georg F. Puchta. Scrutinizing the sources immediately reveals the distortion that the image of German legal scholarship and legislation of the nineteenth century has suffered at the hands of Franz Wieacker, Privatrechtsgeschichte der Neuzeit (1967)."

2 On the difficulties and imperfection of legal translation, cf. Šarčević, Susan: Challenges to the Legal Translator, in: Tiersma, Peter M. / Solan, Lawrence M.: The Oxford Handbook of Language and Law, 2012, pp. 187–199, on the special nature of legal texts, pp. 189 f.

associated pejoratively with a strictly doctrinal, deductive reasoning within the law, a so-called *Begriffsjurisprudenz*, a term[3] which alone is hard to translate. However one might think about the degree to which such jurisprudence existed and continues to exist, the usage of this type of language remains a fact, so that legal diction and reasoning referring to the product of mainly nineteenth century pandect-science cannot be easily translated to the letter.[4] In fact, each use of such vocabulary would actually require us to give either the native term for all readers who are familiar with it, or an in-depth explanation for all those who are not. The first approach would result in a text with a substantial part not in English and thus raises the question, why to translate at all, the second approach is basically an entirely different, probably much longer text.

3 The often used translation "jurisprudence of concepts" can at least be misguiding, as "Begriff" has to be distinguished from "Konzept", because "Begriff" has a more direct relation to the word, or more general, the sign which in turn stands for the idea or the concept. The English word "concept" does not seem to have the kind of implication that "Begriff" has, cf. The New Shorter Oxford English Dictionary, Vol. 1, New York 1993, p. 467, which defines "concept" as "[a] product of the faculty of conception; an idea of a class of objects, a general notion; a theme, a design." Thus, using "concept" omits this intermediate step, which removes one possible additional level of abstraction that an author may, but also does not need to have in mind when using the word "Begriffsjurisprudenz". For more on this distinction, see the next fn. regarding semiotics; cf. Hasso Hofmann, in: Canale, Damiano et al. (eds), A Treatise of Legal Philosophy and General Jurisprudence: Vol. 9: A History of the Philosophy of Law in the Civil Law World, 1600–1900, 2009, p. 312: „*Begriffsjurisprudenz*, the ‚jurisprudence of concepts'" (author's emphasis); Ziegert, Klaus A.: Sociological Jurisprudence, in: Gray, Christopher B. (ed.): The Philosophy of Law: An Encyclopedia, Vol. 2, 1999, p. 815: „‚jurisprudence of legal concepts' (Begriffsjurisprudenz)".

4 One possible way to describe this problem is by using the model of semiotics with the legal term being a mere sign or symbol, cf. for a brief introduction Herberger, Maximilian / Simon, Dieter: Wissenschaftstheorie für Juristen. Frankfurt am Main 1980, pp. 205–225; in the context of a multinational law, cf. Engberg, Jan: Word Meaning and the Problem of a Globalized Legal Order, in: Tiersma, Peter M. / Solan, Lawrence M. (fn. 2), pp. 175–186, 176 f., who cites Charles Sanders Peirce. However, the origins of the model go back at least to Aristotle, cf. Jensen, K. B.: Semiotics, in: Smelser, Neil J. / Baltes, Paul B.: *International Encyclopedia of the Social & Behavioral Sciences*, 2001, pp. 13887–13891, 13887. Aristotle distinguished „spoken sounds" and „written marks" from „affections in the soul" as well as from „actual things", cf. Aristotle, De Interpretatione, in: Barnes, Jonathan (ed.): The Complete Works of Aristotle, The Revised Oxford Translation. Vol. 1, Princeton 1984, p. 25.

What you find here,[5] is a compromise to enlarge the group of potential readers without rewriting the whole original article that was presented at the conference. The conceived meaning of English legal terminology depends, as in every language, on reader's legal background, jurisdiction, epoch, and so on. Therefore, we either chose to use a literal translation, that at least gives a rough idea of what is meant, or we used (part of) a term that was or has been in use, e.g. in the current U.S. Bankruptcy Code, even though our selection is, also due to a lack of corresponding legal background, by no means perfect, nor can it ever be given the great variety of potential readers from various jurisdictions.[6]

I. Introduction

In his large textbook on the history of private law of the Modern Age, Franz Wieacker dedicates just a few sentences to bankruptcy law, in which he highlights the "original strictness" of the German Bankruptcy Act (Konkursordnung, KO).[7] The first version of this law came into effect in the German Empire on 1st October 1879 had juxtaposed two types of procedure that represented different ways to proceed with the bankrupt and his assets. Both routes could lead to the regular *closing* of the procedure[8] and, as documented in the official motivation of the law, were viewed as equals by the legislator: on the one hand the distribution (Schlussverteilung) procedure in the 5th title of the second book (§§ 137–159 KO 1879); on the other the compulsory composition (Zwangsvergleich) procedure in the 6th title (§§ 160–187 KO 1879). This regulatory structure remained in place when an amended version of the law came into effect on 1st January 1900 (§§ 149–172, 173–201 KO 1900).

---

5 We would like to thank *Sophie Costella* for the translation's draft, which was finally revised by us.

6 One example is „Zwangsvergleich", the topic of the article, being translated into „compulsory composition". Whereas „composition" is a technical term, e.g. in English bankruptcy law in the nineteenth century, and still seems to have the meaning of "[t]he settling of a debt etc. by some arrangement.", *The New Shorter Oxford English Dictionary*, vol. 1, New York 1993, p. 462, the combination with "compulsory" seems not to occur in a major authentic English source of law.

7 Wieacker, Franz: Privatrechtsgeschichte der Neuzeit. 2nd ed. Göttingen 1967, p. 467.

8 It is important to distinguish this from the dismissal of the procedure in the 7th title (§§ 188–192 KO 1879, §§ 202–206 KO 1900), which could also occur in two ways: through dismissal because the assets were not sufficient to cover the cost of the procedure (§ 190 KO 1879, § 204 KO 1900), or upon application from the bankrupt with the agreement of all bankruptcy creditors (§§ 188 f. KO 1900; §§ 202 f. KO 1900).

For the distribution procedure, § 152 para. 1 KO 1879 (§ 164 para. 1 KO 1900) mandates a rigid rule that seems to corroborate Wieacker's assessment: "Following closing of the bankruptcy procedure, the bankruptcy creditors who have not been satisfied can assert their claims against the bankrupt without limitation." The Bankruptcy Act did not provide for a discharge of residual debt for natural persons that would have a comparable structure to the regulatory concept in the German Insolvency Act (§§ 286–303; 304–314 InsO 1999) or the US Bankruptcy Code. In addition to the original sums owed, interest on arrears and procedure and enforcement costs could quickly add up. This effect, which is known as the modern debtor's prison (Schuldturm) in the context of debt enforcement,[9] has a profound social dimension, not least because the financial survival of relatives of the bankrupt – above all young children – can be vitally affected.

The law laid the distribution procedure in the hands of the bankruptcy administrator. Once the procedure was opened, the bankrupt lost the authority to administer and dispose of those of his assets that were part of the bankruptcy estate. The latter included all of the debtor's assets subject to foreclosure at the time the procedure was opened. From then on, these assets were destined to be used to satisfy bankruptcy creditors (§§ 1–3 KO 1879; §§ 1–3 KO 1900). The only exception were those assets that could not be seized in line with civil procedure law. Perhaps Wieacker was thinking of this genuinely caring limitation, which left the bankrupt and his family just enough to survive, when he characterised the relevant law as strict and uncompromising, but not inhumane.[10] The distribution procedure in the KO did not grant the bankrupt any further legal entitlement. § 118 KO 1879 (§ 130 KO 1900) gave the relevant provision in the 3rd title of the 2nd book:

> "Until a decision is reached by a creditors' meeting, the administrator can, with the permission of the court or, if a creditors' committee has been appointed by the court, with its permission, grant the bankrupt and the family of the same a meagre living from the bankruptcy estate."

---

9 With, Hans de / Nack, Armin: Der Moderne Schuldturm. *Zeitschrift für Rechtspolitik (ZRP)* 1984, pp. 1–3; Singer, Reinhard: Vertragsfreiheit, Grundrechte und der Schutz des Menschen vor sich selbst. *Juristenzeitung (JZ)* 1995, pp. 1133–1141, 1138; for a critic on the term see Medicus, Dieter: Der moderne Schuldturm? Rechtsdogmatische Überlegungen zur Privatautonomie im Recht der Bankgeschäfte. (Schriftenreihe der Bankrechtlichen Vereinigung, 3) (1992), p. 88; cf. also the principle judgement of the German Federal Constitutional Court, BVerfGE 89, 214–236 on how securities held by close relatives constitute a violation of morality (Sittenwidrigkeit).

10 Wieacker (fn. 7): p. 482.

If such subsistence allowances were granted in an individual case – whether it was by the administrator and court, the creditors' committee, or later the creditors' meeting –, they belonged to the administration expenses that were to be paid in advance from the bankruptcy estate, before bankruptcy creditors were paid. Among these administration expenses, the subsistence allowances ranked in competition with other administration expenses only in very last place, even after the "court costs for the collective procedure" and the "expenses for the administration, deployment and distribution of the assets" (§ 51 KO 1879; § 58 KO 1900). "Retention of the current home" also came under the provision, but as Higher Regional Court Judge Julius Senst explained in his manual on bankruptcy, "usually only for the initial period following the onset of bankruptcy".[11] This arrangement could mean great hardship.

In the distribution procedure, the needy bankrupt was not only forced to rely on the consideration and social conscience of the creditors and the administrator, but also condemned to a passive role. In the regulatory model of the KO, he did not exist as a stakeholder in the bankruptcy procedure, but is found in the codification only as a potential object of action, no different to his assets that were subject to confiscation. Therefore, the court could not only force him to appear before it, but also take him into custody (§ 97 KO 1879; § 106 KO 1900).

The role of the administrator appointed by the bankruptcy court included taking over possession and administration of all assets and deploying them (§ 107 KO 1879; 117 para. 1 KO 1900). Final distribution with the permission of the bankruptcy court was to take place as soon as the deployment of the assets was complete (§ 149 KO 1879; 161 KO 1900). Following distribution, approval of the final account of the bankruptcy administrator and the final creditors' meeting, the court had to decree the closing of the procedure (§§ 150 f. KO 1879; §§ 162 f. KO 1900). All the bankrupt could do was fervently hope that the bankruptcy administrator would succeed in achieving a sufficient yield in the deployment to not only cover the court and administrator costs and all other administration expenses, but also to satisfy the bankruptcy creditors.

II. The compulsory composition procedure

In the case of compulsory composition, however, the bankruptcy administrator was certainly not in a position to control the entire procedure. There, as Leipzig-based professor Ernst Jaeger, a leading expert in bankruptcy law, put it drily, the

---

11 Senst, Julius: Verwaltung von Konkursen. 8th ed. Berlin 1925, p. 314.

law assigned him “only a supporting role”.[12] Instead, another actor takes centre stage in the procedure – the bankrupt himself. Yet this is not the only major difference between this and the distribution procedure. If the bankrupt succeeded in bringing about a legally binding composition, he was only liable to the bankruptcy creditors for the amount of the agreed composition quota once the bankruptcy procedure had been completed. Apart from that he was free of debt.

A compulsory composition that was accepted and confirmed as legally binding by the court led to the closing of the bankruptcy procedure (§ 175 KO 1879; § 190 KO 1900). Unless the composition included a provision to a different effect, “the bankrupt regained the right to command the bankruptcy estate freely” (§ 177 KO 1879; § 192 KO 1900). The effect of the composition was then “for and against all non-privileged bankruptcy creditors”, including those who had voted against its acceptance or had not participated in the procedure at all (§ 178 KO 1879; § 193 KO 1900). It had to grant all these creditors the same right (§§ 168 KO 1879; § 181 KO 1900).

The law offered the bankrupt the option of making “the non-privileged bankruptcy creditors” a “composition proposal”, thus ensuring that he retains the initiative. In this proposal, he had to state “how the creditors are to be satisfied and how and in what way this is to be safeguarded” (§§ 160 f. KO 1879; §§ 173 f. KO 1900). The first, introductory provision was as follows (§ 160 KO 1879; § 173 KO 1900):

> “Once the general verification appointment has been held and as long as the execution of final distribution has not been approved, a compulsory composition can be concluded on the proposal of the bankrupt between himself and the non-privileged bankruptcy creditors.“

The compulsory effect depended on two basic requirements: (1) The “majority of the creditors with voting rights present at the appointment” had to explicitly agree. (2) The total of the claims of the consenting creditors had to be “at least three-quarters of the total of all claims with voting rights” (§ 169 KO 1879; § 182 KO 1900). Ernst Jaeger aptly called this “majority compulsion”, that was allowed under the law when certain protective measures were taken.[13]

If, following completion of the procedure, the bankrupt did not voluntarily fulfil the claims to which a bankruptcy creditor was entitled in line with the compulsory composition, each individual bankruptcy creditor could enforce a claim to the debtor’s estate (§ 179 KO 1879; § 194 KO 1900). However, the creditors were

---

12 Jaeger, Ernst: Lehrbuch des deutschen Konkursrechts. 8th ed. 1932, unaltered reprint Berlin 1973, § 31 I, p. 192.

13 Jaeger: Lehrbuch (fn. 12), § 31 I, p. 191.

not permitted to return to their original claims from before the bankruptcy procedure, which became void through the effect of the composition (remission composition) if not only a pure moratorium was agreed (forbearance composition). A "claim to revoke the compulsory composition for reasons of non-fulfilment of the same" was also explicitly excluded (§ 181 KO 1879; § 195 KO 1900). The law grants more extensive rights only against verifiably dishonest bankrupts:

> "If the compulsory composition is brought about through fraud, each creditor can contest the remission of his claim in line with the composition without this affecting the rights granted to him in the composition." (§ 182 I KO 1879; § 192 I KO 1900).

However, an appeal of this kind was "only permissible if the creditor was, without fault, unable to claim the reason for appeal" in the court proceeding regarding confirmation of the composition (§ 182 II KO 1879; § 192 II KO 1900). "The remission produced by the compulsory composition" was revoked for all creditors by act of law in an extreme case: the legally binding conviction of the bankrupt for fraudulent bankruptcy (§§ 183 I, 209 KO 1879; §§ 197 KO 1900 in conjunction with §§ 283, 283a StGB). In accordance with § 209 KO 1879, the circumstances that determined a fraudulent behaviour were certain actions by the bankrupt with the intention of disadvantaging his creditors, such as manipulating account books, concealing or clearing away assets, or fabricating claims that were "fictional in whole or in part".

Despite this, the implementation of a compulsory composition was not generally subject to an examination of the bankrupt's past behaviour. In the controversial legal policy debate that preceded the introduction of the Bankruptcy Act, however, this kind of examination of the bankrupt based on a range of worthiness criteria was demanded, especially by those who saw a compulsory composition primarily as a good deed for the bankrupt,[14] rather than a bundle of good deeds for everyone involved. Preventing the compulsory composition for regulatory reasons would, however, also have meant negating any benefits of a composition for the creditors. No such regulations were made, at least not in the original version of the KO in 1879 (see IX. below on the reform of 1898).

---

14 For example Lesse, Theodor: Der Akkord in der Concursordnung des Norddeutschen Bundes. Berlin 1867, pp. 1, 4–5, 28–29.

III. The key role of the bankruptcy administrator

In one aspect, however, the bankruptcy administrator was of crucial importance even in the compulsory composition procedure, playing a part that deserves more attention than Jaeger's description of it as a "supporting role" would suggest. If, for good reason, the legislator wanted to allow the bankrupt to regain his free business activities as quickly as possible,[15] he could not create any barriers to the continuation of bankrupt companies. In exceptional cases, a restructuring composition was still possible even when the business remained closed in the months between the opening of bankruptcy procedure and the conclusion following legally-binding confirmation of the compulsory composition by the court. An example could be an owner-run second-hand bookshop or antiques shop that did not need to worry about goods going off or the loss of suppliers and trained staff. Normally, however, closure would create an irreversible set of circumstances.

The German Bankruptcy Act certainly relied on the well-understood self-interest of the creditors and the skills of the bankruptcy administrator. Until a decision was made by the creditors' meeting, whether the bankrupt's business was closed down or continued came down to the judgement of the administrator (§ 118 KO 1879; § 129 KO 1900). In this regard, the Bankruptcy Act did not give any particular guideline for the administrator; it did not reserve a right of approval for the court,[16] "in order to avoid an excess of care from the law and courts".[17] Given this freedom, the vague incentives of personal liability on the one hand and remuneration on the other were essential for the bankruptcy administrator. An unbalanced case law could therefore easily lead to improper incentives.[18]

It is generally agreed in literature that the quality of the administrator's work is one of the most important factors affecting the yield of the bankruptcy procedure, regardless of the many subtleties of the normative organisation of substantive bankruptcy or insolvency law. In line with this, even Ernst Jaeger called the selection of an administrator a "fateful question in bankruptcy"; this famous adage

15 Cf. Hahn, Carl: Die gesammten Materialien zu den Reichs-Justizgesetzen. vol. IV, reprint Berlin 1898, Motive, p. 348.

16 Petersen, Julius / Kleinfeller, Georg: Konkursordnung für das Deutsche Reich. 3rd ed. Lahr 1892, §§ 118–120, Section II, take an aloof view of this legislative decision: in their opinion, the law "deliberately" omitted the immediately involvement of the court.

17 Hahn (fn. 15): IV, Motive, p. 358 (there in the context of court confirmation of compulsory composition).

18 On this, Alles, Matthias: Die Haftung des Konkursverwalters. In press (Frankfurt, expected 2015).

is quoted by scholars in agreement to this day.[19] A well-known assertion from a report on the practice of English insolvency law points in the same direction: "The success of any insolvency system [...] is very largely dependent upon those who administer it." This Corc Report from June 1982 became the foundation of the newer English legislation and has also influenced reform of German insolvency law.[20] The ESUG,[21] which intends to strengthen the influence of the creditors over the choice of administrator, is also based on this premise.

The Bankruptcy Act left the selection of the bankruptcy administrator to the free judgement of the bankruptcy court (§ 70 KO 1879; § 78 KO 1900; cf. § 56 InsO). The literature on the history of bankruptcy law admittedly reveals nothing about the appointment practice or revenue related to work as an administrator at the time of the Bankruptcy Act. One substantial source is a report from 1909 in the Leipziger Zeitschrift für Handels-, Konkurs- und Versicherungsrecht (Leipzig Journal of Trade, Bankruptcy and Insurance Law). In it, Ernst Jaeger reports on the information he had gained from German bankruptcy courts in a written survey conducted throughout the Empire.[22] Unfortunately, there is not sufficient space for more detailed consideration of this source here.

---

19 Jaeger, Ernst: Kommentar zur Konkursordnung und den Einführungsgesetzen. 6th & 7th ed., vol. 2, Berlin 1936, § 78 Note 7; cf. e.g. Uhlenbruck, Wilhelm: Aus- und Abwahl des Insolvenzverwalters – Eine Schicksalsfrage der Insolvenzrechtsreform. *Konkurs-, Treuhand- und Schiedsgerichtswesen (KTS)* 1989, pp. 229–252, 229; Laukemann, Björn: Die Unabhängigkeit des Insolvenzverwalters. Tübingen 2010, p. 27; on Laukemann's work see the review by Ulrich Falk, *JZ* 2011, pp. 464 f.

20 Corc, Kenneth: Report of the Review Committee, Insolvency Law and Practice. London 1982, para. 732; cf. also Piepenbrock, Andreas: Empfiehlt sich angesichts der Wirtschaftskrise die Einführung eines gesonderten Restrukturierungsverfahrens?. *Zeitschrift für Vergleichende Rechtswissenschaft (ZVglRWiss)* 2009, pp. 247–251; Laukemann (fn. 19): pp. 239, 241–248, 316 f.; Henke, Johannes: Effektivität der Kontrollmechanismen gegenüber dem Unternehmensinsolvenzverwalter. Tübingen 2009, p. 1.

21 Gesetz zur weiteren Erleichterung der Sanierung von Unternehmen (act for the further facilitation of reorganisation of companies) of December 7, 2011, BGBl. I 2011, p. 2582.

22 Jaeger, Ernst: Laien als Konkursverwalter. *Leipziger Zeitschrift für Handels-, Konkurs- und Versicherungsrecht (LZ)* 1909, pp. 1–15; The survey was triggered by a paper by the Vienna law professor Pollak, a protagonist of lawyers' privilege when awarding bankruptcy administrations; Pollak, Rudolf: Laien als Konkursverwalter. *LZ* 1908, pp. 660–671; cf. also Pollak, Rudolf: Über die Bestellung des Masseverwalters. *Zeitschrift für das Privat- und öffentliche Recht der Gegenwart* 1897, pp. 335–356.

IV. Expediency of the compulsory composition

When it comes to bankruptcy law, Ernst Jaeger is unquestionably one of the great representatives of German law in the twentieth century. With his great commentary, he had, as even the generally critical Kohler had to admit, "achieved the best", although it "contradicts some of my ideas".[23] Jaeger defined the "concept and being" of compulsory composition, which were controversial from a legal doctrine, constructivist point of view,[24] as follows:

> "Zwangsvergleich [compulsory composition] (Zwangsausgleich, Nachlaßvertrag, Akkord, Konkordat) is a contract, approved by the bankruptcy court, between the bankrupt and the non-privileged bankruptcy creditors regarding a certain satisfaction of these creditors in place of bankruptcy distribution (§§ 173, 174). Compulsory composition is a legal transaction, not a judicial finding, and not a connection between legal transaction and judgement. (…) It is usually a remission and forbearance composition in one."[25]

Jaeger had an unequivocally positive assessment of the function and conception of this legal institution with regard to legal policy. In the 1932 edition, he wrote:

> "The expediency of compulsory composition is clear: the creditors are usually satisfied more abundantly and quickly than when bankruptcy is executed; the bankrupt is returned to free gainful employment earlier and, with avoidance of significant losses of value and costs and usually with ultimate discharge, can be preserved as an entity in commercial law; the trade obstruction, that often impedes large circles, stops."[26]

For these reasons, he believed that compulsory composition appears "a desirable solution to bankruptcy that cannot be thwarted by the selfishness or foolishness of a minority of creditors". This is why the law permits "the force of the majority" under certain protective measures. There could be "a significant benefit" simply "if operation of the company need not be entrusted to third parties", but remained in the hands of the bankrupt, he continues. The costs would also often be significantly

---

23 Kohler, Josef: Leitfaden des deutschen Konkursrechts. 2nd ed. Stuttgart 1903, p. VI.

24 On this (also) from a legal history perspective, cf. Madaus, Stephan: Der Insolvenzplan. Von seiner dogmatischen Deutung als Vertrag und seiner Fortentwicklung in eine Bestätigungsinsolvenz. 2011 (Habil., Universität Rostock 2010), on compulsory composition as a preceding provision pp. 56–82; Bauer, Peter M.: Der Insolvenzplan. Untersuchungen zur Rechtsnatur anhand der geschichtlichen Entwicklung (Diss. University of Augsburg 2008/09), 2009. Both papers are dominated by doctrinal, constructivist questions, which make the works similar to what was attributed to the nineteenth century as "jurisprudence of concepts".

25 Jaeger: Lehrbuch (fn. 12), § 31 I, p. 190.

26 Jaeger: Lehrbuch (fn. 12), § 31 I, p. 191.

reduced, and at the very least the "particular effort of deployment" of the bankrupt's assets would certainly be avoided.[27] If one considers Jaeger's fundamental attitude towards compulsory composition, it is easy to make an observation that Schubert called "surprising": even in 1938, leading experts in insolvency law from academia and practice in the Supreme Court of the German Empire (Bley, Jaeger, Kiesow) had "vehemently defended traditional bankruptcy law in their internal appraisals for the Imperial Ministry of Justice", despite the criticism of the law that had been going on for decades, even into the NS period.[28]

A fundamentally different attitude towards compulsory composition is reflected in a lecture held by the Berlin lawyer Gustav von Wilmowski (1818–1896).[29] He was clearly not convinced by the doctrine and legal policy justification of compulsory composition, although he generally had a lot of praise for the quality of the legislative motivation in his successful commentary on the Bankruptcy Act, whose first edition was published in 1878. In the introduction, he highlighted the fact that the "noteworthy excellence of the motivation" made the commentary significantly easier.[30] However, he argues:

> "No explanations will be able to prove the legal or even merely logical necessity for the individual creditor to give up his individual rights because the majority of the creditors demands it."[31]

He believed that a reason for the law to curtail the subjective rights of the individual creditors and expose them to a compulsion to yield to the majority of creditors

> "could only be found in consideration of interests; in a consideration – partly of equity for the bankrupt, partly of the interests of the creditors – that ought not to be deprived of enjoying an arrangement beneficial to them due to the selfishness of single individuals."[32]

Wilmowski was not alone in this view.[33] In contrast, however, the legislative motivation states that "even in common law [ius commune]", compulsory composition had established itself in practice "despite objectives raised constantly by the theory":

---

27 Jaeger: Lehrbuch (fn. 12), § 31 I, p. 191 fn. 1.

28 Schubert, Werner: KTS 1993, pp. 344–348; citation from the summary, p. 349.

29 More in detail about Wilmowski, cf. Falk: Konkursübel (fn. 1).

30 Wilmowski, Gustav: Deutsche Reichs-Konkursordnung. 1st ed. Berlin 1878, Vorwort.

31 Wilmowski, Gustav: Zwangsvergleich und Besonderheiten im Konkurse. *JW (Juristische Wochenschrift)* 1879, pp. 259–263, 259.

32 Wilmowski (fn. 31), p. 259.

33 Cf. application by Theodor Lesse at the 6th German Jurist Congress (Deutscher Juristentag) and the assessment enacted on it by Stubenrauch, M. von: Verhandlungen

> "The needs of life have overcome the theoretical concerns; and these do not stand up to legal scrutiny either. However, where individuals exercise their rights independently, no majority of votes applies. But bankruptcy creditors do not remain as individuals with their rights; the bankruptcy claim of all of them brings them into a legal community, and binding majority decisions by such a group are valid even in formal law, or at least in the higher values of substantive justice."[34]

Legal doctrine has been unable to add much more than this,[35] with the exception of complex, interest based, often economic, justifications, which Wilmowski obviously rejected. As much scepticism as there was towards the restriction of individual claim rights, Wilmowski could present few arguments against the expediency of compulsory composition.

In contrast, the legal commentary written by Supreme Court Judge Julius Petersen (1835–1909)[36] in cooperation with private lecturer Georg Kleinfeller presents an unreservedly positive view of compulsory composition. The 3rd edition from 1892 contains the following function designation:

The longer on-going bankruptcy proceedings removed the bankrupt's control over his assets, the more his gainful employment was impeded or destroyed. If a composition ended the bankruptcy procedure and allowed the bankrupt to regain his freedom of actions quickly, business partners or family members would find it easier to make sacrifices for him. In that case, the advantage for the bankruptcy creditors would be that the bankrupt was enabled "to compensate their losses through renewed business activity". It could also be desirable in the interests of the economy as a whole "for the payment deadlock, which is rarely limited to the person of the bankrupt alone and often creates large ripples, is solved as quickly as possible". Admittedly, the compulsory composition route was "not applicable in every

des Sechsten Deutschen Juristentages. vol. 2 (1866), pp. 40–44 and Lupp, loc. cit., pp. 134–139; Kompe, W.: loc. cit., pp. 164–176.

34 Hahn (fn. 15): IV, Motive, p. 350.

35 An overview is provided by Braun, Eberhard in: Gottwald, Peter (pub.): Insolvenzrechts-Handbuch. 4th ed. 2010, § 66 Rn. 9–12, who also touches on the view of the legislator of the InsO 1994.

36 Petersen was initially a lawyer (from 1868), Chief Judge at Strasbourg State Court (from 1871) and Chief Judge at Colmar Higher State Court (from 1880); at the Supreme Court, he was a judge from 1883–1900, initially in criminal division I and then IV, from 1886 to his retirement in civil division II, cf. Lobe, Adolf: Fünfzig Jahre Reichsgericht. Berlin/Leipzig 1929, pp. 356, 393, 395. He also provided comments on the code of civil procedure and the law on stock corporations; see Meyers Großes Konversations-Lexikon, vol. 15 (1908), p. 656 f.; not to be confused with George Rudolf Peterßen, president of civil division III.

individual case", in contrast to "that of the distribution" of the bankruptcy estate. "However, where it can be used, it appears the most beneficial for all involved."[37]

V. The bankruptcy court

Another party involved in compulsory composition has been largely disregarded up to now. The term "bankruptcy court" actually conceals the fact that it referred to a single judge at a trial court (Amtsgericht). With the opening of the procedure, he was responsible for "the selection of the administrator, a role as difficult and responsible in each individual case"[38] (§ 70 KO 1879; § 78 KO 1900), as well as for optional appointment of a preliminary creditors' committee (§ 79 KO 1879; § 87 KO 1900), to whom the momentous choice between continuation and closure fell (§ 118 para. 2 sentence 2 KO 1879; § 129 KO 1900). Together with supervision over the administrator, a limited control of legality,[39] the role of the court could be mainly characterised by its mere "appointment and monitoring responsibility".[40] The court could therefore, as Petersen and Kleinfeller wrote, "exercise after all an indirect influence".[41]

In addition, however, the Bankruptcy Act allowed the court, on application, to deny effectiveness to a majority decision made by the creditors if it "contradicted the collective interest of the bankruptcy creditors" (§ 91 KO 1879; § 99 KO 1900). To the legislator, this rule appeared so central for the compulsory composition that it put it explicitly in writing once again in § 173 KO 1879 (§ 188 KO 1900):

> "Forcing the creditors who are not in agreement or who disagree to relinquish their rights merely through the will of others with equal rights, without a decision by a judge, would indeed be an impermissible intrusion on acquired rights, […]. The court may not

---

37 Petersen/Kleinfeller (fn. 16): Vorbem. §§ 160–187, Section 1; see also Becker, Christoph: Insolvenzrecht. 3rd ed. München 2010, Rn. 49; appropriately, Schmidt, Reinhard: Ökonomische Analyse des Insolvenzrechts. Wiesbaden 1980, p. 65 fn. 1, indicates that the German legislator was guided "early"– i.e. when creating the Bankruptcy Act of 1879 – by economic "incentive effects".

38 Hahn (fn. 15): IV, Motive, p. 279.

39 This dominant interpretation certainly does not follow from the words of the statute: "The administrator is supervised by the bankruptcy court." (§ 75 KO 1879; § 83 KO 1900) However, cf. Hahn (fn. 15): IV, p. 281; Seuffert, Lothar: Deutsches Konkursprozessrecht. Leipzig 1899, p. 161; Kuhn, Georg / Uhlenbruck, Wilhelm: Konkursordnung. 11th ed. München 1994, § 83 Rn. 6.; in contrast, Endemann, Wilhelm: Das deutsche Konkursverfahren. Leipzig 1889, p. 421, appeals "for an expanded supervisory role for judges".

40 Laukemann (fn. 19): p. 16.

41 Petersen/Kleinfeller (fn. 16): §§ 118–120, Section II.

allow binding power against all others to an accord that conflicts with the collective interest of all creditors.“[42]

In the provision, the legislator had given the courts the explicit assignment to examine and weigh up interests since October 1879. This will also have something to do with the fact that the Supreme Court used the idea of interests as an argument in bankruptcy cases as a matter of course. Functionally, this was intended to ensure that minorities were also protected through a substantive judicial review. After all, "it would remain an impermissible intrusion if the judge's examination only extended to whether the prescribed procedure was observed and whether the accord concluded lawfully and without fraud.“[43]

The question certainly arose of how the bankruptcy judge was to assess the interests of the creditors rather than the creditors themselves. "The examination certainly may often be difficult; but neither is it impossible for the judge to appreciate the actual and legal situation under consideration nor is it for the majority of the consenting creditors to do so." Practice, in any case, made do with a reasonable rule that has also found its way unchanged into § 245 para. 1 no. 1 of today's Insolvency Act.[44] According to this, the collective interest of the creditors is in all events violated "if the creditors were better off with the assets being paid out than in the case of compulsory composition.“[45] It remains unclear how often the judges actually made use of their authority, but the threat of the final distribution as the alternative must have prevented some compositions that would otherwise only have come about due to illegitimate special interests.[46]

VI. The practice of compulsory composition

Secondary literature in law provides little help in search for information on the practice of compulsory composition. For example, Horst Eidenmüller, a proven

42 Hahn (fn. 15): IV, Motive, pp. 355 f. (author's emphasis).

43 Hahn (fn. 15): IV, Motive, p. 356.

44 With an explicit reference to the Bankruptcy Act, Justification for the government draft of an Insolvency Act, Bundestags-Drucksache 12/2443, p. 290.

45 According to Jaeger, Ernst: Kommentar zur Konkursordnung. 5th ed., Berlin vol. 2 (1914), § 188 Note. 6 and Petersen/Kleinfeller (fn. 16): §§ 170–174, Section 3, p. 514.

46 One key application area must have been the involvement of relatives: Jaeger: loc. cit. (fn. 45) provides an example for his comment with a judgement from Dresden Regional Court, *Zeitschrift für deutschen Zivilprozeß*, vol. 8 (1885), pp. 494–495, according to which a composition that came about through the votes of relatives "certainly could also have served the interests of the other bankruptcy creditors at the same time." (p. 495).

expert in corporate reorganisation, states in the Münchener Kommentar zur Insolvenzordnung (Munich Comment on the Insolvency Act), that:

> "The idea of dealing with insolvency consensually within insolvency procedure monitored by a court is old. It was possible before the InsO [Insolvency Act 1999] came into force, on the basis of a composition in a composition procedure under the VerglO [Composition Act 1927/35], a compulsory composition in bankruptcy procedure (§§ 173 ff. KO) and a composition within collective execution procedure (§ 16 GesO [Collective Execution Act 1990]). However, the structure of these procedures was designed in such a way that it had practically no significance as an instrument of Sanierung [reorganisation] of a corporate legal entity ([...]) anyway."[47]

Firstly, it is worth noting that compulsory composition in accordance with the Bankruptcy Act is mentioned in the same breath as the composition procedure in the Composition Act and composition pursuant to the Collective Execution Act. Although Eidenmüller does distinguish between them to some extent, he does not once mention the fact that compulsory composition came into force as early as 1879, yet the Composition Act not until 1927/1935, almost half a century later, not to mention the Collective Execution Act of 1990. Given these time differences, however, it is no wonder that retrospective judgement has mainly been based on perceptions of the most recent decades of the Bankruptcy Act.[48]

Since the 1970s, if not before, German bankruptcy law has been living the miserable existence of the undead, dramatically described by bankruptcy administrator Joachim Kilger as the "bankruptcy of bankruptcy".[49] Between 1976 and the introduction of the Insolvency Act, the proportion of bankruptcy procedures that were

---

47 Eidenmüller, Horst in: *Münchener Kommentar zur Insolvenzordnung*, 3rd ed., vol. 3, München 2014, Vorbemerkungen vor §§ 217–269 Rn. 3. Similar, Lüer, Hans-Jochem in: Uhlenbruck, Wilhelm: Insolvenzordnung. 13th ed., München 2010, Vorbemerkungen zu §§ 217–269 Rn. 1 f.: "It was only in the post-war years after 1945 that awareness gradually began to spread that the insolvency procedure could also have a function conserving the estate." Cf. also Römermann, Volker in: Nerlich, Jörg/Römermann, Volker: Insolvenzordnung. 25th EL, München 2013, Vorbemerkungen vor §§ 217 bis 269 Rn. 25: "The lack of an instrument for the reorganisation of insolvent companies had proved particularly fatal."

48 On the effect of hindsight bias in cognitive psychology from a legal history point of view, see Falk, Ulrich: Urteilsverzerrungen: hindsight bias und anchoring. Einleitende Fragen zu einem interdisziplinären Problem. in: Brodersen, Kai (pub.): Vincere Scis, Victoria Uti Nescis. Aspekte der Rückschauverzerrung in der Alten Geschichte. Berlin 2008, pp. 9–17. On this set of problems currently, Falk, Ulrich / Alles, Matthias: Verhaltensökonomik und Anwaltsrhetorik, *Zeitschrift für Wirtschaftsrecht (ZIP)* 2014, pp. 1209–1219.

49 Kilger, Joachim: Der Konkurs des Konkurses. KTS 1975, pp. 142–167.

not even opened due to a lack of assets was never less than 70%– reaching a peak of 78% in 1987.[50] From the few procedures opened, a significant share was later suspended due to lack of assets. For example, of all the bankruptcy procedures that ended in 1987, 21% were suspended due to lack of assets.[51] The number of compulsory compositions was so low that the Federal Statistical Office no longer recorded them separately.[52] It was therefore only the image of the practical irrelevance of the entire bankruptcy procedure, and with it compulsory composition as one of its most important elements, that remained in the collective memory. Whether deficiencies in the "structure" of the procedure, which had not changed significantly since the introduction of the Bankruptcy Act and could therefore be blamed on the original legislator, can be derived from this is another question. A closer look on the first years of its application may shed some light on this issue.

The official statistical material, which is available from 1881[53] and has been analysed in parts up to 1913,[54] gives us the following picture: up to and including 1899, the proportion of bankruptcy filings that were disallowed due to a lack

50 Federal Statistical Office (Statistisches Bundesamt), STATIS-Archiv-CD, Zeitreihe 0993034 (bankruptcies rejected due to lack of assets) and 0993001 (bankruptcies in general). The picture does not change significantly if one only looks at company bankruptcies. The proportion of rejections due to lack of assets remained here at over 69% from 1976, reaching its peak of 76% in 1987.

51 Federal Statistical Office, STATIS-Archiv-CD, Zeitreihe 0276001 (bankruptcy with assets), 0276034 (bankruptcy without assets) and 0276067 (remission compositions). The number for companies was also 21%. In 1981, this number was even almost 30%.

52 Some data compiled in Madaus (fn. 24), pp. 85 f.; For example, the legal sociology study by Gessner, Volkmar, et al.: Die Praxis der Konkursabwicklung in der Bundesrepublik Deutschland. Köln 1978, p. 228 for 1975 determined a proportion of 3.2% compulsory compositions among all procedures concluded.

53 These are German judicial statistics published by the Imperial Justice Office up to 1919. The data was based on information provided by the state judicial administrations for their Higher Regional Court districts, *Deutsche Justiz-Statistik*, vol. I (1883), p. 55. The Imperial Statistical Office also collected its own statistics from 1891. Instead of relying purely on internal data from the judiciary, evaluation was based on analysis of the public announcements in the Deutscher Reichsanzeiger, cf. *Vierteljahreshefte zur Statistik des Deutschen Reichs*, 2nd year (1893), III. Heft, p. 67, before a counting card system was introduced for the courts in 1895, *Vierteljahreshefte zur Statistik des Deutschen Reichs*, 5th year (1896), I. Heft, p. 155. Unfortunately, space below is limited for an analysis of the varying quality of the various statistics.

54 A less intense analysis is undertaken by Madaus (fn. 24), pp. 83–37, though he does provide an overview up to 1998. He dedicates only a few lines to the initial period of the Bankruptcy Act up to 1913.

of assets remained at just under 10% throughout.[55] Thereafter, up until 1913, the proportion rose almost consistently to more than twice that: over 23%.[56] The procedure was therefore still functional when the First World War broke out. The average number of bankruptcy procedures opened was around 6,000 per year between 1881 and 1899, compared to around 8,500 between 1901 and 1913.[57] The proportion of procedures that ended with compulsory composition was just under 25% on average, ranging from 29% in 1886 to 21% in 1904.[58] Compared to the vanishingly small number in the mid-twentieth century, therefore, compulsory composition had been a significant practice. From 1895, the satisfaction quota for simple bankruptcy creditors was also recorded. Up until 1913, quotas of over 30% were achieved in final distributions in an average of 20% of procedures; over 40% of procedures saw quotas of less than 10%. These quotas did not change significantly over time. The picture is different for compulsory composition: quotas of over 30% were achieved in 35% of procedures, while just 9% saw quotas of less than 10%.[59]

---

55 The number of bankruptcies dismissed due to lack of assets can only be determined through extrapolation for the years up to and including 1894, as the figure only began to be recorded with the counting card system from 1895. As far as can be told, no estimate has yet been made. The figures published in the *Deutsche Justiz-Statistik*, vol. I–VIII (1883–1897) provide the basis for the calculation of rejected filings for opening procedures (concluded through opening or rejection) and fluctuated between 13% and 15% between 1881 and 1894. Because the opening of procedures could also be rejected for other reasons, for example where there was no reason for bankruptcy, there is an upper limit here for the proportion of rejections due to lack of assets. For 1895, there are parallel figures both from the Deutsche Justiz-Statistik and from the new recording by the Imperial Statistical Office, *Statistisches Jahrbuch für das Deutsche Reich*, vol. 17 (1896), p. 142. This allows the figure quoted in the text, around 10%, to be estimated with a correction factor in a calculation that cannot be explained in more detail here for 1881 to 1894. The estimate fits in with the figures known from the counting card statistics for 1895 to 1899.

56 *Statistisches Jahrbuch für das Deutsche Reich*, vol. 20–38 (1897–1915).

57 1881–1890: *Deutsche Justiz-Statistik*, vol. I-VI (1883–1893); 1891–1913: *Statistisches Jahrbuch für das Deutsche Reich*, vol. 13–36 (1892–1915).

58 As fn. 57. The proportion of compulsory compositions is calculated from the statistical information.

59 The quotas were collected with the counting card system and published for the first time in the *Vierteljahreshefte zur Statistik des Deutschen Reichs*, 5th year (1896), IV. Heft, p. 142 in 5 to 10% groups. The 10% and 30% thresholds were selected as data was collected for these across the entire investigation period.

In analysing this data, the authors are well aware of their limited econometric expertise. However, on the basis of the aggregated statistical data, some plausibility considerations can be conducted that can certainly be critically scrutinized. On the one hand, the rise in asset-lacking bankruptcies from 1900 is very noticeable, raising the question of whether the introduction of the German Civil Code (BGB) and the changes to the law, including the revised Bankruptcy Act, that went with it were significant here. A convincing explanation for the increase remains to be found. On the other hand, the better financial results of compulsory composition are evident, although this does not mean that exactly the same procedures would have generated poorer results if they had ended with final distribution. More information on the individual bankruptcies and a random sample analysis (as far as possible) would be needed to prove this hypothesis. Yet it is difficult to fully ignore the likelihood, that "although the composition route cannot [...] be applied to every individual case", "where the case situation allows it to be used", it emerges "as the most beneficial for all involved".[60]

An attempt will also be made to investigate the thesis that compulsory composition "certainly had practically no significance as an instrument of reorganisation for a firm"[61] in a little more detail. Up until the bankruptcy statistics of 1926, no separate figures were published for business bankruptcies, although these figures could also be intricately generated for the preceding years using the list of occupational groups. However, the statistics for 1926 reveal that just 8% of bankruptcies opened in that year related to people who were not businessmen: 955 in total.[62] The total number of compulsory compositions concluded in 1926 was 1770.[63] This suggests the conclusion that, even in the very unrealistic extreme case that all 955 non-business procedures ended with compulsory compositions, a large number of businesspeople must still have followed the same path. The idea is vulnerable, as not every bankruptcy opened ended in the same year. However, just 5% of the bankruptcies concluded in 1926 took longer than two years, with 68% taking less than a year.[64] There were no economic upheavals as in 1922/23 during this period, so the distortion is not too strong.[65] Given the proportion of

60 Hahn (fn. 15): IV, Motive, p. 349.

61 Eidenmüller: loc. cit. (fn. 47).

62 *Vierteljahreshefte zur Statistik des Deutschen Reichs*, 36th year (1927), II. Heft, p. 84.

63 A total of 7639 procedures were closed, 23.2% through compulsory composition, cf. *Vierteljahreshefte zur Statistik des Deutschen Reichs*, 36th year (1927), II. Heft, p. 86.

64 *Vierteljahreshefte zur Statistik des Deutschen Reichs*, 36th year (1927), II. Heft, p. 89.

65 Only 984 bankruptcies were initiated in 1922 and just 270 in 1923. However, the figure rose sharply again in 1924 back to the pre-war level and saw another sharp rise in 1925,

just 8% consumers, businesspeople must account for a very substantial portion of compulsory compositions concluded – although this finding relates only to a short period of time and needs to be substantiated through more research.

Finally, the statistics also confirm that the duration of the two procedure routes diverged considerably, as expected. While around 50% of compulsory compositions between 1892 and 1894 were concluded within six months of opening, final distribution achieved the same speed in just 16% of cases. Almost 75% of compulsory composition cases were concluded within nine months.[66]

No grave structural problems attributed to the regulatory model are expressed in the statistics analysed here, at least not in the period up to the outbreak of the First World War, and even less so up to the introduction of the German Civil Code. "So bankruptcy law worked. It was not without reason that the Bankruptcy Act was considered the most successful of the four Imperial Judicial Laws at the time."[67] This is Madaus' summary of his own short reflection on the Imperial Era in the historic outline of his study on the insolvency plan "Von seiner dogmatischen Deutung als Vertrag und seiner Fortentwicklung in eine Bestätigungsinsolvenz" (On its dogmatic interpretation as a contract and its development into confirmation insolvency).[68]

However, much remains unanalysed; important questions are yet to be asked. For example, the statistics also provide information on regional differences in bankruptcy practice, which ought to be analysed. The detailed information on the value of assets, the amount of debt and on procedure costs could also allow interesting conclusions to be drawn on developments between the enactment of the Bankruptcy Act and its de facto repeal in legal reality. In contrast, the statistics contain no data on the all-important bankruptcy administrators, their professions,

---

before changing little in 1926, *Vierteljahreshefte zur Statistik des Deutschen Reichs*, 36th year (1927), II. Heft, p. 84.

66 *Vierteljahreshefte zur Statistik des Deutschen Reichs*, 4th year (1895), II. Heft, p. 13. The information comes from the analysis of the Deutsche Reichsanzeiger and Königlich Preußischer Staatsanzeiger by the Imperial Statistical Office. Some of the "mischiefs that have emerged through this type of collection" are described by Lindenberg, C.: *Jahrbücher für Nationalökonomie und Statistik*, New Series Vol. 9 (1884), p. 69.

67 Madaus, (fn. 24): p. 84 – for the second sentence with reference to Kohler, Josef: Lehrbuch des Konkursrechts, Stuttgart 1891, p. 64.

68 The subheading of his work (fn. 24). What is surprising in this statement, however, is the harsh criticism of the regulatory model of compulsory composition, pp. 95–97, which offered "not enough time, means or legitimation to assert a reorganisation concept", not least because it was "orientated towards fast deployment" and had to "end with financial proceeds for the creditors" (p. 95).

or their individual qualities and course of action. However, an analysis of the German Imperial Gazette (Deutscher Reichsanzeiger) and its bankruptcy announcements (§§ 103, 151, 175 KO 1879; §§ 111, 163, 190 KO 1900) could provide useful information here. Finding data about the rights to separation from the estate and to separate satisfaction from collateral, which were ignored in the statistics, just as the Bankruptcy Act excluded them from the procedure, would be more difficult.

The Supreme Court jurisdiction on compulsory composition, a very difficult issue in legal doctrine, also requires intensive research.[69] The official collection of decisions alone contains 24 relevant judgements from the period 1879–1899,[70] including an extremely interesting judgement from the United Civil Senates of 15th February 1886, which deserves very detailed study from a comparative law, methodical and specifically bankruptcy law point of view. Many of the other judgements are also of great interest, including with regard to the subtle differences that appear between individual senates. There is no room for a more detailed study here, but it is worth at least mentioning the basic legal policy tendency that all judgements share: the acceptance of the two-pronged regulatory model of the Bankruptcy Act.

The loyalty that the Supreme Court also showed towards compulsory composition stood in sharp contrast to the critical attitude towards the law held by Viktor Rintelen (1826–1908), a Reichstag deputy of the centre. With an unwavering sense of mission, Rintelen made numerous attempts to make the idea plausible that the concept of the Bankruptcy Act, "in my view and that of my friends, is based on entirely false economic perceptions".[71] This needs to be returned to soon.

---

69 On research regarding the Supreme Court, see for an overview Falk: Fallstudien zur Judikatur des Reichsgerichts um 1900. Karlsruhe 2011, pp. 12–14. A great deal of analytical material is compiled but sadly not synthesised in Falk, Ulrich /Mohnhaupt, Heinz (pub.): Das Bürgerliche Gesetzbuch und seine Richter. Zur Reaktion der Rechtsprechung auf die Kodifikation des deutschen Privatrects (1896–1914), Frankfurt am Main 2000. The publishers did not go beyond outlining the problem (pp. VII–X).

70 RGZ 1, 183–187 (1879 – I. ZS); 3, 34–53 (1880 – I. ZS); 6, 66–69 (1882 – V. ZS); 6, 227–230 (1881 – I. ZS); 7, 35 f. (1882 – II. ZS); 7, 80–83 (1881 – I. ZS); 7, 88–93 (1882 - I. ZS); 11, 173–177 (1884 – II. ZS); 14, 172–179 (1886 – VZSe); 16, 68–72 (1886 – V. ZS); 22, 153–155 (1888 – I. ZS); 22, 325–334 (1888 – V. ZS); 23, 43–48 (1889 – IV. ZS); 23, 119–121 (1889 – III. ZS); 27, 113–116 (1891 – II. ZS; 28, 96–100 (1891 – I. ZS); 28, 130–135 (1892 – I. ZS); 29, 38–41 (1892 – II. ZS); 30, 22–25 (1892 – I. ZS; 31, 40–44 (1893 – VI. ZS); 31, 119–122 (1893 – I. ZS); 39, 17–25 (1897 – VI. ZS); 39, 105–108 (1897 – I. ZS); 42, 118–121 (1898 – VI. ZS).

71 Hahn (fn. 15): VII, Reichstagsprotokolle, p. 267.

VII. The problem of privileges

The law had exempted all other creditor groups that held a higher position than the simple, non-privileged bankruptcy creditors from the effect of compulsion (§ 160 KO 1879; § 173 KO 1900).[72] Looking back, a weak point in this regulatory model is clearly discernible: compulsory composition could only meet the expectations held of it by the legislator in procedures in which there were so many unencumbered assets that the bankruptcy creditors could be offered a satisfaction quota with majority appeal. The estate therefore had to not be already more or less entirely eaten up by privileged claims[73] – not least by rights to separation from the estate and to separate satisfaction from specific collateral.[74]

Yet this occurred more and more frequently as the decades passed. Due to the nationwide spread of certain types of security interest, predominantly revolving global collateral, German bankruptcy practice entered the permanent state of crisis deplored as the "bankruptcy of bankruptcy". This also made the historic legislator's regulatory model of compulsory composition obsolete. However, the extent to which this development can be attributed to the historic legislator of the Bankruptcy Act is again another question altogether.

Given the text of the law and the legislative materials, development in this direction is actually surprising. The Bankruptcy Act had explicitly stated that the pawn in possession of the creditor should be the only item of the personal estate to endure in bankruptcy (§ 40 KO 1879; § 48 KO 1900). The limitation was to be applied not only to physical items but also to claims, and should apply "generally

---

72 Petersen/Kleinfeller (fn. 16): §§ 175–177, Section 2.

73 The argumentation of Schmidt, (fn. 37): pp. 38, 63, seems characteristic here: The conception of the Bankruptcy Act deserves "a largely positive assessment", as long as one does not consider the rights to separation from the estate and to separate satisfaction of privileged creditors. Once these privileges are included in the economic assessment, "justified negative judgements" result.

74 The rights to separation from the estate and to separate satisfaction were to be distinguished from the general privileges for five types of claims (§ 54 KO 1879; § 61 KO 1900), led by those for wages and salary. However, the practical significance of these general privileges appears to have been very limited, at least up to the First World War. Among the bankruptcy procedures closed in 1895, only an average of 2.3% of the total debt was made up of privileged claims. These were satisfied in full in 91.2% of the procedures, *Vierteljahreshefte für die Statistik des Deutschen Reich*, 5th year (1896), IV. Heft, pp. 139–141. In 1913, the figures were 1.6% and 81.7% respectively, *Vierteljahreshefte zur Statistik des Deutschen Reichs*, 23rd year (1914), III. Heft, p. 33. Further exploration of the legal facts would be welcome.

and unconditionally".[75] The legislative motivation put a lot of effort into attempting to prevent any circumvention that threatened the principle through "symbolic" pledging.[76] These efforts were also reflected in the strict requirements for liens under state law in §§ 14–16 of the introductory act for the Bankruptcy Act of 1879, which only became superfluous when the German Civil Code became effective in 1900.

The priority rights that derailed the Bankruptcy Act model had made use of a circumvention construction – a fiduciary transfer of title. The economic purpose was certainly one and the same. The text of the Bankruptcy Act does not refer to this at all, and the legislative motivation on the rights to separate satisfaction also remains silent on the matter. A reference can be found in the minutes of the Reichstag commission that was to discuss the draft for the Bankruptcy Act. The national-liberal deputy Hullman, later High Imperial Commercial Court and Supreme Court Judge,[77] asked,

> "why the creditors were not protected against sales of property that took place without a transfer of possession and served solely the purpose of giving a creditor certainty in the payment of his claim. To no small extent, he [Hullmann] believed that the provisions in the introductory act regarding the pawn could be circumvented if the bankrupt couched the pledge in the form of a sale with a repurchase option."[78]

The question was addressed to the representative of the Federal Council present, Carl Hagens, who is credited with developing the Bankruptcy Act and the legislative motivation to varying degrees[79]:

> "In the case of a covert transaction – displacement in the form of sale – the administrator would be able to assert the same rights against the apparent purchaser as the bankrupt. Otherwise, most state legislations would only permit a constitutum possessorium or a pactum reservati dominii for property with limited effectiveness. Furthermore, cases of this kind were always rare and affected only individual objects, so that, for the draft, the

---

75 Hahn (fn. 15): IV, Motive, p. 191.

76 Hahn (fn. 15): IV, Motive, pp. 191–197. Even the term "symbolic" was demonstratively put in quotation marks, in order "not to put the case for it" (p. 197).

77 Hullmann also wrote one of the first commentaries on the Bankruptcy Act to be published in 1879.

78 Hahn (fn. 15): IV, Motive, Reichstags-Kommission, p. 548.

79 In the view of Jaeger, Ernst: Die Konkursordnung 1879–1904: *Deutsche Juristen-Zeitung* 1904, p. 905, the draft is "predominantly" due to Hagens. Based on archive material, a somewhat different conclusion is drawn by Meier, Anke: Die Geschichte des deutschen Konkursrechts, insbesondere die Entstehung der Reichskonkursordnung von 1877. Frankfurt am Main 2003, pp. 197–199.

occasion was not urgent enough to intervene in civil law in order to rule out this kind of transaction.“[80]

If there was another opportunity to give greater prestige to the possessory principle in the legislation process, it was squandered at this time. Hagens certainly underestimated the willingness of creditors to circumvent the restrictions. Intensive further research is required into how the lack of appropriate safeguards in the law and Hagens' error of judgement can be explained.

VIII. Composition for bankruptcy avoidance

One might agree with Uhlenbruck in considering it an error in legal policy that the legislator failed to introduce an additional pre-bankruptcy composition procedure aimed at preventing bankruptcy from occurring.[81] From the point of view of the time, there were respectable arguments in favour of such a pre-bankruptcy procedure.[82] Then again, concerns that still carry considerable sway in today's discussion[83] should not be underestimated. Here, we will provide merely a brief reminder of four objections that contributed to the responsible federal ministries (Justice/Economic Affairs), at least temporarily, moving away from efforts to create a separate reorganisation act following a colloquium on 8th June 2010:[84]

---

80 Hahn (fn. 78): loc. cit.

81 Peter Gottwald writes of a "wrong decision" in: Gottwald (fn. 35): § 1 Rn. 15; almost nothing on this issue is offered by Meier (fn. 79), pp. 168, 174, 204; Pape, Gerhard et al.: Insolvenzrecht. 2nd ed. 2010, Kap. 7 Rn. 10; cf. also Kap. 3 Rn. 1; on the development "under particular consideration of the Composition Act of 1927 and 1935" (introduction, p. 21); extensively Eisenhardt, Moritz: Sanierung statt Liquidation, Frankfurt am Main 2010.

82 An assessment from Mannheim Chamber of Trade from March 1871, which "spoke out very much in favour of compulsory composition to avoid bankruptcy" on a request from the Imperial Chancellor's Office, deserves consideration here, cited by Thieme, Jürgen: Zur Entstehung der Konkursordnung, in: Einhundert Jahre Konkursordnung, Köln 1977, p. 54 fn. 59.

83 On the arguments in the sections below (1)-(4) Eidenmüller, Horst: Reformperspektiven im Restrukturierungsrecht, *ZIP* 2010, pp. 654–656, who also indicates the dangers of excessive reorganisation, over-regulation and impending breaks in the system; rejection from Spliedt, Jürgen D.: Ist die außergerichtliche Sanierung pleite? – Ein Vergleich zur Sanierung im Insolvenzverfahren. in: *Zeitschrift für Insolvenzverwaltung und Sanierungsberatung (InsVZ)* 2010, pp. 27–39; Piepenbrock (fn. 20): pp. 246–272; Jaffé, Michael: *Zeitschrift für das gesamte Schuldrecht (ZGR)* 2010, pp. 248–263, 260, fn. 37.

84 Cf. Schmerbach, Ulrich: Das „große“ Insolvenzgericht. *Zeitschrift für das gesamte Insolvenzrecht (ZInsO)* 2010, pp. 1670–1673; INDat-Report 5/2010, 6 ff.; Frind, Frank: Sechs

(1) The potential for abuse is obvious. Robust managing directors are incentivised to organise their business more profitably by urging creditors to waive claims, without having to "pay the price" of submitting an insolvency petition themselves beforehand. (2) Although this abuse can be counteracted by suitable regulations, it requires a dense monitoring that would impact on the efficiency of the reorganisation procedure. (3) There is no doubt that the financial expense involved in a high quality pre-bankruptcy procedure is considerable. In all cases in which the attempt at reorganisation fails, this expense unavoidably weighs on the estate. (4) In addition, all attempts to bring about reorganisation later after all are ill-fated from the start.

Finally, although consideration from a comparative law point of view can certainly bring structures to light that could prove debatable in Germany, too, it also teaches us that reform legislation in neighbouring countries that have taken action "still has not yielded the hoped-for success".[85] A legislator who considers compulsory composition as an instrument of reorganisation in an opened procedure as essential and rich in opportunity must also be aware of the threat of conflicting objectives. It is no great leap to suppose that one cannot have both at once. "Under the condition of a bankruptcy procedure that does not impede free movement," the legislative motivation puts it concisely, "a composition procedure outside it is p a r t i a l l y s u p e r f l u o u s , p a r t i a l l y i m p e r m i s s i b l e ."[86]

IX. The debate on compulsory composition in the amendment to the Bankruptcy Act (1898)

Following controversy surrounding the introduction of the Bankruptcy Act in 1879, there were, once again before the reform of 1898, those in favour of an advanced composition procedure prepending and potentially averting bankruptcy. But they were unable to penetrate far "given the demanded tightening in the Reichstag".[87] However, the amendment to the 1879 Bankruptcy Act to adapt it

Maßnahmen um die Sanierungsfunktion der InsO zu stärken. *ZinsO* 2010, 1161–1169. For differences between these proposals and the ESUG amendments (fn. 21), cf. Eidenmüller (fn. 47): Rn. 68–73.

85 Quotations in Piepenbrock (fn. 20): pp. 257 (on France), p. 272.

86 Hahn (fn. 15): IV, Motive, p. 383 (author's emphasis).

87 State Secretary in the Imperial Office of Justice Arnold Nieberding according to a report in the "Berliner Neueste Nachrichten", quoted in Eisenhardt (fn. 81): p. 91. The statement was apparently made on 14.10.1897; Eisenhardt does not state the date of the report.

to the German Civil Code of 1st January 1900 amounted to more than just legal technicalities. Josef Kohler, professor of law in Berlin at the time, noted the following in the preface to the second edition of his 1903 guidelines on bankruptcy law, looking back at the first edition in 1893: "From a statutory point of view, there are significant innovations, however unremarkable the additions to the Bankruptcy Act might appear".[88]

The provisions on compulsory composition (§§ 160–187 KO 1879; §§ 173–201 KO 1900) had undergone changes motivated by legal policy without external pressure for change from other laws. Instead, this was preceded by a controversial discussion in legal policy that had been ignited in 1898 during consultation on the amendment to the Bankruptcy Act in the plenary debate in the Reichstag. Representatives of the centre, led by the aforementioned deputy Viktor Rintelen, had criticised the existing design of compulsory composition as misguided in terms of legal policy. In order to develop a solution, the issue was passed on to a committee which, apparently after much wrangling, agreed on some changes.

Werner Schubert rightly emphasised the epistemic value of discussions in which "considerations in legal policy, legal criticism and legal comparison" were talked about openly: they "bring together the status of development of the time more vividly than literature purely on legal doctrine can do."[89] Even then, strident stakeholders played a role in shaping these debates in legal policy.[90] Schubert describes these stakeholders in the context of secured credit law as "circles with an interest in a change to the law".

Rintelen was a vehement opponent of compulsory composition as a regulatory model, seeing it as too favourable towards the bankrupt. He believed that it permitted the improper continuation of too many small companies that ought to have been the object of market-cleansing liquidation, because they harmed their creditors and thus indirectly the common good, especially at the expense of the body of stable small and medium-sized companies. In short, he felt that compulsory composition "was permitted too easily".[91] The Imperial government pointed out to him that the regulatory model of the Bankruptcy Act had proven itself according to the bankruptcy statistics of the Imperial Statistical Office. Rintelen also encountered resistance from the social democratic members in the Reichstag.

---

88 Kohler: Leitfaden (fn. 23). p. V.

89 Schubert, Werner: Die Diskussion über eine Reform des Rechts der Mobiliarsicherheiten in der späten Kaiserzeit und in der Weimarer Republik, *Zeitschrift der Savigny-Stiftung*, German Section 107 (1990), pp. 132, 133.

90 Schubert (fn. 89): p. 165.

91 Hahn (fn. 15): VII, Motive, Reichstagsprotokolle, p. 269.

In the plenary hall, their spokesman pointed out that "especially smaller tradesmen who had the economic misfortune to have to enter bankruptcy" would "be harmed much more than under the current law" if Rintelen's demands were met.[92]

The changes actually made to the rules of compulsory composition were very ambivalent. The composition was now to be discarded ex officio if it did not allow the creditors at least one fifth of their claims given that the result was attributable to dishonest behaviour on the part of the bankrupt. If the behaviour had been merely reckless, the court retained a margin of discretion (§ 187 KO 1900). However, this provision "only attained very limited practical significance," stated Ernst Jaeger a few years after its introduction.[93] Moreover, he sharply criticised a second tightening, after which the bankrupt's spouse and his or her claims were excluded from voting on the composition (§ 183 KO 1900). According to Jaeger, this thought had "a very questionable justification" and stunted the voting rights for claims "whose acquisition was entirely unobjectionable", despite the fact that the existing options for denial offered "sufficient protection as well as the advantage of free consideration of the situation in each individual case". The latter referred particularly to the review of collective interest of the creditors (§ 173 KO 1879; § 188 KO 1900).

The fact that the number of compulsory composition procedures remained just as high after the amendment could also be explained by other changes which pointed in the opposite direction and which therefore lead to the ambivalent assessment of the reform as a whole. According to § 110 KO 1900, the court could link the composition appointment with the first creditors' meeting and the general verification appointment. Because the first meeting usually had to be within a month (§ 102 KO 1879; § 110 KO 1900), the compulsory composition procedure could be terminated very quickly after confirmation by the court. In addition, the new § 130 KO 1900 offered a certain guarantee for the bankrupt that the administrator would not close down his business despite a plausible proposal for compulsory composition, given the court's newly gained power to prevent the administrator from closing the business. The increase in predictability this brought about for the bankrupt slightly compensated for the lack of debtor's control over the estate during the procedure. The theory put forward by Eisenhardt that compulsory composition was "significantly tightened" by the amendments therefore seems, in summary, to overestimate its consequences.[94]

---

92 Quoted according to Hahn (fn. 15): VII, Reichstagsprotokolle, pp. 264–283 (279 – deputy Singer).

93 Jaeger: Kommentar (fn. 19), § 187 Note 2.

94 Eisenhardt (fn. 81): p. 89.

X. Conclusion

Given this background, it seems strange to read the following in a legal history doctoral thesis on the history of the Bankruptcy Act, in the "Commencement and reactions" section: "On 13th August 1880, the Berliner Tageszeitung reported a significant increase in the number of bankruptcies." Those familiar with the motivation behind compulsory composition will prick up their ears at how the paper on the content of the newspaper report continues: "The new Bankruptcy Act is apparently too bankrupt-friendly and sees no negative consequences for the bankrupt's honour."[95] Experts in reorganisation today would probably see the newspaper report as an indicator of success: today there is agreement that entering insolvency procedures as early as possible significantly increases the chance of business retention and reorganisation.[96] In the first years in which it was in force, the design of the Bankruptcy Act, which was aimed at retaining companies and certainly not at divestiture, may have achieved exactly that.

---

95 Meier (fn. 78): p. 197. The doctoral thesis does nothing more than state the content; no attempt is made at analysis. However, it would have been impossible for the author, Anke Meier, to provide a conclusive explanation, as she had previously omitted compulsory composition as part of the Bankruptcy Act. The paper dedicates just 12 lines to this regulatory instrument in the Bankruptcy Act, which give an account of the statutes from an early state of legislation, the draft of a Gemeinschuldordnung [Collective Debt Act] (1873), op. cit., p. 145. The thesis offers somewhat more text on the composition procedure of the Prussian Bankruptcy Act of 1855, op. cit., pp. 99 f. However, very little light is shed on the functional significance, either.

96 This is the assumption drawn from multiple investigations conducted by the largest German credit insurance firm (Euler Hermes) and the Zentrum für Insolvenz und Sanierung at the University of Mannheim: Ursachen von Insolvenzen. Gründe für Unternehmensinsolvenzen aus der Sicht von Insolvenzverwaltern, *Wirtschaft Konkret*, No. 414 (2006), p. 7; cf. also *Wirtschaft Konkret*, No. 418 (2007): Rettung aus der Insolvenz; *Wirtschaft Konkret*, Nr. 107 (2009): Insolvenzen in Zeiten der Finanzkrise; Egeln, Jürgen, et al.: Ursachen für das Scheitern junger Unternehmen in den ersten fünf Jahren ihres Bestehens, Mannheim 2010, available as PDF on the homepages of the ZEW (Zentrum für Europäische Wirtschaftsforschung) and ZIS. Very instructive: Bitter, Georg et al.: Die Zukunft des Überschuldungsbegriffs. Expertenbefragung im Auftrag des Bundesministeriums der Justiz. *ZIP* 2012, pp. 1201–1209; see also Bitter, Georg / Röder, Sebastian: Insolvenz und Sanierung in Zeiten der Finanz- und Wirtschaftskrise, *ZInsO* 2009, pp. 1283–1292.

Peter von Wilmowsky

Insolvency Law: Its Roles and Principles

This paper presents the understanding of insolvency law that developed around thirty years ago in American legal literature[1] and is now considered the "classic account" there.[2] It is little acknowledged in German legal doctrine, despite its potential for defining the role(s) of insolvency law with greater precision. While German legal doctrine limits itself to the "equal treatment of the creditors" and thus to just one of insolvency law's principles (and one with a limited scope of application),[3] the approach that is the subject of this paper attempts to include all functions of insolvency law, as well as their limits.

When a debtor who runs a business ("firm") becomes insolvent, a range of issues need to be addressed. These can be divided into two groups: the issues relating to the deployment of the debtor's assets (i.e. the future of the debtor's firm), and the issues concerning the distribution of the proceeds generated by the deployment decision (which comes down to the allocation of the loss caused by the insolvency).

I. The difference between asset deployment and asset (or loss) distribution

The need to differentiate between asset deployment and asset (and loss) distribution derives from non-insolvency law: As long as a debtor (who runs a firm) is solvent, it is universally accepted to look at investment decisions and financing

1 Jackson, Thomas, *The Logic and Limits of Bankruptcy Law*, Harvard University Press: Cambridge, Massachusetts, 1986; Adler, Barry / Baird, Douglas / Jackson, Thomas, *Cases, Problems, and Materials on Bankruptcy*, Foundation Press: New York, New York, 4th edition 2007, pp. 21–30; Jackson, Thomas / Scott, Robert, "On the Nature of Bankruptcy", *Virginia Law Review* Vol. 75, 1989, pp. 155–204; Baird, Douglas, "A World Without Bankruptcy", *Law and Contemporary Problems* Vol. 50, 1987, pp. 173–193. – Overviews: Goode, Roy, *Principles of Corporate Insolvency Law*, Sweet & Maxwell: London, 4th edition 2011, Chapter 2, Part 4; Finch, Vanessa, *Corporate Insolvency Law*, Cambridge University Press: Cambridge, 2nd edition 2009, Part I, Chapter 2.

2 Adler, Barry, "Financial and Political Theories of American Corporate Bankruptcy", *Stanford Law Review* Vol. 45, 1993, pp. 311–346.

3 Infra text at n. 37.

decisions separately. This differentiation is displayed on every company balance sheet.

The asset side lists the assets in which the debtor has invested, such as land, machinery, intellectual property rights, shares in subsidiaries, goods, receivables and cash (§ 266 (2) HGB).[4] If the debtor becomes insolvent, a decision must be taken on how these assets are to be used in the future (asset deployment decision).

The equities and liabilities side of the balance sheet records the financial sources of the debtor, divided into equity and debt (§ 266 (3) HGB). It informs us how the assets (listed on the asset side) have been financed. In the case of insolvency, a decision must be taken regarding how the proceeds yielded by the asset deployment decision are to be distributed among the debtor's financiers (shareholders and creditors).

As long as the debtor is solvent, the separation of the asset side and the equities and liabilities side expresses the fact that investment decisions and decisions regarding financing are made independently of one another. The question in which assets the firm should invest (because they hold a promise of success) has nothing to do with the question which type of financing is to be preferred. If the differentiation is applied to insolvency, it becomes apparent that asset deployment and asset distribution are independent from each other: The way the insolvency debtor's firm is re-deployed has no impact on the ratio by which the value of the firm is distributed among the debtor's financiers.[5]

II. The asset deployment branch of insolvency law

The insolvency case must result in an asset deployment decision. If the debtor's assets make up a firm (a business enterprise), it needs to be decided whether the firm is to be continued or is to be terminated. The role of insolvency asset deployment law is to define the prevailing criteria, the decision-makers and the measures needed to implement these deployment options.[6]

---

4 HGB: Handelsgesetzbuch (German statute on commercial law).

5 Jackson 1986, op. cit. n. 1, pp. 22–27. Overview: von Wilmowsky, Peter, *Europäisches Kreditsicherungsrecht*, Mohr Siebeck: Tübingen, 1996, pp. 219–222. For the connection with the irrelevance hypothesis of Modigliani and Miller, see Baird, Douglas, "Bankruptcy's Uncontested Axioms", *The Yale Law Journal* Vol. 108, 1998, pp. 573–599 (at p. 582 n. 31).

6 This paper supposes that insolvency law is created by the legislator, and is mandatory. However, this is subject to question. Could it not be left to private contracts (such as agreements between the creditors and the debtor or the articles of association of the debtor company) to lay down the rules which will apply in the case of the debtor's

1. Criteria

The criteria that should decide on the firm's continuation or termination raise one of the fundamental questions of insolvency law: What is the objective, or are the objectives, of insolvency proceedings?

a) *Satisfaction of creditors*

If the objective is to satisfy the creditors' claims as far as possible, the essential criterion becomes the yield that the asset deployment option will achieve. The yield that would result from continuing the firm (going-concern value) must be compared with the yield that would be achieved by terminating the firm (termination value). If the going-concern value is greater than the termination value, the decision will be taken to continue, and vice versa. The going-concern value results from the profits that the firm will generate in future. It is not their nominal value that is decisive, but the present value at the time of the asset deployment decision, derived from discounting the future profits.

The fact that the going-concern value has to be included in the asset deployment decision rebuts views that interpret insolvency as a sign of the lack of viability of the debtor's firm. According to these views insolvency indicates that the market has eliminated this company for being not worthy of continuation.[7] It is certainly

insolvency? Authors arguing in favour of a "contractual" insolvency law created privately and autonomously include: Adler, Barry, "Finance's Theoretical Divide and the Proper Role of Insolvency Rules", *Southern California Law Review* Vol. 67, 1994, pp. 1107–1150; Adler, Barry, "Bankruptcy Primitives", *American Bankruptcy Institute Law Review* Vol. 12, 2004, pp. 219–244; Schwartz, Alan, "A Contract Theory Approach to Business Bankruptcy", *The Yale Law Journal* Vol. 107, 1998, pp. 1807–1852. – Authors rejecting this approach include: Tabb, Charles, "Of Contractarians and Bankruptcy Reform: A Skeptical View", *American Bankruptcy Institute Law Review* Vol. 12, 2004, pp. 259–272; Block-Lieb, Susan, "The Logic and Limits of Contract Bankruptcy", *University of Illinois Law Review* Vol. 2001, pp. 503–560. – An overview is given by Tabb, Charles, *The Law of Bankruptcy*, West Academic Publishing: St. Paul, Minnesota, 3d edition 2014, § 11.1.

7 See, e.g., Schmidt, Karsten, „Überschuldung und Insolvenzantragspflicht nach dem Finanzmarktstabilisierungsgesetz", *Der Betrieb* Vol. 2008, pp. 2467–2471. Schmidt argues: The term "insolvency" serves to separate firms that are and are not worthy of continuation; "insolvency" indicates that the debtor's firm is not worth continuing (p. 2470). "Over-indebtedness" invariably demands that the debtor's firm be eliminated from the market (p. 2467).

possible that a firm is no longer able to survive in the market; in this case, the termination value is higher than the going-concern value. But the opposite is just as possible. The insolvency (illiquidity or over-indebtedness) of the debtor tells us nothing at all about how (through termination or continuation) the debtor's firm would best be used.[8] A classic example is the insolvencies of the American rail companies, whose continuation promised a higher yield than their termination (especially given the shape of their real estate which would be almost impossible to use for a different purpose).[9] The insolvency proceedings against Eurotunnel and Global Crossing came to the same result; in these cases, too, there was no better way to use the assets (the rail tunnel under the English Channel and the fiberglass cables laid under the oceans for Internet communication, respectively) than to continue the respective commercial activity.[10]

b) Public interest

The insolvency of a company affects not only the interests of the company's creditors, but also the public interest. If the company's business is closed down, unemployment may rise, the competitive environment worsen, the economic structure of the region change, distortions in industrial policy occur or other economic disadvantages arise. Should these interests not also be taken into account when deciding how the debtor's firm is to be deployed? The answer is no. Insolvency (asset deployment) law is not the proper forum for considering matters of the public interest and exerting influence on entrepreneurial decisions.

The termination of firms is not a phenomenon that is limited to insolvencies. Most businesses are closed down outside insolvency proceedings, i.e. while solvent. If the management of a firm realises that the firm is no longer worth operating (e.g. because it manufactures a product for which there is no longer a demand), it is their job to terminate this activity. If they waited until insolvency occurred, they would be neglecting their statutory duties as corporate directors and the contractual duties resulting from their employment contracts. The legislator is free to combat the social costs triggered by the termination of firms, to

---

8 Cf. Drukarczyk, Jochen / Schüler, Andreas, "Die Eröffnungsgründe der InsO", in: *Kölner Schrift zur Insolvenzordnung*, ZAP-Verlag: Münster, 3rd edition 2009, pp. 28–84 (at ¶¶ 113–114 and ¶ 143): In insolvency proceedings, companies with reasonable chances of continuation do not go down.

9 Flessner, Axel, *Sanierung und Reorganisation*, Mohr Siebeck: Tübingen, 1982, pp. 94–95.

10 Baird, Douglas, *The Elements of Bankruptcy*, Foundation Press: New York, New York, 4th edition 2006, pp. 230–231. (Not included in the subsequent editions.)

develop appropriate firm closure laws and thus to involve private individuals in financing public interests. It may enact continuation obligations based on employment, competition, regional, industrial or economic policy reasons, and thus work to control investment. If these measures are to be suitable for meeting their goals, however, they must apply equally both within and outside insolvency; they must be independent of insolvency. Limiting their applicability to firms whose owners are undergoing insolvency proceedings would be unfounded. Protection against unemployment and other encroachments on the common good cannot differentiate between cases in which a firm is closed down while its owner is insolvent or is solvent. The opening of insolvency proceedings is not a suitable starting point for protection laws regarding the closure of firms.[11] This kind of protection law should be independent from insolvency law. Should it come into existence in the future, it would also be applicable in the case of insolvency and, along with the interests of the creditors, play a role in the decision regarding continuation or termination of the debtor's firm.

German insolvency law limits itself to the interests of the creditors, in that it defines the satisfaction of the creditors as the (only) objective of the insolvency proceedings (§ 1, first sentence, InsO).[12]

2. Decision-making authority

Who shall decide whether the insolvency debtor's firm should be terminated or continued? Choosing between termination and continuation is a question based on a forecast: no-one can predict the future, so the decision may turn out to be the

11 This is the position developed by the American insolvency law theorists who call themselves 'proceduralists'. Selection: Jackson 1986, op. cit. n. 1, pp. 21–27 and 209–210; Baird 1998, op. cit. n. 5, at pp. 576–599; Jackson / Scott 1989, op. cit. n. 1; Rasmussen, Robert, "Empirically Bankrupt", *Columbia Business Law Review* Vol. 2007, pp. 179–246. – The opposite position, which answers the question with yes, is held by the 'traditionalists'. See, for example: Warren, Elizabeth, "Bankruptcy Policy", *The University of Chicago Law Review* Vol. 54, 1987, pp. 775–814; Warren, Elizabeth / Westbrook, Jay, "Contracting Out of Bankruptcy: An Empirical Intervention", *Harvard Law Review* Vol. 118, 2005, pp. 1197–1254; Goode 2011, op. cit. n. 1, ¶¶ 2–15 to 2–19; Flessner, Axel, "Philosophies of Business Bankruptcy Law", in: Ziegel, Jacob (editor), *Current Developments in International and Comparative Corporate Insolvency Law*, 1995, pp. 25–26; Stürner, Rolf, in: Kirchhof, Hans-Peter, et al. (editors), *Münchener Kommentar zur Insolvenzordnung*, C.H. Beck: München, 3rd edition, Volume 1, 2013, Einleitung ¶ 3.

12 InsO: Insolvenzordnung (German Insolvency Act).

wrong one. It should therefore be made by those stakeholders that will bear the risk of failure. Who they are depends on the criteria by which the asset deployment decision is made. If matters of the public interest are taken into account, a public body, such as the insolvency court or an administrative authority, will be selected to make the decision. This applies to French law that assigns the decision-making authority to the insolvency court both in so-called salvage proceedings ("procédure de sauvegarde") and in reorganisation proceedings ("procédure de redressement").[13] If the objective is to satisfy the creditors, however, they should be called upon to make the decision. After all, they will bear the costs if their estimation of the future profits and therefore of the going-concern value proves incorrect. Following this logic, German law places the decision regarding asset deployment in the hands of the creditors (although there are slight variations depending on the deployment option that is chosen).[14]

3. Neutrality of insolvency (asset deployment) law

If the insolvency proceedings shall lead to the deployment decision that, according to the creditors' estimation, promises the highest yield, the following principle ought to apply: Insolvency asset deployment law must be designed in such a way that the creditors are able to make their decision without bias; the legal rules should not take sides by providing an advantage or disadvantage to one asset deployment option or the other. Achieving this kind of neutrality is more difficult than it initially appears. It requires measures to be taken both for the duration of the proceedings (4) and for the individual asset deployment options (5).

4. Time period of the insolvency proceedings: continuation of the debtor's firm during the proceedings

The principle of neutrality demands that the creditors find the firm intact at the end of the insolvency proceedings. A closure of the firm during the insolvency

---

13 Art. 626-1 and Art. 631-19-1 C. com. – C. com.: Code de commerce (French statute on commercial law).

14 The creditor bodies entrusted with the asset deployment decision are: (1) Termination: authority of the "Creditor Meeting", § 157 InsO. (2) Continuation through conveyance to a new legal entity: authority of the "Creditor Committee", alternatively the "Creditor Meeting", § 160 InsO. (3) Continuation by the debtor (reorganisation): authority of the "Groups" formed within the insolvency plan proceedings (creditors whose claims will not be reduced by the insolvency plan are not eligible to vote), §§ 237, 243, 244 InsO.

proceedings, either by the decisions of the insolvency receiver (or the debtor-in-possession) or by the workings of the insolvency law, would push the final asset deployment decision (to be taken by the creditors) towards the option "termination of the firm". Starting up the firm's activities again (for the option "continuation of the firm") would require additional effort and expense, which would place the option "continuation" at a disadvantage. Consequentially, the law needs to both create the legal environment that permits the firm's continuation during the proceedings and require the insolvency receiver or debtor-in-possession to continue the firm (while the proceedings are going on).

a) *Suspension of the creditors' individual asset deployment rights (automatic stay)*

If, during the insolvency proceedings, the creditors were able to take possession of assets of the debtor (which are bound in the debtor's firm) in an uncoordinated manner, the firm would come to a standstill. The assets used for the firm's activities would be ripped apart. Rational individual decisions on the part of the creditors would result in each one of them ultimately being in a worse condition than if they had acted in a coordinated way. Insolvency asset deployment law that fits its purpose must therefore prohibit the creditors from exercising their individual rights to seize the debtor's assets during the insolvency proceedings.[15] Whether or not creditors are protected by security interests should play no role in this case. In contrast to American law, which mandates the "automatic stay" in a single provision for all groups of creditors and all types of rights to seize assets (including the right of setoff) (§ 362 B.C.),[16] in German law it is spread across several statutory provisions. The ban on individual collection rights, directed at unsecured creditors, is stipulated in § 89 InsO. The extent to which the holders of security interests are stripped of their rights to seize the encumbered asset is determined by § 166 InsO, with respect to security interests in movables, and by §§ 30d, 153b ZVG, with respect to mortgages.[17] In principle, these provisions prohibit the secured creditors from enforcing their security interests against the collateral. However, the differentiations made in detail (and without sufficient reason) in § 166 InsO do create significant loopholes.

15 The creditors' seizure of the debtor's property (i.e. its firm) can be compared to the shared use of a renewable resource (a fish pond, for example). See Jackson 1986, op. cit. n. 1, pp. 11–14.

16 B.C.: Bankruptcy Code (USA).

17 ZVG: Gesetz über die Zwangsversteigerung und Zwangsverwaltung (German statute on execution against immovable property of judgment debtors).

In the case of security interests in personal property, § 166 (1) InsO requires that the debtor holds the collateral in his possession. In this case, the ban on individual access does not cover, for example, security interests in shares, because, typically, it is the secured creditor and not the debtor who possesses the shares. Should the secured creditor enforce its security interest and sell the shares (§ 1228 (2) BGB),[18] which is not barred by § 166 (1) InsO, an inter-corporate structure (i.e. the power of directing the subsidiary company, that the debtor was able to exercise through its shares) can no longer be continued. § 166 (2) InsO, which deals with security interests in intangibles, is too narrow as well. It is incomprehensible why only the assignment of receivables is covered there, but not the creation of pledges in receivables. Nor is there an obvious logic behind the exemption of security interests in those intangibles that are not receivables, such as trademarks and other types of intellectual property rights.[19] And there is a further loophole: As regards title retention clauses, the seller's right to repossess the goods can be stayed only for the period between the filing of the insolvency petition and the insolvency court's order of relief (preliminary insolvency proceedings) (§ 22 (2), first sentence, no. 5 InsO), but not during the insolvency proceedings following the court's order of relief (main proceedings) (cf. § 51 InsO).

b) *Continuation of the firm during the proceedings*

The insolvency receiver's task is to continue the debtor's firm during the proceedings. This applies equally to both the preliminary proceedings (between the insolvency petition and the court's order of relief) and the main proceedings (following the court's order of relief) (§ 22 (2), second sentence, no. 2, and § 158 (1) InsO). The same applies to proceedings run by the debtor-in-possession. During the proceedings, the firm can only be terminated if the insolvency court (in the preliminary proceedings) or the creditors' committee (in the main proceedings) agree.[20]

18 BGB: Bürgerliches Gesetzbuch (German Civil Code).

19 Cf. Marotzke, Wolfgang, in: Kreft, Gerhart (editor), *Heidelberger Kommentar zur Insolvenzordnung*, C.F. Müller: Heidelberg, 7th edition 2014, § 166 ¶ 31; Marotzke, Wolfgang, *Das neue Insolvenzrecht – dargestellt am Beispiel der Mobiliarsicherheiten*, Juristische Gesellschaft Mittelfranken e.V.: Regensburg, 1999, pp. 27–28.

20 Marotzke, Wolfgang, *Das Unternehmen in der Insolvenz*, Luchterhand: Neuwied / Kriftel, 2000, ¶¶ 2–42 and ¶ 122.

5. Asset deployment options: a level playing field

The neutrality of insolvency asset deployment law also means that each deployment option be available on an equal footing, so as to establish a level playing field for these options. While no particular legal instruments are required for termination, continuation demands a series of measures.

a) Termination

The decision to terminate the debtor's firm means that the assets of the firm will be sold piecemeal and the proceeds will be distributed to the debtor's creditors. The debtor looses all its assets. In case the debtor is a corporation (as opposed to a natural person), it will be removed from the companies' register. "Termination" thus implies that the (corporate) debtor will cease to exist. This means that, to the extent that the creditors' claims were not satisfied from the proceeds of the insolvency proceedings, the claims will expire as well. Hence, the rule of German insolvency law that the debtor's debts survive the insolvency proceedings (to the extent that they were not satisfied in the proceedings) (§ 201 (1) InsO) does not have any effect in the case of corporations as debtors.

b) Continuation

Concerning the deployment option "continuation" there are two ways how to continue the debtor's firm: continuation by another legal entity and continuation by the debtor.

aa) Continuation by another legal entity: going-concern sale

One way of continuing the firm is to sell it (i.e. all of its assets) as a going concern to another legal entity ("asset deal"). As in the case of termination, the insolvency estate will then consist of a sum of money (the proceeds from the going-concern sale) that will be distributed to the creditors. Now without assets, the debtor will be extinguished through removal from the companies' register, and, in consequence, those creditor claims that could not be satisfied will expire. Up to this point, the effects are the same as those of termination. In order for it to remain so, without the going-concern sale being legally more difficult than termination, the acquirer of the firm must be protected from becoming liable for the insolvency debtor's liabilities. If the acquirer were liable, these liabilities would increase its costs and might thus tilt the scales in favour of termination. Consequently, the rules of civil law that hold the acquirer of a firm liable for the seller's liabilities need to be limited. Two examples shall be given: Those claims of employees of the debtor that relate to the time before the insolvency petition was filed should be excluded from the acquirer's liability stipulated in § 613a (1) BGB.[21] The statutory liability which is triggered by the acquirer's use of the seller's trade name (§ 25 (1) HGB) should not apply in the case of insolvency.[22]

bb) Continuation by the debtor: reorganisation

The option that the debtor's firm can be continued not only by a different legal entity but also by the debtor itself (known as reorganisation) offers some benefits. For one, the transaction costs associated with the transfer of all assets comprising the firm are avoided. For another, continuation through a going-concern sale meets its limits when assets cannot be conveyed – such as (in German law) the right of use from rental, lease or licencing contracts (§ 399 BGB), the rights granted by public law licenses (e.g. in the fields of transportation or the mobile telephone system), or the power of the debtor to issue instructions to a subsidiary corporation under an inter-corporate control agreement (§ 308 AktG).[23]

However, reorganisation cannot be achieved in standard insolvency proceedings; the Insolvenzordnung does not allow for it. Instead, insolvency *plan* proceedings must be pursued (§ 1 (1) with § 217 InsO). This does not alter anything in terms of the objective of the insolvency proceedings (to satisfy the creditors); the insolvency plan merely provides an additional means to the end.

In order for reorganisation to be available as an asset deployment option, insolvency asset deployment law must take a range of measures.

(i) Reduction in the claims of the creditors

The claims of the creditors must be reduced to the value of the insolvency assets (i.e. the debtor's firm). Otherwise, the debtor would remain insolvent (due to over-indebtedness) even after resolution of the insolvency proceedings, so that new insolvency proceedings would have to start immediately. In the cases of the other asset deployment decisions (termination and continuation through a going-concern

---

21 Annuß, Georg, in: Staudinger, J. von, *Bürgerliches Gesetzbuch – Kommentar*, Sellier – de Gruyter: Berlin, 2011 edition, § 613a ¶ 343 (but with justification through insolvency distribution law).

22 Roth, Wulf-Henning, in: Koller, Ingo / Kindler, Peter / Roth, Wulf-Henning / Morck, Winfried (editors), *Handelsgesetzbuch – Kommentar*, C.H. Beck: München, 8th edition 2015, § 25 ¶ 4c (but with justification through insolvency distribution law).

23 Bitter, Georg / Laspeyres, Anne, „Rechtsträgerspezifische Berechtigungen als Hindernis übertragender Sanierung", *Zeitschrift für Wirtschaftsrecht* 2010, pp. 1157–1165. – AktG: Aktiengesetz (German statute on stock corporations).

sale), this reduction in claims is brought about by separating the debtor corporation from its assets and then removing it from the companies' register. Because reorganisation means that the debtor corporation remains in existence, insolvency law has to provide for a reduction in claims. This has been achieved through § 227 InsO as an exception to the continued liability of § 201 InsO.[24]

(ii) Distribution of the value of the firm to the creditors

In contrast to termination and going-concern sale, a reorganisation does not result in money proceeds that could be distributed to the creditors. Rather, it is the firm's value that needs to be distributed to the creditors. There are two ways of doing this.

- The claims of the creditors are not extinguished entirely, but remain at the level at which they are covered by the value of the firm. The effect of this is that future profits (on which the calculation of the going-concern value was based) will benefit the creditors alone (but not also the shareholders of the debtor). The disadvantage of this course of action is that a figure has to be put on the value of the firm, as continued by the debtor (because this figure determines the maximum level of the remaining claims). The evaluation problems associated with this are considerable.
- The simpler option is to assign the value of the firm concern to the creditors by transferring to them the shares in the debtor corporation, that were previously held by the debtor's shareholders (debt-equity swap). No figure needs to be put on the firm's value here, as the claims of the creditors are completely wiped out in return. § 225a (2) InsO gives the creditors the legal power to obtain the company shares.[25] However, this provision needs to be limited: If the debtor was not in excessive debt (but rather was illiquid), dispossession of the company shares that exceeded the total of the creditors' claims would contravene the constitutional guarantee of property (Art. 14 of the German Basic Law); a limitation in line with the constitution is needed in these cases.[26]

---

24 *This* discharge of residual debt has nothing to do with the discharge of residual debt mentioned in § 1, second sentence, and in §§ 286–303 InsO. The latter is a social policy measure that aims at preventing a *natural* person from being in debt all his or her life. This regulatory purpose is not addressed in the discharge of a *corporation's* residual debt addressed in § 227 InsO.

25 Some authors, however, are sceptical. See, e.g., Müller, Hans-Friedrich, „Gesellschaftsrechtliche Maßnahmen im Insolvenzplan", *Zeitschrift für Insolvenzrecht* Vol. 2012, pp. 419–452 (at pp. 440–451).

26 On the insolvency proceedings against Suhrkamp-Verlag, a German publishing house, which apparently was not over-indebted, see, e.g., Landgericht Frankfurt am Main,

(iii) Continued existence of the debtor

The 'reorganisation' option demands that the debtor remain in existence. If the debtor is a corporation, the problem arises that the insolvency petition alone triggers the corporate law proceedings that will lead to the deletion of the corporation from the companies' register (dissolution proceedings of corporate law).[27] It is true that these proceedings are immediately suspended for the duration of the insolvency proceedings.[28] But the only way to exit the dissolution proceedings under corporate law is for the shareholders to decide to continue the corporation.[29] The shareholders will evidently not be interested in doing so, as their shares (in the case of over-indebtedness) no longer have any value. If the provisions of corporate law remained as the only ones, the shareholders would have considerable potential for extortion: they would only decide to continue the corporation if they – contrary to the order of priority of the debtor's financiers – received a portion of the firm's value.[30] In order to make reorganisation law practicable, the (German) insolvency law reform act of 2012 authorized the debtor's creditors to assume all powers vested by corporation law in the debtor's shareholders, in particular to decide in the insolvency plan to continue the debtor corporation (§ 225a (3) InsO). As a matter of principle, however, corporation law should be changed to make not the insolvency petition, but the creditors' decision to either terminate the firm or transfer it to another legal entity a reason for dissolution of the corporation.

September 10, 2013, 3–09 O 96/13, ¶ 73, and Bundesgerichtshof, July 17, 2014, IX ZB 13/14.

27 Filing of the insolvency petition is one of the grounds for dissolution in corporate law: § 728 (1) BGB (BGB-Gesellschaft); § 131 (1) no. 3 HGB (Offene Handelsgesellschaft and Kommanditgesellschaft); § 60 (1) no. 4 GmbHG (Gesellschaft mit beschränkter Haftung); § 262 (1) no. 3 AktG (Aktiengesellschaft). -- – GmbHG: Gesetz betreffend die Gesellschaften mit beschränkter Haftung (German statute on close corporations).

28 § 730 (1) BGB (BGB-Gesellschaft); § 145 (1) HGB (Offene Handelsgesellschaft and Kommanditgesellschaft); § 66 (1) GmbHG (Gesellschaft mit beschränkter Haftung); § 264 (1) AktG (Aktiengesellschaft).

29 Continuation resolution: § 728 (1) BGB (BGB-Gesellschaft); § 144 (1) HGB (Offene Handelsgesellschaft und Kommanditgesellschaft); § 60 (1) no. 4 GmbHG (Gesellschaft mit beschränkter Haftung); § 274 (1) with (2) no. 1 AktG (Aktiengesellschaft).

30 Brüning, Marc, *Gesellschafter und Insolvenzplan*, Kovac: Hamburg, 2006, pp. 119–138.

III. The distribution branch of insolvency law

The law of insolvency distribution is concerned with the question of how the value of the debtor's firm (i.e. either the termination or the going-concern value) should be distributed among the debtor's creditors. Here, too, the focus is on the criteria which should govern this distribution.

1. Criteria of insolvency distribution: the hierarchy among the debtor's financiers

If the debtor's assets are not sufficient to satisfy the creditors' claims (over-indebtedness), the order of priority that exists among the creditors decides who receives how much or, conversely, who has to bear what loss. The question of how the order comes about may provide temptation to see this as one of the roles of insolvency law. But this is not the case. The order among the debtor's financiers was established before the insolvency proceedings, and insolvency (distribution) law would be wise to respect this hierarchy.

2. Principle: respecting the hierarchy established before insolvency

Before the debtor became insolvent, he defined the order of priority among the creditors through agreements with his creditors. Security interests granted by him guarantee the holder priority: the value of the collateral primarily serves to satisfy the secured claim. Only the remainder will go to the unsecured creditors. There are also agreements in the other direction: If the debtor agrees with a creditor that the creditor is subordinate, such creditor's claim will only be satisfied in the case of insolvency once all unsecured creditors have received full payment. This ranking derives from the subordination agreement, and need not be repeated in the insolvency statute. The debtor's shareholders, too, have been allocated their place in the financial hierarchy outside the insolvency proceedings. Corporate law stipulates that the firm's assets can only be distributed among the shareholders once the claims of all creditors, including the subordinate ones, have been met in full.[31]

Through these instruments, the law outside insolvency law creates a hierarchy among all financiers. There is no reason to change this when the debtor becomes insolvent. Each of the aforementioned agreements governed an exchange of values.

---

31 § 733 BGB (BGB-Gesellschaft); § 155 HGB (Offene Handelsgesellschaft and Kommanditgesellschaft); §§ 70, 72 GmbHG (Gesellschaft mit beschränkter Haftung); § 271 (1) AktG (Aktiengesellschaft).

Those who obtained security interests provided the debtor with a consideration in return, in the form of a reduction of the interest rate due by the debtor. Through a subordination agreement, the debtor gained (in return for paying a higher rate of interest) a reduction in his senior unsecured liabilities and was therefore able to offer his senior unsecured creditors better chances of satisfaction, which in turn brought him more favourable interest rates in this segment. If the distribution hierarchy in place before insolvency were to be changed by insolvency law, the exchange of values that took place before the insolvency proceedings would lose its foundation: the acquirer of a security interest would have given his consideration (i.e. the reduction of the interest rate) without receiving the agreed benefit (the priority in distribution) in return. In the case of subordination, the debtor would have given his value (a higher interest rate) without gaining the benefit of improved credit conditions for his senior unsecured creditors. Only if security interests and subordination agreements are honoured by insolvency distribution law can the competition for the value of the debtor's assets work properly. This is very clear in the case of security interests: they are the legal instrument that initiates a competition for priority rights in the debtor's assets. The effect of this competition is that the priority rights are acquired by those creditors who offer the greatest benefit to the debtor.

There are certain groups of creditors who should not be subjected to this competition. The victims of tort actions on the part of the debtor are a notable example. Because they did not grant credit to the debtor voluntarily, the law should grant them statutory security interests, other distributional privileges or an insurance solution in their favour. However, German law, as it stands today, does not protect them. Another example of an involuntary creditor is the debtor's maintenance creditors (for example the debtor's children). Their case is taken up by the rules on the enforcement of court judgments; these rules withdraw those parts of the debtor's property (such as salary claims) which are needed to fulfil the maintenance obligations from the creditors' competition; these attachment limits then also apply in the case of insolvency.[32] The responsibilities that public environmental law imposes on the debtor for the clean-up of contaminated sites are based on pollution of the natural environment and therefore also on involuntary credit. By declaring these responsibilities a "public burden", the statutes of the German federal states on clean-up of contaminated sites give them a statutory priority which even trumps the holders of mortgages in the affected real estate

32 §§ 850–851d ZPO; § 36 (1) InsO. – ZPO: Zivilprozessordnung (German statute on civil procedure).

(§ 10 (1) no. 3 ZVG).[33] Finally, the debtor's employees must be mentioned. They are not able to reasonably take part in the competition for the debtor's assets. If they do not assert themselves in this competition, it is only with considerable effort and expense that they can switch debtors or spread their credit risk across multiple debtors. German law does not assign them any statutory security interests in the debtor's property; rather their salary claims for the last three months preceding the insolvency proceedings are insured through a state-run insolvency insurance (§§ 165–172 SGB III).[34] In contrast, the state tax authorities (as creditors of the debtor) do not need protection. They can avoid the granting of credit by imposing advance tax payments.

If insolvency (distribution) law were to create its own rules of distribution, it would invite 'forum shopping' and thus be an abuse of the insolvency proceedings. Those creditors who received a better distributional position in the insolvency proceedings than they had before the insolvency would be tempted to file an insolvency petition even when there was no insolvency event and therefore no reason to pass the entrepreneurial decision-making authority from the owners to the creditors. Conversely, if creditors received a worse distributional position in the insolvency proceedings, they would refrain from filing an insolvency petition, even though insolvency proceedings would be necessary given the debtor's debt situation.

As a general rule, insolvency law should abstain from developing its own distributional rules. It should refer to the priority rights established outside insolvency instead. Insolvency distribution law should thus be limited to respecting the distributional hierarchy established before the insolvency proceedings. It is the law outside insolvency law that, in principle, determines the relationship among the debtor's financiers.

3. Exceptions: interventions by insolvency (distribution) law

If insolvency distribution law considers changing the distribution hierarchy that existed before insolvency, such changes ought to be based on purposes of insolvency law. Two interventions are worth mentioning.

---

33 von Wilmowsky, Peter, „Gesetzliche Sicherungsrechte für Altlastsanierungspflichten?", Juristen-Zeitung Vol. 1997, pp. 817–825.

34 SGB: Sozialgesetzbuch (German statute on social security).

a) Pro-rata distribution among the unsecured creditors

As regards the relationship among the (senior) unsecured creditors, outside insolvency priority is established by "first come, first served": Whoever is first at obtaining a judgment and enforcing it (through the remedies of collection law) against the debtor's property enjoys priority over the other unsecured creditors. In insolvency, this rule is suspended and a pro-rata satisfaction is mandated instead: The (senior) unsecured creditors' claims will be satisfied in proportion to their amounts.[35]

It is no easy task to identify the reasons that support the pro-rata rule. The most plausible explanation appears to be that this rule produces efficiency gains by reducing monitoring costs. If insolvency (distribution) law did not mandate a pro-rata distribution, the unsecured creditors would be forced to constantly monitor the debtor for signs of impending inability to pay and the other unsecured creditors for collection actions, as well as to prepare themselves for a dash for the debtor's assets at any time. Mandatory equal treatment relieves them of these costs. If one figures a world without transaction costs, the unsecured creditors would agree this rule of distribution among themselves. This explanation does not apply to secured creditors. Creditors who, before the insolvency proceedings, acquired a security interest in one of the debtor's assets can expect payment from the encumbered asset and do not have to rely on monitoring the business activities of the debtor and pre-empting other creditors in accessing the debtor assets. The secured creditors are therefore not among the creditors in whose interest the pro-rata rule was made.[36]

---

35 In German law, there is no statutory provision on the pro-rata distribution; but this rule is generally recognised. See e.g. Ehricke, Ulrich, in: Kirchhof, Hans-Peter, et al. (editors), *Münchener Kommentar zur Insolvenzordnung*, C.H. Beck: München, 3rd edition, Vol. 1, 2013, § 38 ¶ 10. Other terms: bankruptcy dividend; pari passu distribution; rule of „par condicio creditorum".

36 Jackson 1986, op. cit. n. 1, pp. 15–16, 29–31; Jackson, Thomas, "Bankruptcy, Non-Bankruptcy Entitlements, and the Creditors' Bargain", *The Yale Law Journal* Vol. 91, 1982, pp. 857–907 (model for investigating distribution questions with the help of a functional creditor insolvency distribution agreement); Baird, Douglas, *The Elements of Bankruptcy*, Foundation Press: New York, New York, 5th edition 2010, p. 80; Finch 2009, op. cit. n. 1, pp. 599–674; Mokal, Riz, "Priority as Pathology: The Pari Passu Myth", *The Cambridge Law Journal* Vol. 60, 2001, pp. 581–621. – Häsemeyer develops other justifications for the pro-rata principle (failure of private autonomy, influence of the creditors on the debtor's assets) and derives another field of application (which extends to the holders of security interests).

The view that prevails in German insolvency jurisprudence appears to exaggerate the importance of the pro-rata rule. Attempts are made to relate every aspect of insolvency law to it.[37] But these attempts are doomed to fail. Even in insolvency distribution law, the pro-rata rule falls short – it can only claim validity in the relationship between unsecured creditors, while in all other cases the priorities that were established before (and thus outside) insolvency are decisive. If one looks at insolvency asset deployment law, the pro-rata rule is without any explanatory value at all. It is not connected in any way to the problems that need to be solved with respect to asset deployment.

b) *Costs of the insolvency proceedings: priority*

The effort and expense involved in conducting insolvency proceedings, including continuing the debtor's firm during the proceedings, deserves an improvement in position in the hierarchy of the financiers. The expenses mentioned create the conditions for an informed and undistorted decision on asset deployment by the creditors. Because this is in the interests of the creditors who have no security interests, a distributional rank below that of the secured creditors but above the unsecured creditors is justified. This is the (preferential) status of "administrative expenses" as defined in §§ 53–55 InsO.

IV. Conclusion

On the asset deployment side, the role of insolvency law is to withdraw from the debtor the authority to decide on the further use of his assets and to transfer this authority to the creditors. If the debtor's assets are a firm, three asset deployment options must be available, just as they are outside insolvency: the termination of the firm; its continuation by another legal entity; and its continuation by the debtor. Insolvency law should act neutrally, without preferring or neglecting any of the asset deployment options. These options require a series of measures, from stopping the creditors from exercising their individual collection and enforcement rights against the debtor's property, to the principle of continuing the debtor's firm throughout the insolvency proceedings, and to a reorganisation law which allows

Cf. Häsemeyer, Ludwig, *Insolvenzrecht*, Carl Heymanns: Köln, 4th edition 2007, ¶¶ 2.24–2.27. Rebuttal by von Wilmowsky, Peter, „Buchbesprechung", *Zeitschrift für Wirtschafts- und Bankrecht* Vol. 2004, pp. 547–548.

37 Inter alia: Foerste, Ulrich, *Insolvenzrecht*, C.H. Beck: München, 6th edition 2014, § 1 ¶ 8; Bork, Reinhard, *Einführung in das Insolvenzrecht*, Mohr Siebeck: Tübingen, 6th edition 2012, § 1 ¶ 2.

the creditors to replace the shareholders. On the distribution side, insolvency law must respect the hierarchy that was established before the insolvency under non-insolvency law. Any intervention in this must be justified by insolvency law. Such justifications include the pro-rata distribution to unsecured creditors and the preference for the expenses of the insolvency proceedings.

Differentiating between asset deployment and loss distribution clears the way for an efficient legal doctrine of insolvency law. There is no issue in insolvency law that cannot be mapped more clearly and better managed with the help of this differentiation than without it.[38]

38 Even in difficult and controversial sub-fields, such as insolvency contract law, insolvency conflict of laws and insolvency environmental law, the separation provides reliable orientation. Cf. von Wilmowsky, Peter, „Insolvenzvertragsrecht: Die Grundstruktur", *Zeitschrift für Insolvenzrecht* Vol. 2011, pp. 453–479 (at pp. 454–455); von Wilmowsky, Peter, „Internationales Insolvenzrecht: Plädoyer für eine Neuorientierung", *Zeitschrift für Wirtschafts- und Bankrecht* Vol. 1997, pp. 1461–1472; von Wilmowsky, Peter, „Insolvenz und Umwelthaftung", *Zeitschrift für das gesamte Handelsrecht* Vol. 160, 1996, pp. 593–625.

Contributors

Jasper Kunstreich is a PhDl student in Economic and Social History at the University of Oxford. His doctorate on the emergence of the German bankruptcy regime in the 19th century is supervised by Professor Avner Offer and Professor Joshua Getzler. Before coming to Oxford, Jasper Kunstreich studied History, Law, and Political Science at the University of Heidelberg.

Albrecht Cordes is professor of Medieval and Early Modern Legal History and Civil Law at the Goethe University Frankfurt/Main. His research activities focus on late medieval and early modern legal history, and mainly on the history of commercial law and the legal history of the Hanseatic League. He is director of the Institute for legal history at the Goethe University, board member of the Hansischer Geschichtsverein, and member of the steering committee of the LOEWE Research Focus "Extrajudicial and Judicial Conflict Resolution". Latest publication with Serge Duchy (eds), Eine Grenze in Bewegung, München 2013.

Ulrich Falk is director of the Institut für Unternehmensrecht (Institute for Corporate Law), member of the academic council of the Zentrum für Insolvenz und Sanierung (ZIS, Centre for Insolvency and Reorganisation) and member of the Historisches Institut (Historical Institute) at the University of Mannheim. He has been teaching and conducting research in Mannheim since 2002. From 1992 to 2001, he was a scholar at the Max-Planck-Institute for European Legal History in Frankfurt am Main. In the 2009/10 academic year, he held a research professorship from the state of Baden-Württemberg, building up an inter-faculty project group on the history of the insolvency proceeding (business management, economics, law). In 2010/11, he was a Senior Fellow at Alfried Krupp Wissenschaftskolleg Greifswald. His research in legal history focuses on the early modern age and the 19th and 20th centuries.

Wolfgang Forster holds chair of civil law, comparative history of law and philosophy of law, at the department of law of the University of Tübingen. Main publication: Konkurs als Verfahren. Francisco Salgado de Somoza in der Geschichte des Insolvenzrechts. Köln 2009 (Norm und Struktur, 32). Current project: Agostinho Barbosa (1590–1649) im Kontext der frühneuzeitlichen Rechtswissenschaft.

Mechthild Isenmann research assistant at the Department of Economic and Social History at the University of Leipzig, selected publications: (with Eberhard Isenmann), Das Innenverhältnis einer spätmittelalterlichen Handelsgesellschaft und die Ausweitung interner Konflikte – Hans Arzt und Gesellschaft, Anton Paumgartner und die Reichsstadt Nürnberg (1447–1471), in VSWG 101 (2014), S. 432–487; Vom Nutzen und Schaden des Reichtums. Junge Nachfolger in oberdeutschen Familiengesellschaften des 15. und 16. Jahrhunderts, in: Schulte, Petra; Hesse, Peter (Hrsg.), Reichtum im späteren Mittelalter. Politische Theorie, ethische Handlungsnormen und soziale Akzeptanz, (VSWG Beihefte 232) Stuttgart 2015, pp. 167–187. Involved in the DFG funded research project: „Strategien, Mittel und Wege oberdeutscher Handelshäuser der inner- und zwischenfamiliären Konfliktlösung oberdeutscher Handelshäuser im 15. und langen 16. Jahrhundert".

Håkan Jakobsson is a PhD student at the Department of History at Stockholm University. Recent publications: H. Jakobsson, "Kalescher, karosser och lustjakter: utformning och beställning av lyxartiklar hos den svenska aristokratin 1660–1667", pp. 47–73, in Det svenska begäret. Sekler av lyxkonsumtion, P. von Wachtenfeldt & K. Nyberg (eds.) (Carlsson Bokförlag: Stockholm 2015). K. Nyberg & H. Jakobsson, "Financial networks, migration and the transformation of the merchant elite in 18th-Century Stockholm", pp. 72–94, in T. M. Safley (ed.), The History of Bankruptcy: Economic, social and cultural implications in early modern Europe, (Routledge: London & New York 2013). Current research-project: The introduction and utilization of Dutch experts and knowledge in the Swedish state administration 1570–1670.

Christoph Kling is a PhD student of Ulrich Falk and research assistant at his chair for Civil Law, Rhetoric and European Legal History at the University of Mannheim. In 2014/15, he completed a LL.M. programme at Harvard Law School and continued his current work on a doctoral thesis dealing with bankruptcy in the 19th century.

Klas Nyberg is professor and director of the Centre for Fashion Studies at Stockholm University. He is an economic historian and researcher in the field of textile history, consumption history and material culture. His most recent publications are Det svenska begäret: Sekler av lyxkonsumtion, P. von Wachtenfeldt & K. Nyberg (eds.) (Carlsson Bokförlag: Stockholm 2015) and Från kläde till silkesflor. Textilprover från 1700-talets svenska fabriker, E. Stavenow-Hidemark & K. Nyberg (K. Nyberg ed.) (Kulturhistoriska bokförlaget: Stockholm 2015).

He leads the research programme "The Genesis of Fashion. The role of state-sponsored manufactures in the rise and spread of fashion in the Nordic region in the early modern period."

Viera Rebolledo-Dhuin wrote her PhD. on "Book Trade and Credit: Book Professions and their Networks in Paris, 1830–1870" (*La librairie et le crédit. Réseaux et métiers du livre à Paris, 1830–1870*, 3 vols.), secondary school teacher in a bi-national French-Spanish section, recently detached to the research program intituled: "DEF19: *Dictionnaire des éditeurs français du XIX*[e] *siècle*", financed by the ANR (National Research Agency). Main research fields: Book history; business history, esp. small enterprises, luxury industry/fashion goods; bankruptcies, crises, history of the law (esp. commercial law); social history of credit, commercial discount, informal credit, credit inter-enterprises; history of Paris, Parisian sociability and history of elites; formal and statistical methods, esp. demography of firms, prosopography and network analysis.

Magnus Ressel is assistant professor at the chair of Early Modern History (Prof. Schorn-Schütte) at the University of Frankfurt/M. He obtained his PhD on the relations of Northern Europe with the Barbary Corsairs at the Universities of Munich and Paris (Sorbonne I). He has published mostly on economic, social and maritime history. Recent publications: Zwischen Sklavenkassen und Türkenpässen. Nordeuropa und die Barbaresken in der Frühen Neuzeit. Berlin/New York, 2012 (= Pluralisierung & Autorität 31); British Dominance of Merchant Shipping between Northern and Southern Europe, 1720–1750, in: International Journal of Maritime History 25,2 (2013), pp. 117–142. Current project: The German merchant community in eighteenth century Venice.

Dave De Ruysscher holds the chair of legal history at the Vrije Universiteit in Brussels. His research interests foremost concern the history of commercial law (bankruptcy, marine insurance, company law). His main publications are "From Usages of Merchants to Default Rules: Practices of Trade, *Ius Commune* and Urban Law in Early Modern Antwerp", *The Journal of Legal History* 33/1 (2012), 3–29, and "Bankruptcy, Insolvency and Debt Collection Among Merchants in Antwerp (*c.* 1490–*c.* 1540)", in Th.M. Safley (ed.), *Bankrupcy in Early-Modern Europe*, Abingdon, Taylor & Francis, 2013, 185–199.

Margrit Schulte Beerbühl is professor at the department of historical studies II (modern history) at the Heinrich Heine University of Düsseldorf. She has published widely in the fields of British social and economic history, Anglo-German relations, merchant networks, British naturalization policy and history of consumption. Among her publications are: *The Forgotten Majority. German Merchants in London, Global Trade, and Naturalization 1660–1815*, New York/London 2015. Current research projects: Secret Anglo-German trade networks during the Napoleonic Wars and The first worldwide speculation bubble of 1799.

Erika Vause is Assistant Professor of History at Florida Southern College in Lakeland, Florida, United States. She researches debt and credit in Revolutionary and post-Revolutionary France and has published in journals including *French Historical Studies, Law and History Review* and the *Journal of Society History*. She is currently working on a book project which examines how anxieties about usury, debt imprisonment, pawnshops and bankruptcy helped define critiques of emergent capitalism in nineteenth-century France.

Peter von Wilmowsky LL.M (Berkeley); Goethe-University Frankfurt am Main, Germany; Chair for Civil Law, Insolvency Law, European and International Commercial Law; recent publications on contracts in insolvency law; his current research project is on derivatives in insolvency law.

Register

www.ingramcontent.com/pod-product-compliance
Ingram Content Group UK Ltd.
Pitfield, Milton Keynes, MK11 3LW, UK
UKHW011005120926
8556IPUK00027B/50

9 783631 658253